The Latin American Identity and the African Diaspora

THE LATIN AMERICAN IDENTITY AND THE AFRICAN DIASPORA

ETHNOGENESIS IN CONTEXT

ANTONIO OLLIZ BOYD

CAMBRIA PRESS

Amherst, New York

Copyright 2010 Antonio Olliz Boyd

All rights reserved
Printed in the United States of America

No part of this publication may be reproduced, stored in or introduced into a retrieval system, or transmitted, in any form, or by any means (electronic, mechanical, photocopying, recording, or otherwise), without the prior permission of the publisher.

Requests for permission should be directed to:
permissions@cambriapress.com, or mailed to:
Cambria Press
20 Northpointe Parkway, Suite 188
Amherst, NY 14228

The image on the front cover is by Jean Baptise Debret. Esclaves negres, de differentes nations. Voyage pittoresque et historique au Bresil. 1834-39. Reproduced by permission of the Print Collection, Miriam and Ira D. Wallach Division of Art, Prints and Photographs, The New York Public Library, Astor, Lenox and Tilden Foundations.

Library of Congress Cataloging-in-Publication Data

Olliz Boyd, Antonio.
　The Latin American identity and the African diaspora : ethnogenesis in context / Antonio Olliz Boyd.
　　　p. cm.
　Includes bibliographical references and index.
　ISBN 978-1-60497-704-2 (alk. paper)
1. Latin American literature—Black authors—History and criticism. 2. Caribbean literature—Black authors—History and criticism. 3. Blacks in literature. 4. Identity (Psychology) in literature. I. Title.

　PQ7081.A1O45 2010
　860.9'89608—dc21

2010016256

In memory of
Clara Ana, my mother
Rose, my godmother
Virgilio "Pupu" Rodriguez
Max Nathan
Marvin Wachman

I am what I am because you cared. I shall never forget.

> "I don't know what it means to be a Black woman in the Spanish-speaking Caribbean. I know how it feels. It feels as if you exist in virtual reality, as a symbol of 'our shared African heritage'..."
> —Mayra Santos-Febres, Afro-Puerto Rican novelist in *Daughters of the Diaspora*

Ethnogenesis:
Same ship, different ports or same trip, different ships.

> "When I began looking for a job after college, I discovered that being a white Latina made me a nonthreatening minority... My color was a question only of culture... And what was a Hispanic?.... There is no such culture..."
> —Julia Alvarez, Dominican novelist in *Half and Half: Writers on Growing Up Biracial and Bicultural*

Table of Contents

Acknowledgments ix

Prologue xv

Essay I: Aesthetic Blackness in the Creative Literature of the Latin/Hispanic Reality 1

Essay II: The Aesthetics of Language as an Experience of the Afro Latin/Afro Hispanic Reality 81

Essay III: An Aesthetic Experience: The Reality of Phenotypes and Racial Awareness in Dominican Literature
Julia Alvarez and Loida Maritza Pérez 157

Introduction to Essay IV 203

Essay IV: A Latin Identity, An African Experience: The Tabom Brazilians of Ghana 217

Epilogue 301

Notes 317

Index 321

Acknowledgments

¡*Mil Gracias*!...*Obrigadíssimo*! Many thanks to the myriad novelists, poets, and essayists from Latin America who have overtly or covertly expressed their connection to Africa for me to ponder, digest, and consider as a fact of life. The widely expanding concentric circles of the African Diaspora lead back to the African Continent in search of self.

> *Nuestro folclor afroespañol, hispanoafricano, tiene guitarra y tambor y se resuelve en el son cubano.* (Excilia Saldaña, *Kele Kele*)
>
> (Our folklore is Afro-Spanish, Hispanic-African; with guitar and drum it resolves itself in the music of Cuba.)

The Ghana Connection

Quite by chance, an article on the Internet affirmatively suggested the possibility of locating an established group in Ghana that had reversed the Diaspora from the Americas back to the Continent. Ghanaian friends, ex-students, and colleagues offered their services in answer to my query: Have you heard of such a group? Thanks to Alex Aning (Asante), Moses

Panford Jr. (Fante), and Gabriel Asoanab Abudu (Bissa), my inquisitive aim was pointed in the right direction. Their contacts in Ghana, especially those of Dr. Aning, made my nebulous dream become a vividly living reality. Without these supportive Ghanaian contacts, the location (in Ghana) of the descendants of African returnees from the Diaspora would have remained a mystery. In addition to offering cultural advice, Dr. Panford graciously proofread and edited the first draft on Latino phenotypes, as well as the outline and subsequent development of the draft on the Tabom "returnees." His "native" point of view, coupled with his training in literary criticism, gave me the confidence of knowing that I was heading in the right direction and had shown respect for and comprehension of the subject matter. Dr. Abudu, for his part, assured me that all Ghanaians are acquainted with the Gold Coast's role in American slavery, and in songs and poetry give passing thought to the return of spirits to their homeland(s). In addition, the material on Guillén, Morejón, and Saldaña, that he so willingly made available to me, was of immense aid. Finally, it was a trip to Ghana to read a paper at the First International Conference on Afro-Hispanic, Luso-Brazilian, and Latin American Studies at the University of Ghana in Accra, where thoughts, doubts, suggestions, and introductions were to become concretized into manuscript form.

Contacts in Ghana
In Ghana proper, nothing would have been accomplished without the brotherly welcome and gracious reception that I was offered by his Excellency, the chief of the Tabom clan, Nii Azumah Nelson V. My questions for him were many; his answers were freely given. The chief's kindness in giving me a personal tour of the Brazil House site in the Tabom neighborhood of the Jamestown section of Accra not only made the history of returning ex-slaves come vividly alive, but also assured me of his sincere interest and desire to cooperate with my project. Due to the chief's guidance, I found that there were still Tabom subjects in the Jamestown area that revered the chief's imposing link to their history and viewed his iconic public image as their historical connection. Many thanks also to

the chief's brother, Mr. Alexander Aruna Nelson, for accepting me into his home and sharing the memory of his family's journey from Brazil to the land of the Gã. I owe him a mountain of gratitude for allowing me to peruse, with his commentary, the invaluable collection of photographs and documents of his ancestors, the Brazilian Africans. However, none of my efforts in Ghana would have come to fruition without the capable assistance of Mr. Abobo Williams, who was then a student at the University of Ghana but is now pursuing graduate studies at Ohio University. Abobo is trained in the literatures and cultures of his homeland and is a fluent speaker of one of Ghana's endemic languages, Akan, as well as two of that language's most popular dialects: Twi and Fante. Likewise, he is a native speaker of his family's Dagaare language, in which I express my heartfelt thanks to him: "Barka Abobo." Furthermore, his perfect command of English not only made him a most capable interpreter and guide but also made it possible for me to breeze through the protocol of first-time introductions with a minimum of cultural mishaps. Abobo's translation also helped me in our interactions with the taxi drivers who drove us to our appointments; they were speakers of Ewe but also spoke Twi. Additionally, it was Abobo who relied on his acquaintance with some of the elders in his hometown, Takoradi, to retrieve the poems, songs, and sayings related to slavery that were incorporated into this project. Mr. Edmond Adoko, an Akan elder, graciously offered to cooperate in this respect. I am likewise grateful to Abobo's elder brother, Jonathan "Kunwanie" Williams, for pitching in to help in retrieving and sending some much-needed research material that was only available from Mr. Adoko after Abobo had left Takoradi to return to Accra. Finally, I am indebted to Michael Narh Luther-Tetteh for his belief in me as someone genuinely interested in the ethnic groups of his country and his confidence in my research capability. Michael's interesting accounts of tribal history and culture helped me to experience how he viewed his role in Ghana's multiethnic "*crisol*" and to envision how the Tabom were able to connect the dots that followed their position as African natives, then Africans in the Diaspora, and finally as Diaspora-African returnees without a loss of self and purpose. Translations from English to Gã, and Gã to English were handled through the expert linguistic ability of Michael as was acquisition of the original, professional photographs for the Tabom group.

THE UNITED STATES CONNECTION

Here in the States, I am grateful for the tireless technical support of Andrew von Ramin-Mapp. I sincerely appreciate his candid statement, "I don't repair computers, dust off keyboards, or clean monitors, but I'll be glad to help you with anything technical." And technical assistance was never lacking. "Jefe," you and I both know that this manuscript would probably never have materialized without your mentoring. Not only did my research horizons expand but my ability to face my own computer challenges has improved a thousandfold because of your patience and guidance. Danke, thank you, obrigado, and gracias.

IN TOTO

It should not be difficult, in retrospect, to remember all the different contributors whose "*granito de arena*" or grain of sand helped to stimulate my intellectual energy. Yet, try as I may to acknowledge this debt, I am sure someone will become a victim of the "senior moment" with which time of its own accord endows us. I do wish to thank Mrs. Gloria Jackson for her encouragement and for reading a portion of the manuscript. Mrs. Jackson, you'll see that some of your suggestions were incorporated. And to Anthony "Piquico" Sánchez, know that your unabashed approach to explaining Quisqueya's black folk cultural environment was a welcome respite from the academic apologies that I usually received. *Seguro que me comprendes. Te estoy eternamente agradecido.* Nor have I forgotten the intellectual stimuli I received from the constructive comments of Richard Jackson, Jerome Boyd, and Brian Sims. Finally, to Mark Fields (Marcos Campos) and his connections in Lima, thanks for locating the much-needed materials from Peru.

All of the previously named are present in the complexities of this project.

A Special Thanks and "Obrigado" Apart

James Henry Kennedy is someone that I could always count on to know the right answer to my many questions about Brazil, his adopted country. And thankfully, if the answer eluded him, his myriad contacts in the area of Brazilian culture were there to help him to help me. In essence, Professor Kennedy is one of the most erudite Brazilian culturists that I have ever met. My requests to refer to his holdings of Brazilian books, articles, magazines, and newspaper collections were never denied.

I must also acknowledge a source that I will not hesitate to contact again when the need arises: the Orange County (Florida) Library System. Not only was I amazed at how efficiently the Interlibrary Loan system functioned, but the luxury of having materials delivered to my door was unique. My sincerest gratitude to everyone involved.

Nota bene:

I, the author, am responsible for all translations from Spanish to English, unless otherwise noted. Likewise, I am to be held accountable for the Portuguese language entries that required an English translation. At times, I consulted with Professor Kennedy for his learned input where indecision rested with idiomatic phrases and cultural terms in Portuguese, but ultimately the final decision of what to include, revise, or reject in the area of translations/interpretations was my obligation. I alone am answerable for the final result, positive or negative.

Prologue

"Ellos son blancos se entienden." (Spanish)
"Eles que são brancos, se entendem." (Portuguese)
("They understand each other, they're all White.")
—An aphorism culled from the author's
personal experience with folk sayings of Latin America

An aphorism is often accepted as a concise expression of a social truth. Yet, these pithy sayings, like most units of language, have the tendency to reveal both intent and effect when reviewed with critical considerations for their surface arrangement and deeper structural levels. For example, the saying that introduces this section of my study makes it obvious that the "speaker" and the "spoken about" are actors in separate social environments who nevertheless share a context controlled by precepts of race. In questions of race, this surface level/deep structure approach to an apothegm more often than not reveals more about a society's true psychology of race than the pronouncements of "racial democracy" or "race-neutral" identification that one finds in the "politically correct" declarations of most Latin American societies. Both Spanish-speaking Latin America and its Portuguese-speaking geographical associate, Brazil, actively support issues of race while denying, at the same time, the existence of practices of racial victimization. Yet there are many expressions that can be extracted from the folk mythology of both areas that carry inferences of a racial dichotomy. For the most part, they demonstrate the convoluted psychology of folk maxims that carry the intention of jocular diversion along with the deleterious and misconstrued result of implying a social truth in a contextual atmosphere of "racial harmony." For example, in Spanish-speaking areas one hears:

> *El negro, si no la hace a la entrada, la hace a la salida.*
> (If a nigger doesn't mess up at the beginning, he'll mess up at the end.)

In Brazil, the thought is the same, although with a slight edge of volatility:

> *O preto que não caga na entrada, caga na saida.*
> (The nigger that doesn't shit things up in the beginning will shit them up at the end.)

Of course, the determination of the entertaining or didactic aesthetics of such pronouncements depends on the listener's social position.

However, my main interest in the presentation of the following essays concerns the image and social effect of the aesthetics of blackness that one finds in the creative literature of Latin America. For the aphorisms presented earlier, the question of entertainment versus didacticism might have been simplistically rhetorical, but in the area of creative literature, an exposition in this sense requires more expansion. Is it also rhetorical, then, to ask if the end result of creative literature is aimed only at entertaining the reader, or is there also a didactic goal? Given that most short stories, novels, epics, poems, dramas, and memoirs are constructed as an author's reaction to an analysis of experiences, concepts, or an imagined world, the literary target can serve to pique an interest or present a truth as the writer perceives it. It is with this last element in mind that I have looked at the reality of the Afro Latino image in various examples of Latin American creative writing (i.e., novels, poems, short stories, and song lyrics) wherein the fictive cosmos alludes to a concrete and real space. The imagery of the Afro Latino person registers, upon careful reading, as a form of *noesis* or perception, perhaps truth by design. In short, we are led to approach the author's organization of his or her fantasies as recognition of the Afrodescendant's symbological factor in the national societies where Spanish and Portuguese are the modes of communication in the Americas.

With the previous thought in mind, I crafted the four essays in this study to be correlated in overall theme and concept. However, they can and should each be read as separate discourses. Their organization is within the pragmatics of a common literary experience, that is to say, the integration of Afrodescendants into the literary spaces of Latino culture as symbols of national identity. The context of the first three essays is based on the creative writing of authors with a Latin American mindset, wherein we go from a specific geopolitical environment (e.g., Cuba, Puerto Rico, Dominican Republic, or Mexico) to promote by hypothesis that the topics discussed can also apply to the entire area termed Latin America, in part if not as a whole. Under this guise, the specific terminology—*Latin America*—includes all the countries in the Americas where Spanish and Portuguese are spoken. The basic tenet I am proposing is to establish, with some validity, the extent to which the national psyche has accepted or rejected (as can be shown in one specific case) the ethnic Afro Latino and Afro Latinism as icons of the national culture.

Most natives of the Spanish-speaking and Portuguese-speaking areas of the Americas are not oblivious to the fact that there are black and partially black natives in their regions. Yet the phenotypic distinctions that would affirm an infusion of African genes apparently are not so discernible to the non-native observer, or even to a sizeable group of non-native academicians. Many of the latter claim to specialize in Latino or Hispanic studies and make suppositions about the culture that distort the Afrodescendant presence. Perhaps their stance is politically motivated since the same color gradations are apparent in U.S. nationals and are cause for differential treatment toward those who are not accepted as white.

Nonetheless, Africans were introduced into the Latin American area in the early sixteenth century, long before the institution of slavery became part and parcel of North American politics and the culture of its economy. As a matter of fact, Plymouth, Massachusetts, and Jamestown, Virginia, did not become a reality for early settlers from England until 100 years after Africans had been transported to the Americas by the Spaniards and the Portuguese. By 1510 the first sizeable group of Spanish-speaking Africans (*ladinos*) arrived in Hispaniola from Spain. By 1518 non-Spanish-speaking Africans were being shipped directly from the Continent. Cuba received its first large group of slaves in 1520. Notably, the first major slave revolt in the Americas broke out in 1522 on Hispaniola, on the sugar plantation of Diego Columbus, Christopher's son. In both Cuba and Hispaniola, slave revolts began almost as soon as the Africans could plan an escape route or devise a means of retaliation. In 1533 a revolt at the Jobabo mines in the Oriente area of Cuba was recorded as eventful, although only four slaves, allegedly, took part. In his article, "The Slave Trade in Mexico,"Aguirre Beltran, the Mexican researcher of African populations in his country affirms, "The first slaves to arrive in Mexico accompanied their masters in the enormous task of the Conquest. They came from the island of Cuba, to which they had been brought under royal licenses several decades after the discovery of America" (429).

The island of Cuba and the island called Hispaniola, which later became Haiti and the Dominican Republic, were not the only Latin areas that saw the wheels of their colonial economy turn with the forced labor of African captives. Each and every country in Latin America that survived as a colony of Spain (or of Portugal, in the case of Brazil) and that early in the nineteenth century acquired independence from their European colonizers promoted their economy with slavery. Yet, when Aguirre Beltran published "The Slave Trade in Mexico" in 1944, the editor of the journal in which it appeared (*The Hispanic American Historical Review*) felt that more concentrated studies needed to be made on the African's presence in the Americas, and especially on the so-called Spanish-American mainland:

> Since the Negro has been more adequately studied in Brazil and the Caribbean, this issue of *The Hispanic American Historical*

Review has been organized around the subject of the Negro on the Spanish-American mainland. (24.3, Aug. 1944, Editorial page)

Most of what was presented in that issue focused principally on linking the African directly to slavery within a historical, anthropological, and sociological perspective. Integration as a person into his or her respective community did not seem to merit being studied in any depth. The Afro Latino is seen mainly as an object to be clinically dissected considering only the guidelines of history, anthropology, or sociology. In "The Slave Trade and the Negro in South America," Fernando Romero, in citing the weaknesses of previous studies, concludes that the list of countries that require investigative studies to determine the physical presence of the African person in South America should be increased to include Ecuador, Chile, Uruguay, and Argentina. As he declares, "Such omissions do not seem desirable to the writer [i.e., Romero], for these countries also received a large number of Africans..." (370). Later studies, with different methodologies and interests, have confirmed that there is a definite and viable African image in the aforementioned regions. The thematic path we have followed in the essays of the present work extends the African image found at the surface level to include a deep-structured total integration within a national space. For example, in the essay on "phenotypes," it would be impossible to acknowledge the gradations in skin color that one finds in the Dominican Republic and most Latin American countries without accepting the root cause(s) that produced the distinctions. The indigenous Indian, the usual scapegoat for the basis of color variations in Latin America, is present in some countries, but not in all. To wit, the range of *mulatos, pardos, morenos, trigueños*, and even the prototypical Latin phenotype would have been difficult to produce without an African presence.

I consider it important to show that authors native to diverse Latin American cultures do find that their use of the Afro Latino image can provide their literary canvases with subtle symbols of nationalism and even of racism without resorting to the stridency of political populism. After all, literature is a slice of life that has been given direction and meaning from a percipient's (i.e., author's) point of view. Still, when accepting an author's claim for the ethnoracial perspective of his or her country as predominantly black, somewhat black, or not black at all, published demographical statistics can be misleading in all of Latin America, precisely because of another observation that Romero makes and asserts with a quote by a fellow observer of race: "Any study of the Negro in Spanish America encounters the initial difficulty of determining who is a Negro" (375). Quite unexpectedly, this perception of Latin America's carefully guarded psychological misgiving about the ethnic and racial image it would be comfortable projecting becomes the subtext of the article that originally was proposed by Romero as a historical investigation (369). It would appear that his concerns for evidence of a declared racial connection, as well as the failure of this to be as forthcoming as anticipated, impeded his approach to obtain facts and truths:

> Moreover, as long as social prejudice existed, and as long as social stratification was based upon degrees of pigmentation, it was natural for every South American to try to appear Caucasian, or very close to it. The Negro, accordingly, passed himself as mulatto, and the latter declared himself "white." (374)

Thus, in his discussion of Peru and its census figures, Romero determined that:

> And since on the other hand, existing racial prejudice led every offspring of mixed unions to seek classification as a "white" [...] within the figure for Caucasian inhabitants, many individuals are included who are not of this race. All of this has as its consequence the fact that the percentages of Negroes that appear in the censuses of 1876 and 1940 are false through defect. (379)

It was not without reason that Susana Baca, a contemporary black Peruvian singer, would assert that even though she grew up surrounded by black music, she could find no mention of Afro Peruvians in the history books of Peru (see Essay I).

Therefore, since most Latin American countries vacillate in recognizing wholeheartedly the African-descendant population in their midst and moreover decry the proliferation of African genes in their genetic constitution or base, the image of an Afro Latino as an actual person, with genetic ties to Africa, remains an enigma whose existence is often difficult to fathom for the masses in the United States. This perception pertains to most North Americans, both black and white. Political correctness, however, has attempted to refocus the racial distortion by adopting and adapting the term "Hispanic," a nomenclature that has elicited much debate in the Spanish-speaking world. Consequently, we have determined, a priori, that the cultural construct of an Afro Latino reality must have remained confined within the geographical purview of the political, social, and linguistic boundaries of the Latin American paradigm. It seems as if people in the United States never noticed, or remained confused by, the black Latin baseball players of the major leagues or the boxers, like "Kid Chocolate," who visit this country. Then again, we are more than aware that during the Second World War, Puerto Rican troops recruited by the United States were placed in color-stratified units: the fairer-skinned ones who spoke English were considered "white," or close enough to be admitted as such. And those that were determined to have the unmistakable physical characteristics of black people were assigned to African American battalions. Would it be a conundrum, then, to consider the Afro Latin and the African American to be co-genotypes within a shared genetic basis? There are signs, although feeble, that the invisible is slowly becoming visible. In a commentary recently published in *Black Enterprise*, a journal directed to the business-oriented African American population, there was the observation that

> traditionally, marketers see black people as a monolithic group. Few studies examine black diversity in terms of age or social status; fewer still acknowledge our cultural diversity. After all, we are Caribbean, Afro Latino, and African, as well as African American. (Hutson 52)

Depending on the mindset, where matters of race are solidified in a commonly held thought, the clear and undisputable fact might go unnoticed that all the groups mentioned in Hutson's remark share a singular genetic base: African. Until the cultural diversity of black people is accepted, some national groups will not be considered to have African-descendants in them. The uncertainty of racial parameters as they pertain to Latin Americans is not a topic of discussion for most Americans who subscribe to the rhetoric of "Hispanism," as if the term in some measure promoted a decree of racial singularity. Nonetheless, it has to be considered that an Afro Latino, by the narrowest of definitions, refers in the main to someone with genetic ties to Africa by birth or descent, and who has also been endowed with a sociocultural heritage (current or in disuse) from the Latin culture of the Portuguese-speaking or Spanish-speaking Americas. This, I declare, is a form of "ethnogenesis." Likewise, it has to be taken into account, as Romero confirmed over sixty years ago, that one's physical appearance (in Latin America) *might* determine one's racial assignation, although this is not absolute. Both racial blackness and racial whiteness, in Latin America, can become correlative at some point in the charting of skin tones and the graphing of the accompanying morphology of hair quality and facial features. Since the Latin American author lives and shares his space with conationals of diverse races—or, in a sense, ethnicities—we considered it pertinent to look at the author's aesthetic approach to race or the ethnicities of his or her country and the resultant creative literature. We observed the semiotic context, implanted in the literary space, with language as symbols that betray the rejection or acceptance of race/ethnicity by the national psyche, and especially the place that phenotype assumes as an artistic construct in the hierarchy of national symbols.

The fourth essay has been organized with the goal of diminishing the concept of Afro Latinism as mythos only, arguing that it should be viewed as a vital experience. It is here that we turn to an African space in real time as opposed to a fictive context. True, an African presence in the Latin space does validate the basic mythology that one finds in the literary concept of such Cuban films as *Guantanamera* and *Patakin*, with perspectives that may have come straight out of the African-related *Kulturgeschichte* of Cuba, or of Brazil with a film such as *A Deusa Negra*. Does Africa contain, nevertheless, a reality that can be conjoined to that of its Latin counterparts and serve as inspiration? It should be noted that the examples we offer in the fourth essay establish the contemporary presence of an Afro Latino link with the African continent's history and present, and with possibilities for the future, perhaps as it may pertain to the creative literature written by Latin American authors of diverse ethnic groups: black, mixed, and white. It is in this spatial reality that we confront the returnees' psyches, their strengths and weaknesses, their sensitivities, their social status, and the vagaries of human experiences without the spatial, political, and psychological constraints of slavery that still plague the Latin kinship. The new environment does not share the Latino space's sociopsychological atmosphere of noetic perceptions of enslaved race and ethnicity. We look for roles of behavior for survival, such as the African spirituality observed in Essay I. We observe the prominence or absence of phenotype as demonstrated in Essay III, or if there will be a sense of hierarchy based on economics and a perception of royalty and class entitlement.

But is it logical, some might question, to consider the symbology of an African identity in the creative literature of Latin America, and the actual existence of descendants of returnees to Africa from Latin America under the same rubric of African Latin identity? If we find that the image of the African Latino and the Latino African carries a correlative relationship, it is not without reason to explore the possibilities that such a concept offers for establishing an identity that is germane to both African and Latin heritages. In Essay IV, as we explore the world of Latino returnees to the African continent, we hypothesize how a black Latin psychology would have evolved without the encumbrance of a slave mentality .

Our curiosity about the possibility of locating Latino returnees to Africa was piqued by references to the fact that the Brazilian poet Luiz Gama was the son of Luiza Mahin, whose origins were claimed to be in Ghana. We read that she had been a hunted revolutionary figure in the fight against the enslavement of Africans in Brazil, and subsequently learned that the poet's mother might have returned to the Continent. However, the available literature presented this more as a probability than as fact. Nonetheless, the Kingdom of the Mahi is not unheard of, although there is some speculation as to whether the Mahi migrated to the Yoruba territory of present-day Nigeria from a region associated with today's Ghana (formerly called the Gold Coast). The background of the poet's mother and her African affiliation are not fantasy. Yet would Luiza Mahin return to the Gold Coast or to Nigeria after taking part in a rebellion against slavery and oppression in Brazil, we asked? Our supposition was that after a prolonged sojourn in Brazil, she could in all probability return to the Gold Coast or Nigeria a free Latina African, as opposed to remaining a fugitive, Portuguese-speaking African Latina in Brazil.

When it comes to the possibility of Africans returning to the Continent with their "latino" acculturation, the most common presumption, in the creative literature, seems to be that African enslavement to the Americas was a one-way journey and ties to the Continent were truncated completely. This thought and its ensuing aesthetics are underscored by the fact that in recent history none of the African countries, except Ghana, has ever made an overt appeal to Afrodescendants in the New World Diaspora to resettle in their nation and retrace the roots of their ancestors. This concept can perhaps be amended to include The Gambia. This West African country has of late made an effort to capitalize on the fame of Alex Haley's *Roots* and encourage African Americans of the United States to explore their heritage in the land of the novel's protagonist, Kunte Kinte, not as resettlers but as cash-spending tourists. Neither country, apparently, has given serious consideration to the Afro Latin as an integral element of the overall ethnic image of Africans and African descendants in the Diaspora. Contrary to popular notions, however, we are aware that there were large numbers of liberated Africans who did return to Africa in the nineteenth century, principally settling in Sierra Leone and Liberia. They did so with the assistance of England and the United States, and not at the expressed invitation of endemic groups already located in those areas. Furthermore, they were returnees from English-speaking countries and did not share in the culture or languages of the Latin American sphere. As a matter of fact, those African-descendant groups that American and British organizations returned to Africa tended to remain at social and political odds with the native peoples they found in their areas of settlement. For this group of returnees, apparently, the intention that led them to promote a concept of ethnic differences was aimed at maintaining an identity for themselves apart from that of the national groups that were already established in the spaces they would share.

Would Latino returnees demonstrate a similar reaction? For those freed individuals who returned from regions of British and United States control, there was the perception that a hierarchical ethnic separateness would promulgate and sustain the presumed status associated with the acquisition of British and North American cultural habits and mindsets. Along with this, there is the outsider's view that subjacent in the attitudes of economic and social entitlement harbored by the returnees is an undeniable element of *colorism*. It is common knowledge that European and African miscegenation among the returnees and their descendants was a fait accompli, just as in the Americas (north and south), in Europe, and on the African continent. Latin America, however, has additionally been endowed with a recognized phenotypocracy where social and economic entitlements are exigent. Would this mindset carry over to resettlement in Africa?

Either because manumission was only theoretical or because their rebellious acts put them at odds with the authorities, in the nineteenth century, the abandonment of some Latin territories became a viable alternative for many ex-slaves. Lingering cultural traits, vivid oral histories for some, and personal memories for others caused the image of Africa to be relived with nostalgic longings and a yearning to return. There were areas, they felt, such as Nigeria, Benin, Togo, and the Gold Coast, which would now enable them to relive a dream of belonging. Consequently, the return to Africa became a reality. Today there are descendants of those returnees to Africa whose group or clan identity depends mainly on their ancestors' sojourn in the Latin world. While these diasporic Latinos or Latino Africans have not been given a niche sui generis in the fictional imagery of Latin America's creative literature, their existence is both real and historic and merits consideration along these lines. If the aesthetics of artistic creativity have a strong foundation in the artist's social reality, then the Latino African should be drawn into the space of recognition and artistic design. As the saying goes in Latin America: "*Lo que ojos no ven, el corazón no siente.*" ["What the eyes don't see, the heart doesn't feel"].

With the previous thoughts in mind, I have posited that the presence of both the Latino in Africa and the African in Latin America merits inclusion in the artistic creation of a true perspective of the African Latino image, not as subsets of each other but as correlative ethnic groups. These were the guidelines of the first three essays, which led to the exposition in the fourth and final essay on the "Tabom" of Ghana, descendants of Afro Brazilians who in 1836 lay claim to their ethnic roots as a rationale for the justifiable reassimilation of black Latins into the folds of native African cultures.

Works Cited

Aguirre Beltran, Gonzalo. "The Slave Trade in Mexico." *The Hispanic American Historical Review* 24.3 (Aug. 1944): 412–431. Print.

Hutson, Brittany. "A Unique Consumer Market." *Black Enterprise* 42.1 (Aug. 2009): 52. Print.

Kennedy, James H. "Luiz Gama: Pioneer of Abolition in Brazil." *The Journal of Negro History* 59.3 (Jul. 1974): 255–267. Print.

Romero, Fernando. "The Slave Trade and the Negro in South America." *The Hispanic American Historical Review* 24.3 (Aug. 1944): 368–386. Print.

Tillis, Antonio D. "Afro-Hispanic Literature in the US: Remembering the Past, Celebrating the Present, and Forging a Future." *IPOTESI, Juiz de Fora* 12.1 (Jan./Jul. 2008): 21–29. Print.

The Latin American Identity and the African Diaspora

Essay I

Aesthetic Blackness in the Creative Literature of the Latin/Hispanic Reality

> Su génesis data del *Auto de los Reyes Magos* (s. XII) y el personaje negro es uno de los constantes del teatro español del Siglo de Oro. Su evolución culmina en las renovaciones del teatro lopesco... (Moses E. Panford, Jr., *Manuel Vicente Guerrero: El Negro Valiente en Flandes*)
>
> (The Black man's debut appearance dates from the *Drama of the Three Wise Men* (XIIth century), and his characterization remains a constant figure in the Spanish theater of the Golden Age. The evolution of his development as a theatrical image culminates with innovations in the theater of Lope de Vega...)

By the time of the discoveries of the Americas and the African's transfer from the Continent to Hispaniola (today's Haiti and the Dominican Republic) and subsequently to South America in the sixteenth century, his acculturation and visibility in the social context of Spain and Portugal already had a long and continuous history in the creative literature. As the quotation that opens this chapter (taken from a monograph by Moses E. Panford, Jr.) shows, the black figure as a literary and theatrical constant appeared to be both culturally anticipated and a depiction of the social reality of the Iberian environment of the day. However, when considering issues of ethnic diversity in a given society in the atmosphere of today, most studies that focus on race, racial groups, ethnicity, and ethnic groups in a particular society utilize either sociological methods or a historical timeline as a guide or as the emphasis of their direction. Yet creative literature as an integral element of the social environment in which it is produced can likewise function as an informative medium, with both time and space as contextual parameters. Furthermore, when the author's exposition is adjusted to the time slot of his characterization, the creative construct can likewise offer insight into the historical period of the artistic production. Consequently, when the conjunct of time, space, and character roles is interpreted as the exemplum of a sociological presence within a specified framework of historicity, a literary expression or image of this nature can certainly be accepted as the opinion that guides the author's art. Such an approach has been found to express the inherent lyricism of a writer in the production of his or her creation based on a personal perception of locale and moment.

For example, two recent studies among the various others that have been added to the growing body of literature that strengthens the validity of an African-descendant image in Latin America are: Stinchcomb, *The Development of Literary Blackness in the Dominican Republic* (2004), and Hernández Cuevas, *África late en la mexicanidad* (2007) [Africa Pulsates Within the Mexican Identity]. Both books focus on the creative literature of a specific Latin American country with the intent of establishing therein an Afro Latin presence as fact. While one viewpoint is presented from the perspective of a North American scholar who is not native to the environment and the other from that of a Latin American academic born and raised in the culture, the opinion of each, in questions of an identifiable Africanity in situ, coincides without controversy: Africa is a vibrantly integral aspect of Latin America's reality both culturally and spiritually, and presents evidence of her physiognomic incursion into the area.

From another point of view, the Dominican-American writer Junot Diaz deftly characterizes this vision of the reality of an Afro Latin existence with a style that stretches the boundaries of the interplay between the magical and the real. It is the technique with which he interprets his observation of Africa's influence in the life of the Dominican characters in his 2007 work *The Brief Wondrous Life of Oscar Wao*. Africa's spiritual reality makes a decisive entry into the overall thematic drive of Diaz's creation with a magical presence. This dual imagery of the factual and the marvelous is perceived with the very first words that introduce the context and concept of this novel: "They say that it came first from Africa, carried in the screams of the enslaved" (1).

Although this stereotypical "it" is introduced without a solid shape or form, it does have a name and a purpose when it sets foot in the New World, that is, Hispaniola. Hispaniola is unquestionably the *site*, the epicenter, and the ground zero of the author's cultural reality. It is likewise the area where Spanish invaders first set foot in the Americas and concomitantly introduced African slavery to the New World. This introduction brought with it the mystical and spiritual force of the enslaved African. Coupled with a name and purpose, the author has also designed a destiny for this metaphysical expression. The reader intuitively grasps the force of the Diaz "it" as he, the author, defines and reveals the concept's drive and purpose by means of the actions of being, of doing, of perceiving, and being perceived. Thus an African puissance, so to speak, is transformed, in this sense, into a dual ontological energy of commencement and conclusion. Consequently, not only the actions of Diaz's characters, but their physical being and, not surprisingly, their fates are all driven by the "it" that has been established as the force majeure of the context: "Maritza, with her chocolate skin and slanted eyes, already expressing the *Ogún energy* that she would chop at everybody with for the rest of her life" (14; emphasis added). Ogún is found in the pantheon of gods (i.e., Orichas/Orixas) that African captives brought with them to the Americas and that served to ensure a certain spiritual strength that in turn was passed on to their descendants. It has been said that in no other realm are African cultural forms more evident in Dominican society than in spiritual expressions (Torres-Saillant 132).

Fukú americanus is the classical entry that the author assigns to this transcendent force, transformed from its African image to accommodate the conditions of a new geographical and social environment. But in the local vernacular—that is, the popular speech of the Dominican Republic—this spiritual "it" is referred to simply as *fukú*, and is approached by Diaz in accordance with the reality of Dominican folklore and experiences: "*fuku* [is]...generally a curse or a doom of some kind; specifically the Curse and the Doom of the New World" (1). However, in quotidian terms, *fukú* appears to have both a negative as well as a positive aura. Given that the scourge of slavery in the Americas was introduced with Santo Domingo as the gate, Diaz feels justified in declaring that "Santo Domingo might be fukú's Kilometer Zero, its port of entry, but we are all of us its children, whether we know it or not" (2). The perception that the reader intuits is that *fukú*'s purpose is in some way connected to the transfer of the African's essence to an alien and hostile environment; and for Diaz, all inhabitants of Kilometer Zero—that is, Santo Domingo, and by extension all of Hispaniola (in other words, Haitians as well as Dominicans)—fall under the sway of *fukú*'s potency.

According to the belief system of most African philosophies that were transferred to the Americas along with Africa's sons and daughters, the Supreme Being of all creation has dispensed *aché* (Spanish), or *axé* (Portuguese) to everyone. In this cosmovision, *aché/axé* is perceived as life force, power, grace, or blessing. In some philosophies, Orichas/Orixas or assistants to the Supreme Being are responsible for the guidance of each individual. While this explanation may appear somewhat simplistic and makes reference only to the Spanish- and Portuguese-speaking communities in the Americas, this explanation in fact refers to a complex metaphysical system that has survived in West Africa over millennia and in all of the Americas since the introduction of African slavery. Central to the worldview of these philosophies is the idea of destiny. Destiny, however, is not just the end result but also the path that leads one to the end result. Herein lie the forces of thoughts, ideas, words, and actions that become integrated to determine one's fate or one's personal aura. Is *fukú*, then, the hand of fate, the hand that leads to destruction, or is *fukú* one's positive karma that leads to success? Or, can our energy matrix be a combination of the two? Just as he, the author, specifically assigned Ogún to Maritza and to no one else in the novel, Diaz is quite successful in showing that, in Kilometer Zero (i.e., Hispaniola), each person's Oricha is different and acts according to a preplanned destiny. The personality traits of Diaz's characters do not overlap. Oscar Wao, the principal figure, is blessed with the attributes of an African bloodline that evolves into an Afro Latino reality, and his *fukú* bestows on him the karma that ultimately decrees his fate. While the penultimate chapter of *The Brief Wondrous Life of Oscar Wao*, "Curse of the Caribbean," appears detached from the ending, it is, nonetheless, the instance where Oscar's *fukú* reveals its definitive hand.

The spiritual presence of *fukú* as a perception that can be invasively malignant at times may assume various phonemic shapes throughout the Americas without compromising the spiritual base, be it *fufu* or *juju*. It is a concept fully understood in all environments that received the African captive and are now home to his descendants. In his study of the black African element in Puerto Rican Spanish, Manuel Alvarez Nazario begins his explanation of the term with the entry *Fufú*, and associates it with "Black people along the coasts of Puerto Rico and even in English-speaking North America" (288–289) as a referent to witchcraft and malignant spirits. However, it is in the Caribbean area of Colombia, in Venezuela's Falcon State, and in Santo Domingo where the switch to *fukú* becomes most evident, according to Alvarez Nazario's research (288–289). While the art of Junot Diaz is fiction, the fundamental base for this art relies in large measure on the historic verisimilitude of the African in the American space as an Afro Latin reality.

From an examination of the cited entries and from other available bibliographies it can be concluded that novels, poetry, and even song lyrics, although fictive in content, can be understood as an artist's interpretation of his or her reality. For example, Diaz's fictional world leads to an admission of an African presence in his Dominican milieu. This reality is, of course, shaped by a cosmovision that the author may or may not share with other members of the macrocosmic national group or microcosmic social subgroup. For the average Dominican, for example, an assertion of having an African base, physically or spiritually, can be a cause for heated debates or absolute denial. Considering this, one often finds that for some authors, reality is the result of a reaction to the norms and cultural traits of the group's cosmos. This concept, used as a basis or hypothesis for the presentation of the Afro Latin reality that follows, helps to focus the understanding that writings about or by the Spanish- and Portuguese-speaking African descendant will not be aesthetically uniform or even psychologically of one accord. It is determined that sensitivity to his or her sociocultural atmosphere can be, and often is, an element of motivation for the artist and consequently helps to formulate his or her aesthetic theory.

In a pioneering study on the concept of black aesthetics as seen in selected works of a representative sampling of nonwhite Latin American authors, it was determined that

> in Latin America, the systematic study of blackness as a subjective concept, as the expression of an author's personal reaction to his surroundings is further obfuscated by the Latin American approach to black esthetics and racism. Few studies treat the internal theme of the author as part of an ethnic continuum. (Boyd, "The Concept of Black Esthetics" 9)

It was further concluded that the concept of black aesthetics is a reaction to being sealed in black in opposition to being sealed in white. In these terms, one sees artistic reactions as stimuli. The stimulus becomes a motivator under the guise of self-evaluation within a given society (1). In Latin America, it should never be overlooked that self-evaluation as an African descendant is either an act of commission or of omission based solely on precedent or prescribed social norms. Working within these boundaries one adjusts to the fact that an Afro Latin reality remains fluid in Latin America, given that an obviously non-Caucasoid individual in Puerto Rico, for example, may be euphemistically classified as *"trigueño"* ["tannish"], while conversely that same person in the Dominican Republic is unquestionably accepted as *"blanco,"* meaning "white," with all of the prerogatives and social attributes that that society reserves for its lighter-complexioned members. This is but one example of a corpus of racial attitudes one finds throughout the Spanish- and Portuguese-speaking Americas. In all fairness, it must be made clear that most Latin American societies do not overtly authorize racist attitudes in this day and age. The emphasis here is on "most." However, one has to deal with the covert in Latin America, and covertly, for most countries, the structure and pattern of acceptance and success follow the degree of one's consanguine affiliation to a Caucasoid and/or non-Caucasoid ethnic group. Studies have shown that no person can be explained outside the frame of reference that includes the organic heritage, the social heritage, the human nature, and the unique experience of that person (Boyd, "The Concept of Black Esthetics" 13). Consequently, admitting that the presence of Africa in Latin America is a reality organizes the summation of all of the foregoing. It is a reality that manifests itself in the area's basic culture, in the language, in the karma and religiosity, and, most importantly, has played an important role in shaping the imagery of the national phenotypes that the outside world considers to be the Latin American prototype.

* * * * * *

Little does the outsider suspect, however, that the culture and phenotype classified as "Hispanic" or "Latin" in the autochthonous sense are the denouement of a few centuries of close interaction among the Africans, Europeans, and indigenous Indians that have peopled the region. The proportions are not equally balanced in all regions. Some areas, such as Mexico and Central America, are decidedly more European and indigenous Indian, but do have an African element diffused within the ethnic composition. Other areas, including the Spanish-speaking Caribbean (Cuba, Dominican Republic, and Puerto Rico), have a generous admixture of African genes attached to a European base and a latent if not a complete absence of indigenous Indian stock. Yet, Puerto Rico appears to be less African, in phenotype, than the Dominican Republic. Cuba, with its vibrant African presence and strong psychological tendency to separate the miscegenated from the European-appearing person, lies somewhere in the middle of its two sister countries. Nonetheless, all three share a genotypic and phenotypic Afro Latin reality that is inescapable. Miscegenation of the races is the process that has mestized the European genetic base (i.e., created mixed-race individuals, or "mestizos") to produce the chromatic range in pigmentation that eludes ethnoracial typing by the unaware. As for the vast landmass of the South American continent, from Venezuela down to Chile, African genes are certain to appear in today's sophisticated DNA processing. Colombia, in this respect, has the third-highest number of African descendants after Brazil and Cuba.

Portuguese-speaking Brazil, in contrast, is not only Africanized culturally, linguistically, and phenotypically, but its spiritual karma owes as much if not more to the ancestral concept of a Supreme Being brought over on the slave ships from Africa than to practices of Christianity, Judaism, or Islam. Recent scientific studies by Brazilian researchers have proven that for the Brazilian populace there exists the hazard of ethnoracial misinterpretation when "equating color or race with geographical ancestry, and using interchangeably terms such as white, Caucasian, and European on the one hand, and black, Negro or African on the other" (Parra et al. 181). Brazilians, according to this study ("Color and genomic ancestry in Brazilians"), form one of the most heterogeneous populations in the world. This is basically due to five centuries of interethnic mixing of peoples from Europe and Africa with the autochthonous Amerindian (179).

This does not mean, however, that there is complete acceptance or admission of an African-derived heritage as an integral element or as the basis of the ethnic composition of all peoples in the areas where Spanish and Portuguese are the linguistic means of communication. Most tend to look askance when questioned about an African element in their country's ethnicity. What pigmentation does not reveal, a psychological defense of denial or preclusion becomes the national modus operandi. In other words, one hopes to be accepted as white based on appearances and not on a supposed African-related bloodline. Such an approach is confirmed by a statement that the black Peruvian singer Susana Baca gave to the *San Francisco Chronicle* on September 24, 1997: "Peruvian radio is dominated by foreign music...I was surrounded by black music, but I never heard it on the radio, and I could find no mention of Afro-Peruvians in the history books." Her rendition of "Zamba Malató," with phrases and vocabulary in an African language, appears to pay homage to ancestry and in-group tradition. As the liner notes for the album indicate:

> The Zamba Malató is a style believed to be derived from the traditional landó...the music has African words that, like everything in the oral tradition, have lost significance or have been distorted in their pronunciation....(Susana Baca)

It is the oral tradition, in most countries, that perpetuates the connection to Africa that distance and chronology tend to mitigate or that the dominant society had hoped to eradicate by a policy of silence and/or denial.

The publication identified at the beginning of this essay, *África late en la mexicanidad*, forces us to consider whether Latin America's connection to Africa is mere supposition or if the disquisition its author offers supports the proposed imagery in the title. Perhaps one of the most commented upon volumes concerning the presence of African populations in the Americas has been Gonzalo Aguirre Beltran's *La Población negra de México* [The Black Population of Mexico]. If the concept of Hernández Cuevas is coalesced with the research of Aguirre Beltran, one can better understand, for example, how a term such as "Bamba" in Richie Valens' popular hit, with the line *"para bailar la bamba se necesita una poca de gracia..."* ["to dance the bamba you've got to have a little bit of grace"], can be accepted as the vestige of an African legacy that Mexico received from the presence of African slaves on its soil. This legacy continues to pulsate through the veins of the Mexican identity. Legend has it that "La Bamba" is a traditional folk song and dance originally sung by slaves as they worked in Vera Cruz, Mexico during the seventeenth century. Aguirre Beltran has located a territory in the south of Zaire (today's Democratic Republic of the Congo) with a province called Bamba. Its inhabitants were known by the tribal name of Ba-Mbamba, and during the era of captive African labor some were sent to Mexico grouped under the name Bamba (Aguirre Beltran, *La población* 140). Evidently, there is some currency to the folk history of "La Bamba" as a form of music and dance. David Haro, also a Mexican lyricist and singer, has penned the following verses for a *décima* (a poetic form) entitled "Mozambique":

> *Somos negros de la costa tropical*
> *Bamba, bamba e*
> *Llevamos sangre de la que regó Cuauhtémoc*
> *Somos mexicanos*
> *Cantamos sones*
> *Bailamos la rumba*
> *Veracruzanos de color*
> *Y pelo crespo* (Sones de Mexico, *Fandango*)

> (We are blacks from the tropical coast
> Bamba, bamba yeh
> We carry the blood of Cuauhtémoc within us
> We are Mexican
> We sing the "son"
> We dance the rhumba
> Vera Cruzans of color
> And kinky hair)

Yet in spite of the affirmation indicated by the lyrics, there is a long history of reluctance in Mexico to embrace the Afromestizo (mixed African and Amerindian) identity. In "Afro-Mexican History: Trends and Directions in Scholarship," the author found that the black person in early Mexican society was "viewed ambivalently, that is, as being both a part and not a part of the nation; their experiences possessed an added voyeuristic effect" (Vinson 2). Nonetheless, in a pictorial essay that appeared in the April 2007 issue of *Inside Mexico*, it was noted by the Mexican photographer Alberto Ibañez that: "The Afromestizo community is part of the skin of our country, a face that appears to be looking to the sea, searching for its origin" (18). Additionally, there is the affirmation that:

> The African heritage in the Mexican identity remains patent along with the nation's Amerindian, Asian and Spanish legacies, amongst others; and these, in a sense, are the amalgams or archives of previous encounters of diverse human groups. This fact leads us to conclude that the mixing of races is a phenomenon that transcends the question of "appearances," precisely in that dimension where "appearances are deceptive." (Hernández Cuevas 94)

Brazilian researchers have also concluded that "In Brazil, at an individual level, color, as determined by physical evaluation, was a poor predictor of genomic ancestry, estimated by molecular markers" (Pimenta et al. 194).

It is precisely this duplicity of appearances that has made the concretization of the Afro Latin identity so elusive. One must always be mindful of the fact that particular phenotypes in the "Hispano/Latino" ethnography, as genomic studies have shown, are not an end result, but are only the visible evidence of a genetic instancy that can further destabilize or be physiognomically transformed with an unexpected outcome. The acceptance or rejection of the miscegenated individual's physical appearance depends on his or her cultural environment. Notwithstanding this, there is an established precedent in Latin societies of recognizing miscegenation as an intermediate stage within the range of blackness, even if the miscegenated individual might hope to be categorized finally into the upper echelon of the racial scale (i.e., with a classification of whiteness). This mindset can even be found in *Lazarillo de Tormes*, a sixteenth-century tale of early Spain written by an anonymous author. In order to put food on the table, Lazarillo's poor and widowed mother begins to cohabit with Zaide, a black man, whose contributions to their pantry make life much better for both mother and son. These contributions, which lead to an improved lifestyle, turn Lazarillo's distrust and fear of his stepfather—mainly due to his color—into admiration and respect.

A biracial son is the result of the union between Zaide and Lazarillo's mother. Lazarillo finds his half-brother to be quite attractive—*"mi madre vino a darme un negrito muy bonito"* ["my mother presented me with a beautiful little black boy"]—and shows him brotherly love and affection without any hint of racial prejudice. The brother, though, finds his father's black color to be intimidating (*"Madre, coco"* ["Momma, the bogeyman"]) and gravitates more favorably toward his white mother and white half-brother Lazarillo. Lazarillo, however, comments that the brother should look at himself first before denigrating his father's color. He also understands that his brother probably shares this tendency with others in the ethnoracial environment of his sixteenth-century Spain:

> Yo, aunque bien muchacho, noté aquella palabra de mi hermanico y dije entre mí: "¡ Cuántos debe [sic] de haber en el mundo que huyen de otros porque no se veen a sí mismos!" (Rico 17–18)

> (Although I was still a young lad, I made note of my little brother's remarks ["momma, the bogeyman"] and said to myself: "I wonder how many there are in this world that flee from others because they don't look at themselves!")

Lazarillo's observations concerning racial differences and the psychological dilemma of the mixed-race individual serve to confirm the historical fact of the early presence of blacks on the Iberian Peninsula, which precedes the appearance of the African in the Americas. Some researchers allege that many of the Moors that invaded the peninsula and stayed between the eighth and fifteenth centuries were black. Regardless of whether the term "Moor" has ethnic or racial connotations, research has proven and rendered indisputable that both Spain and Portugal made incursions into Equatorial Africa prior to the sixteenth-century context of Lazarillo's anecdotal reference to his time and space, as the following comment makes clear:

> ...de 1441 a 1505 teriam sido levados de África para Portugal pelo menos umas 140,000 cabeças humanas, possivelmente acima de 150 000. (José Ramos Tinhorão 85)

(...between 1441 and 1505 there could have been taken to Portugal from Africa some 140,000 human beings, possibly more than 150,000.)

When one reads that in both the sixteenth and seventeenth century, 10 percent of the registered population in Lisbon, Portugal's capital, was black (Loude 33), the statistics cited by Tinhorão appear sufficiently credible. While the transportation of black slaves to the Americas is recorded as beginning in earnest in the sixteenth century, in Europe African labor had started many years before. The first African slaves arrived in Portugal some fifty years before Columbus sighted the lands of the New World, before Vasco da Gama returned from his voyage to India, and prior to Pedro Alvares Cabral's landing on the shores of the Land of the Holy Cruz, later baptized as Brazil (33). With further reference to Lazarillo's observation regarding his biracial half-brother, interracial unions in both Spain and Portugal had already become a fait accompli, with miscegenated offspring a not unheard of result. Many Islamized Africans came with the invasion of the Arabs in the eighth century, while other Africans were recorded to have been in the area prior to the invasion of the Arabs in 711 A.D.. Meanwhile, during the same period, sexual unions between the European male and the African female were not unusual even before the African female left the Continent to be sent to her destiny in Europe or Latin America. Consequently, one speaks today of an Afro Latin/Afro Hispanic ethnicity that displays a broad gamut of skin tones. Nonetheless, prior to this contemporary reality reference can also be made to an Afro Iberian actuality as the established precedent for the present-day image of inconclusive phenotypes. An actuality is found much earlier than Lazarillo's sixteenth-century Spain:

> The semantics of early Spanish literature written in Arabic, or perhaps better defined as Arabic literature written in Spain during the eighth to the fifteenth centuries, in no uncertain terms attest to Afro Iberian identities within the process of cultural transmission. (Boyd and Abudu 291)

The following lines, taken from the poem "The Raven and the Lily" by Ibn Hamdin of twelfth-century Spain, comment on the perceived image of an interracial union of that era, even though the language attempts to subterfuge the intent:

> I saw perched on a lily a raven whose presence
> announced a year of misfortune.
> What an honor for the ebony brush that
> applies the ointment.
> Yet what vilification for the delicate ivory
> receptacle of the ointment (Boyd and Abudu 287)

The context for these lines is as enlightening toward an understanding of twelfth-century racial aesthetics in Spain as the lines themselves, which delicately portray a pornographic image of a black man in sexual union with a white woman. The manuscript from which the lines are taken states that a black slave (Abdun Aswad), in order to file a complaint against his white wife, appeared before the twelfth-century Spanish jurisprudent Ibn Hamid. Cultural lacunae obscure the dimensions of implied racism in the cited lines, since it is not made clear that the husband and wife have an equal social status—they are both slaves. Southern Spain, at this historical moment ruled by the Almoravids (Moors), was under the jurisprudence of Malikite Islamic Law, which decreed that a slave man could only marry a slave woman. Within the social context, the jurist feels that the "ebony brush" is honored while "the ivory receptacle" is vilified. With the not-too-subtle appeal to racial differences, his meaning is all too apparent (Boyd and Abudu 288). Although they are both slaves, his black color vilifies her; her ivory color honors him. In the Latin world, recognized interracial unions and bi- or multiracial offspring enjoy a long but silent, hidden, and often embarrassing history that started even before the Americas were settled, as examples from "The Raven and the Lily" and *Lazarillo de Tormes* so clearly show.

In today's world, Latin America's vast array of almost-white or almost-black phenotypes—with cultural classifications such as *jabao, grifo, indio-blanco, moreno claro, moreno oscuro, mulato claro, mulato oscuro, moro, chino* (in the ethno-phenotypic sense "chino" does not refer to an Asian in some Latin American countries), *morocho, trigueño, indio con facciones de negro, negro con pelo lacio, ondulado o suavemente enrizado, negro de facciones finas, moreno adelantado, pardo, fula*, or the red-haired *bachaco* mulatto of Venezuela—is but a miniscule listing of indeterminate categories of color that are produced in the miscegenation process, and often appear as descriptors in the creative literature. One finds these skin tones and designations of racial characteristics catalogued throughout Spanish-speaking Latin America. Brazil's listing, while much more expansive, follows a similar paradigm of inconclusive ethnoracial patterning.

As indicated, the African presence in Latin America, together with acts of interracial procreation, is not a recent phenomenon for the Spanish- and Portuguese European base, as seen in Spain's sixteenth-century *Lazarillo de Tormes* and in references to earlier centuries. An unknown number of black and "mulatto" servitors were in the entourage of Hispaniola's first governor, Nicolas Ovando, when he landed on the island in 1502 (Rout Jr. 24). The first slaves brought from Spain to the Americas had already begun to show signs of being the issue of biracial unions. During a recent trip to the Elmina Castle on Cape Coast, Ghana, the learned docent made it graphically clear that before African women were shipped to Europe, and subsequently to the Americas, many were forced to submit to sex acts with their Spanish and Portuguese slavers while being held captive in forts and dungeons. In their lectures, the guides emphasized that the question of biracial offspring did not appear to be a matter of much discussion or concern for the slaver/rapist. Mixed-race children were both a happenstance result and an incriminating fact of the female slave/white captor relationship.

* * * * * *

In Latin America, racial identity—or who is or is not black—seems to have always been and continues to be a matter of appearances. The noticeable presence or noticeable absence of African genes is considered, without a doubt, the principal factor of ethnic and racial classification. The emphasis is on "noticeable." Both in the past and in the present, social adjustments of treatment and acceptance are based on the chromatic scale. The higher in the scale toward an identity of European whiteness that one progressed in the past (and progresses in today's social environment), the more positive the social rewards. This seems to be precisely the point that the Venezuelan poet, political activist, senator, and minister of foreign relations Andrés Eloy Blanco (1896–1955) seemed to express with his popular verses entitled "Angelitos Negros" ["Little Black Angels"]:

> *Pintor nacido en mi tierra*
> *con el pincel extranjero*
> *pintor que sigues el rumbo*
> *de tantos pintores viejos.*
>
> *Aunque la virgen sea blanca*
> *píntame angelitos negros,*
> *que también se van al cielo*
> *todos los negritos buenos.*
>
> *Pintor, si pintas con amor,*
> *por qué desprecias su color,*
> *si sabes que en el cielo*
> *también los quiere Dios.*
>
> *Pintor de santos de alcoba*
> *si tienes alma en el cuerpo,*
> *porque al pintar en tus cuadros*
> *te olvidaste de los negros.*
>
> *Siempre que pintas iglesias*
> *pintas angelitos bellos*
> *pero nunca te acordaste*
> *de pintar un ángel negro.*

In a summarized English interpretation, the poet questions the actions of a native painter:

> Although you are an artist born in this land, this country, your paintings seem to have a foreign aura. Even though the Blessed

Aesthetic Blackness in the Creative Literature   17

Virgin "may" be white ["sea blanca"], you should also have little black angels surrounding her. They likewise go to heaven.

"If you are painting with love," continues the poet, "why do you despise their color? You know that God also wants them in heaven." However, as already noted, the deciding factor in who is embraced or rejected as the prototypical Latin or the representative native is a matter of physical features, not the sociocultural makeup of the individual. Eloy Blanco continues with his admonishment to remind the artist that he always seems to overlook little black angels in favor of "little pretty angels" ["*Siempre...pintas angelitos bellos*"]. Little pretty angels? Is this an uncontrollable parapraxis on the part of the poet, or the simple admission of a culturally controlled concept? It is clear that for the poet (or his Latin culture), black is a synonym for ugly and white is a synonym for pretty. This is unquestionably apparent as Andrés Eloy Blanco juxtaposes "angelitos negros" against "angelitos bellos."

Where the acceptance of an Afro Latin identity is at the core, race relations in Latin America have always been confusing for the outsider and indeterminate for the native practitioner. Often a black or racially mixed person, on an individual basis, will be accepted and accorded the recognition and respect reserved principally for the Caucasoid-appearing person. Yet his ethnic group, identified as Afro- or African-related, neither advances socially nor benefits from the social merits acquired by the isolated member of the group. Simón Bolívar, the father of Venezuela's independence movement and the acclaimed liberator of South America, never hid the fact that his personality and character were formed by two black women who worked in his house—his wet nurse and a nanny, namely "la negra Hipólita" (1763–1835) and "la negra Matea" (1773–1886). Today both women, in an unofficial capacity, serve as national icons of abnegation and have been conferred the ultimate honor of being buried in the Bolívar crypt alongside the president's family.

To add to this confusion however, the converse is also found. It is no secret that Fulgencio Batista, Cuba's president prior to Fidel Castro, was designated multiracial, and in this mixture African genes were always given consideration. Batista's phenotype was by no means European. More than one observer or biographer has listed Batista's racial background as including European, African, Indian, and Chinese ancestors. Given the racial composition of Cuba as a nation, this fact would make him 100% Cuban. Yet not even as president of the nation could Batista acquire membership in the racially elitist Havana Yacht Club, due to the miniscule amount of his European (viz. Spanish) genetic makeup. Closer to 2010, Hugo Chávez, another South American president, has found stiff opposition to his governance by the Caucasoid-appearing upper- and upper-middle-class individuals of his country. Politically, opposition to the president's policies is blamed on his alleged socialist agenda. In addition, some have received quite negatively the president's multiracial appearance and his declared acceptance of mixed-race roots. In a revealing paper prepared by Ana Chalá for the Commission on Human Rights and read at the Ninth Session of the Sub-Commission on Promotion and Protection of Human Rights, Working Group on Minorities, she unabashedly asserted that "Hugo Chavez is the first multiracial president of Venezuela and is called 'Negro' (N . . . r) [a racial epithet] by his detractors because of his African-Indigenous features." The author affirms in her study that the cultural presence of an African background is still felt in Venezuela's approach to spoken Spanish and its popularly observed religious activities (Chalá 32).

The denigration of groups and individuals in the attempt to negate an Afro Latin reality in Latin America is an issue that creates constant conflict in the broad socioethnic perspective of the area. Some countries, such as Argentina, have attempted to erase from national memory all indictments of having cooperated with the slave trade. What validity would an Argentine national find in a title entry such as: "The first genocide in Argentina and why the colored nation disappeared. In the XIXth century between 1850 and 1870, there was a culture of negritude"? How relevant to the concept of contemporary race relations in Argentina and its denial of ever having had an African presence can be seen in the following statement, translated from the article in reference:

> Socialism arrived in Rio de la Plata long before European immigration. It was the black community of Buenos Aires, liberated under the National Constitution of 1853…ex-slaves, who in 1858 offered the first ideas and doctrines of a utopian socialism. This was six years before the International Workers' Association was created in Europe in 1864, and spearheaded by Marx, Engels and the anarchist Miguel Bakunin.
>
> On 18 April 1858, a black intellectual, Lucas Fernandez, created and directed a weekly journal called *The Proletariat*, with the purpose of addressing class interests, i.e. the interest of the 'colored class.'
>
> Argentine leftists have some doubt about these black pioneers, erased from history and from memory. (Corbiere, "El genocidio en la Argentina")

While Argentina has aggressively attempted to rid its memory of all vestiges of the slave society that helped to propel its economy forward, most other American countries seem to have accepted their Afro Latin reality, albeit reluctantly. Bolivia, Uruguay, Paraguay, Mexico, and Chile still are being coerced, as the result of ongoing and published research, to admit to an African presence. For them, the possibility of denying a connection to a black heritage is more tenuous now than ever before. In those countries, as in most of the Diaspora, the African has left a mark where his or her person was received that is like "cables of perdurable toughness," to adapt a phrase from a translation of Shakespeare's Iago (France 77). For example, the concept of the tango as a stylized dance form is ingrained as strongly in the national psyche of Argentina as the Rio de la Plata is as a symbol of that country's topography. Further, most researchers have determined that tango is a word and a dance of Yoruba origin, and thus readily accept its African roots. Many in Argentina with Eurocentric cultural inclinations vehemently reject this provenance.

While the *bamba* of Mexico and the tango of Argentina are mere words used within a national corpus of European origin, they are indeed traceable as having been deracinated from the African continent along with the enslaved peoples that brought them as concepts of a lived reality. As such, each concept appears in its respective lexical niche in the Americas as linguistic vestiges of a cultural and physical manifestation that has lost its indigenous perspective on the contemporary scene. That there is a psychological need for some countries to still attempt to deny a linkage between Africa and their modern societies is part and parcel of the image that the enslavement of Africans in Latin America has wrought. But, as Lovejoy in "The African Diaspora: Revisionist Interpretations of Ethnicity, Culture and Religion under Slavery" informs us:

> [A]n effort is being made to bridge that almost unbridgeable gap that separates the academic study of slavery and the slave trade from a full and general appreciation of the heritage of Africa in the Diaspora and the modern world. (2)

This research and study of the aesthetics of the Afro Latin world has shown that evidence of an African lineage in Latin America goes far beyond the phenotypic image. Aspects of the area's creative literature confirm that a strong black identity in South America, Central America, and the Spanish-speaking Caribbean is both definitive and vibrantly quotidian at various levels—including spiritual, linguistic, and philosophical, among others—even without overt admission. One can find tangible features of an African heritage integrated into the fibers of contemporary life in these regions of the Americas and perceive that these aspects go a long way toward shaping the cultural demarcation of many countries. As Lovejoy also points out, "[f]or many slaves in the Americas, Africa continued to live in their daily lives" (8). It is this lived experience that has become a cultural force in the day-to-day context of many Latin American environments. For some, this experience passed down from generation to generation has become the psychological and social dynamic that creates a sense of ethnic solidarity. Perhaps this sense of ethnic cohesion and unity can be explained in real terms by referring to an interview between a white sociologist and a black Uruguayan university student. In answer to the question of what characterized, specifically, the Afrodescendant experience in Uruguay, the reply was:

> The most interesting fact is the clear evidence that amongst all blacks in Uruguay there is this feeling of belonging to an ethnic aggregate with whom things are shared. Not everyone places emphasis on the same things, but there is a sentiment of kinship. They all say that belonging to an ethnic group "is something that is felt." This shows that there is a sense of alliance because of common rights [and] common needs. (La Onda Digital, "Diálogo con la sicóloga Susana Rudolf")

This sense of shared needs and shared rights is perhaps one of the principal modules for determining group bonding in the construct of an Afro Latin identity. More likely than not, the realization that one is participating in or has participated in the construct of mutual affiliation will stem from an acceptance or recognition of one's historical link to an African history, a history that was transported to the Americas under the conditions of belonging to a captive group. Although it may not be overtly expressed, the psychological sentience for an ethnoracial group connection tends to remain subjacent, although not totally absent. Often it is subjectively felt. For the creative artist, more than likely his or her awareness of an ethnoracial affiliation will be couched as the subtext of the artistic expression. In this manner, the artist's sentiments will seem less oratorical, less sententious. While not overtly expressed, for the black Colombian writer Manuel Zapata Olivella, the displaced phenotype becomes pivotal to the storyline in his novel *Chambacú corral de negros* [Chambacu, a Ghetto of Black People]: "*Dominguito le creció en el vientre como una maldición. El pelo rojo y la piel lechosa. Ajeno en la isla. 'El hijo del blanco Emiliano'. Nació sin padre*" ["Little Dominguito grew in her womb like a curse. His red hair and his milk-colored skin. So foreign on the island. 'The son of the white man Emiliano.' He was born fatherless"] (22). The implications are multiple, although parsimoniously indicated. Miscegenation, a reality that is often ignored in some Latin environments, is the glaring entity of focus in this vignette. This child grew in his mother's womb as a curse. Why? At birth, his red hair and milky white coloring gave him away as not being the child of a co-islander. Chambacú, as Zapata Olivella tells us, was an island whose inhabitants were all black. The author uses his perception of the environment as subtitle: *un corral de negros* [a ghetto of black people]. The historical link that the island's inhabitants have with each other is obvious in the author's construction. Dominguito, as the child was named, was the son of Emiliano, an outsider, a white man. The child's phenotype had made his paternity suspect, and unequivocally suggested interracial breeding. That in and of itself could have been seen as a curse in this all-black society. Only his mother's ties to her black community saved Dominguito. Curiously, in other Afro Latin societies a phenotype of this nature would have been considered an advancement and hence a step away from the embrace of Africa in a history and psychology that entailed enslavement. As a matter of fact, the cultural expression used to denote generational skin color that changes from dark to light within the group, in many Latin American countries, is precisely "*adelantar la raza*" (to improve the race, i.e., make it lighter in complexion). For Zapata Olivella to say that red-haired, milky white Dominguito was the son of a white man was superfluous in a certain sense, but necessary artistically to intimate that the father was someone with whom the black people of Chambacú were familiar, and who was not one of them racially.

As an Afro Latin writer, Zapata Olivella intentionally exposes one of the avenues of miscegenation in the Latin American world: relationships through rape or concubinage of white men with black women, even though the race of the latter, as a whole, is despised or belittled by the socially dominant group. The Afro Latin reader will surely raise additional questions concerning the phenotype of Dominguito. By itself, "*piel lechosa*," that is, milk-colored skin, does not definitively guarantee, for the Afro Latin reader, that this child's coloring is the sole result of a white ancestor in the immediate past, or that he will be accepted as white. In all Latin American cultures, there are a plethora of words to describe the individual whose skin tone might be in a range of acceptable whiteness but whose total phenotypic morphology indicates a near or distant African ancestor. While color is of paramount significance, there are other physical determinants such as the shape of the nose, the fullness of one's lips, and the amount and type of curl to one's hair that also pronounce a linkage to an African ancestral base. However, the color of the Afro Latin individual can range from very black (*negro retinto*) to almost white (*jabao, mulatto claro, pardo,* etc.). Consequently, when another Colombian writer, Carlos Arturo Truque, describes a character in his short story "Vivan los compañeros" ["Long Live the Comrades"] as "*el negro Ayala*" ["Ayala, the black man"], there would be little to distinguish him phenotypically from other people found in the Colombian context of this story. However, in need of specifics to highlight and denigrate the racial imagery of Ayala, Truque focuses on a physical feature attributed to most blacks, but often reserved in literary descriptions as an overt pejorative: "*el jetón Ayala*" ["big-lipped Ayala"] (124). Even when the reader learns that Ayala, in this short story, has outstanding qualities, is quite astute, and very intelligent, his one unredeeming characteristic and major impediment is the fact that he is black. Evidently, Truque's omniscient voice intends to register or indicate a generalized disapproval and distrust of all blacks in his society, morphed into the negative characterization of Ayala, "*el Negro engreído*" ["the self-centered Negro"] (130):

> El mismo Ayala nos recibe en una choza...Es alto... Tiene los brazos muy largos, pero delgados y con venas protuberantes; la cara es igualmente delgada y huesosa, de color negro ceniza, característica de negro enfermo. (132)
>
> (Ayala himself receives us in a hut...He is tall.... His arms are very long but thin with swollen veins; his face is likewise thin and bony, it is an ashy black color, like that of sick black people.)

Aesthethic blackness in the creative literature of the Latin/Hispanic reality is by no means one-dimensional. While Truque is usually listed as an Afro Latin writer, the aesthetic construction that directs his imagery of the sole character identified as black in "Vivan los compañeros" does not adhere to the ethnic schema usually employed by racially sensitive

Afro Latin writers for comparable characterizations. More often than not, when the black or nonwhite author uses distinguishing signs of physiognomy in the construction of a character—among other symbols—they serve as a guide to the person's ethnicity without resorting to caricatures or inane descriptions (Boyd, "The Concept of Black Esthetics" 224). However, absolutely nothing was accomplished literarily with Truque's descriptors such as *"jetón"* ["big-lipped"] or *"color Negro ceniza... característica de Negro enfermo"* ["ashy black color...like that of sick black people"] for Ayala except to draw attention to the author's negative mindset where blackness is concerned. Could this be a case of the *insoluble identity question* that critics find so prevalent in some Afro Latin depictions (Lewis 176–177; emphasis added)? Or is it another dimension of the miscegenated individual comparing his or her blackness to the blackness of the non- or slightly mixed-race individual?

When diagrammed as a skin tone with stereotypical characteristics, black, for some Latin American writers who perceive themselves as socially black but phenotypically not quite black enough, connotes a subtle posture of quiet rebellion against being grouped under the rubric of generic blackness. Or, it can denote a vacillating self-acceptance of being black in the absence of being recognized as *mestizado*, that is, a mixed-race person. Such is the impression of himself—in this case, quiet rebellion—that Truque projects with Ayala, who is constructed with a semiotic imagery of being a grotesque representative of black people collectively—*"característica de Negro enfermo"* ["a characteristic of sick black people"]—without an obvious raison d'être. Truque's use of the modifiers "astute" and "intelligent" do not counterbalance the negative symbology. Why would this approach to characterization be needed if not to highlight the unspoken statement: "he is black, and you also call me black"? This disposition where questions of race and color are concerned demonstrates just how ingrained the attitude that molds perceptions of race and color has become in the Latin world and the effect it can assume in the fictive world of creative literature.[1] At some point in a person's life, they might have an epiphany that monolithic blackness is perhaps not what they perceive for themselves. In Truque's life, as he points out in the autobiographical essay "Mi testimonio" (My Testimony), a negative incident that he unexpectedly experienced as a young student, and which he felt was unjustified, made him the victim of a crushing invective, replete with unwarranted racial epithets: "*¡Negro sinvergüenza...Póngalo a trabajar, señora. ¡Esa porquería no va a servir para nada¡*" (19). ("Shameless nigger...[Take him out of school] and send him to work, lady. That piece of garbage will never amount to anything!")

The inference that one intuits from reading "Mi testimonio" suggests that Truque questions the social treatment meted out to a certain class of individuals without considerations of merit or justification. Evidently, Truque never recovered either from the episode or the hurtful remark, for as he candidly says in the same testimony: "*Y fui desarrollando un crudo egoísmo que hubiera llegado a destrozarme, si no hubiera tenido la pasión de llenar cuartillas*" ["I began to develop a somewhat crude form of egotism that might have destroyed me had I not had a passion for filling up notebooks"] (20).

Writing for Truque became a consolation, a catharsis, an escape from the bitterness that continued to consume him. The tenor of his "testimonio" belies his opening statement: "*Quien lea esta líneas, creo, no podrá atribuirlas a la amargura o al resentimiento*" ["Whoever reads these lines will not be able to attribute them, I think, to bitterness or resentment"] (17).

The world of the Afro Latin is always unstable when it comes to questions of color and race. Hence, for the creative artist, emphasis on pigmentation and physical features becomes a ready-made device to express subjective imagery of race or ethnicity, especially for the individual that understands the aesthetics of the Afro Latin space. When Zapata Olivella highlights the term "*piel lechosa*" it is a clear sign, for him, that this person's color is not within the normal range of the prescribed racial physiognomy of being genetically Caucasoid. Since Dominguito was born to a black mother in a black-oriented environment, the subjacent implication is the question of how this fact will control his self-identification in the Latin world. How will others in this atmosphere or beyond it perceive him as a light-skinned person with red hair that is kinky? If his hair were straight, regardless of the *"piel lechosa,"* then his status would be similar to that of a white man.

The vagaries of miscegenation are not limited to Colombia, as demonstrated by a popular song that has made the rounds throughout Latin America. Under the authorship of a Puerto Rican singer/lyricist, Bobby Capó, the theme "Capullo y Sorullo" [the flower bud and the fool] has appeared in the traditional music styles (cumbia, merengue, etc.) of many Latin countries, including Mexico, Honduras, and El Salvador, to name but a few. An excerpt from the lyrics reads as follows:

> *Había una vez en mi pueblo, un matrimonio*
> *Rubio como la mantequilla*
> *Yo puedo dar mi fe y testimonio*
> ....
> *Del matrimonio nacieron 9 hijitos*
> *8 salieron rubiecitos*
> *Yo lo vi, y nadie me lo dijo*
> *que el noveno resultó ser bien negrito*
> *El marido soportó por muchos años*
> *Pero a la larga el silencio le hizo daño*
> *Y decidió confesar a su mujer*
> *Así lo hizo y ustedes van a ver*
> *Oye capullo a todos los quiero igual.*
> ....
> *Todos son angelitos*
> *Y los llevo en el alma*
> *Pero hablemos del negrito*
> *Sin perder la calma*
> *Dime capullo, ¿es mío el negrito?*
> ....
> *Y ella le contestó*
> ....
> *Oye sorullo, el negrito es el único tuyo*
> ....
> *¿Cómo va a ser?*
> *Aquí la bomba explotó*
> *el matrimonio acabó*

Aesthetic Blackness in the Creative Literature 27

Ella se fue con los 8
Y él con el negro cargó.
(Capó, *Canta Bobby Capó*)

(Once upon a time in my little town, there was a married couple as blonde as the color of butter/I can vouch for this/9 children were born to this couple/of which 8 came out blonde/I saw this myself and no one told me so/but the ninth was born quite black/The husband tolerated this for many years/But in the long run, silence got the better of him/And he decided to make his wife confess/ That's what he did, and now you're going to see/"Listen, my little flower bud,/I love them all as equals./They're all little angels/And they're all right here in my heart/But talk to me about the little black one/Without getting all upset/Tell me, my little flower bud: Is the little black one mine?"/And she answered him/"Listen here fool, the little black one is the only one that's yours."/How can that be?/Here's where the bomb exploded/It undid this couple's union/She left with her 8 and he went off with the one that was black.)

Here, as the case is clearly made by the lyricist, the emphasis is not so much on the wife's presumed adulterous nature but on the presumption of racial purity that results in revealing the inherent black genetic strain alleged to be an integral part of the Latin American genotype. It cannot escape the culturally attuned listener of this song that both progenitors were presumed to be white. Curiously, they are designed by the lyricist to be the Latin-type Caucasoid—"blond as butter"—and not the prototypical Nordic blond (i.e., "blond, and white as snow"). Spanish-speaking Americans are all too cognizant of the perceived differences that are alleged to exist between their ethnic groups and comparable groups elsewhere. In their world, Latin American whites are accepted as such even if absolute paleness is not nature's end result or if a genomic analysis might infer other racial strains, as the lyricist suggests. Bobby Capó incidentally has been listed as being Puerto Rican of African descent. It is possible that the scenario he presents in these lyrics may have been drawn from a real-life situation in his native environment. An artistic reality often has its genesis in a day-to-day actuality.

Questions of miscegenation and its manifestation in the different national literatures are not difficult to observe in the various creative writings of the Latin American region. The manner in which this concept will be depicted depends, of course, on the personalized aesthetics of the author. With Zapata Olivella, miscegenation was seen as stark and violent. "Zapata Olivella's ethnic viewpoint is both an outgrowth of the geographical limitations that control his context and the realization of himself as an integral part of the artistic stimuli within this geocontextural dimension" (Boyd, "Manuel Zapata Olivella" 315). However, with his compatriot Truque, it is the absence of miscegenation in the black Colombian individual that he sees as uncivilizing and negative. Both writers are themselves nonwhite. Another nonwhite writer, Mayra Santos-Febres, a native of Puerto Rico, approaches the question of race mixing and color, especially in the Caribbean setting, with an entirely different agenda. She is able to capture the nuances of miscegenation without incrimination or victimization. For her, the process is merely a fact of life. It is a reality in the Latin/Hispanic Caribbean that does not require a detailed explication. In her novel *Cualquier miércoles soy tuya* [I am Yours on Any Wednesday], the reader is introduced to this approach with the compassionate description of a young male prostitute whose angelic physical appearance does not betray his demoniacal machinations. An older man arrives on the scene accompanied by *"un efebo que parecía un ángel caído del cielo"* ["A little Adonis that looked like an angel fallen from above."] (14). Her physical description of this "little angel" carries semiotic innuendoes of ethnicity that someone outside of the culture might overlook:

> el niño era del color exacto de la canela. Tenía los labios llenos y rosados, una nariz pequeña de muñequito de cerámica que adornaba su cabeza perfectamente rapada al cuero...En aquella cara se destacaban unos ojos achinados que miraban al horizonte ... con la arrogancia desentendida de un príncipe bantú. (14)
>
> (The young boy was the exact color of cinnamon. His lips were full and pinkish, a small little nose like that of a porcelain doll garnished his head, perfectly shaved to the scalp...His slanted

eyes stood out prominently on his face as he gazed off into the distance with the disengaged arrogance of a Bantu prince.)

In an ethnic sense, what Santos-Febres has presented her readers is the image of someone who is definitely not white and who is seen through the lens of a person aware of those elements that conjoin to determine whether a heritage of blackness is remotely possible or is overtly evident. To say that an individual is *"canela"* [cinnamon] in color places that person in a range of skin tones that is not too dark but not too light, which at times can be racially indeterminate. But this determinant, coupled with lips that are full and a nose that is small, together with eyes that are Asian-like in appearance, create the impression of the possibility of some racial mixture. However, like most people with this particular physiognomy, hair quality can be the very factor that distances one from or concretizes the close relationship to an African forebear. Consequently, the author, aware of cultural tendencies in this respect, sees to it that this character disguises any further telltale signs of race by having him shave off all his hair. This is a common practice among some natives termed *"jabao"* in Cuba and Puerto Rico, as well as *"grifo"* in Puerto Rico (i.e., intermediate to light-skinned individuals with the tightly curled wooly hair that is considered to be prototypically African). The female gender resorts to methods of decurling and hair straightening. Males in this ethnic range likewise resort to methods of destructuring the telltale curl or removing entirely the incriminating evidence. But, just to be sure that her intentions are understood as to the ethnoracial characterization of this "angelic figure," she likens him to a Bantu prince [*"un príncipe bantú"*]. While the possibilities of a comparative image were entirely at the artistic discretion of the author, the choice of an African association (Bantu) was deliberate and aesthetically directed.

Unlike some writers in the Spanish-speaking Caribbean, Santos-Febres avoids stereotypical color designations or broad, generic classifications that tend to devoid the African-related person in the Diaspora of his or her individual human quality. For example, Haitians, in the Afro Latin world, are usually depicted in the creative literature as the typical example of the nonmiscegenated individual that phenotypically verges on the grotesque. However, in the hands of Santos-Febres, her Haitian character, Tadeo Chamdeleau, is given a phenotype that would place him in any black-related environment of the vast African Diaspora, including Spanish-speaking or Portuguese-speaking spaces. He has a *"mandíbula ancha, coronada por unos labios grandes color chocolate..."* ["A wide jaw, crowned by large lips, the color of chocolate"] (13). The comparative difference between this character and the angelic little male prostitute is that for this one there is no apparent, artistically inferred indication of miscegenation (large lips the color of chocolate), but his appearance is not inhuman or bizarre. In the depiction of the other, miscegenation is an obvious fact (full, pinkish colored lips, Asian-like eyes); still, the thought of "a certain something, perhaps intangible" that links him to an African heritage is in the author's mind. Latin Americans have the tendency to operate on mental ascriptions of race and ethnicity and usually make an effort to circumscribe overt classifications.

The Afro Latin community has had close to five hundred years of continuous living with Europeans and indigenous Indians in the Americas. Given that racial barriers in the area have been quite fluid where sexual relations are a commodity of convenience or simply the result of human attraction, the telltale phenotypes that are the resultant products of interracial unions are an established fact. This has resulted in generations of visible evidence, with myriad connotations of ethnicity and race. Mayra Santos-Febres speaks knowingly of the statistics, couched in descriptions and ethnic references. With artistically created demographics, perhaps based on personal observations, in this novel she alludes to the gamut of colors that the many years of interracial and intraracial unions have produced: *"niños barrigones de todos los colores del arco iris"* ["Little children, of every color in the rainbow, with distended bellies"] (51).

Santos-Febres manages to capture the nuances of miscegenation in the Afro Latin reality without the dogmatic exhortation of incriminations or victimization of the participants. Immediately after introducing the concept of children of every color in the rainbow, she focuses on the characterization of Sambuca, whom she describes with the sensitivity of ethnic comprehension as *"era un mulato oscuro"* ["He was a dark-skinned mulatto"] (51). For the non-Latin world, a "mulatto" is presumed to be a biracial individual of intermediate racial characteristics that place him or her midway along the chromatic chart of black to white or white to black. In the Afro Latin environment, a *"mulato oscuro,"* or dark-skinned mulatto, is not a chromatic aberration. It is one of the real resultant expressions of inter/intraracial possibilities. However, the author justifies the image for the culturally attuned and explicates for the culturally unaware:

> ... se estiraba el pelo con brillantina y fijador, para domar los rizos gordos que coronaban su cabeza...Tenía los ojos color caramelo, como los de su padre, Doroteo Cámara, un negro... (51)
>
> (...he would straighten his hair with hair cream and gel in order to tame the fat curls that crowned his head...He had light-colored eyes like his father, Doroteo Cámara, a black man...)

Once again, the morphology of color plus hair quality determines the identifying nomenclature assigned to an individual, with a subjacent inference of racial mixing. Quietly, Santos-Febres emphasizes the results of generations of intraracial unions that deliver a recognized product but at the same time offer unexpected permutations to the myriad variations in the genomic theme. The racial angle in this vignette that introduces Sambuca has been well thought out and plotted. In an unobtrusive manner, just before the appearance of the *"mulato oscuro,"* the name *"Falú blancos"* ["the white Falu family"] is offered to the reader. Will there also be a black family with the surname Falú? In an indirect manner, the author leads the reader to understand that yes, there are black and white Falús. The matron of the white family is the employer of Sambuca's mother. The two share both first and last names, Georgina Falú, with no further explanation at this juncture. The logical deduction would be that there is a familial relationship between the two women. However, the author offers no additional clues. The relationship would perhaps remain extraneous to the storyline if it were not for the fact that Doroteo, Sambuca's father, is called "black." His mother, Georgina Falú, is likewise seen as a black woman by Doroteo. The reader will undoubtedly question the origin of Sambuca's non-African genes that softened the curl to his hair and gave him the light eyes. Was it only the father? Was it a combination of the gene pool that the father and the mother carried, although both were socially considered to be black? The Afro Latin community, as Santos-Febres has indicated, has not only a cultural history that was spawned in the Americas, but likewise has a genetic history that was created by involuntary and voluntary sexual contacts in the Spanish-speaking environment of Latin America.

In this particular instance, Puerto Rico is the context for the author's references to color and identity. However, the inferences she posits could well apply to most countries in Latin America that share a template of European-Spanish and African cohabitation in the main, with the indigenous Indian as another genetic possibility. In summation of her observations, Santos-Febres finds that the prototype of the Puerto Rican individual is the product of generations of human hybridity: European, African, and indigenous overlapping. Thus, this hybrid being has come to autodefine the Puerto Rican persona in classical terms as follows:

> ... [S]oy puertorriqueño, es decir, isleño hasta cierto punto, negro negado y blanco sin serlo. Un híbrido, la mitad de algo, el doble del doble. Es decir, un ser acostumbrado a deambular por el laberinto que tejió sobre los mares el hambre de los monarcas, monarcas europeos, monarcas africanos, monarcas gringos. (Santos-Febres 171)
>
> (...I am a Puerto Rican, meaning, an islander who up to a certain point is a black [person] in denial, and a white [person] without being so. [I am] a hybrid, the half of something, a double of the double. That is to say, [I am] someone accustomed to wandering through the labyrinth that the greed of European monarchs, African monarchs, and Gringo monarchs created on the seas.)

My translation of this statement, taken from Santos-Febres' *Cualquier miércoles soy tuya*, is an example of the thought process purposefully directed at capturing the sense of the psychoracial history that one perceives throughout her novel. In an interview, the author reveals a more individual perception of her own personal space in the Afro Latin reality:

> Yo no creo en marginalidades fijas, quizás porque pertenezco a varias. Soy mujer, negra, caribeña y quién sabe qué otras cosas más que me colocan en un margen. (Morgado 3)
>
> (I don't believe in exclusive spaces, probably because I belong to several. I am a woman; I am black; I am from the Caribbean, and who knows what else there may be that sets me apart.)

One perceives from this that the Afro Latin reality, in creative literature, considers not only the question of an identifying phenotype but also suggests a mindset that accepts Africa as a genetic and cultural base for the region. However, the aesthetics that control the dimension and imagery of this reality will of necessity conform to the artistic cosmovision of the creator. This conviction, in turn, is directed by the cultural constraints of his or her native space. Milca Esdaille, in an interview that she conducted with Dominican writers Julia Alvarez, Junot Diaz, and Loida Maritza Pérez, approached the subject of a lack of communality between Afro Americans and Dominicans, who in the main are also Afro-related, with this thought:

> It's our African lineage that is most enduring, still vibrant in our skin and hair. Ninety percent of the roughly ten million Dominicans, living at home and abroad, have African ancestry. This is the key link between the collective stories of African Americans and Dominicans. As a friend in college was fond of reminding me, "same trip, different ships." (Esdaille, "Same Trip, Different Ships")

While this might be Esdaille's personal philosophy where the African Diaspora and shared African traits are concerned, it is not a worldview that all native artists in the Dominican culture would follow. Nonetheless, it might very well be a concept with which Diaz, Alvarez, and Pérez would concur. Based on the ethnic designs in the works they have written, the Afro Latin in general, and the Afro Dominican in particular, view members of their national society under a rubric of racial acceptance solely on the basis of a shared language—Spanish. President Barack Obama of the United States, who is patently biracial, is much lighter in skin tone than many Dominicans who view themselves as nearly white, and definitely not black. Yet, Dominican newscasters consistently refer to the American president as black. It is true that he has a direct connection to a nonmiscegenated white parent and a black African parent who is recognized as being nonmiscegenated and not the descendant of slaves in the Americas. For many Dominicans, in contrast, it would require a genealogical study to obtain the directness of their fusion of white genes (e.g., Spanish, French, Italian, English, Dutch, etc.). Their relation to Africans stems mainly from the island's original slaves. Nonetheless, African-related individuals from neighboring non-Spanish-speaking areas are also viewed by Dominicans with suspicion, and are not accorded the benefits of fraternal inclusion based on a presumed shared ethnicity. It is known, however, that both groups—the Spanish-speaking and the English-speaking nonwhites—are directly descended from captive Africans. The Dominican author Ramon Marrero Aristy, in his novel *Over*, follows this cultural tenet of implied inferiority and ethnic separateness in the construction of a dialogue between a Dominican, a Haitian, and an English-speaking Caribbean worker. The Dominican speaks to the Haitian:

> Cállate la boca, mañé del diache, que tu no tiene que meterte en la conversación de la gente...

The Haitian retorts:

> La dominicane son palejele—gruñó el haitiano decepcionado.

The Dominican challenges the retort:

> Parejero no, degraciao. Que a utede y a eto condenao cocolo deberían quemarlo junto. (Marrero Aristy 70)
>
> ("Shut your mouth, you *fu...ng c...cks...ker*, you ain't got no business jumping into the conversation of civilized people..."/"All

Dominicans are stuck-up," grumbled the disappointed Haitian./ [The Dominican challenges the retort with:] "We ain't stuck-up, you miserable little nothing! You and those English-speaking Caribbean niggers should all be burned up together.")

The venom that the Dominican directs against the two non-Dominican blacks is captured by Marrero Aristy with use of the injurious epithets "*mañé*" and "*cocolo*." These malicious sayings have become ethnoculturally oriented and are meant to show not only ethnic differences (although the Dominican might perceive them as racial) and rejection, but also to inflict psychological pain upon other blacks, principally because of a Dominican tendency to exclude and demean the non-Spanish-speaking black person. At the surface level, the translation of the dialogue into English might diminish the full weight of the negatively laden imagery. At their deep structure foundation, the invectives are cutting and meant to inflict psychological pain. It is worth noting that based on the speech pattern that the Dominican uses, with the implied phonology of the popular class, the assumption can be made that he is uneducated and not racially white, but instead prototypically African-related like the majority of the population. His folk culture is nationally formed and controlled. In view of this, the author provides the reader with a footnote that explains the occasions when the offending terms are used (i.e., "*mañé*" for the Haitian and "*cocolo*" for the English-speaking black person from the neighboring islands in the Caribbean where Spanish is not the national language). Still, Marrero Aristy avoids giving the etymology for either term. The origin of these lexical items, derived from the baser sociolect of the lowest strata of Dominican popular society, underscores the contempt that these two black groups merit from Dominicans who share their racial base.

Race does not necessarily conform to skin tone, but skin tone can imply race for Dominican racial classifications. Black Dominicans who phenotypically show little or no miscegenation are suspiciously thought to be Haitian until their Latin roots (culturally, that is), are verified. Jorge Duany, in one of several studies on Dominicans and questions of race, highlights the well-known case of José Francisco Peña Gómez, who at one time was a presidential candidate for the Dominican Revolutionary Party (PRD). His alleged Haitian origin and very dark skin tone produced such virulent racism against him that his defeat in the electoral campaign of 1996 was almost a given (Duany, "Reconstructing Racial Identity" 152). In her well-received novel *Geographies of Home* (1999), Loida Maritza Pérez deftly tackles the question of Dominican ethnicity and racial confusion. The protagonist Iliana María and all her siblings have different phenotypes, even though they have the same mother and father. The author's descriptions are blunt, raw, and purposefully designed to focus on the innate drive of Dominicans toward color and physiognomy:

> The longer she watched herself the more repulsed she became. Before, she had been able to manipulate her reflection so as to see only her pale skin, shades lighter than any of her sisters' and only slightly darker than Gabriel's [white American] wife. The color of her skin had made her blind to her kinky, dirt-red hair, sprawling nose, her long, wide lips. (18)

Those readers who are familiar with the reality of Dominican phenotypes will readily accept this imagery as not being exaggerated. The physical features of the character, and the implied self-loathing because of these features, are an inherent characteristic found in many Dominicans. The fact that they may be confused with other peoples in the African Diaspora who have similar traits never dawns on them until they leave the enveloping ethnic embrace of their Dominican culture. This is a dominant feature of Pérez's approach to ethnicity in *Geographies of Home*. The opening lines of the novel stress the point clearly:

> The ghostly trace of "NIGGER" on a message board hanging from Iliana's door failed to assault her as it had the first time she returned to her dorm room to find it. (1)

Aesthetic Blackness in the Creative Literature

In other words, the epithet used by American students to refer to Iliana's race had somehow become commonplace to her, although still not acceptable. While Pérez uses her literary construct to place her characterizations in a realistic, although artistic, context (see Essay III), Jorge Duany views the same concept in concrete sociological terms:

> When people move across state borders, they enter not only a different labor market and political structure but also a new system of social stratification by class, race, ethnicity and gender...As a mulatto Dominican colleague told me recently, she "discovered" that she was black only when she first came to the United States; until then she had thought of herself as an india clara, literally a light [-skinned] Indian in a country whose aboriginal population was practically exterminated in the 16th century. ("Reconstructing Racial Identity" 147)

Once having moved past the goalposts of their native ethnic culture, Dominicans must adjust to other racial terminologies beyond the customary "white or colored" national assignments. Again, Duany's findings state that:

> In Puerto Rico, although the traditional system of racial classification is similar to that of the Dominican Republic, most Dominican immigrants [to Puerto Rico] are viewed as blacks or colored (in local lore, prietos, morenos and trigueños). (148)

This does not exclude or ignore the fact that in Puerto Rico there are people with the same African-oriented phenotype, which places them comfortably within any of the multiple areas where the African Diaspora is found:

> Elsewhere I have documented the difficulties faced by most Dominicans in Puerto Rico on account of their skin color...The main problem is that the vast majority of Dominicans consider themselves indios [literally "Indians," figuratively brown-skinned], whereas most Puerto Ricans classify them as black or mulatto....

> Puerto Ricans tend to represent Dominicans as darker-skinned than themselves, underline their Negroid facial features and hair texture, and treat them accordingly...Hence Dominicans often experience the intense stigmatization, stereotyping, prejudice, discrimination, and exclusion to which all people of African origin are subjected in Puerto Rico and other countries. (Duany, "Dominican Migration to Puerto Rico" 259)

With continued interest in the aesthetics of the artist to determine how subjacent tendencies are revealed where race, ethnicity, and blackness are concerned, concepts were selected from the writings of Rosario Ferré to see exactly how this propensity is presented. Ferré is by no means an Afro Puerto Rican author like Mayra Febres-Santos, discussed earlier. Still, she is a native Puerto Rican like Febres-Santos and not unwilling to use the Afro Puerto Rican image as either a primary or secondary figure in assigned roles in her novels. In a review of a study of her life and art (*Rosario Ferré: A Search for Identity*), the critic did not hesitate to affirm: "Rosario Ferré has been in the vanguard of fiction, criticism, and theory in recent years and has helped Puerto Rico assume a more respectable place in Latin American literature" (Lang 670). As an activist, she is known for her aggressive defense of the rights of women. Still, when it appertains to Afro-Caribbean women, some observers feel that their characterizations by Ferré leave a lot to be desired: "...the characters are still part of a society that discriminates against people based on their gender and race" (Gosser-Esquilín 52). Granted, there are black people in Ferré's works: blacks who are Puerto Rican, blacks who have been brought from Africa to Puerto Rico, and near-whites who have an infusion of African genes. However, her gratuitous depiction of black people with cartoonlike imagery does little to strengthen her storylines or lend an air of verisimilitude and contributes much to demean the seriousness of true artistic intent. For example, in *La casa de la laguna* [The House by the Lagoon], one finds the following:

Aesthetic Blackness in the Creative Literature 39

> Los antepasados de Petra eran oriundos de Africa, y cuando la gente se admiraba de su gran fuerza física, ella se reía...tenía la piel oscura, pero no como chocolate aguado, sino como el ónix profundo...Cuando Petra sonreía, era como si una herida blanca rasgara la oscuridad de la noche. (73)
>
> (Petra's ancestors were originally from Africa, and when people would admire her great physical strength, she laughed...she was dark-skinned, not like watered-down chocolate, rather like a jet-colored onyx...When Petra smiled, it was as if a white gash had lacerated the darkness of the night.)

Why is it that the African, or a black person in general, is usually perceived by the non-African-related creative artist as jet black, black as night, black as coal, or black as tar as if by some prescribed code? Ferré acquiesces to the convention and does not disappoint the reader who shares her one-dimensional mindset toward an African's color. A few pages after her reasonless description of Petra, the reader meets one of this character's ancestors, her grandfather Bernabé: "Bernabé era más negro que el *alquitrán* y era muy *inteligente*" ["Bernabé was blacker than *tar*, and was very *intelligent*"] (75; emphasis added). The statement seems to imply his tar-black color is a contradiction to his intelligence level. Such images that continue to follow the racial coding of nineteenth- and early-twentieth-century attitudes offer little to support the overall construction of this novel, but do much to render the ethnic sensitivity of the author as suspect. It seems that such occurrences in Ferré's writings are not the result of unintentional happenstance, nor can their appearance be attributed to ethnic naiveté. In her volume of bilingual poetry, *Language Duel/Duelo del Lenguaje*, Ferré has a curious entry under the title "La sombra de la culpa," which she has translated as "The Shadow of Guilt." It is curious in the sense that the verses and images that one finds to be racially offensive in Spanish are omitted in the English translation, for which the author herself is responsible. The following examples correspond to (a) the original verse in Spanish as published by the author; (b) my translation into English of the original

Spanish; (c) the author's published translation in English, which she has placed beside the Spanish version:

(a)	(b)	(c)
—Madre, ¿ porqué los negros andan descalzos?	"Mother, why do Black people go around with no shoes on?"	"Mother why do Blacks go around the house barefoot?"
—No son como nosotros, hija. Los trajeron de bárbaros países y siguen siendo bárbaros.	"They are not like us, my dear. They were brought from savage countries, and they continue to act like savages."	"They were born in the wild, dear. They don't like to wear shoes."

Any bilingual reader will readily see that (a) and (c) are not in agreement; and even (c) might raise an eyebrow, depending on the ethnoracial culture and sensitivity of the reader who is fluent in Spanish and English. It is obvious when comparing (a) and (c) that in (c) the author's intent, directed at monolingual readers of English, is to separate herself from a black population. From the same poem, one can also excerpt the following:

(a)	(b)	(c)
El silencio de la selva les acolchaba los pasos, pero yo pensaba que era porque no usaban zapatos. Eusebia planchaba las camisas de mi padre con ensalmos de Macumba dejaba en ellas el zumo de los pantanos de Africa.	The silence of the jungle stifled their steps, but I thought that it was because they didn't wear shoes. Eusebia would iron my father's shirts with incantations of Macumba and drench them with the swamp waters of Africa.	The silence of the jungle went everywhere Eusebia's skin was a swamp; her sweat steamed my father's shirts every time she ironed them.

While the version in Spanish continues to focus on Africa's backwardness and exoticism, in (c), the author's translation, there is emphasis on the presumed differences between "them" and "us." It is the same distancing that will be apparent in Essay II with Luis Palés Matos. Of course, Ferré has structured references to the African's color in the poem in question, just as she does in the novel:

(a)
y de Brambon recuerdo la manera en que su piel se confundía con el Packard Negros con los pies rosados

(c)
and when I think of Brambon, I remember the perfect way his skin blended in with the Packard Blacks with pink skin under their feet

Here the author's English translation is slightly more explicit than the Spanish offering since it does not leave the image truncated ("Blacks with pink skin under their feet," while the Spanish in a more literal translation offers only: "Blacks with pink feet"). Neither the Spanish nor the English is structured to veer from the overall construction and thematic of "they/them" as grotesque, outlandish, distorted, aberrant. Ferré is aesthetically symmetrical in her perspective of the Afro Latin, especially the Afro Puerto Rican.

What has been reported for Puerto Rico and the Dominican Republic are not isolated images of the full scope of the African Diaspora in the Hispanic world. When José Alcántara Almánzar, the author of "Black Images in Dominican Literature," says that "[t]he Dominican has a scale of values in which the white person occupies the highest position, and the black the lowest" (Alcántara Almánzar 165), the same statement can be applied to any Latin American country, regardless of the demographics for the black presence. Nor is the Dominican Republic the only Spanish-speaking Latin American environment where euphemisms have been created to mask the degree of African-relatedness that is suggested by the different tones of pigmentation. Even the Puerto Rican author Ferré—with her affinity for describing human skin tones as "black as tar" or that become "confused with a [black] Packard car"—finds the need to make a selection from among the different mulatto types that one finds in the world of "Hispanismo"—that is, *mulato, mulato oscuro*, and *mulato claro* (mulatto, dark-skinned mulatto, and light-skinned mulatto). In her novel *La casa de la laguna*, there is a description that illustrates a necessary ethnic choice for her character: "*Por fin escogió a Tony Torres, un mulato claro de facciones finas*" ["Finally he chose Tony Torres, a light-skinned mulatto with keen features"] (181). Undoubtedly, the monolingual reader of Spanish will readily intuit the image as that of an almost-white person, if the complete morphology of right color, nose, lips, and grade of hair meet the requisites deemed necessary by the pigmentocracy of that society. Consequently, the onus of demeaning an ethnoracial counterpart cannot be placed entirely on the Dominican Republic. However, there is no denying that it is a country of miscegenated individuals, and that a black Dominican considers himself superior to the black outsider such as the Haitian. In this regard, it is commonplace for many to freely employ derogatory expressions that reveal a pathological repulsion towards their own African past, and to the black Dominican and Haitian culture (Alcántara Almánzar 165). Consequently, skin color is not only related to social status, but also determines national acceptability. What happens if race, which inevitably is related to skin color in Latin America, is indeterminate? Do mixed-race Latin Americans, Dominicans in particular, with similar phenotypes give any consideration to their ethnoracial standing for the concept of a prototypical Afro Latinism? Creative literature, when it exposes the mindset of an author within his or her culture or projects the national culture as context, can present a realistic concept of race and ethnicity either as the thematic force or as an adjunct to the schema.

* * * * *

It was previously determined in this essay that for a study of race relations in a given national milieu, and for the reaction of that environment's inhabitants toward the question of race and color, it is customary to examine sociological and psychological studies and their relationship to the historical framework. Juxtaposed to these considerations, it is found that both a society and its history can create the mindset that forms the societal modus operandi of a people. For example, where race and ethnicity have been codified to produce hierarchical strata that guide social behavior, this ethnoracial template conforms to and determines the aesthetic direction of that society. It is inevitable, in this respect, that the literary arts will in some measure reflect national aesthetics in the context of works created by the lived experiences of novelists, poets, dramatists, and lyricists in the national environment. This has led to the hypothesis that "a rigorous consideration of aesthetics, in the study of literature, is perhaps unavoidable when searching for dimensions that offer the clearest guide to an author's literary intent" (Boyd, "The Concept of Black Esthetics" 1). In other words, the relationship between ethnicity and aesthetics provides a dimension in the rapport established between the artist and the public that draws both closer to the subjective inclination of each where race and society are concerned. This approach, however, does not reveal the sole dimension of an artistic creation:

> Literature, the author's end product as an artistic medium, must of necessity be viewed from different angles in order to capture all dimensions. Without a doubt, societal and cultural factors are basic to expression. Expression is basic to dimension in literature. If the author's aesthetics and those of his ethnic group are considered to be immediate factors in the evolution of the general society and culture, then to fully comprehend and appreciate the author's intent, one should look at him/her in terms of that author's personal aesthetic orientation. It must not be overlooked that this orientation is developed through an involuntary ethnic affiliation. (3)

It is through such an examination that the Afro Latin reality, portrayed in the creative literature of a national environment, can be projected and demonstrated as the outcome of a real-life actuality. However, at the surface level it does not distinguish between those Latin American authors who write about a perceived Afro Latin reality and those who write while living within and experiencing the Afro Latin reality. To write on a black subject in Latin America does not necessarily decree ethnic participation, as Jean

Franco points out in *The Modern Culture of Latin America: Society and the Artist*. She states, "The avant-garde poets who introduced the fashion ['talking real Negro'] were usually white writers…" (cited in Boyd, "The Concept of Black Esthetics" 12). Despite the social barriers and the risk of being misunderstood, there is, however, a definite dimension of black aesthetics in Latin American literature. It is important to understand that aesthetics is couched in terms of a subjective entity for self-evaluation and is not specific to the phenotypic appearance of the author. This concept is unapologetically borne out in the writings of Julia Alvarez and Junot Diaz, for example. Both are light-skinned Dominican authors and by Dominican standards would be unwaveringly classified as "white Dominicans." In keeping with most Western standards, Diaz and Alvarez are considered to be prototypically Hispanic or Latin. From their art, it is clear that both are patently sensitive to the questions of race and racism in the Dominican Republic, and they do not skirt issues where the hierarchy of color comes into focus. Both approach the subject of skin color in Dominican society with an aboveboard honesty and directness that is usually found in writers much darker than they. For a fuller and more satisfying approach to reading the literature of Latin America where Afro Latinos are an integral element, the guiding *lemma* or motto is, "a black attitude in creative writing is an aesthetological dimension." It depends largely on how well the artist understands and accepts the effects imposed on his or her society by the biological and social determinants of skin tones as a cultural component of his or her national psyche. Consequently, it is concluded that the black attitude/aesthetic is a psychological, political, and sociological interpretation by the author of their literary milieu.

* * * * *

Blackness, in the creative literature of most Latin American countries, is inferably embedded within its cultural construct as an aesthetological dimension, much the same as it is in the general community. In the general society and the society as a literary construct, some embrace their categorization of being black; some merely accept it tacitly; others deny it and assign

Aesthetic Blackness in the Creative Literature 45

themselves to culturally devised niches for psychological assuagement. For example, Regino Pedroso, the artist who wrote the following verses had options that would have enabled him to evade a direct reference to an African ethnic dimension. Nonetheless, he preferred the following stance:

> *Negro, hermano negro,*
> *tú estás en mí, ¡habla!*
> *Negro, hermano negro,*
> *yo estoy en ti; ¡ canta !*
> *Tu voz está en mi voz,*
> *tu angustia está en mi voz,*
> *tu sangre está en mi voz...*
> *¡También yo soy de tu raza!*
> (R. Pedroso, "Hermano negro," as quoted in Lee 231)

> (Black man, black brother,
> you are a part of me. Speak up!
> Black man, black brother
> I am in you. Sing!
> Your voice is in my voice
> Your pain is in my voice
> Your blood is in my voice...
> I also belong to your race!)

The perceived affiliation is more than physical. The poet celebrates and embraces his blackness with a union that is spiritual, psychological, and full of emotional intensity. As such it controls and determines the subjective direction of the poetic voice. "I"/"my" is conjoined with "you"/"your" not only to autodefine blackness but to confirm it as a pervasive personal condition: "Your voice is the voice of my poetry. Your pain is the pain in my poetry. Your blackness is the blackness in my poetry. I am you." For the artist, evasion is not an option when one recognizes and submits to the profundity of one's blackness. But acquiescence, nonetheless, carries responsibilities:

> *¿No somos más que negro?*
> *¿No somos más que jácara?*

> *¿No somos más que rumba, lujurias negras y comparsas?*
> *¿No somos más que mueca y color, mueca y color?*
> ("Hermano negro," as quoted in Lee 233)

> (Aren't we more than just blackness?
> Aren't we more than just song and dance?
> Aren't we more than just rhumba, Negro lust
>   and the folly of carnival?
> Aren't we more than just grinning teeth and a black face, grinning
>   teeth and a black face?)

Blackness carries the responsibility of dignity, observation, and self-respect. To underscore this thought, the poet reminds his black brother that one's image can and should be self-controlled:

> *Negro, hermano negro,*
> *silencia un poco tus maracas.*
> *Y aprende aquí,*
> *y mira allí.*
> . . . .
> *Negro, hermano negro,*
> *enluta un poco tu bongo.*
> ("Hermano negro," as quoted in Lee 233)

> (Black man, black brother
> muffle the sound of your maracas a little
> And learn from this one
> Take notice of that one.
> . . . .
> Black man, black brother,
> deaden the sound of your bongo a little.)

Given that the poet communes in thought and spirit with his black brother, what might seem like admonishments are actually serious suggestions for a decolonization of the mind. Blackness, for this poet, is more than the clownish picture that others paint of the black man: a maraca-shaking, bongo-pounding insouciant. Life requires one to observe and learn from others ("*aprende aquí y mira allí*"). However, unlike the societal norm,

Aesthetic Blackness in the Creative Literature 47

nowhere in the poem is there a hint of differences between or allusions to a perceived hierarchy based on color gradations or ethnic boundaries decreed by nationality. A black man is a black man, mixtures notwithstanding. For this artist, blackness has its Diaspora to which all black people are linked through the institution of "slavery" (defined by the artist as *"explotación"* ["exploitation"]). Common sufferings bind black men together more than race (i.e., color), and while the imagery of color and race is present, they are expressed in terms of being both causation and condition:

> *Negro, hermano negro;*
> *más hermano en el ansia que en la raza.*
> *Negro en Haití, negro en Jamaica, negro en New York,*
> *negro en La Habana, dolor que en*
> *vitrinas negras vende la explotación.*
> . . . .
> *Da al mundo con tu angustia rebelde. . .*
> *tu humana voz. . .*
> *¡y apaga un poco tus maracas!*
> ("Hermano negro," as quoted in Lee 233)

> (Black man, black brother;
> more of a brother because of suffering than race.
> Black man in Haiti, Black man in Jamaica, Black man in New York,
> Black man in Havana, exploitation sells your pain in black
>   showcases.
> . . . .
> Let the world hear your restless cry,
> your voice that is human,
> and quiet the sound of your maracas a little.)

For the poet, it is not color (*raza*) that binds him to his black brother as much as the experiences of their common suffering (*el ansia*). Phenotypically, Pedroso did not share the same physiognomic traits of most mixed-race Cubans. Regino Pedroso (1896–1983) was born in Union de Reyes (Matanzas), Cuba, the son of a Chinese father and an Afro Cuban mother. Raised by his mother and her family in a predominantly black environment after his father abandoned Cuba to return to China, Regino apparently learned from his milieu that to be Afro Chinese and Cuban held no great social advantages, even though his ethnic appearance was slightly different than that of the average Afro Cuban.

Matanzas, as an important sugar-producing area, had one of the highest populations of African slaves in the country. Due to this, the area strongly retains its African traditions and has a firm connection to its African roots. Most societies in Latin America allege to subscribe to a tripartite system of ethnoracial classifications: black, mixed-race (mulatto, mestizo, etc.), and white. Cuba is no exception. There are, nonetheless, social variables that allow acceptance into a particular niche and/or enable progression into an upwardly situated stratum. Pedroso's poetry indicates that, apparently, he had developed a mindset of social stratification that was personal. His art was shaped accordingly to this mindset. Mid-nineteenth century Cuba saw its mixed-race structure revised somewhat with the arrival of Chinese laborers, who were predominantly male. Placed in a milieu where interaction with Africans was unavoidable, some entered into marital unions with African or African-descendant females. Consequently, the physical appearance of Asians and their biracial offspring was no longer uncommon in Cuba when Pedroso was born. A certain rapprochement between the two groups is even suggested as the basis for a Chinese-Cuban religious philosophy. The syncretic Chinese-Cuban "saint" Sanfancón eventually entered into a symbiotic existence with other saints and deities of Euro-African extraction: "Thus followers of Santería continue to pay respects to Sanfancón in some of the remaining Chinese societies on the island, and popular culture has it that Santa Bárbara [in Spanish culture] is Changó [in African culture] is Sanfancón [in Chinese culture]" (Scherer 9). For Orientalist researchers, the name Sanfancón, or San Fang Kong, represents a Western corruption of Cuan Yu, who, after his death became the "Venerated Ancestor Kuan Kong" and eventually the "patron" of all Chinese immigrants to Cuba (Scherer 9). Undoubtedly, this concept was a product of African and Chinese interaction more so than the result of Spanish indoctrination.

Low-skilled, indentured Chinese servants had been imported into Cuba between 1847 and 1874 to work the sugar plantations alongside black slaves. Their arrival is related to a period when it had become somewhat difficult to bring in fresh supplies of African captives due to British agitation against trafficking in black bondsmen. In Cuba, these Chinese indentured workers, or "coolies," as they were known, suffered the same hardships on the plantations as the Africans. Given that the paradigm for forced labor had already been established by the time of their arrival, Chinese workers likewise suffered the abuse and harsh conditions, the ruthless exploitation, and the despicable derogation to which the Africans were subjected. Chinese labor in Cuba in the nineteenth century was slavery in every social aspect in spite of being listed under the rubric "indentureship" (Knight 119). Asian indentured servants, living in conditions that were tantamount to slavery, became victims of the same social stigmas that were applied to black slaves and their descendants. There can be no denying the fact that "slavery and indentured labor were synonymous" (119). Consequently, Chinese workers were known to endure practices caused by racial prejudice and racist-engendered discrimination. As a result, the Chinese, not unexpectedly, on many occasions joined forces with Africans in acts of violent protest. The Chinese were known to rebel on plantations much the same as the African captives. It was not until after the promulgation of the Treaty of Peking in 1879 and the establishment of a Chinese consulate in Havana that legal discrimination against the Chinese began to cease (Corbitt 131), de jure. Be that as it may, racist attitudes against the Chinese worker persisted, since it is common knowledge that although legal decrees may curtail racist behavior, in no country do laws necessarily preclude discrimination or racism. Statutory pronouncements have absolutely no control whatsoever over attitudes, mores, and social customs that are based on antipathy toward another because of race or color.

Already one has seen how Pedroso in "Hermano negro" manages to transfer the sentience of his African ancestry to the constructs of his poetry (I/my = you/yours). Did he acknowledge an Asian heritage also? Yes, he did, and in no uncertain terms. Still, he appeared to understand that Asian roots prescribed no more advantages than an ancestral provenance from Africa. There were just as many negative paradigms attached to being Chinese as there were to being African during this period. Besides, legal slavery had only ended some ten years before Pedroso was born. The Chinese coolie was treated much as if he were a slave, and racism and discrimination lingered as factors to be contended with long after abolition:

> *Surge de largos años de humillación.*
> *Soy de tu misma raza hombre amarillo;*
> *tuvimos por abuelos los mismos mandarines*
> *venales y enfermizos,*
> ....
> *Tú has despertado en mí lo que hay de Asia;*
> *adormecido estaba por el Pan-americanismo y el*
> *Hispano-americanismo,*
> *más yo vengo de allí en connubio con África:*
> *dos grandes continentes humillados y vencidos...*
> (Regino Pedroso, "Salutación a un camarada Culí,"
> as quoted in Lee 236–237)

(Countless years of humiliation are the background.
Yellow man, I am also a member of your race.
We probably had the same corrupt and sickly Mandarin
  grandfathers.
....
You have awakened in me what there is of Asia.
It lay dormant because of Pan-Americanism and
Hispanic-Americanism,
but I have abandoned them in solidarity with Africa:
two great continents, humiliated and vanquished.)

If the manner in which the general populace understands the term "Hispanic" today were the guide for Pedroso, then it might have been to the poet's advantage to hide behind the race-neutral, ethnopolitical classification of Hispano. But as he indicates, the poet prefers to be considered African and Chinese in specific terms, rather than appeal to the racial neutrality of Hispanic-Americanism. In these verses, the poet avoids a hierarchical scale of assumed superiority versus a consigned inferiority based on phenotype or skin tone. Race, in his construct, takes precedence over ethnicity. A Hispanic identity fuses ethnicity into a racial concept even though racial integrity acknowledges one's personal genetic composition. Thus, Pedroso willingly commits to solidarity with his Asian roots: "*Mas, sangre de tu sangre, yo vivo en fiebre ahora tu fuerte gesto y tu tragedia…*) ["But, as blood of your blood, I now feel the fire of your valiant struggles and your distress…"] (Lee 237). Yet, at the same time, it is plain that both his African and Asian lineages are an equal part of him. As social equals, both heritages shared the same negative effects of humiliation and servitude. Where an allegiance to the concept of Pan-Hispanism at one time might have been his ethnic direction, he has abandoned this philosophy to accept and embrace his African and Asian roots, the essence of who he is racially. It was said that when asked to list his skin color, Pedroso wrote "*negro amarillo*" ["Yellow black"] (Lee 231). Did he mean to infer "a yellow black man" or "a black yellow man"? In Pedroso's approach, there does not appear to be any appeal, whatsoever, to the region's arrogation of "*mestizaje*" [mixture] or genetic leveling as the means to render indeterminate the incriminating strains of an undesired race. Beyond his poetic voice, the fact does not escape the most casual eye that Cuba is a country of African and Latino mixtures. In this sense, Nancy Morejón has determined in her essay "Nación y Mestizaje" ["Nationhood and Race Mixtures"] that:

> El negro—a mi juicio—aporta esencias muy firmes a nuestro coctel, y las dos razas que en la isla salen a flor de agua… Por lo tanto, el espíritu de Cuba es mestizo. Y del espíritu hacia la piel nos vendrá el color definitivo. Algún día se dirá "color cubano." (226)
>
> (The black man—in my opinion—has made essential contributions to our cocktail mixture, and to the two races [European Spanish and African] that have floated to the surface,…Consequently, Cuba's spirit is mixed. And from the spirit to the skin will surface our defining color. One day it will be called "the Cuban color.")

Morejón is not unique in her way of thinking. Other Latin Americans, including other Cubans, understand that this racial configuration can also apply to them and their color, but are somewhat disinclined to include it in the national dialogue of their art.

When considered in terms of commonly held attitudes that negate the Afro Latino as a viable dimension in his respective society, artists like Junot Diaz, Nicolás Guillén, and Regino Pedroso tend to skew the deprecatory image of the black man in Latin societies by exposing in their art the depth to which Africa has penetrated the national psyche of their country and from which few, if any, escape effects that have now become innate. Still, it is difficult for many who are outside the culture—and especially in the United States—to conceive of the so-named Hispanic American or Latin American person, color gradations notwithstanding, as having a direct relationship to Africa, be it racially, spiritually, or philosophically. This opinion is held in spite of the fact that the area's cultural understanding and involvement with the African continent can be shown to transcend acceptable daily staples such as the African-based cuisine of "rice and beans" or "*mondongo con yuca*" [a stew of tripe or chitterlings with cassava], and pelvic-thrusting dances done to the frenzy of the "bongo" beat.

Concomitantly, for many whose principal ethnic identity is Hispanic (politically acceptable in the United States) or Latin, the reality that an African imprint is nationally all-pervasive or is an undeniable reality and a fundamental basis of their national conception, either racially or spiritually, undoubtedly causes untold psychological modifications and adaptations in order for there to be self-acceptance. Immigration to the United States compounds the issue of personally accepting African genes. This is mainly due to the fact that Americans in the United States have not begun to assimilate into their concept of race the fact that their viewpoint of "Hispanic" contradicts their own definition of what classifies a person as "black." But a three-tiered society of (a) black, (b) white, and (c) not black or white is one of the more popular arrangements for ethnoracial juxtapositions on a national basis in Latin America. Be that as it may, neither Diaz, Guillén, nor Pedroso preclude the image of Africanity in their works, as if omission of having African ancestry were a commitment based on the status of being miscegenated. While in many

Latin American countries miscegenation that manifests itself at the upper tier/tiers of the color scale (i.e., a complexion of lighter skin) is deemed to be a saving grace from the perils of Africanness, Diaz, Guillén, and Pedroso consider it to be artistic exactitude to include Africa within the full scope and range of their country's ethnoracial actuality. There are other creative artists—from their countries and in other areas of Latin America—who employ various artistic media such as music and the plastic arts to show that they are also willing to confront the concept of Africa in the Latin American ethos as an aspect of verisimilitude.

* * * * * *

Nonetheless, there are entire countries whose premise for nationhood and citizenry denies the existence of an Afro Latino individual as relevant to the representation of their national image. With this reference to areas that undergo a psychological modification and adaptation for self-acceptance, it appears to parallel the present-day mindset of Mexicans. The masses readily accept the image of a mixed-race majority with a mixture that has its origin in the offspring of the European Spanish male and the indigenous female. The ruling class elite, a numerical minority, look askance at such a mixture for their own particular ethnic base. They psychologically contend that their lighter hue aligns them closer to a European forebear than to the swarthiness of the New World indigenous being. Neither the Eurocentric elite nor the mixed-race masses, for the most part, overtly accept the possibility of having African genes in their genetic makeup, or to an infusion of African culture as part of the national patrimony. There are, nonetheless, Mexican researchers who are in disaccord with this stance. Gonzalo Aguirre Beltran, known for his research on the African presence in Mexico, explains in his essay "Bailes de Negros" ["Black People's Dances"]:

> Se sabe que México recibió inmigración negra que vino de Africa y asiática que fue introducida por el puerto de Acapulco; pero jamás se da beligerancia a esta gente; es juicio común que pasó sin dejar huella. (2)

(It is a known fact that Mexico received immigrants from Africa and from Asian countries, and that they entered through the port of Acapulco; but never is there any acknowledgment of these people; the common thought is that they left no traces [of their presence] at all.)

The predominant mindset for most Mexicans assumes that whatever deviation from the skin tone of the European norm has given rise to the phenotype of the masses (referred to by Mexicans as *"color quebrado"*— incomplete coloration) is due exclusively to the interbreeding of the Spaniard with the indigenous female. In other words, some variation of the "Cortes-Malinche" syndrome accounts for the non-Caucasoid color of the average Mexican. Malinche was the indigenous woman who became lover and translator for Mexico's Spanish invader Hernán Cortés and subsequently bore him a son, Martín Cortés. When the European wife of Cortés appeared in the New World, Malinche was pawned over to Cortés' captain, Juan Jaramillo, for whom she gave birth to a daughter named María. Few Mexicans are unaware that Malinche has been termed the symbolic mother of the new Mexican people, based on the two "mestizo" children she produced. Malinche's offspring culturally represent the start of the area's genetic alteration. However, the acceptance or rejection of influences that result in national miscegenation and/or cultural exchanges are not lost on Aguirre Beltran when he declares that:

> La importancia que entre nosotros tiene el indio y lo indio nos lleva a ignorar cualquier otra contribución a la cultura nacional, a más de la occidental, y esto reza particularmente con el negro. Durante el siglo pasado y principios del presente nuestros pensadores llegaron a aceptar ideas racistas de las que excluyeron al indio pero no al negro. La contribución cultural africana es recusada o simplemente no reconocida. ("Bailes de Negros" 2)

(The importance we give to the Indian and things that are Indian forces us to ignore all other contributions to our national culture except for concepts from the west, and this is particularly true when it comes to the black man. Throughout the last century and the beginning of the present, our thinkers began to entertain racist ideas from which they excluded the Indian but not the black man. The cultural contribution of the African [in Mexico] is [either] rejected or just not recognized.)

There are Latin American countries that have been known to rely on an indigenous Indian ancestry to explain away phenotypes that they considered too dark, or in the case of a country like the Dominican Republic to account for the miscegenated appearance of Dominicans who were not "white" enough to be declared bonafide Caucasoids, but were "lighter" than the prototypical African phenotype. This alternative approach enabled the Dominican to latch on to the term *indio* (Indian) to identify someone they considered lacking the complete morphology for European whiteness or for those who did not have the definitive skin tone identity attributed to African blackness. Silvio Torres-Saillant, in his race-focused essay "The Tribulations of Blackness: Stages in Dominican Racial Identity," declares:

> Ethnically, the Indians represented a category typified by nonwhiteness as well as nonblackness, which could easily accommodate the racial in-betweenness of the Dominican mulatto. Thus the regime [Trujillo's regime, 1930–1961] gave currency to the term indio to describe the complexion of people of mixed ancestry. (139)

Even after the demise of Trujillo, "*indio*" as a color is still functional in the mental attitude of most Dominicans. Yet they are not the only Latin Americans who rely on an indigenous Amerindian relationship to explicate the gradations of color that prevent them from attaining a "white-appearing" majority in the sociopolitical sense. A prototypical national color that excludes the darker-skinned results of the African/European or European/Indian progeny is felt by most Latin Americans to be the true representation of their iconic image. Thus, in reference to her observations of the years of cultural and racial miscegenation in Cuba, poet Morejón can speak of a "Cuban color" as the definitive ethnic neutralizer, or national identifier (Morejón 226).

Based on rationalizations of this type, for the Dominican Republic, one can refer to an "Indian color" with the same referential base. For Morejón, undoubtedly a "Cuban color" is nothing more than recognition of the cultural and genetic melding of the African, European, and in some cases the Amerindian to form a Cuban whole. She supports her observation by citing from Guillén's "Canción del bongó" (The Song of the Bongó):

> *En esta tierra, mulata*
> *de africano y español*
> . . . .
> *Siempre falta algún abuelo*
> *cuando sobra algún Don*
> *y hay títulos de Castilla*
> *con parientes en Bondó*
> *vale más callarse, amigos,*
> *y no menear la cuestión*
> *porque venimos de lejos,*
> *y andamos de dos en dos.*
> (Morejón 226–227)

(In this mulatto country
that's both African and Spanish
. . . .
There's always a hidden grandfather
or one nobleman too many
with titles from Castile
while having relatives in Bondó.
It's better not to say anything, my friends
nor even raise the question
because we've come a long way
[and now] walk side by side.)

Castile is the poet's metonym for Spain, while Bondó is Guillen's metonymic reference to Africa. It is the fusion of Africa and Spain that has made Cuba into a country of mixed-race individuals, he feels. Morejón in no uncertain terms agrees and declares that Cuban culture (undoubtedly, she would find the national literature to be a fundamental aspect of Cuban culture) cannot be seen as native without the input of black awareness:

> Opino por tanto que una poesía criolla entre nosotros no lo será de un modo cabal con olvido del negro. (226)
>
> (Therefore in my opinion, our endogenous poetry is in no way complete if we leave out the black man.)

But in the case of the Dominicans, "*color indio*" is the same as declaring that *indio* is a sign of positive progress toward the elimination of the African-descended phenotype, which many Dominicans find embarrassing, when not outright repugnant. Mexico's approach to color, in contrast, highlights the "mestizo" as the biological result of European and indigenous Amerindian unions. The supposedly distinct color of this group is often used to indicate the resulting range of "*mestizaje*," seen as a product of Amerindian/European racial mixture. Mestizo, consequently, is considered both a racial group and an identifying color (*color mestizo*) and overarchingly becomes much the same as for the race/color indications of black and white where no color is uniform for a particular race. Mestizo coloring likewise runs a gamut that is unpredictable in siblings and other relatives. However Mexico, early in its history of recognizing the offspring that resulted from unions between Europeans and Africans (mulattos) or Amerindians and Africans (mulattos or mestizos), found it to be more palatable, psychologically, to co-opt the term mestizo and have it apply to the offspring of all mixed-race descendants, especially after the War of Independence (Hernández Cuevas 115). In this sense, usage and psychological need continue to function, up to the present, as a single unit. The *Pequeño Larousse Ilustrado*, a dictionary published in Mexico, lists the terms "mestizo" and "mulato" as synonyms (Hernández Cuevas 29fn15).[2] Consequently, it was after New Spain's (i.e., Mexico's) independence from Spain, the mother country, in 1821, that offspring resulting from the many permutations created by relationships between Africans, Amerindians, Asians, and the Spaniard were officially classified as "mestizos," that is, "mixed-race" individuals (in the literal Spanish to English translation). For some societies in the Americas, there can be as many as sixty-four arrangements and variations resulting from the mixing of the races (see F. James Davis, *Who is Black*, 37). However, it is in Magnus Morner's listing in *Race Mixture in the History of Latin America*, published in 1967 that some light is shed on how miscegenation in eighteenth-century Mexico was viewed:

> Spaniard [male] and Indian [fem.] produce a mestizo
> Mestizo [male] and Spanish [fem.] produce a castizo
> Castizo [fem.] and Spaniard [male] produce a Spaniard (58–59)[3]

Here, it appears that the criteria for designations of race are based on a particular phenotype. Consequently, the possession of mestizo genes does not eliminate the possibility of returning to the *appearance* of being a Spaniard. This must certainly be based on a comparison of physical characteristics and served as a basis for determining which image would be prototypical. When mixtures are with African types, one sees:

> Spanish [fem.] and Negro [male] produce mulatto
> Spaniard [male] and mulatto [fem.] produce morisco (i.e., Moorish)
> Morisco [fem.] and Spaniard [male] produce albino
> Spaniard [male] and albino [fem.] produce tornatrás (i.e., a step backward) (58–59)

In this section, Morner shows stronger evidence of the reliance on specific phenotypes that expose the non-European factor in the mixture. Even so, within the reality of miscegenation, the differences between the physical characteristics of one group and that of another might be minimal or even overlap. Although Morner gives some eight to ten other listings of interracial mixtures with African genes, some are questionable as to their visual appearance. For example, albinos in most societies are usually identifiable racially even though there is an absence of pigment in their skin and hair. There are white albinos with Caucasoid characteristics as well as black albinos with identifiable

African-descendant physical traits. What did the eighteenth-century listings actually indicate? Of course, the observations Morner lists are empirical and far from being the results of a systematic and scientific study. But in the long run, what one gathers from the study he presents is that the eye observes and determines society's approach to race and classification. However, observation is not uniform and can certainly lead to confusion.

The classifications that Morner offers in his study had already been reviewed by Aguirre Beltran, the Mexican researcher, with the caution that the given inventory of names was merely an exercise in nineteenth-century erudition and created more confusion than clarification (*La Población negra de México* 175 177).[4] It is known that there were and are occurrences of "race passing" in Latin America, just as in North America. Consequently, when Larousse published "mestizo" and "mulatto" as synonymous expressions—despite the fact that "mestizo" carried a higher status than "mulatto"—there appears to have been some previous overture toward a resolution of this type, if folk history is considered to have been the basis. Mexico, like most Latin American countries, has sustained issues of race and identity that appear to have become submerged in the sea of racial confusion in today's society. While ethnicity and color have always revolved around issues of social and economic hegemony, some Mexican nationals have found it more convenient to allow the controversy to become subterfuged because of that country's sensitive relationship with their pathologically race-conscious neighbor to the north and its one-drop rule. In this sense, to be Hispanic in the country to the north is a more convenient escape hatch than having to explain the true nature of Mexican "*mestizaje*" as a national identity. The social symbology for Mexico, where race is concerned, also appears to focus on a three-tiered society: white (preferably Spanish in origin), indigenous (ignoring the fact that they do not all have the same pigmentation), and a fusion of the two groups to produce the prototypical "mestizo" or mixed-race individual. The Asian and African genetic influences are conveniently obliterated through the omission of historical data or information or willful neglect.

Aguirre Beltran concluded that African genes had become so fully integrated into Mexico's genetic chart that for the average layperson a recognition of black characteristics in the makeup of the general population, especially in terms of *"mestizaje,"* would be difficult to single out as such (277). Hernández Cuevas offers the reader a more contemporary perspective of ethnic naming, and likewise shows that Mexican literature confirms the presence of Africa among its genetic traits. He comments:

> Up to the present day, "chino" makes reference to kinky, tightly curled hair. Chinaco, pinto, prieto, moreno, zambo, coyote, cafre, jarocho, tapatio, grifo, infame, vil, pelado, lépero, amongst other derogatory names refer to those "castas" [mixed-race ethnic groups] with "color quebrado" [suspect pigmentation], the offspring of the infinite mixtures of black Africans with Amerindians and in some cases with Spaniards. (59fn42)

This litany of race-oriented terms sheds light on some interesting observations on Mexico and race that have been overlooked, ignored, or downplayed by some of the area's culturists or dismissed as improbable in their reasoning. There are terms mentioned in the previous quotation as racially disparaging toward nonwhite Mexicans that are also used in other areas of Latin America for the same purpose: to denigrate someone because of his or her color. For example, in most Spanish-speaking environments, *prieto*, which means "black," is felt to be more injurious when assigned as a racial classification than *"negro,"* which also means "black." The term *"prieto"* (in Spanish, and *"preto"* in Portuguese) used as an epithet is recognizable by most Latin Americans. *"Negro"* as an established racial identifier is likewise understood and used by all Spanish- and Portuguese-speaking Latin Americans but can be understood as an epithet depending on the context. Conversely, *"zambo"* (alternatively spelled *sambo*) is known to be an indicator of a phenotype that betrays African/Amerindian miscegenation, while *"grifo"* results principally from a genetic heritage of African/European mixtures. The deep structure connotation of race and color inherent in most of these terms is often comprehensible only to those who are psychologically capable of operating within their culture's established paradigms for race and color.

Within this same trend of ethnic terminology there exist in Mexican ethnic appearances *chino* and *china* as determinants that denote a nonwhite phenotype that is not precisely Asian. In seventeenth- and eighteenth-century Mexico, *mulato* and *chino* meant virtually the same thing. *Chino* had become the appellative for the offspring of a black man and Amerindian female (Aguirre Beltran *La población negra de México*, 179). In another instance, *chinaco* is synonymous with being Mexican of African heritage (Hernández Cuevas 5). Consequently, it has been reasoned that to be "*chino*" in Mexico means that one has distinguishing characteristics, such as hair quality, which reveal African genetic traits (115). *Chino* becomes *chinaco* when /-aco/ as a morpheme of disparagement extends the primary meaning. An analogous example can be made with the American English derogatory term "pickaninny." Originally "*pequeno*" in Portuguese—a term for something small, little, insignificant, childlike—it can accept the morpheme /-ino/ to depreciate further the value of the primary meaning, and offers *pequenino* (i.e., pequen (o) + -ino) as the Portuguese slavers' derogatory term for their black human cargo, or a black child of little economic value. The corrupted pronunciation of the Portuguese term by English slavers converts *pequenino* into *pickaninny*. From all indications, *chinaco* did not make reference to the Caucasoid-appearing Mexican, but principally to the miscegenated individual of African descent who was at the bottom of the social ladder (Aguirre Beltran, *La población negra de México* 179).

Failure to understand or recognize Mexico's racial history can result in gaffes or misstatements by a translator, in particular when passing along information or cultural concepts. "Corridos in Southern California," an article published on the Mexican *corrido*, a narrative folk ballad, illustrates the translation challenges that can confront a person who is not willing to acknowledge certain truths of race, or is ignorant of them. The author of the article, Terrence L. Hansen, cites various *corridos* in his essay and presents their lyrics in both the original Spanish and his English translation. In his translations to English, race and color are noticeably effaced, as if on purpose. The omissions are apparently not out of ignorance, but for some other reason that would keep intact Mexico's image of not having a genetic relationship with Africa. In Hansen's citation of the lyrics for the "Corrido de Doña Elena," one can find:

Fue don Fernando el Francés	Fernando the Frenchman bold
un soldado muy valiente que	so valiant and brave was he who
combatió a los *chinacos* de	fought against the *liberals* of
México independiente.	Mexico, land of the free. (205)

While *liberals* as a translation for *chinacos* only reveals a fraction of the image that the word entails for an aware native, for the outsider, this might very well be an acceptable interpretation (Hernández Cuevas 115). In Mexican-Spanish the term *chinacos* was often employed to refer to a non-Caucasoid physical appearance. The lyricist does not make this clear in his English translation since the word he uses—"liberals"—refers to those soldiers that fought on behalf of the Mexican government in the War of Reform (1858–1861) and is not as ethnically specific as "chinacos." However, the author's attitude toward issues of color and race in Mexico becomes more clearly evident in his translation for the *corrido* "Jesús Cárdenas":

Ranchito de San Antonio	On the ranch of San Antonio
estado de Nuevo Leon	Nuevo Leon, name of the state,
murió la *güera* Chabela	*fair* Chabela had to die for treason,
por jugar una traición.	this was her fate. (221)

Here, it is obvious that the translator understands the ethnoracial value of the Mexican popular term "*güera*" and gives it full acceptance by interpreting it as "fair." Chabela is "fair" in the sense of being light in complexion, with hair that is blond. In Mexican Spanish *güero/güera* is popularly used to refer to someone fair and blond. The intended physical morphology of this translation into English is apparent. However, in another version of the same *corrido*, Chabela, "the fair one," confronts Jesús face-to-face:

Jesús sacó su pistola para darle de balazos Chabela le respondió: Véngase *prieto* a mis brazos.	Then Jesus took out his pistol and to shoot her he took aim. Chabela gasped and then cried: "Come to my arms, I'm to blame." (223)

Monolingual/bilingual Spanish speakers are provided with a color description (*prieto* = black) for Jesús that is overlooked in the translated English version. One cannot assume that the translator is unaware of current terminologies for physical descriptions in Mexican Spanish. If "*güero*" was within his lexical range, "*prieto*" undoubtedly had to be a part of his active lexicon also. "*Prieto*" functions as a color descriptor in the standard Spanish of all national versions of the language. Consequently, speakers of Spanish with the inherent sensitivity of the native speaker perambulate the barriers that separate *prieto* = color, or race in a derogatory sense, from *negro* = race, or color in a general sense, with relative ease. In all fairness, it should be mentioned that "*prieto*" can at times connote a stylized sense of endearment (such as "*mi querido prietito*"; i.e., "my dear little dark one") for the native Spanish speaker of the Mexican variety, regardless of race. Here again, its use entails special control so as to avoid connoting an offensive reference, culturally. Still, the association with color and race is not too far removed. While an argument can be made for the translation of "*prieto*" as "my dear" in this *corrido*, were that the case, there should be no rationale for its omission in the English translation. Perhaps one of the reasons why blackness and African-relatedness are so misunderstood in general by people who do not share in the culture is the reluctance by native Latin Americans to reveal something they consider to be a blot on their racial origins.

Consequently, the question becomes: Why is there reluctance on the part of the translator to associate blackness as an ethnic classification with the Mexican image, or to be remiss in interpreting the term with its stylized meaning? A work such as *El color de nuestra piel* [The Color of

Our Skin] by Celestino Gorostiza (1904–1967) shows exactly how cognizant Mexicans are of the differences of skin color within their population. For most Mexican nationals, the different skin-tone shadings are indeed meaningful in terms of social acceptance, social progress, and emulation. Unlike the translator of the *corridos*, Gorostiza approaches pigmentation and its social effect from an insider's awareness. Notice how the title of his drama bears the inclusiveness of *"nuestra piel"* ["our skin"] as opposed to an external vision which would have resulted in the phrasing "your skin" or "their skin." Embedded in the dialogue of this work are several cautions that refer to the author's understanding of how the question of color operates in the Mexican social atmosphere. It has been mentioned before that most Mexican culturists presume that the country operates on a tiered racial scale that evolves from European (white), the Amerindian, and the biracial (mestizo) individual. However, Gorostiza uses terms such as *"prieto"* and *"negro"* with impunity, and solicits the native speaker's comprehension of *"prieto"* and *"negro"* as either a color or a presumed race. When Hector, the lighter-skinned and blond brother addresses his darker-complexioned brother Jorge with: *"¿Quihúbole, negro?"* (31) ["What's up, nigger?" or "What's up, blackie?"], what image comes into focus in the mind of the monolingual Spanish speaker? Is *"negro"* a reference to color or to race, or to color indicating race, and does the context preclude the term being received as an epithet? When the playwright allows Carlos, the whiter, upper-class suitor *"fino de facciones"* (25) (i.e., with thin lips and pointed nose) of the swarthy-complexioned sister to moralize:

> *Pero, afortunadamente, en Mexico la cuestión del color no representa ningún problema y no tiene ninguna importancia...Hasta en una misma familia hay prietos y güeros, y nadie se fija ni habla de ello.* (33)

> (However, fortunately Mexico does not have a problem with color. It doesn't matter at all. There are black-skinned people and blond types in the same family and no one notices or talks about it.)

Aesthetic Blackness in the Creative Literature 65

can one consider the concept of race and color to be entirely absent from the social mindset of Mexican society?

As the theme of the play develops, the reader or theatergoer witnesses a different set of prerogatives that respond to this question. Carlos' family rejects his proposal of marriage to Beatriz on the grounds that she is too dark and debunks, in essence, his moralizing statement on Mexico's lack of a problem with color and ethnicity. Additionally, Hector's constant derision of his elder siblings, Jorge and Beatriz, because of their darker complexion finds unusual support in his own family circle. Don Ricardo, the father, overtly shows that his preferred child is Hector, the *"güerito"* (i.e., the little blonde son), and makes a mental effort to see himself as lighter than he actually is. Don Ricardo comfortably associates himself and his light-skinned, blue-eyed son with a family tree of allegedly *"criollo"* (Spaniards born in the Americas) ancestors:

> *¿Estás tú loco? Yo no soy mestizo. ¿De dónde crees tú que sacaste los ojos claros? Mira a mi padre. Criollo puro. Tú lo heredaste a él.* (35)
>
> (Are you mad? I am not biracial. From where do you think you got those light-colored eyes? Look at my father; an unadulterated Spaniard. You inherited them [the light-colored eyes] from him.)

In real life, the correct set of inherited genes might be only just a wish, bolstered, at best, by a psychological exigency. Later, it is learned that Don Ricardo's wife presents him with the supposition that Hector might not even be his biological offspring.

With his thematic construct, Gorostiza has ensured that colorism, based on the hierarchy of superior to inferior skin colors, is a social absolute that is usually passed from generation to generation. In this respect, Don Ricardo lectures his "blond, blue-eyed" son:

> *Eso que haces no está bien. Faltas al respeto a tu casa, a tu familia...y te degradas tú mismo al ponerte al tú por tú con una prieta mugrosa de éstas...Si el mundo está lleno de mujeres...blancas... bonitas...limpias...* (14–15)

(What you are doing is not right. You are being disrespectful to your home, to your family...and you lower yourself when you stoop to the level of one of these dirty, black women. Why the world is full of clean...white...pretty...women.)

While the dramatist does not place overt or special emphasis on the impact of African blood in Mexico's racial history, in the development of the dialogue he reveals to the culturally aware reader or theatergoer that he is conscious of its genomic possibilities in the country's genotypic chart (34). "*Prieto*" and "*negro*," as they function in his literary lexicon, are not empty words without a national raison d'être.

To further illustrate the view of the aesthetics of color as a thematic concept in the art of a Mexican writer, one can look at a novel by Francisco Rojas González (1904–1951), *La Negra Angustias* [Angustias, The Black Woman], originally published in 1944. Its psychocontextual framework reveals through the analysis of its black protagonist a more definitive approach where race and color are concerned. Not only does Rojas González demonstrate an insider's view of ethnic awareness and of the colorism that motivates conditional social acceptance or rejection, he also illustrates prevailing attitudes that appertain to blackness in the Mexican context. Angustias Farrera, the protagonist of *La Negra Angustias*, is Mexican-born and the daughter of a white Mexican mother and a black Mexican father—or is he also biracial? Because of a dual assignation that makes him black at times and at others mulatto, this is not clear unless mulatto is the same as black:

> ¡*Válgame Dios, Antón Farrera! –respondió la vieja...No más véale la color. Mulata como usted. La madre que—que en paz descanse—era blanca y fina; de ella sacó las facciones y de usted...lo* prietillo. (13)
>
> (May God help me! Anton Farrera, the old woman answered. Just look at her color, a *mulatta* just like you. Her mother—may she rest in peace—was white with delicate features. She took her facial features after her, and her *blackness* after you.) [emphasis added]

Aesthetic Blackness in the Creative Literature 67

Wouldn't the fact that the old woman saw Angustias' father as mulatto be an indication that he is biracial? Miscegenation had been an ongoing process in Mexico since the introduction of Africans into the area during the sixteenth century.

The author alternates between calling both father and daughter at times black, and other times mulatto. But neither Angustias nor her father, Anton Farrera, operate on the assumption that they are downtrodden because of their color. Their struggles are aimed at liberating themselves from a world of want because they are the economically oppressed victims of a stifling poverty that appears more class oriented than racially motivated. The author never clearly expresses whether their impoverishment is tangential or fundamental to their blackness. Other Mexicans—mestizos, *indios*, and even lower-class *blancos* [whites]—are just as illiterate and socially bereft. Nor is Angustias' environment peopled only with other blacks. Rojas González immerses her in an environment of protoypical Mexicans—in the main, "mestizos"—with whom she shares a common goal. Their shared objective is to rid themselves of material need and social deprivation.

Angustias inhabits a world of such diverse phenotypes that few non-Mexicans can conceive of or even perceive the varying descriptions:

> *Surianos de todas las regiones de Guerrero y de Morelos se hallaban reunidos en Cuatla: costeños pintos con las más exóticas coloraciones del vitiligo; indios tlapanecos altaneros, cazurros y orgullosos de su linaje; negros de la Costa Chica, parlachines y traviesos; mestizos de la sierra, tan serenos y temerarios en la pelea como sombrios y trágicos en la paz; criollos alegres, valentones y descarados; mulatos impulsivos y majaderos....todo el mosaico étnico que componía la población mexicana de aquellos días...* (119)

(Surianos from every region of Guerrero and Morelos had congregated in Cuatla: people of color from the coast with the most exotic skin colors; arrogant, Tlapaneco Indians, taciturn and proud of their heritage; Blacks from the Costa Chica, chatty and mischievous; Mestizos from the highlands as dispassionate and fearless in battle as they are somber and forlorn in peace; happy-go-lucky Creoles, conceited and cheeky; impulsive and dumb mulattos... the entire ethnic patchwork that made up the turbulent, rural population of the Mexico of that period...)

However, given that the focus of the author's thesis is on Angustias the person, exactly how does he construct her ethnic image? There is no doubt that she is Mexican. She is a native-born Mexican woman who fought valiantly and competently in the revolutionary struggle of the underclass [*los de abajo*] for economic freedom and respect of person, as well as for her personal agenda of gender liberation. Ethnically, however, she is black with "*la cara renegrida*" ["A shiny, black face"] (13). Rojas González places more emphasis on the physical characteristics of Angustias—in order to stress her blackness—than he does on factors that would reveal her fundamental human qualities. Stereotypically, she has "*pelo enmarañado*" ["stiff, wild hair"], "*piernas negras como dos troncos de ébano*" ["legs as black as two logs of ebony wood"], "*carnes negras y prietas*" ["flesh that was genetically as well as organically black"], "*gruesos labios*" ["thick lips"], "*su boca carnuda*" ["a big, fleshy mouth"], in addition to an "*epidermis renegrida*" ["a shiny, black epidermis"]. On various occasions she is racially denigrated: "*–Para Blanca Nieves está muy prieta...*" ["She's awfully black to be a Snow White..."]; "*...si ya hasta manosear se dejó la negra mustia!*" ["...that degenerate nigger even allowed them to feel her up all over!"]; "*Sí, aquí sobran dos gentes...esta negra del infierno y el alcahuete de Modesto*" ["Yes, there are two people too many here...that nigger woman straight out of hell and Modesto who tries to hook people up"]. Finally, the common epithet "*changa retinta*" ["jet-black monkey"] underscores the venom with which the Mexican public views the African-descendant background of Angustias and makes reference to this racial background. Even though it was Angustias who later captured the phrase and applied it to herself (88), it is, structurally, Rojas González who determines the linguistic imagery that should be attached to his representations. In this instance, the self-implied racial invective projects an element of social defiance as Angustias hurls it back at her enemy with the understanding that she is neither harmed nor humiliated by the phrase. Therefore, notwithstanding Angustias' use of the term, it does reveal the aspersions with which Mexicans would refer to the black people in their midst.

The physical characteristics of Angustias serve as an impetus in the primary thesis of her construction: she is inescapably black physically, at least in the mindset of the author. Yet, in close alliance with this outlook, one also finds a psychological bent that is equally as important in the author's literary configuration of the African-descendant individual. The secondary premise, based on the author's mental configuration of Angustias, leads to the conclusion that blacks in the Mexican environment are seen to willfully allow the white man to control them and usurp their dignity. Of their own volition, they become, in literal terms, the slaves of whites. Rojas González unhesitatingly posits this assertion as the denouement of his literary study. Toward the end of the novel, there is a shift in the construct of Angustias, wherein one sees a complete reversal of character. She is no longer seen as the commanding, domineering, macho-hating woman who leads a band of rebellious revolutionaries in search of their rights. At one time, she thought nothing of ordering someone to be castrated as punishment for sexual harassment. She was not against refusing the amorous advances of a powerful white man: "*¿Desprecia una negra un hombre blanco y cabal como Don Efrén?*" ("Can a black woman reject [the advances] of a powerful white man like Don Efren?") (64) Yet, the white-skinned, blond, and blue-eyed schoolteacher who brought her the "civilizing" benefits of reading and writing would subsequently evolve into her nemesis and master after she married him. He exploits her fame and popularity for his own economic gain, deceives her with other women, and in front of other people degrades her image as a leading figure of the Mexican Revolution:

> *Angustias, ven, átame la correa de mi zapato...La mulata, sencillamente, alegremente, cortó la charla con las mujeres para ir hacia su marido. Se hincó en una rodilla y sobre la otra puso*

> *el zapato sucio y gastado del profesor, para anudar cuidadosamente la cinta desatada.* (202)

> (Angustias, come, fasten the belt on my shoe…The mulatta, happily and without much ado, broke off her conversation with the other women to go to her husband. She knelt down on one knee and placed the teacher's dirty and worn-out shoe on the other, in order to carefully redo the belt that had come undone.)

Angustias was completely oblivious to the effect this had on those who had looked up to her because of the compelling strength of her character:

> *Después, todas las mujeres se vieron entre sí sorprendidas y, desde ese instante, la figura de la negra Angustias quedó para ziempre a la zaga, sorbiendo el polvo que alzaban los pies del profesor.* (202)

> (After this, all the women looked at each other in surprise, and from then on, the person of Angustias, the black woman, always trailed behind the teacher sucking in the dust that his heels kicked up.)

With the construction and imagery of Angustias organized around her race and ethnicity, Rojas González confirms not only the presence of blacks as an integrated component of the general population of Mexico, but also affirms the negative perspective from which they are viewed by the literate classes. Recognized by some critics as an author who "wished to propose *mestizaje* as a solution to the race problem in Mexico" (Schmidt 657), the view of Mexico as a nation of mixed races is patently present in the hypothesis that Rojas González has proposed for the protagonist of *La negra Angustias*. Although Angustias functions under the rubric of *"negra"* (i.e., "black"), there is no doubt she was intended to be construed as a product of Mexican *mestizaje*, or race mixing. *The Pequeño Larousse* dictionary conjoined *mulato* and *mestizo* as synonymous in meaning. In this construct of Rojas González, African genes are subsumed by the cauldron of Mexican *mestizaje* much the same as in other areas of the Spanish-speaking world, where enslavement of the African was a fait accompli. The mother of Angustias was designed to be the Caucasian prototype (white, with delicate features) (13), but her father is nonwhite in no uncertain terms. As mentioned, at times he is seen as black and at others as mulatto.

Late in the development of the novel, it becomes obvious that the author's intent is to explore the occurrence of race mixing in Mexico, with an African factor in the mix. Besides Angustias and Manuel and the parents of Angustias, there is another couple with a child whose ethnoracial heritage is unclear. *Mestizaje* is a strong possibility, even though the racial background of the parents remains unknown and is only slightly suggested for the reader. Introduced simply as "*una muchacha simpática y fornida*" ["a likeable and well-built young girl"] and "*un mocetón recio como eral*" ["a strapping young man, as powerful as a young bull"], their offspring is described as "*un niño de pecho gordinflón y* prieto" (186) ["A young breastfed child, chubby and *black.*"] I have placed the child's color in italics to draw attention to the fact that no other clue is supplied as to the racial background of this young family. Yet the author felt that it was important to the overall schema of his literary construction to highlight the color of the child, or imply the ethnicity of one or perhaps both of the parents. And in the case where "*prieto*" is an implication for some readers of someone who is swarthy or Mediterranean-dark, out of all of the possibilities that the author could have implied, in no uncertain terms did he intend for the image to be that of a little blond, blue-eyed child. On a subsequent trip to this young family's home while the husband was absent, Manuel, the blonde, blue-eyed schoolteacher, conveniently encourages his wife Angustias to retire to a room that had been prepared for the two of them. After making sure that she has fallen asleep, he goes out to the kitchen and makes advances to the young mother who is alone in the house with her child. Here again, the author's suggestion of the young mother's acquiescence implies a covert societal accusation. It is for the reader to determine whether the "black child's" mother actually submitted to Manuel's sexual overtures and should thus be judged as dissolute in the absence of her husband. Can this be a suggestion that the black woman is easy prey for the white prowler? Would the reading public of that day have had the tendency to stereotypically associate the loose morals of the young mother with a suspect ethnic image? In following the Afro Latino concept designed by both Rojas González and Celestino Gorostiza, one is reminded that literary constructions are purposefully diagrammed to connect points of reference, or to provide clues for an author's deep structure agenda versus a surface construct that implies an intended comprehension in an artistic manner. Race is fundamental in the construction of *La Negra Angustias*. Given that the goal of the literary composition is to create meaning, what meaning should the representation of the young mother of dubious ethnicity have for the reader? As Fajardo-Acosta has made clear in the essay "Understanding Literature," published on his World Literature Web site:

> An important feature of literary texts which distinguishes them from other kinds of persuasive discourse is the fact that they operate not through direct statement and explicit revelation of their contents but instead through indirect allusion...Literary texts thus convey meaning to their readers in ways which go far beyond the mere literal or "surface" level of signification.... Meaning in literature is therefore something that needs to be determined not merely on the basis of a face-value understanding of the words in it but through a complete evaluation of the signifying complexity of the entire text [images, symbols, allusions, and suggestions]. (5–6)

But the question remains: What literary goal does the author strive for with the vignettes of mothers and offspring? On this note, Rojas González is more specific. The ultimate paragraph of this novel declares:

> *Dentro de una cunita, un pequeño de piel morena y ojos verdes escuchaba embelesado el dulce canto materno, que se trenzaba con los gorjeos del mirlo prisionero.* (220)
>
> (In his little crib, a little brown-skinned child with green eyes, listened bewitched to his mother's sweet lullaby as it intermingled with the gurgling sounds of the imprisoned blackbird.)

Aesthetic Blackness in the Creative Literature 73

This scene has undoubtedly been structured to provide suggestive imagery for the implied miscegenation of Angustias and Manuel's child. However, there is no disputing the fact that their child is Mexican, a Mexican of the future with his black, Afro Latino roots encaged behind his green eyes and *moreno*/mestizo color, much the same as the little black child of the welcoming young couple. Their ethnic and racial background was not made explicit; nonetheless, they are also Mexican. The author did not overtly construct visible blackness for the mother and father, as if to confirm that one's genetic background can often be concealed (encaged). Blackness, nonetheless, can be substantiated in the genetic chart of Mexico with a logical explanation that stems from the episode of African slavery in the country's past. It is a past that has made literary figures like Angustias an element of reality and a symbol of Mexico's racial patrimony.

In the racial climate of today's Mexico, phenotypes are not always visibly commensurate with the genetic heritage one has received from a biological heritage, especially in the case of miscegenation. For both Rojas González and Gorostiza, the illusive nature of genetics and color is clearly seen in their final resolution to reduce the national icon of race to a mestizo image wherein *"mestizaje"* subsumes *"mulataje"* and the progression of *"prieto"* [black] becomes *"moreno"* [brown]. This ethnic duality of race mixing ultimately emerges as the mestizo symbol of Mexico. Subsequently, what the artistry of literature meaningfully confirms with its treatment of topics that skillfully conceptualize colorism and covert racism, others affirm with cogent data and philosophical truths. Thus, to substantiate the presence of an Afro Latino image in an unsuspecting environment, a researcher of the African presence in Mexico declares:

> [Of the] 200,000 slaves introduced into the country during the three long centuries of colonial domination…The majority ha[ve] diluted their blood by their unions with aborigines and whites, thus giving rise to the mixture of bloods that forms the biologic basis of Mexican nationality. (Aguirre Beltran, "The Slave Trade in Mexico" 431)

Works Cited

Aguirre Beltran, Gonzalo. "Bailes de Negros." *Revista de la Universidad de Mexico* 25.2 (Oct. 1970): 1–49. Print.

———. *La población negra de México*. México, D. F.: Fondo de Cultura Económico, 1984. Print.

———."The Slave Trade in Mexico." *The Hispanic American Historical Review* 24.3 (Aug. 1944): 412–431. Print.

Alcántara Almánzar, J. "Black Images in Dominican Literature." *New West Indian Guide/Nieuwe West-Indische Gids* 61.3–4 (1987): 161–173. Print.

Alvarez Nazario, Manuel. *El elemento afronegroide in el español de Puerto Rico: Contribución al estudio del negro en América*. San Juan, P. R.: Instituto de Cultura Puertorriqueña, 1974. Print.

Baca, Susana. *Susana Baca*. Luaka Bop, 1997. CD.

Boyd, Antonio Olliz. "The Concept of Black Esthetics As Seen in Selected Works of Three Latin American Writers: Machado de Assis, Nicolás Guillén and Adalberto Ortiz." PhD diss., Stanford University, 1975. Print.

———. "Manuel Zapata Olivella." *Dictionary of Literary Biography: Modern Latin-American Fiction Writers*. Volume 13. Ed. William Luis. Detroit: Gale Research Inc., 1992. 313–321. Print.

Boyd, Antonio Olliz, and Gabriel Asoanab Abudu. "Afro Iberian Identity in the Early Literature of Spain: Precursor to the Afro Hispanic Identity." *Imagination Emblems and Expressions: Essays on Latin American, Caribbean and Continental Culture and Identity*. Ed. Helen Ryan-Ranson. Bowling Green, OH: Bowling Green State University Press, 1993. 283–299. Print.

Capó, Bobby. *Canta Bobby Capó*. Seeco, 1999. CD.

Carpentier, Alejo. *Ecue-Yamba-O*. Madrid: Alianza Editorial, 1989. Print.

Chalá, Ana. *People of African Descent in South America*. Paper prepared for the Commission on Human Rights, Sub-Commission on Promotion and Protection of Human Rights, Working Group on Minorities. 8 May 2003. Web. 6 Jan. 2008.

Corbiere, Emilio J. "El genocidio en la Argentina: Lucas Fernández, precursor del socialismo en el Rio de la Plata." Web. 5 Jan. 2008.

Corbitt, Duvon C. "Chinese Immigrants in Cuba." *Far Eastern Survey* 13.14 (Jul. 12, 1944): 130–132. Print.

Cyrus, Stanley A. "Ethnic Ambivalence and Afro-Hispanic Novelists." *Afro-Hispanic Review* 21.1–2 (Spring–Fall 2002): 185–189. Print.

Davis, James F. *Who Is Black?* University Park: The Pennsylvania State University Press, 1991. Print.

Diaz, Junot. *The Brief Wondrous Life of Oscar Wao*. New York: Riverhead Books, 2007. Print.

Duany, Jorge. "Dominican Migration to Puerto Rico: A Transnational Perspective." *Centro Journal* 17.1 (Spring 2005): 242–269. Print.

———. "Reconstructing Racial Identity: Ethnicity, Color and Class among Dominicans in the United States and Puerto Rico." *Latin American Perspectives* 25.3 (May 1998): 147–172. Print.

Escamilla Vera, Francisco. "Andrés Eloy Blanco (1897–1955)" n.p. Web. 4 May 2010.

Esdaille, Milca. "Same Trip, Different Ships—Dominican Authors and African Americans—Interview." Web. 5 May 2007.

Fajardo-Acosta, Fidel. "Understanding Literature." World Literature Web site. Web. 25 May 2007.

Ferré, Rosario. *La Casa de la Laguna*. Edición española. New York: Vintage Books, 1996. Print.

———. *Language Duel/Duelo del Lenguaje*. New York: Vintage Books, 2002. Print.

France, Ana Kay. "Iago and Othello in Boris Pasternak's Translation." *Shakespeare Quarterly* 28.1 (Winter 1977): 73–84. Print.

Gorostiza, Celestino. *El color de nuestra piel*. Eds. Luis Soto-Ruiz and S. Samuel Triflo. Toronto: Collier-Macmillan Canada, Ltd., 1966. Print.

Gosser-Esquilín, Mary Ann. "Nanas Negras: The Silenced Women in Rosario Ferré and Olga Nolla." *Centro Journal* XIV.2 (Fall 2002): 49–63. Print.

Hansen, Terrence L. "Corridos in Southern California." *Western Folklore* 18.3 (Jul. 1959): 203–232. Print.

Hernández Cuevas, Marco Polo. *África late en la mexicanidad*. Lewiston, NY: The Edwin Mellen Press, 2007. Print.

Knight, Franklin W. *Slave Society in Cuba During the Nineteenth Century*. Madison: The University of Wisconsin Press, 1970. Print.

Lang, Peter. "Rev. of *Rosario Ferré: A Search for Identity*, by Suzanne S. Hintz." *World Literature Today* 70.3 (Summer 1996): 670–671. Print.

La Onda Digital de Uruguay. No. 203, 14 al 20 de Setiembre de 2004. "Diálogo con la sicóloga Susana Rudolf y la estudiante Noelia Maciel." Web. 25 May 2007.

Lee, Debbie. "Regino Pedroso and the Creation of a Triple Consciousness." *Journal of Hispanic Higher Education* 2 (2003): 225–240. Print.

Lewis, Marvin A. *Afro-Hispanic Poetry 1940–1980: From Slavery to "Negritud"in South American Verse*. Columbia: University of Missouri Press, 1983. Print.

Loude, Jean-Yves. *Lisboa na cidade negra*. Trans. Manuela Mendonça Torres. Lisbon: Publicações Dom Quixote, 2005. Print.

Lovejoy, Paul E. "The African Diaspora: Revisionist Interpretations of Ethnicity, Culture and Religion under Slavery." *Studies in the World*

History of Slavery, Abolition and Emancipation 2.1 (1997): 1–23. Print.

Marrero Aristy, Ramón. *Over*. Santo Domingo: Ediciones de Taller, 1980. Print.

Morejón, Nancy. "Nación y Mestizaje." *AfroCuba: Una antología de escritos cubanos sobre raza, política y cultura*. Eds. Pedro Pérez-Sarduy and Jean Stubbs. San Juan: Editorial de la Universidad de Puerto Rico, 1998. Print.

Morgado, Marcia. "Una entrevista con Mayra Santos Febres." Web. 25 May 2007.

Morner, Magnus. *Race Mixture in the History of Latin America*. Boston: Little, Brown and Company, 1967. Print.

Panford Jr., Moses. "Hacia una revalorización de *Ecue-Yamba-O* de Alejo Carpentier: una perspectiva fanti." *Anales del Caribe* 21–22 (2003): 66–77. Print.

———. *Manuel Vicente Guerrero: El negro valiente en Flandes (introducción, edición y notas)*. Boulder, CO: Society of Spanish and Spanish-American Studies, 2003. Print.

Parra, Flavia C., et al. "Color and Genomic Ancestry in Brazilians." *Proceedings of the National Academy of Sciences (PNAS)* 100.1 (7 Jan. 2003): 177–182. Print.

Pérez, Loida Maritza. *Geographies of Home*. New York: Viking Penguin, 1999. Print.

———. Geographies of Home. "An Interview with Loida Maritza Pérez." Web. 30 May 2002.

Pérez-Sarduy, Pedro, and Jean Stubbs. *Afrocuba*. San Juan: Editorial de la Universidad de Puerto Rico, 1998. Print.

Pimenta, Juliana R., et al. "Color and Genomic Ancestry in Brazilians: A Study with Forensic Microsatellites." *Human Heredity* 62 (2006): 190–195. Print.

Poet, J. "Baca Keeps Afro-Peruvian Music Alive." *San Francisco Chronicle Review* (24 Sept. 1997). Web. 9 May 2008.

Rico, Francisco, ed. *La Vida de Lazarillo de Tormes: y de sus fortunas y adversidades*. 17th ed. Madrid: Ediciones Cátedra, 2003. Print.

Rojas González, Francisco. *La Negra Angustias*. México, D. F.: Fondo de Cultura Económico, 1998. Print.

Rout, Leslie B., Jr. *The African Experience in Spanish America: 1502 to the Present Day*. Cambridge: Cambridge University Press, 1976. Print.

Santos-Febres, Mayra. *Cualquier miércoles soy tuya*. Barcelona: Mondadori, 2002. Print.

Scherer, Frank F. "Sanfancón: Orientalism, Confucianism and the Construction of Chineseness in Cuba, 1847–1997." *Centre for Research on Latin America and the Caribbean* (Jul. 1998): 1–13. Print.

Schmidt, Donald L. "The Indigenista Novel and the Mexican Revolution." *The Americas* 33.4 (Apr. 1977): 652–660. Print.

Sones de Mexico. "Fandango" lyrics. Web. 5 May 2010.

Stinchcomb, Dawn F. *The Development of Literary Blackness in the Dominican Republic*. Gainesville: University Press of Florida, 2004. Print.

Tinhorão, José Ramos. *Os Negros em Portugal: Uma presença silenciosa* 2da ed. Lisboa: Editorial Caminho, SA, 1997. Print.

Torres-Saillant, Silvio. "The Tribulations of Blackness: Stages in Dominican Racial Identity." *Latin American Perspectives* 100 25.3 (May 1998): 126–146. Print.

Truque, Carlos Arturo. "Mi testimonio." Trans. June M. Legge. *Afro-Hispanic Review* 1.1 (Jan. 1982): 17–22. Print.

———. "Vivan los compañeros." Ed. Eduardo Pachón Padilla. *Cuentos Colombianos*. Bogotá: Instituto Colombiana de Cultura, 1973. Print.

Vásquez, Chalena. "Presencia africana en la cultura de la costa peruana." Web. 9 Sept. 2007.

Vinson, Ben, III. "Afro-Mexican History: Trends and Directions in Scholarship." *History Compass* 3 (2005): LA 156, 1–14. Print.

Zapata Olivella, Manuel. *Chambacú corral de negros*. 4th ed. Medellín, Colombia: Editorial Bedout, S. A., 1974. Print.

Essay II

The Aesthetics of Language as an Experience of the Afro Latin/Afro Hispanic Reality

> *Mientras que a nosotras nos duele la cabeza, a ellas les da jaqueca...y cuando les da una sirimba salen corriendo para el sicólogo y nosotras directico pa' la consulta del santero... ¡Así es la vida, cariño!* (Pedro Pérez-Sarduy, *Las Criadas de la Habana* 63)

> (While we get headaches, they develop migraines ...and when they have a *sirimba* [panic attack], they run off to the psychologist; we make a bee-line to a session with the root doctor. That's life my dear!)

Words and phrases derived from African linguistic sources, when employed in the creative literature of a given community as an expression of the national image or an element of native culture, strongly suggest a relationship—past or present—with Africa. For example, the term *sirimba*, as used in the opening quotation, is present in the active or passive vocabulary of most Cuban natives. It is understood to describe a recognized condition of "nerves." Accessible to most Cuban nationals, this word did not enter the national lexicon by way of Spain, but arrived on the slave ships along with their cargo from the African continent.

When it comes to Latin America as a whole, there is no contesting the fact that persons from Africa were a living part of that area's quotidian context. In a vast majority of the Latin countries, there are still descendants of these Africans—although some are now miscegenated with other races—that substantiate the cogency of an ongoing Afro Latin presence. Thus, when Alvarez Nazario writes in his study *El elemento afronegroide en el español de Puerto Rico* [The Black African Component in Puerto Rican Spanish]:

> *Obedece la presente obra al deseo de definir y analizar la huella que ha dejado el esclavo africano de antaño en el español puertorriqueño, mayormente en la expresión de nivel popular (con relación al vocabulario y en menor medida a la fonética)*. (7)

> (This study answers a need to define and analyze the imprint that the African slave of yesteryear has left on the Spanish language of Puerto Rico, especially at the popular level, with regards to its vocabulary and to a lesser extent its phonetics.)

One can find patent confirmation of another one of the distinguishing characteristics left by the African existence or experience that has endured to become pervasive in the Latin cultural environment. This observation for Puerto Rico, it should be noted, has not excluded other Latin areas, as the article "Some Lexical Linkages between Africa and Venezuela" confirms:

> As will be demonstrated, the evidence presented here points to diverse African origins of words used in Venezuela, i.e. both from the Sudanic and the Bantu families, with some languages seemingly contributing more than others to the lexicon. (Megenney 385)

Aesthetics of Language as an Experience 83

In general, Megenney confirms that the African presence in Latin America was extensive and strong enough to influence spoken Spanish and Portuguese wherever the African was found. In another article, entitled "Common Words of African Origin Used in Latin America," he acknowledges that "...if only in the form of a few borrowed words cemented into the superstrate language, we might be safe in assuming a number of about 150–200" (1). This calculation seems to refer to the probable number of languages and dialects that made lexical contributions to the Spanish and Portuguese languages spoken in the Americas. In addition, Megenney's observations confirm—for those that doubt the reality of an African population in Latin America with recognized experiences—that Sub-Saharan people were enough of a force to make their cultural presence felt and absorbed into the total concept of a regional culture. The article offers "...a list of words which are generally well known and found with a relatively high frequency of usage throughout most of Spanish America or Brazil as the case may be" (1). However, the words are not in regional context and thus, in a sense, deprive native Spanish/Portuguese linguistic environments of their overall effect or contribution for a regional expression. Consequently, when vocabulary derived from an African-based language is employed in prose, poetry, and song lyrics alongside expressions with lexemes in standard Spanish, one perceives an air of autochthony for national consumption (e.g., Cuban, Venezuelan, Colombian, etc.) and even for the nonnational familiar with the cultural environment of a particular country. It is in such a context that one would understand "Canción festiva para ser llorada" ["A festive song of lamentation"] by Luis Palés Matos, the Puerto Rican poet:

> *Cuba ñáñigo y bachata*
> *Haití vodú y calabaza*
> *Puerto Rico burundanga*
> (Palés Matos 24)

The African terms *ñáñigo*, *bachata*, *vodú*, and *calabaza* are not exclusive to the Puerto Rican cultural scene, and they denote definitively an aesthetic image of blackness. While these expressions are likewise employed with comparable value in other Latin environments, it is the combination *"Puerto Rico burundanga"* ["messed up, useless Puerto Rico" or "Puerto Rico full of worthless junk"] that calls one's attention to the author's aesthetic relationship with his verses. Could this perspective have emanated from an experience in his immediate environment, given that he is Puerto Rican and native to the locale he has called into question? Although the Africanisms are logically and perceptively used, one questions the poet's identification with this part of his national culture that he has explained with African terminology. Is it Puerto Rico's alignment with the blackness of other areas (i.e., Cuba and Haiti) that renders it *"burundanga"* or is it simply the presence of blackness in Puerto Rico that gives it the aura of worthlessness? Perhaps this particular word choice stems from the poet's assessment of the poem's tone based on other aesthetic criteria? Certainly Palés Matos must have had other choices in his artistic portfolio of available African lexemes that rhymed.

In contrast, the late Cuban singer Celia Cruz, in her rendition of the song "Burundanga." declares:

> *Songo le dio a Borondongo*
> *Borondongo le dio a Bernabé*
> *Bernabé le pegó a fuchilanga*
> *le echó a burundanga*
> *les hinchan los pies*
> *monina*
> (Cruz, "Burundanga")

This is an arrangement of names and actions with archetypal African vocables that culminates in *"burundanga"* to generate for the listener a sense of "scandal" or "uproar" in keeping with the Cuban meaning of the term. This juxtaposition of African terms creates a context into which the singer/lyricist interjects herself with the African-based appellative *"monina"* meaning "brother," specifically, "soul brother." This closeness is explained in subsequent verses with the admonition: *"Abambele practica el amor...Porque entre hermanos se vive major"* ["Let's show some love, Abambele...Because one lives better as brothers"]. In each example offered, the African expressions selected by the poet/lyricist are to be considered more for their metonymical imagery than as word-for-word replacements of comparable terms in Spanish. The grouping of African terms in the earlier lyrics, perceived as the metonym, comprehensively affirms a cultural heritage—an African cultural heritage—brought to the Americas, revised, and continued. The manner in which this legacy is utilized, however, rests with the subjective mindset of the poet and/or lyricist and accords with his or her comprehension of the word choice and identification with it. Identity can be understood as a conglomerate of factors that gives a person a set of qualities or characteristics that enables that self to be the same or different from other individuals. In the case of Celia Cruz, there is no vacillation. She aligns herself with the imagery of her lyrics by appealing to the concept of brotherhood implicit in the term *"monina,"* adapted from the liturgical literature of the Abakua, an Afro Cuban religious organization. In comparison, one can look at the notion of identity and Africanness as considered by the Afro American writer Langston Hughes and his Cuban counterpart Nicolás Guillén. Both writers, contemporary peers, were racially miscegenated, and each affirmed an adherence to "blackness" as a cultural legacy. One identified with Africa as a symbol of primitive forces; the other adhered to the reality of Africa as the core of his essence. In his autobiographical treatise, *The Big Sea*, Hughes writes:

> She [the white patron] wanted me to be primitive and know and feel the intuitions of the primitive. But unfortunately, I did not feel the rhythms of the primitive surging through me, and so I could not live and write as though I did. I was only an American Negro—who had loved the surface of Africa and the rhythms of Africa—but I was not Africa. (325)

Consequently, any recourse to Africanisms that one finds in Hughes' works should be approached and accepted as nothing more than poetic constructions rather than inherited cultural sentience.

Contrarily, Guillén always made it a point to confirm that Africa was an integral part of his identity. An example of this direction can be seen in the poem that attests to his ethnoracial heritage, "Balada de los dos abuelos" ["The Ballad of the Two Grandfathers"]:

> *Africa de selvas húmedas*
> *Y de gordos gongos sordos*
> *–¡Me muero!*
> *(Dice mi abuelo negro.)*
> *Aguaprieta de caimanes*
> *verdes mañanas de cocos*
> *–¡Me canso!*
> *(Dice mi abuelo blanco.)*
> (Valdés-Cruz 113)

> (Africa of humid forests
> And big muffled gongs
> –I'm dying!
> (Says my black grandfather.)
> Swamp waters with crocodiles
> Mornings green with coconuts
> –I'm tired!
> (Says my white grandfather.))

The poet's black grandfather is not approached with mythological evasiveness or romanticized lyricism, but is described as a sentient, human being with an identifiable geographical backdrop: Africa. This, in a sense, gives the poet possibilities for evoking Africa and African concepts as fundamental to his identity. This kinship, so to speak, remains a constant in his poems and writings. The Hughes and Guillén examples could lead to the suggestion that the admission of Africa as an entity of self-identification depends in large measure on how one rationalizes a personal relationship with the African space. Not all Latin American countries willingly accept an African lineage. Peru, in this sense, is somewhat complex and serves as a case in point. There are Peruvian writers, such as Mario Vargas Llosa, who are not Afro Peruvian but acknowledge the black person to be an element of the national identity. In his works,

Vargas Llosa unhesitatingly characterizes black people as native to the environment. This is especially obvious in his novels that present Peru as the literary backdrop. *Conversación en la Catedral* [Conversation in the Cathedral] and *La ciudad de los perros* [The Time of the Heroes] are a representative sampling of his literary thesis as it relates to race and ethnicity:

> Nothing teaches us better than literature to see, in ethnic and cultural differences, the richness of the human patrimony, and to prize those differences as a manifestation of humanity's multifaceted creativity...[B]ut it is also an experience of learning what and how we are, in our human integrity...in relationships that link us to others, In our public image and in the secret recesses of our consciousness. (Vargas Llosa, "The Premature Obituary of the Book: Why Literature?")

Aside from the Vargas Llosa approach, others among the country's creative writers, historians, and researchers in the social sciences tend to focus more on the Amerindian and Indian mestizo populations at the expense of the African descendant. There are, nonetheless, numerous reminders of Africa's presence in the national fabric of the Peruvian whole. The landmark study by Fernando Romero, *Quimba, Fa, Malambo, Ñeque: Afronegrismos en el Peru* (1988) [Quimba, Fa, Malambo, Ñeque: Africanisms in Peru] provides a national readership with proof of how integrated the African, his or her descendants, and recognizable lexemes have become in the country's culture. Most *limeños* (i.e., natives or residents of Lima) would understand the intangible quality of the term "*Quimba*," and a majority, if not all, would attribute its imagery to Peru's black population, even if non-African-related *limeños* cannot agree on whether the concept carries negative or positive social attachments. When perceived as an expression of "soul" (e.g., *esa muchacha canta con quimba*/that girl sings with soul) or intuited as a spirited action to which one is psychologically attuned (*para mí el centro ejecutó un ataque quimboso*/the way I see it, the center executed his play with grace and passion), then recent displays of *Quimba* in the contemporary artistic life of Peru are accepted with innate cultural comprehension by all Peruvians, not only those who overtly identify as black or black-related. Eva Ayllón, an internationally acclaimed Afro Peruvian singer, released a CD in 2009 entitled "*Kimba*[sic] *Fá*" which is understood to be equivalent in meaning to "soul with joyous passion") True to the recording's cultural heritage, the tracks are not only laced with syncopated, percussion-driven sounds—with the title song "*Quimba Fa, Malambo, Ñeque*" showcased—but the entire disc is representatively Peruvian with a recognizable mixture of both Creole [*música criolla*] numbers as well as Afro Peruvian [*festejo*] beats. If Peru has begun to overtly acknowledge all the components of its ethnic image, at least where the arts are concerned, then Ayllón's musical entry greatly helps to fill the niche. Prior to the release of Ayllón's "*Kimba Fá*," a black theater group in Peru, *Teatro del Milenio* [The Theatre of the Millennium], produced a play entitled "*Kimbafá*" [*Quimba fá*], and offered yet another version of the "*Quimba*" concept. "*Quimba*," in this production, is presented as a more ubiquitous incursion into Lima's popular strata and, as such, runs the gamut of daily life experiences.

From a review of the play, one learns that the Theatre of the Millennium proposed, with this staging, to introduce a new artistic technique that would move away from the imagery of past performances, wherein black identity and culture solely related to slavery and runaway slaves:

> If Kimbafá is the story of what has been excluded from history books and what has been marginalized in the metropolis, the play also makes a performative argument that what is marginalized is also what is ubiquitous…Kimbafá highlights blackness as a unifying presence throughout the city as if to argue that limeños might take a lesson from a page in Afro Peruvian history on how to deal with the isolating effects of city life…[T]he work [likewise] argues that in Lima, rhythm is everywhere, everyone is a character, and Afro Peruvian stylings are a principal influence over the sounds and scenes of city life…[T]he play sends a powerful message about the foundational, everyday place of Afro Peruvians [and the Black experience] in contemporary Peru. (Garza 2–3)

Aesthetics of Language as an Experience   89

With the popular acceptance of the African term "*Quimba*," there is no denying that Peru has an abstruse approach to blackness in its country, a country where the Amerindian image reigns supreme as the preferred national icon of ethnicity. Along with this fact, from all media accounts it did not appear to be unwarranted, though unusual, for Peru's president, Alan Garcia, to award the late singer Arturo "el Zambo" Cavero the country's highest symbol of national recognition, The Order of the Sun of Peru, which is usually reserved for presidents and other high-ranking dignitaries. Posthumously, this Afrodescendant Peruvian singer and musician from the popular social stratum joins the ranks of the country's most distinguished sons of national influence.

Bolivia, by comparison, today has fewer African descendants than Peru. Yet it is also possible to isolate elements of an Afro Bolivian lexical heritage that has now become integrated into the popular speech of most Bolivians. For example, the term "*saya*" as a form of music and dance cultivated by Afro Bolivians as part of their culture is now well known. Non–Afro Bolivians also dance it and are familiar with both the word "*saya*" and the distinctive music. However, that has not always been so prevalent. Percentage-wise, black Bolivians are said to be less than two percent of a majority Indian and mestizo population. Nonetheless, their presence in Bolivia has been continuous since the sixteenth century, when Africans were first brought to the area by Spaniards to work in the silver mines of Potosí. Ignored from the 1851 abolition of slavery to the present, it appears that their image has now been resurrected in an effort to make them not only a part of Bolivia's national scene, but to have them become incorporated into the larger African diaspora as well (Busdiecker 106). An interesting anecdote, in this respect, makes reference to Bolivia's president, Evo Morales, who found himself among a group of black Bolivianos while campaigning for the presidency in 2002. Reports indicate that there was nothing in Morales' speech that acknowledged an Afro Bolivian presence, even though they had been invited to the campaign activities to welcome him. At the conclusion of his address to the public, upon being asked to do so, Morales did agree to dance the *saya* with a young woman on each arm, representatives of the Afro

Bolivian community. His comment was: "I feel like I'm in Africa" (Busdiecker 113). Why Africa? Did Morales find the Afro Bolivian dance and the image of this community incompatible with his country's Amerindian and mestizo models, even though elements of African culture (the *saya*, for example) have become integrated into the lexical corpus of the nation? He was not unfamiliar with the cultural dance in which he participated. In addition to the term *"saya"* that has become a standard expression on the popular scene, other music and dance expressions of African origin like the *"zemba"* (in other areas of the Americas called samba and *semba*), *"cueca negra"* of Central African origin, and the *"mauchi"* (a funeral song) have contributed to a heightened consciousness of Bolivian blackness (Rodriguez 319). Consequently, when one experiences the appearance of this African-based lexicon in the creative literature of Bolivia, it should be accepted as a natural progression based on similar appearances of popular African lexemes in the national literatures of other Latin American countries.

For instance, the quote that begins this essay, taken from Pérez-Sarduy's *Las Criadas de la Habana* [The Maids of Havana], shows in precise terms how language from extra-Castilian sources assumes, over a period of constant usage, the contours of being well-established within the national linguistic paradigm. One can refer to the terms *jaqueca* and *sirimba* as used by a character from *Las Criadas de la Habana*. Although Caridad is black, her use of *"jaqueca"* and *"sirimba"* is not racially restricted. In other words, the two terms cannot be misconstrued to solely represent elements of an African-Cuban vernacular Spanish (i.e., something akin to Cuban Ebonics), if there were a linguistic element of this nature.

"Jaqueca" functions with precisely the same linguistic value on the Iberian Peninsula as it does in Latin America. It is my understanding that the word, Arabic in origin, was absorbed within the parameters of the Spanish and Portuguese languages, as was a large corpus of other Arabic-based lexical items. This process occurred during the period when both Spain and Portugal were occupied—from the eighth to the fifteenth centuries—by Arabic-speaking Arabs and Moors. In today's spoken Spanish, the term *"jaqueca"* has developed into an item of standard

Aesthetics of Language as an Experience 91

communication all over the Spanish-speaking world. "*Sirimba*," however, has an entirely different history of introduction and survival in the speech pattern of ordinary Cubans. The author of *Las Criadas de la Habana* is a black Cuban; however, "*sirimba*" is not restricted to the speech pattern of black Cubans. Consequently, one can be certain that he did not select this particular vocabulary item because of the Afrodescendant origin of the speaker who used it in the novel. Pérez-Sarduy has the tendency to write within the culture of Cuba, for his country has both permeated and nurtured his essence to form and mold the personal identity that one finds expressed in his writings. Therefore, in order to fulfill the requisites of his creative urgency, the language he writes in is culturally Cuban—Cuban Spanish. While Cuba does have mutually intelligible linguistic similarities with other Spanish-speaking neighbors with whom it shares space in the Caribbean (the Dominican Republic and Puerto Rico), each of these countries, for the native speaker, is recognizably independent of the other when the autochthonous vernacular comes into play.

In the case of Cuba, an African influence on daily life is exceptionally strong, especially the philosophies and practices of various African religions that were introduced on the island during a period of almost 400 years of African enslavement. There are religious systems that operate under the name of *Regla de Ocha* or *Santería* (the Rule of Ocha, or Veneration of the Saints), *Regla de Palo*, *Regla Conga* or *Palo Monte*, *Regla Arará*, and *la Sociedad Secreta Abakuá* (the Secret Society of the Abakua), among others, which remain viably current (Martinez Casanova 140). Out of these systems of worship have surfaced concepts, observations, and a vocabulary that have become assimilated within the national lexicon. It is observed that

> [t]here exist terms in "lengua" [i.e., the specific use of an African language for religious expressions] to identify ailments or issues of health that have become incorporated into the word-stock of all Cubans. Consequently from the language of the Conga, [one can identify] *sirimba* [an attack of nerves],...*bilongo* [magic, witchcraft, to cast a spell]...*matungo* [sick, sickly], [and] *nfumbe* [dead]. (Martinez Casanova 146)

What is of special note is Martinez Casanova's affirmation that this vocabulary list, although brief by design in his essay, forms part and parcel of the active or passive lexical corpus in daily use by all Cubans, without distinction of race or class.

It is my opinion, however, that considering the class-oriented social resistance of many Cubans to be overtly associated with cultural references that are African in nature, some of these terms might be more passively recognized than actively employed by all social strata. Still, it is safe to consider that most Cubans, regardless of their societal level, can distinguish between a lexical item or a linguistic concept that is etymologically Spanish and another that is the result of the island's African heritage. Because of this, the argument can be developed that to be ethnically Cuban—that is, Cuban in nationality, culture, and mindset—exposure to the widely used lexicon of African origin is a foregone conclusion and an expectation. This determination has enabled many of the country's creative artists to comfortably craft their art to appeal specifically to the nationalist temperament and a familiarity with African terms. *Ecue-Yamba-O*, by Alejo Carpentier, is a specific example that readily comes to mind. This appeal to the familiar and the expected is precisely the perspective that Pérez-Sarduy offers his readers in *Las Criadas de la Habana*. There are countless examples found in the language that when grouped together create a subjective focus. The aim is directed at the creation of a popular Cuban atmosphere or scenario expressed from the "people's" point of view. For instance, no Cuban would find it difficult to intuit the concept embedded in the phrase: "*Uno se entera de estas cosas por Radio Bemba, que se encargó de regarlo como pólvora fresca por toda La Habana, hasta con lujo de detalles…*" ["One learns of these things by means of radio station Big Lips, whose mission it was to spread the news like wildfire all over Havana, and with minute details"] (66).

In this particular case, not only Cubans but also most natives of other regions of the Spanish-speaking Caribbean will have intuitively concluded that gossip or rumors were the principal source of the news that had been spread around Havana. *Bemba*, a word that was introduced into the area by Bantu-speakers from the Congo during the era of slavery, has with time and usage adapted itself to the morphology of the Spanish language in a way that has enabled it to generate standard items at the popular level. For example from *bemba* [big, broad lips] there has evolved *bembe+tear* (*bembetear*), a verb form that means to gossip, to spread rumors, or run off at the mouth incessantly. The substantive *"bembeteo"* [gossip, or the act of talking incessantly] is equally well known and used. Likewise, the augmentative morpheme (-on) can be added to the base form to create *"bembón,"* which pejoratively indicates "exceptionally big lips." In addition, Spanish morphology also accepts morphemes of diminution and endearment (-cito) that tend to assuage an image and in a certain sense lessen the harshness of the deprecating approach. When Pérez-Sarduy has a biracial character (in Cuban terms, a *mulatta*) refer to an unmiscegenated or slightly miscegenated counterpart with:

> ...me senté por casualidad al lado de una mujer negra, cubana también, bastante bemboncita ella, pero que parecía de lo más educada. (243)
>
> (...by chance, I sat alongside a black woman, also Cuban, whose lips were quite big, but who appeared to be very well-mannered.)

an awareness of ingrained differences with regard to color and social expectations appears slightly overt and not too submerged. Here, the term *"bemboncita"* takes on a cultural image somewhat difficult to translate, but that can be interpreted to indicate the intention of appearing nonpejorative. The *mulatta* figure makes a subjective assessment based on her own physiognomy that must have had "thin lips," and ponders what she considers to be the incongruity of being black but well mannered, or perhaps well educated, given that both concepts are found in the term *"educada."* She, the *mulatta*, was highly educated but did not consider herself to be black before arriving in the United States. Although Pérez-Sarduy's descriptions of how one Cuban black sees another black person are purposefully frank, one perceives in his construction a covert questioning of the social background that has formed such negative perceptions:

> ...*su brillosa cara de un negro chapapote muy negro* (100)
> (...the tar-black shiny face of a very black Negro)
>
> *Parece un conguito* (100).
> (He looks like something from the Congo...)
>
> ...*con cara de azabache* (100)
> (with a jet-black face...)
>
> *Era más prieta que el tizne* (34)
> (She was blacker than soot)
>
> *Negra achiná...muy fondillú ella, de pelo bueno, abundante...* (192)
> (A big-butt, slant-eyed black woman with good hair and a lot of it...)

As in most environments where the European has sexually confronted Africans and their descendants, miscegenation is an inevitable outcome. In Cuba, as Pérez-Sarduy illustrates, the end result of race mixing has produced both a social hierarchy and a specialized vocabulary that attempts to convey a genetic imagery. For example, the term "*jabao*" in the Cuban space conjures up the notion of someone who is light-skinned in complexion and perhaps with freckles but with the remaining physical morphology of hair quality, prominence of nose, and protrusion of lips that betray a decidedly African genealogy. These genotypically oriented images, for the majority of Pérez-Sarduy's Cuban readers, would be clearly imagined in their thought process, based solely on the language of description:

> *Aquella noche, Edelia, una santiaguera jabaita muy simpática...* (35)
>
> (That night, Edelia, a friendly little "high-yellow" woman from Santiago...)

A variation of the previous quote shows the interplay of color and hair quality for this type:

> *Me preguntó Basilia, una sirvienta mulata jabá de pelo malo-malo que trabajaba por Malecón...* (116)
>
> (Basilia, a light-skinned mulatta servant with exceptionally bad hair, who worked over on the Malecón, asked me...)

There are other classifications from the author's immediate environment that enable him to candidly present, for this Afro Latino community, his perspective of a socially inbred awareness of diverse phenotypes. Nonetheless, the skin tone gradations, in particular, fall within Pérez-Sarduy's inescapable yet subtle characterization of blackness:

> *...el caso es que Yamila... era tan mulata...como ella misma, pero con el pelo castaño tirando a rubio natural.* (217)
>
> (...the fact is that Yamila was as much of a mulatta as she, but with chestnut-colored hair that was on the verge of being naturally blond.)

It is known within the Cuban culture of phenotypes and ethnic hierarchies that the slightest variation that indicates a physical relationship with Africa in ascending or descending progressions can psychologically affect a person's acceptance or rejection in that society:

> *aquel mulato indio de pelo lacio natural...* (217)
> (that Indian-looking mulatto with naturally straight hair)
>
> *una mulata de ojos claros...* (137)
> (a mulatta with light-colored eyes...)
>
> *Trigueña de pelo espeso, grueso y bastante rizado...de piel morena y ojos color esmeralda* (135)
> (a swarthy, brown-skinned woman with thick, rough, and very curly hair and emerald-colored eyes)
>
> *...se sentía orgullosa del color canela de su piel...* (216)
> (...she was proud of her cinnamon-colored skin...)

This is but a minute sampling of the examples that Pérez-Sarduy offers his reader for the ethnic stratum that is not perceived as definitively white, but whose members are hesitant to admit racial blackness. This mindset might be considered a tenuous safety net in Cuba, the author infers, but the ethnic and racial reality of the United States presents a conflicting attitude for the mixed-race segment that must be confronted when doubt arises:

> ...*te preguntan la raza a la que perteneces y, por ejemplo, para que te enteres yo aquí no soy mulata, ni mestiza, ni "Hispana," aunque hablemos español...sino "black"...que quiere decir negra.* (203)
>
> (...they ask you which race you are, and for your information, here, [in the U.S.] I am not a mulatta, nor a mestiza, not even "Hispanic" even though we speak Spanish...I am "black" which [in Cuba] means "negra.")

Herein lies the crux of Pérez-Sarduy's observations. The racial standards of Cuba and the United States, although dissimilar, share a common goal in the racial constructions of this African-descendant Cuban author. It appears to him that both countries overtly manifest a psychological exigency to expunge the telltale signs of Africanness and assume a political modus operandi that promotes a classification of white as the national desire to attain social and economic privileges. While Pérez-Sarduy's Cuba does not have a one-drop rule or a bipolar, blood-based black/white distinction, a mental outlook of "white by appearance" does function as the national guideline:

> *Pues Yeya, la gorda putísima de allí al doblar, la que se cree muy blanca porque se tiñe el pelo de rubio...* (172)
>
> (Well Yeya, that big, fat whorish thing that lives around the corner, the one that thinks she's definitely white just because she dyes her hair blond...)

This approach gives way, however, for skin tone gradations to come into play that tend to blur ethnic divisions, but only in a lexical sense.

Psychologically, the imagery still has its clear lines of racial divisions for the Cuban native who finds ethnic differences to be distinguishable not only by skin tones but also according to a standard of physical characteristics. These traits have become integrated into his or her cultural outlook:

> ...*la combinación del trigueño blanco con ojos claros de Jorge con la espléndida mulata de Gracielita nunca había causado mucha gracia en la Habana...(*216)
>
> (...the combination of Jorge, the light tannish-hued white man with light-colored eyes, together with that splendid mulatta Gracielita had never been received too favorably in Havana...)

As Pérez-Sarduy knowingly indicates in his constructions, his culture can accept as *"trigueño"* someone who is not to be perceived as white (*trigueña de piel morena*) in addition to employing the same concept for the culturally acknowledged "whitish-looking person" (e.g., *el trigueño blanco....Jorge*). While to the outsider the overlap in terminology might complicate further the country's racial context, for the average Cuban, at least from the popular sector, the aphorism embedded in the following statement provides a logical answer for any doubt:

> *Oigan caballero...,vamos a dejar el temita ese de la raza, que en definitiva aquí "el que no tiene de congo tiene de carabalí" todos somos cubanos...* (218)
>
> (Listen up, my man...let's drop this little matter of race, since in the long run "he that doesn't have some Congo blood, has blood from Calabar"; we are all Cuban...)

Actually, this saying is tantamount to acknowledging that while you may not look the part, "if you don't have genes from one African tribe, you have them from another." For many in Cuba and in other regions of Latin America, most people are suspected of having or hiding a black ancestor (more specifically of the maternal lineage). As a matter of fact, there are color designations for Latin-type whites that subjectively distinguish them from Europeans or white Americans. For example, when Pérez-Sarduy writes: "*Mery era blanquita como la leche...*" ["Mery was as white as milk," literally, but meaning pale white] (49), it supports the fact that Mery was not Cuban. She had previously been introduced as a Spanish national. And when a black mother receives a gift for her son that she describes as "*aquel rubio americano*" ["that blond American"] (83), there is no need to say that the figurine is white since the image of blond, pale Americans reigns as prototypical in all of Latin America. This approach is countered with an entry that reads: "El Nuevo Herald,...*traía la foto de un blanco cubano de rostro campesino...*" ["*The New Herald*...showed the photo of a white Cuban with the face of a farmer..."] (277), as if to stress the difference between "*el norteamericano blanco*" and "*el blanco cubano*" ["the North American white person" and "the white Cuban"]. The placement of the modifier "*blanco*" delimits what is a normal description, that is to say, "*norteamericano blanco*," as opposed to what the author does not see as normal: "*el blanco cubano*." And when whiteness in Cuba goes beyond the anticipated, it is usually stressed: "...*lo conocían como "Manzanita" porque era gordito, y de tan blanco que era se ponía* colorao *por el sol*" ["He was known as "the little apple" due to his chubbiness, and he was so white he would turn *reddish* when in the sun"] (131). Not without reason does Pérez-Sarduy highlight with italics this character's color, as if to stress its anomaly within the native environment. The subject of color in Cuba, and in most of Latin America, is a delicate matter that is usually relegated to the innermost circles of a family and is rarely, if ever, discussed in public.

Herein lies the dilemma for most people who are outside the Latino/Hispanic culture, especially North Americans in the United States. Misconstruction of the concept of Latinism/Hispanism creates false paradigms that run counter to the reasoning that North Americans insist is biologically cogent. A failure to understand and accept the pervasiveness of African genes and culture throughout all the Americas establishes an archetypical Hispanic model as someone socially constructed to be "nonblack." Graciela—Pérez-Sarduy's characterization of the prototypical

Cuban *mulatta*—reacts strongly to the chromatic distinctions in Cuba and the incongruity of the American stance when she proclaims, as noted earlier: "Here [in the United States], I am not a mulatta, nor a mestiza, not even Hispanic...I am *black* which in Cuba is *negra*" (203). This is the visibility that the Afro Latino has for the American-oriented mindset, in spite of the fact that all natives of Spanish-speaking Latin America should be politically and culturally "Hispanic," according to the American way of reasoning ethnicity. However, to accept all Spanish-speaking natives as Hispanic, regardless of the amount of melanin pigmentation that he or she possesses, would dismantle the race-conscious Americans' philosophies that are based on the dichotomous distinction between black and white people. In short, their reasoning on race would become foundationless. How could the Hispanic ethnicity be explained in American terms when a Hispanic woman recalls being descended directly from Africans from the Continent: *"conmigo no se juega, yo que sí soy negra gangá de nación, carajo"* ["Don't mess with me, damn it, as I am definitely a pure black woman of the Gangá nation"] (110).

The interesting feature of acknowledging an African reality in Latin America, and especially in Cuba, is the fact that through oral histories of living people a traceable lineage can still be ascertained. Usually researchers of Cuban ethnicities, to the exclusion of the Gangá, will focus on the Congo, the Lukumí, and at times the Arará groups because of their prominence in African-based religions, music, and nationally adopted vocabulary in Cuba's culture. It is not unusual, for example, for someone in Cuba to exclaim when upset: *"tengo el congo subío."* Literally translated, it would mean that the person had his or her Congolese temper provoked and is not to be crossed or irritated. There are other investigators (see Basso Ortiz) for whom the Gangá groups were at one time a numerically important entity to be reckoned with in the period of aggressive African enslavement in Cuba. They were reported to have come from the Sierra Leone–Liberia areas, which are far to the west of the locations of the Congolese and the Yoruba (Lukumí in Cuba). The Gangá presence confirmed the diversity of peoples that was prevalent in African slavery. Today, their descendants are reportedly located in Perico, in the Matanzas region of Cuba, and as recently as twenty-five years ago efforts were still being made to revive and maintain the culture. Some, such as the reported great-granddaughter of a recognized slave survivor, have gone to great lengths to retrieve lost or submerged Gangá roots. The great-grandmother in question passed along certain cultural traits that the descendant struggles to keep alive among the younger generations:

> In 1983 she [Linda Diago] formed a folkloric group that has served to activate the interest of the younger generations for the traditions of their elders. [With this effort] they have spread throughout the country the drumming styles, the songs and the dances of the Gangá-Longobá. (Basso Ortiz, "Los gangá longobá" 198)

An infusion of African genes into the body politic of Latin America is not the only legacy that gives that space a heritage that is quite distinct from the cultural base bequeathed to the region by Spain. Africans did not arrive in the Americas as tabulae rasae, or with muted tongues. Ideas, gods, religions, philosophies, and lexicons to express these concepts traveled with them from various locales on the African continent. For example, in his analysis of the Afro Ecuadorian novel, Franklin Miranda found:

> *Por otro lado, desde la cosmovisión bantú, alrededor de la cual se sustenta la afroecuatorianidad, la palabra hablada es dadora de vida. El poder nombrar la naturaleza toda que esta exista, sea aprehensible para la comunidad. Con esto como premisa se entiende porque la brujería se halla tan vinculada a este pueblo: la palabra hablada sirve para conjurar, para hacer magia.* (54)

> (On the other hand, in accordance with the worldview of the Bantu, which is the basis of the Afro Ecuadorian being, the spoken word is the sustainer of life. Recognition of nature, in whatever form it may exist, should be at the community's grasp. With this as a premise, it should be clear why witchcraft is so much a part of this group: it is the spoken word that exorcizes and makes magic.)

It is precisely from this reservoir of beliefs that Adalberto Ortiz, the Ecuadorian author of *Juyungo*, extracts a vignette that characterizes Cristobalina.

As a black woman, she instructs María de los Ángeles, a white woman, on how to entrap the black man with whom María is in love:

> *De eso no te preocupes, hija. Atendeme bien. ¿Conocés vos ese pajarito colorao que mientan brujo? Hacé que te cacen uno. Le sacás el corazón y en esa sangrecita mojás las cuatro puntas de un pañuelo tuyo. Entonces se lo regalás a Lastre y verás cómo lo enchimbás, hasta ponerlo más manso que un pollo choto.* (80)

> (Don't worry my child. Just listen to me. Are you acquainted with that little red bird they say is a witch? Have them catch one for you. Take out its heart, and moisten the four corners of your handkerchief in its blood. Then present it to Lastre, and you'll see how he'll become so messed up in the head that he'll turn as docile as a gentle little chicken.)

There is no doubt that the Bantu cosmovision is also as current in Cuba as it is in other countries to which Africans were transferred. In this sense, while the black race may have been the purveyor of Cuba's African spirituality, its accessibility to nationals of all hues is not questioned on the island, as Pérez-Sarduy shows:

> *Me acuerdo...cuando a Clotilde...que tenía hecho Changó desde hacía cuarenta años...* (156)

> (I remember...when Clotilde...who had become a devotee of Changó some forty years ago...)

> *...Carmita...nos llama para avisarnos de que a su madre, la Vieja, como le decíamos todos, le había bajado Changó...* (157)

> (...Carmita calls us to let us know that her mother, Ole Lady, as we all called her, had become possessed by Changó...)

The spirit and worship of Changó is not a special privilege for Cubans only. Reliance on a relationship with Changó can be found among descendants of Africans throughout their diaspora in the Americas. Amazingly, we have even found that the concept of Changó traveled back to the Continent with the Tabom of Ghana, a group of Africans that had been released from slavery in Brazil in the early nineteenth century. Adherence to the philosophy of Changó worship also forms a part of the spiritual beliefs of the descendants of these returnees who settled in Ghana. There is hardly a Cuban alive who does not recognize the pantheon of African gods that arrived on the island along with enslaved captives from the Congo region and from today's Nigeria. Changó, Yemayá, Ochun, Obatalá, Eleggua, and Babalú, to name but a few, have altars of worship in many of the households of blacks, whites, mulattos, mestizos, *moros, jabaos, trigueños*, and others in that country's pigmentocracy. These African figures of devotion that control so much of Cuba's spiritual psychology are recognized as Cuban spiritual icons, even when overt worship to them is not observable. Their presence retains currency wherever Cuban nationals may be found. At times, it seems incongruent that African gods would be worshipped by Cubans in exile, especially when the exiled individual is viewed as phenotypically white, whitish, or light-skinned mulatto. In *Las Criadas de la Habana*, the author realistically transports evidence of the African-based spiritual guidance that has sustained many Cubans for hundreds of years outside of the national sphere:

> *Yamila y Gracielita...se refugiaron en un rinconcito del club rodeadas de recuerdos de Cuba con las paredes,...adornadas con los* iremes *del culto abakuá, maracas, banderitas y estandartes de Cuba...* (286; emphasis added)
>
> (Yamila and Gracielita...retreated to a little corner of the club [located in Washington, D.C.] surrounded by reminders of Cuba, with walls...decorated with *little iconic figures* from the *Abakuá* cult, maracas, flags, and Cuban banners...)

In Cuba, one does not have to be an active practitioner of African-based religious philosophies to know that the "Abakuá" is a secretive Afro Cuban religious society that was originally formed in the Calabar region of Nigeria. Because of the hierarchy that decrees the social levels of African slaves and their Spanish enslavers, it appears ironic that white Cubans were initiated into the secrets of this African philosophy and formed their own Abakuá section in 1863. As for the *ireme*, with their mise-en-scène as elaborately clothed, devil-like figures, they are an intricate aspect of the Abakuá society whenever they make an appearance and are found represented in paintings and posters. Their relationship to the Abakuá as ancestral spirits that guard and promote the group's cultural values is understood and received as part of a national idiom of culture.

The North American African-descendant community has yet to be studied in this sense and does not appear to offer a comparable image, despite having the same racial origin. The linguistic offerings from African-based spiritual and religious traditions do not seem to have enjoyed the same acceptance as in Latin America. Perhaps the reason can be attributed to a difference in demographics. George Reid Andrews in his review essay "Afro-Latin America: The Late 1900s" suggests one, but by no means the only, cogent rationale for this omission in North American English:

> The numbers tell the story: the heart of the New World African Diaspora lies not north of the border, but south. During the period of slavery, ten times as many Africans came to Spanish and Portuguese America as to the United States. ... [B]y 1990 the estimated 100 million Afro-Latin Americans still outnumbered Afro-North Americans by a factor of more than three to one [i.e., 30 million for the total U.S. population of the same period], and accounted for almost twice as large a proportion of their respective national populations. (363)

Indeed, a strong black presence in South America, Central America, and the Spanish-speaking Caribbean has helped to make language in Latin America—especially in Cuba and Brazil—one of the cultural layers where the African image or presence is most ostensibly viable, outside of the element of miscegenation (Gomez 112). A lexicon infused with Africanisms often defines the substrata of linguistic autochthony in various Latin American countries. In other words, language undergoes a metamorphosis into mechanisms that substantiate what it means to be a native speaker from a particular Latin American country. Where Portuguese-speaking Brazil is concerned, its African-related corpus has likewise become an affirmation of the essence of being Brazilian. Surprisingly, the Caribbean areas of English speakers, as well as speakers of French and Dutch in the same geographical region, are the locales that have long proffered an image of being the principal conveyors of African cultural traits. It has been found, for example, that in Jamaica captives from Africa who were speakers of Twi (from the region of today's Ghana, West Africa) formed the group that provided the political and cultural leadership on the plantations of that British colony. Consequently, when one looks for linguistic traces of this hegemony in the common vernacular of today— Jamaican Creole—it is not surprising that traces of the Twi language will still be evident. Haiti is another case in point. With its overwhelming majority of miscegenated and nonmiscegenated African descendants and the formation of a Creole language as the endemic means of communication, it is to be anticipated that strong remnants of African cultures are to be found in the area. For comparison, one can refer to a study by Winifred Vass concerning the Bantu-speaking heritage of the United States in which she lists some 200 words of Bantu origin that allegedly function in North American English. Recognition of this fact is not always approved or accepted by the average English speaker in the United States. For many, the reality of Africanisms in the functional lexicon of standard English (with the exception of isolated entries such as "goober" for peanut, or "gumbo," which bears an etymological relationship to the Afro Cuban word for the vegetable known in English as "okra"—i.e., "*quimbombó*" in Cuban Spanish) is either strongly disputed or considered to be a study still in progress.

However, a denial of African influences in the national profile of some countries is not unusual. In Mexico, for example, and despite continuous research, many Mexicans still regard with suspicion any suggestion of an African imprint in that country being considered a legitimate piece of historical evidence even though scholars have been able to substantiate a strong African presence in Mexico's ethnic history. One of Mexico's earliest presidents, Vicente Guerrero (1781–1831), traced his African roots through his father's lineage. The father, Pedro Guerrero, worked as a mule driver, a profession that was recognized as being almost solely controlled by Afro Mexicans (Vincent 148). Guerrero, the son, was called the Mexican "Abraham Lincoln" for having issued a presidential proclamation on September 16, 1829, that abolished slavery (153). It probably has escaped the notice of many in Mexico that the state of Guerrero was named for someone whose forebears made the journey from Africa to the New World. Prior to President Guerrero, the annals of Mexican history record that Gaspar Yanga, a native of Gabon, West Africa and the leader of a Mexican slave revolt in 1570, established a maroon colony with nearly 500 Africans who had run away from that country's institution of slavery (154).

Since 1932, the Mexican town originally known as San Lorenzo de los Negros has assumed the name of Yanga, in honor of this rebellious and historical figure from Africa. Would many of those who reside in Yanga today recognize that its founder used the name of his ancestral base, an area located in the southernmost area of Gabon, West Africa? Nyanga, today, is the largest and least populated of Gabon's nine provinces. However, Yanga, Mexico, in the state of Veracruz, is not the only locale in that state that bore witness to the reality of African enslavement. The state of Veracruz was a principal site for settling Africans transplanted to Mexico. With this in mind, it should not appear strange to find towns today with African names such as Mandinga or Mozomba. Written records confirm that many of the slaves imported into New Spain were from the Mandingas ethnic group (Carroll 494). New Spain was the territory north of the Isthmus of Panama, and included Mexico. Around 1735 a group of *cimarrones* or runaway slaves—maroons—created a disturbance in the vicinity of Veracruz and Oaxaca. By the time the revolt was crushed, some six settlements had been formed by the escaped Africans: Rosario, Mata de Anona, San Antonio, San Martin de Mazatiopa, Breve Cosina, and one in the vicinity of Oaxaca under the name Palacios de Mandinga. Whether the name chosen for this last settlement represented a cultural attachment for the Africans or served as a recognizable rallying point for fellow clanspeople has not been made clear (Carroll 494–495). Even today, the region of Veracruz often brings to mind the concept of an area that *might* be ethnically different from the rest of Mexico.[5] For example, few people in today's Spanish-speaking Latin America are unaware that the popular Mexican singer Toña La Negra (Maria Antonia Peregrino) was a true native of Veracruz. Her phenotype kept alive the thought that Africa might have had a strong physical presence in the area at some time in the past. A confirmation of this fact was reflected in the lyrics of some of her most popular songs:

> *Yo soy mulata y orgullo tengo tener la sangre de negro en mis venas.*
> *Yo soy mulata y no me importa que me critiquen si yo tengo bemba.*
> *Yo soy mulata y orgullo tengo de tener piel tostada*
> *Y no me importa si tengo ñata yo soy mulata de verdad.* ("Yo soy mulata")

> (I am mulatta and proud to have the blood of Black people running through my veins.
> I am mulatta and don't care if I'm criticized for my big lips.
> I am mulatta and proud that my skin is tanned
> I don't care if my nose is broad I'm a true mulatta.)

Incorporated into the lyrics of this song is vocabulary with origins in Africa (*bemba* = big lips, *ñata* = big, flat nose) alongside vocabulary from Spain. Most of Latin America is familiar with these terms. And although another popular song, "Angelitos Negros" ["Little Black Angels"], was not written for her specifically, her sensitive and emotive delivery of the powerful social statement in its lyrics, especially in color-conscious Latin America, made it seem as if the lyricist had focused especially on her talents and her understanding of color prejudice as practiced in Mexico and throughout the Americas:

> *Pintor nacido en mi tierra, con el pincel extranjero*
> *Pintor que sigue el rumbo de tantos pintores viejos*
> *Aunque la virgen sea blanca, pintame angelitos negros*

> (Painter born in my country [but] with a brush that is foreign
> Painter who follows the path of painters gone before, even if the Virgin Mary may be white, paint for me some little black angels.)

It was felt that Toña La Negra was at her best when accompanied by her brother, the guitarist Pablo "El Negro" Peregrino. After her death

Aesthetics of Language as an Experience   107

in 1982, a statue was erected in the Parque Zamora in central Veracruz (the city) in homage to her image as Mexico's icon of black sensitivity. In this respect, were it not for the statue of Yanga the warrior, the monument to Toña la Negra would be singular as a symbol of honor to the country's black heritage. Although there have been other Mexican artists who have used lyrics that carry memories of the country's relationship with Africa, none has achieved the status and recognition of La Toña. As indicated in the previous essay, the trend to celebrate African heritage continued with David Haro, a contemporary Mexican singer who utilized his song "Mozambique" to confirm the mixed-race genotype that some in his country try to ignore:

> *Somos negros de la costa tropical*
> *Llevamos sangre de la que regó Cuauhtémoc*
> *Veracruzanos de color, Y pelo crespo...*
> (Sones de Mexico, *Fandango*)
>
> (We are black people from the tropical coast
> We carry the blood of Cuauhtémoc within us
> Veracruzans of color, [a]nd kinky hair...)

Along with this admission, there is the prominent refrain "*Bamba, bamba, e.*" What stands out in both Haro's "Mozambique" and Richie Valens' "La Bamba" (see previous essay), based on a Veracruzan *son jarocho* or Afro mestizo tropical rhythm, is the African term *bamba*. The Afro Mexican phenotypes referred to in the lyrics of Haro and Valens are still found in today's Mexico, especially in the Veracruz and Oaxaca regions of the Pacific coast. As noted by the Mexican photographer Alberto Ibáñez: "The Afromestizo community is part of the skin of our country, a face that appears to be looking to the sea, searching for its origin" (*Inside Mexico*).

Is it the chronological space, traveled by fading memories, that has caused the image of Mexico's Africans to die out in the contemporary consideration of culture? In other Latin American countries, lack of contact with the source and the imposition of time have often interfered with the transfer of culture in spite of oral histories and legends handed down from generation to generation. Uruguay, for example, with an African-descendant community of 170,000–180,000—approximately 6% of the country's total population—exemplifies this concept of ruptured continuity. In a survey conducted by a Uruguayan psychologist and a group of black Uruguayan university students, the question arose as to whether there was a feeling of cohesion or lack thereof among the country's citizens of African descent. The reply left no doubt that solidarity was not an issue: "...amongst all Black Uruguayans there exists a feeling of belonging to an ethnic aggregate among whom things are shared; not everyone places emphasis on the same things, but there is a sentiment of kinship" (*La Onda Digital*, "Diálogo con la sicóloga Susana Rudolf"). When the lyrics of "Milongón de Reyes," as sung by the Afro Uruguayan artist Eduardo da Luz are considered, it is clear that spatial and temporal intervals may have dimmed somewhat the memory of shared oral histories and legends. There are, nonetheless, sufficient remnants to connect the artist to the cultural sensitivity of his listening audience as a display of ethnic unity:

> *Kalungan gue katun ga ga ye yuba*
> *Kalungan gue katun ga ga ye yuba*
> *Kalungan hie balele kalugan ga balambo*
> *Kalacumba cacaroiogue kalungan gue katan ga ga*
>   *ye yuba.*
> ("Milongón de Reyes")

Careful observation reveals that the lyricist has referred to the diverse African cultures of Kalunga, Katunga, Balele, Kala-Kumba, Kakaro-Chokwe, and Balambo. While the orthography for the written lyrics adheres to the lyricist's perceived morphological arrangement, this has not deterred the observer from tracing their origin to actual place names in the Congo-Angolan region of West Africa. And when da Luz goes on to sing:

> *Muchas naciones llegaron tras de su reina*
> *africana*
> *Minas, congo, y bengueles junto a magisos*
> *Hoy San Felipe y Santiago se visten toda a la usanza*

Cabinda, angolas, molembos y mozambiques.
("Milongón de Reyes)

(Many nations came following their African queen
Minas, Congos, Bengueles as well as Majiosos
Today, San Felipe and Santiago are all dressed up in style
Cabinda, Angolas, Molembos and Mozambiques)

one thing is certain from this generational transfer: the Africans that were shipped to Uruguay did not represent one monolithic conglomeration or mass of people assembled under one generic name. Most Africans brought to the Americas came with diverse ethnicities and ethnonyms. These names seemed to have been passed on orally and are orthographically represented in the lyrics as heard. This accounts for the transcription of Kalunga as Kalungan when sung by da Luz. The final *n* evidently represents the nasalization of the preceding vowel, *a*. Nasalized vowels are a standard feature of the Bantu language system, the linguistic force of the area from where the term proceeds.

With Spanish-speaking creative artists, the use of an African-based vocabulary in their art, in many cases, is not an exception. As seen in the example of the Uruguayan lyrics, similar word lists are often used in artistic constructions to simulate the speech patterns of an authentic African language, or to create a literary context of artistic African reality. Presentation alone, however, does not ensure authenticity. Luis Palés Matos of Puerto Rico (1898–1959), for example, used many African-linked lexical references in his Afro Puerto Rican verses. There is one in particular entitled "Majestad Negra" ["Black Majesty"] where his craft is arranged principally with an eye toward the musicality of the sounds and the intent of creating an authentic African prosody through phonemic arrangements:

Por la encendida calle antillana
Va Tembandumba de la Quimbamba
Rumba, Macumba, Candombe, Bámbula.
. . . .

*Flor de Tortola, rosa de Uganda
Por ti crepitan bombas y bámbulas
Por ti en calendas desenfrenadas
Quema la Antilla su sangre nyanyiga.*
(Valdés-Cruz 160)

(Through the burning hot West Indian street
Struts Tembandumba from Quimbamba
Rumba, Macumba, Candombe, Bambula
. . . .
Flower of Tortola, rose of Uganda
The sounds of the bomba and the bambula are
because of you
The wild kalenda [dance] is because of you
Your African blood makes the West Indies burn.)

"Majestad Negra" is obviously structured as homage to Queen Tembandumba, a legendary warrior queen of the Congo, and displays the use of an African-language vocabulary with an artistic intent. When one considers that the context serves as motivation for the listener or reader to focus on an African figure from West Central Africa, then the transfer of this image to some abstruse locale in the West Indies is without reason and raises questions concerning the artistic goal. Was Tortola, a British possession, the only place in the region with an African-descendant population? As the locale of focus, Tortola has nothing to do with the poet's personal space or to any previous reference. True, the Tortola he mentions is in the Antilles, and conforms to the image of *"la encendida calle antillana"* ["a scorching-hot West Indian street"]. But creatively, Palés Matos could have associated the imagery of Quimbamba with his Puerto Rican hometown, the Guayama where he was born and raised. It is a town noted for its considerable Afro-related population. Did he intend to deflect attention away from himself or pretend that Puerto Rico was alien to blackness? It must have been psychologically safer for the poet, who after all was in control of his art, to transfer the concept of blackness to Tortola, a neighboring island, as if the African image could not appear in Guayama, Puerto Rico. Besides this, *"Tembandumba from Quimbamba...rosa de Uganda*" is conceptually incongruous. During the era of her "black majesty," Quimbamba was part of the Congo area of West-Central Africa, while Uganda is more closely associated with East Africa. Furthermore, during the apex of Tembandumba's reign in the seventeenth century, there was no Uganda. The name change from Buganda to Uganda did not take effect until some 200 years later, when the area became a protectorate of the British between 1894 and 1900. This was well after the death of Tembandumba. One is inclined to conclude, therefore, that the poet's choice of lexicon was not a consideration of the generation-to-generation oral legacy of his Afro-Guayaman compatriots, even though an African-based orality with its concomitant vocabulary was in place in that region. One finds that the poet's imagery was created perhaps from the racial safety of personal noninclusion or alliance, and the conjecture of an "imagined" scenario. The end result clearly shows the poet's artistic intention of distancing himself from the ethnic realities of his native environment, and in this way depersonalizes his construct. At the same time, he infuses in his verses a surface level feeling of Africanity for the context by highlighting and focusing principally on the sound patterns inherent in the phonemic arrangement of Rumba, Macumba, Candome, Bámbula, Tembandumba, Quimbamba. The end result is indeed artistic, but not representative of the poet's own Afro Caribbean experience. Although lauded for his skills in drawing attention to the presence of blacks in the Caribbean, his presentation, at least in "Majestad Negra," remains more metaphoric than evocative or symbolic. For some literary critics, although Palés Matos was one of the principal and pioneering figures in the presentation of African imagery in the poetic voice of the Spanish-speaking Caribbean, his art often belied a "Eurocentric bias" that reinforced black stereotypes as caricatures (West-Durán, "Puerto Rico: The Pleasures and Traumas of Race" 55). Clearly, in the previously cited verses, the punctuated, driving sound of the African drum was more important for his construction than the physical imagery that he attempted. The Afro Antillean world of this poet, in particular, is highly mythologized, to the point of being distorted, a thought that is also confirmed in "Puerto Rico: The Pleasures and Traumas of Race" (56).

In spite of Palés Matos' apparent reluctance to confirm a homegrown, native, and personal African presence in "Majestad Negra," an African-based image, in language and people, is accessible in the popular ambiance of ordinary Puerto Ricans and often finds its way into literary expressions. At least some, in turn, support the concept of a historical link to African beginnings and provide a legacy of an Afro Puerto Rican oral tradition. Examples exist that are in overt opposition to the evasive stance of Palés Matos in "Majestad Negra," and take the form of both a cultural and an ethnic admission. In the prologue to the second edition of *Dinga y Mandinga*, a volume of poems by Fortunato Vizcarrondo, Puerto Rico has two basic demographic zones where the presence of African descendants appears to stand out. As listed, there is the region of Santurce, Loiza, and Carolina in the north. In the south, there is the area that comprises San Antón, Salinas, Patillas, Guayama and Arroyo (Vizcarrondo xxvii). Fortunato Vizcarrondo (1895–1977), born in Carolina, Puerto Rico, was well aware of the black, white, and mulatto ethnoracial arrangements of his island. It was he who constructed the poem around the popular Latin American epigram: ¿*Y tu abuela 'onde está*? [And your grandma, where is she?], a not-too-veiled reference to the fact that lingering in the background of many families is a black ancestor who's hidden away:

> . . . .
> *Tu coló te salió blanco*
> *Y la mejiya rosá*
> *Loj lábioj loj tiénej finoj*
> *Y tu agüela a'onde estaj?*
> *¿Disej que mi bemba ej grande*
> *Y mi pasa colorá?*
> *Pero dime, pot la binge*
> *¿Y tu agüela a'onde ejtá*
> . . . .
> *Erej blanquito enchapao*
> *Que déntraj en sosiedá*
> *Temiendo que se conojca*
> *La mamá de tu mamá.*

Aquí el que no tiene dinga
Tiene mandinga... ¡ja, ja!
Por eso yo te pregunto
¿Y tu agüela a'onde está?

Ayé me dijite negro
Queriéndome abochoná
Mi agüela sale a la sala,
Y la tuya oculta ejtá.

(You turned out to be white, in color
And pink, the color of your cheeks
You got lips that are thin
But your grandma, where is she?
You say my lips are big
And my kinky hair is red
But tell me, for the sake of the Virgin Mary
your grandma, where is she?
. . . .
Your whiteness is just a thin veneer
It gets you into high society
But you're afraid that they'll find out
Who is the mother of your mother
In this country if you ain't got some Dinka
You've got Mandinga...Ha, ha!
That's why I'm asking you
And your grandma, where is she?

Yesterday you called me black
Attempting to make me feel embarrassed.
But my grandma sits in the living room
And yours is hidden away.)

To the culturally unaware, Vizcarrondo's semiotic approach to Puerto Rican blackness might be unperceived or misunderstood. The combination of Dinka versus Mandinga is an overt reference to a historical awareness that in the Americas, the infusion of African genes was not limited to one particular African group, but was spread around without distinction. One is reminded with this saying of the same approach witnessed in Cuban literature where the accusatory finger was pointed at the Congo and Calabar (i.e., "*el que no tiene dinga tiene mandinga*" versus "*el que no tiene de congo tiene de carabalí*") and in Peru where it is alleged that if you do not have some Amerindian Inca blood, then you have African Mandinga genes ("*el que no tiene inca tiene mandinca*"). Miscegenation is a known factor in the Latin American genotype; open admission does not come too easily. There are many lighter-skinned Puerto Ricans who, like their counterparts in most of Latin America, usually disclaim a relationship to an African ancestor. The poet attempts to dispel this myth by questioning hidden family ties to blackness (usually via a matriarchal link—hence the "grandmother" reference). However, another cultural observation in these verses shows that the person that had received the brunt of racial disparagement could not have been jet black or even dark brown, since someone with "*pasa colorá*"—that is, red kinky hair, as he describes himself—is usually seen as "*jabao*" or "*grifo*," meaning a fair-skinned person with facial features that denote African descent, and red, kinky hair. Phenotypically, this combination is usually an indication of some miscegenation, be it recent or not, and is a common presence throughout North and South America and the Caribbean. It is the result of a European/African sexual relationship, be it forced or consensual. The area where Palés Matos was born (Guayama), and the district of Vizcarrondo's birth and childhood (Carolina), both have sizeable populations of African descendants. Yet, the lyricism of Vizcarrondo's poem is in direct opposition to the "Majestad Negra" of Palés Matos. One uses his creative voice to include the artist with sensitivity, while the other creates in a manner that attempts to disguise the artist's national sentiments, although the inner voice of both fashions blackness as their context. In an analysis of other Latin American writers, I have found that what appears to be a measure of ethnic integrity for the black writer becomes a failure of historical and social diagnosis for some white writers. In Latin America, as in other areas where there is a definite consciousness of being black or being white, with ascribed patterns of behavior and reaction, there also exists a double consciousness of being nonwhite or nonblack that dictates ethnic aesthetics (Boyd, "The Concept of Black Esthetics" 225–226). Vizcarrondo writes as someone who has a clear sense of being nonwhite in a race-conscious environment.

One of the more recent artists to confirm an African heritage in Puerto Rico with the aesthetics of writing from within a nonwhite culture is Mayra Santos-Febres (1966–), who, like Vizcarrondo, is also a native of Carolina, Puerto Rico. Santos-Febres overtly commits to her blackness and is sensitive to how the characterization of black people is deployed in the creative arts of her country. When questioned about how she compares herself with other Puerto Rican writers of her gender, she replies:

> I honestly don't know. We all write about Puerto Rico quite a bit. And we do share similar preoccupations about gender. But, aside from those sociological coincidences, I don't think that our work is similar at all. ... There is one thing, though, that sets me apart from all the other writers: I am Black. My take on race as a literary theme goes beyond its use as a trope or a symbol of nationhood. (DeCosta-Willis 453)

In other words, race for her is not a figurative or metaphorical symbol in art, but an entity constructed as an expression of life, a life that is lived daily, a life with experiences that shape one's character and decisions. This becomes more apparent in her answer to the question, "In your opinion, what does it mean to be a Black woman in the Spanish-speaking Caribbean, in a U.S. colony such as Puerto Rico?":

> I don't know what it means to be a Black woman in the Spanish-speaking Caribbean. I know how it feels. It feels as if you exist in virtual reality, as a symbol of "our shared African heritage," as if you passed out of an episode of *Roots* and started roaming around the island without any connection whatsoever to the transformations that you see unraveling in front of your eyes. You are the past…So, the existence of a Black writer in Latin America, or in the Caribbean to a lesser extent is pretty precarious. If he or she does not become a token, s/he becomes a symbol of national origin, of the past. I refuse

to be one or the other. ... I am trying hard not to become Tembandumba de la Quimbamba. (DeCosta-Willis 455–456)

Some in Latin America, and even in Puerto Rico, would regard this stance as overtly militant. Santos-Febres, nonetheless, explains herself simply: "I am a feminist. I support Puerto Rican independence. I am anti-racist" (460). And how does she view race relations on her beloved island? While it is obvious from the previous quotes that she does not share the same viewpoint as her fellow feminist compatriots concerning an identity of Puerto Rican blackness, in her art she makes her position unequivocal. In the novel *Cualquier miécoles soy tuya* [I am Yours on Any Wednesday], there is a chapter devoted to the practice of African-based spirituality ("*Orzo Moyugba*"), in which one of the characters autoexamines himself and his spiritual needs:

> *¿Qué se pone uno para un tambor? Yo de blanco, definitivamente no me iba a vestir. No quería parecer creyente, pero tampoco dejar de parecerlo....Para algo soy puertorriqueño, es decir isleño hasta cierto punto, negro negado y blanco sin serlo. Un híbrido, la mitad de algo, el doble del doble.* (171)

> (How does one dress for these drum-beating spiritualist meetings? I am definitely not going to wear white. I don't want to look like a believer; nor do I want to look like a disbeliever....It is a given that I am Puerto Rican, that is to say an islander, up to a point, a black person in denial and a white person even if I'm not. A hybrid, a half of one thing, a double of the double.)

This is the novelist's approach to race for Puerto Ricans. It is so unlike the image that is openly admitted to by others on the island. Undoubtedly, Santos-Febres' explication is the result of her experiences in life. It is a personal recognition and acceptance of patterns beyond parameters confined to ordered social arrangements for considerations of race in the contemporary sense. *Cualquier miércoles soy tuya* is peopled with blacks, mulattos, and white-skinned persons with black features (*negros, mulatos, jabaos*), seen as remnants of an economically imbalanced colonial system: Georgina Falú (*blanca*/white) and her servant of the same name Georgina Falú (*negra*/black), with an implied consanguine relationship between them. Likewise, there is a phenotypic image not often recognized beyond Latin America as a separate entity of racial classification. Individuals of this type are part and parcel of every Latin American environment where the vagaries of African/European or African/Indigenous Indian genetic blending come into focus:

> *Sambuca era un mulato oscuro y esbelto, que se estiraba el pelo con brillantina y fijador, para domar los rizos gordos que coronaban su cabeza de palma real. Tenía los ojos color caramelo, como los de su padre, Doroteo Cámara un negro...* (51)
>
> (Sambuca was a thin, dark-skinned mulatto who straightened his hair with pomade and gel in order to tame the fat curls that crowned his head shaped like a royal palm tree. He had light-colored eyes like his father Doroteo Cámara, a black man...)

The image of a dark-skinned mulatto is not a reality for most observers of race outside the Latin American sphere, especially in the United States, where a mulatto, perforce, is anticipated to be light-skinned.

Is language that denotes color gradations important in the creative art of the Latin American? To the artist that writes with a black aesthetic, either consciously or subconsciously, it is an integral part of the paradigm of blackness. Blackness in Latin America has its basis in the reality of African slavery. The myriad manifestations of its perceptibility are seen culturally—not only in language, cuisine, music, and philosophies of religion, but in the biological outcome of genetic expressions. A genealogical path that substantiates an African ancestor might be an in-house secret in most Latin American families (e.g., the phrase "and your grandma, where is she" is popularly accessible to most Latin Americans). The ethnoracial background of many families would not be readily available for *extra familiam* consumption. To trace this path from a white perspective might offer a result where absolute whiteness or a nonblack appearance is the desired end result. The black mindset operating within the aesthetics decreed by an acceptance of one's African relatedness produces an entirely different morphology of color and ethnic prototypes.

One can see this in the interesting and curious trajectory of ethnicity, skin tones, and phenotypes that the viewpoint of Santos-Febres explicates as well as confirms. She offers the reader a black beginning that produces an ethnic progression that leads from absolute blackness as a color to the unsystematic description of black as a symbol of ethnicity:

> *Como siempre pasa en esta isla, los prietos retintos buscaron mujeres de buen ver, es decir lo más blancas posibles, y se fueron casando.* (49)
>
> (As usually happens on this island, the jet-black men looked for the best-looking women to marry, that is to say, those that were as light-skinned as possible.)

It was inevitable that such a scenario would produce:

> *... niños barrigones de todos los colores del arco iris...* (51)
>
> (...children of all the different colors of the rainbow, and with distended stomachs...)

It is important to understand that the term "as light-skinned as possible" does not necessarily imply absolute whiteness. As a reference for color, in the Latin American mindset, "light-skinned" is a relative factor. The genetic process that Santos-Febres has traced for her readers, nonetheless, leads to the closing description in the chapter where Africa is subtly inferred to be still present in the native background:

> *Su predilecto indiscutible era el Chino Pereira. Le decían Chino porque tenía los ojos rasgados, aunque la piel era del color de madera tostada. Algunos lo creen hijo de Sambuca Cámara, o quizá sobrino...* (57)
>
> (His unquestionable favorite was Pereira "the Chink." He was called "the Chink" because of his slit-like eyes, even though his skin was the color of slightly burnt wood. Some thought he was Sambuca Cámara's son, or perhaps his nephew...)

Was the resemblance so close that "*el Chino Pereira*" could be accepted as the son of Sambuco, the "dark mulatto with the curly hair that had to be tamed with gel"? While on the previous page, Santos-Febres lists typical Puerto Rican foods that have African names (rice with *gandules*, i.e., chickpeas; pickled *guineítos*, a member of the banana family) as food fare for everyday consumption, never do there appear to be pretensions, on her part, of stressing with undue emphasis the reality of an African legacy in Puerto Rico. For Santos-Febres, cultural elements with their origin in Africa are purely the result of an unavoidable integration through heritage and custom. It is important to understand, nonetheless, that the *gandules*, *guineítos*, and *bomba* which one finds diagrammed into her art did not become integrated as national icons due to the island's relationship with Spain and the Spanish language. The African origin from which these cultural artifacts proceeded to become embedded in the national psyche of speakers of Puerto Rican Spanish is clearly explained in the Alvarez Nazario study.

Using African elements to express native tendencies or concepts is not limited to a particular area. In both Cuba and Brazil, the atmosphere that encourages the use of an African-based lexical corpus and cultural imagery is even more pervasive than that which is found in most of the other Latin American societies. The original base of native African speakers, in these two countries, was reinforced over a longer period of time with incoming ethnicities from the Continent. It was not until October 7, 1886, that slavery was finally ended in Cuba by royal decree. As for Brazil, Princess Isabel signed the so-called "Golden Law" that would terminate slavery as a legal practice on May 13, 1888. To put this in proper perspective, the enslavement of Africans ended in the United States in mid-December 1865, when the U.S. Congress ratified the 13th amendment to the Constitution. The fact that both Brazil and Cuba received far larger quantities of African natives and that they continued to arrive for a longer span of time than to other parts of the Americas, including the United States, strengthened the linguistic base of these two countries with a viable glossary of practical words from various

African groups. Much of the lexicon so prevalent in the popular speech patterns of today's Cuba had its origin in the language of practitioners of the Yoruba- and Congo-based religions. The same holds true for many of the African-related terms found in the vernacular of the corresponding popular sector in Brazil. There, the Yoruba-based Candomble religion has been deemed responsible for the introduction of many of the more common words in Brazilian Portuguese that can be traced to an African source.

During the nineteenth century, other countries had begun to rely on the results of natural birth, purchases from other enslavers, or on the sale of captives from other areas of the Americas to satisfy labor requirements. However, Brazil over a longer period continued to receive a fresh supply of Africans both legally and illegally. As for Cuba, the exact number of imported captives into that country, after 1820, cannot be substantiated with documentation. Nonetheless, there are records for the year 1867, which was reportedly the last year in which a documented slave landed on the island (Murray 131). Although the ethnic groups sent to Cuba were diverse, the Bantu nations from south of the equator were the most influential. Within their group are the Bakongo who formed the Palo Monte religious philosophy that is still alive in contemporary Cuba. Likewise, the Yoruba-speaking groups also fostered religious practices that still exist. Thus, one finds that Santería, attributed to the Yoruba in the New World, functions alongside the Palo Monte of the Bantu-speaking Congo groups from Central Africa and the Catholicism of European enslavers. The scope of this essay is not an investigation of the religious practices found in Cuba. Yet, it cannot be overlooked that many of the lexical items so prevalent in the speech patterns of Cubans and used as iconic symbols to promote native imagery in Cuban letters, stem from the lexicon that served the practitioners of Palo Monte, Santería, and other African-based religions on the island.

The quote cited at the beginning of this essay, taken from Pedro Pérez-Sarduy's 2003 novel, *Las Criadas de La Habana*, offers the reader only a miniscule glimpse into the world of Cuban Spanish in active use.

The Spanish language, in Cuba, is singular with its unabashed reliance on Africanisms.

Of course, there are and have been other creative writers and lyricists in Cuba who also use African-based linguistic patterns as the artistic leitmotif for their craft. A prime example is the well-known Cuban poet Nicolas Guillén (1902–1989), who has already been mentioned. His non-Spanish vocabulary items establish a context that delineates or frames his subtext, yet they are always within the range of native Cuban lyricism. At times, his African-based glossary registers nuanced intentions of self-identification along with a goal of ethnic inclusion. In the poem "El apellido" ["The Family Name or The Surname"], Bakongo, Banguila, Kumba, and Kongue—names of African ethnic groups—are used not only to refer to some of the multiple possibilities for a family name, but at the same time in a subtle and covert manner question why the poet's name does not make reference to an African ethnicity. The thought is introduced poetically as follows:

> Ever since my school days/and even before/...they have told me my name.../your name is, and you shall be called/And then they gave me that which [you] see written on this card/the fourteen letters with which I sign my poems... (quoted in Spanish in *Cuba Literaria*, translation by author)

The poet then challenges the logic of having only a Spanish surname (Guillén), and refers indirectly to his mixed-race ethnicity: "... *No tengo pues un abuelo mandingo, congo, dahomeyano?*" ("Don't I have a Mandingo, Congo, Dahomeyan grandfather?") Referred to in the Cuban social system as mulatto, Guillén consequently challenges the rationale of being labeled with only a European Spanish tag: "I am also the grandson, the great-grandson, the great-great-grandson of a slave. But that is for his master to be ashamed of" (*Cuba Literaria*, translation by author). Inherent in these verses, one finds, subtextually, an epistemological questioning of why the assigned European patronymic has more validity than an African family name erased from his heritage by the will of someone else: "Nor [does it matter that] the Mandinga, Bantu, Yoruba, Dahomeyan name of my poor grandfather [was] drowned in the ink of the notary?" (*Cuba Literaria*, translation by author). In this poem, Guillén limits his use of Africanisms to a listing of nations, in the quest for identity: "Could I be Wolof?/Nicolas Wolof, perhaps?/Or Nicolas Bakongo?/Perhaps Guillén Banguila?" (*Cuba Literaria*, translation by author). In this last arrangement, there is the inference of pairing the European master (surnamed Guillén) with an African female (of the Banguila nation). The uncertainty of the nation in which his female genealogy has its origin enables the poet to extend his questioning with the supposition of still another nation: "Perhaps [I am] Guillén Kumbá." The metaphoric use of Africanisms to question his identity and suggest a concept of miscegenation ends with an affirmation that he is who he is in spite of dubious racial origins: "What does it matter, then/What does it matter now/Ay, my insignificant name/with/its fourteen white letters?" (*Cuba Literaria*, translation by author). The full range that Guillén intends to give his construction of Africanisms coupled with standard Spanish can now be appreciated by the manner in which the word "white" is employed as a concept. "White" fits neatly into this semiotic construct with a full range of meanings in the abstract: something racial, something empty, something meaningless and void. It is the poet's decision to determine whether the European patronymic assigned to him has more validity than an African surname erased at someone else's volition: "Neither does it matter/the Mandingo, Bantu Yoruba, Dahomeyan name of my unfortunate grandfather, drowned in the ink of the notary?" (*Cuba Literaria*, translation by author).

Guillén's Afro Cuban compositions display not only an autochthonous, African-based lexicon and an awareness of African ethnicities, territories, and history, but also a spiritual association with this idiom that focuses on the essence of self-identity. Most Cubans have always been aware of religious philosophies that link the country as a whole to ideological roots that originated on the African continent. The tenets of

Santería, Palo Monte Mayombe, and Abakua (an African-based religious philosophy that got its start in Cuba), in one way or another have been found to influence both national thought and actions. But, then, each of these philosophies has contributed in large measure to the rich lexical output found in Cuban speech and song lyrics of the popular segment of its society. However, while the transported cultures of the Bantu/Congo and Yoruba/Lukumi have shown notable influences, only the Abakua, with historical roots among the male leopard societies of the old Calabar region in southeast Nigeria, is endemic to the Cuban national space. Its formation on Cuban soil does not render it less authentically African, nor does this fact minimize the significant addition that the Abakua, as a society, has made to popular speech. In addition, it has been shown that the ceremonial chants, origin myths, and historical events of this group have greatly enriched the national fabric of the country. In summation, one can conclude that the African-based language and many of the cultural concepts of the Abakua that have entered the mainstream of Cuban popular psychology and popular speech (Miller 164) are some of the important elements, which together give the country an authenticity of its own. This is an aspect that makes it so unlike any other country in the region.

Consequently, what has come to be known as Cuban Spanish, because of this addition, is seen by the creative artist as richer in content and more expansive aesthetically. One of the artists from Cuba who pursued this reasoning was Alejo Carpentier, who published his first novel, *Ecue Yamba O*, in 1903 with a theme based on Abakua philosophies. While the motif was never a cultural challenge on ethnoracial terms for the Cuban reader, a Ghanaian scholar, Moses Panford Jr., has questioned the motives behind Carpentier's title selection. From the viewpoint of an African, Panford writes:

> Obviously the title in essence must respond to a certain ideological motivation, given that it ignores the fact that most readers [of this novel] would be middle to upper class white, and not black like the characters he has portrayed. (2)

But herein lies the perplexing situation of race-relations in Cuba. Panford's "Fanti perspective" is logically taken from an African point of view. However, subjacent in the selection of Carpentier's title is his awareness that many Cuban readers have already internalized psychologically the *cubanidad* ("Cubanness") of African terms and practices that permeate Cuban culture, in spite of the demonstrated aversion toward concepts of blackness that many white Cubans harbor.

Black and white Cubans, within their separate spaces, often share philosophies and concepts independently of each other. Cuban-born descendants of Africans formed their first Abakua group as a secret society in 1836 to resist slavery, provide mutual aid for burials, and to purchase the freedom of its members. The society's stance against colonial Spanish rule and their principles of mutual aid both attracted and encouraged white Cubans, especially the more affluent who were vehemently anti-Spanish. As a result, white Cubans also began to form Abakua societies from 1857 onward, and then started to share in the mysteries and secrets of an ontology that had been transferred from Africa and allowed to flourish on Cuban soil. Consequently, it would come as no surprise to most Cubans that diverse segments of the national space would have access to the same African legends, sayings, and practices, with full comprehension of the philosophy's secretive stance at the deep structure level. Eventually, popular speech, popular music, and even the visual arts became infused with symbols and themes that emerged from the Abakua/Lukumi cosmos. A world was revealed that had previously been both secretive and esoteric in nature. In sum, African cultural patterns with their origin in teleological concepts subsequently surfaced as a "quintessential symbol of the nation" (Miller 168).

Those who are foreign to the metaphysical environment in which this specialized lexicon of the Afro Cuban world is generated may fail to understand a word's intent and purpose. Consequently, the person who is outside the cultural environment is faced with a linguistic barrier that impedes communication. This disruption in the exchange of languages and culture becomes an obstacle that prohibits full participation in the intended aesthetics of the literary space. To illustrate this concept, one can refer to a poem by the Cuban poet Nicolas Guillén entitled "Sensemayá," with the refrain *"Mayombe-bombe-Mayombé,"* which is perhaps one of Guillén's most popular poetic creations in the Afro Cuban genre. The common academic approach has been to critique this theme as an example of *"jitanjáfora"* (i.e., nonsense words). On other occasions, the phrase is classified as a grouping of onomatopoeic sounds. Neither classification explains the subjective impulse or motivation of Guillén's construction. Both terms overlook the artist's personal and introspective identification with his medium and fail to comprehend the objective utilization of the context to appeal to his society's cultural awareness of a vibrant philosophy in its midst. The refrain, *"Mayombe-bombe-Mayombé,"* stems from a spiritual doctrine based on an African ideology. It is the doctrine of Palo Monte, inspired by forces of nature, and of which Mayombe is a branch. This philosophy arrived on Cuban soil with Bantu speakers from the Congo region of the Continent and is recognized by many Cubans. It is not a vacuous exercise in the agglutination of meaningless sounds (i.e., *jitanjáfora*). *Sensemayá* is in essence a call to worship, a call to the mystical force that is associated with divine figures. Translations and attempts at literal interpretations of Guillén's African-based lexicon do not always result in making denotative/connotative levels transparent for the culturally uninitiated or culturally insensitive. Furthermore, there are many natives who understand the sense of what is being said even though a word-for-word translation may escape them. The concepts are a lived experience for many. Such is the case with the phrase *"iba ibá/aguede má/mole yá,"* used as the *estribillo* or repetitive chorus in Guillén's poem "La vida tiene sus secretos" ["Life has its secrets"]. Does the poet expect all Spanish speakers to have full access to a literal comprehension of this chorus? Or is he relying solely on Cuban natives, and a select group of this segment at that, to be linguistically familiar with the African lexicon of his community? Guillén's adaptation of *iba ibá* is not esoteric to the point of being cryptic. Still, the extent of the comprehension of the phrase among all Cubans is a matter for debate.

As a closed society in terms of culture and philosophies, the national environment contains individuals from different spheres of life who find themselves born into a theology of black culture despite overt denial of its existence. One of the legacies of slavery in both Brazil and Cuba has been an obvious symbiosis of living among the races that has led to an interchange of religious philosophies between African and European peoples within national boundaries. The cited phrase that Guillén uses is part of a chant in Yoruba to an Oricha venerated in the Santería pantheon. It is a chant with which most Cuban santeros are familiar but whose word-for-word translation few are able to give. It has been pointed out that "Santeros control a lexicon of a few dozen to hundreds of Lukumí words and phrases," and while semantic meaning, as well as pragmatic and connotative meanings might be accessible, they "often cannot be segmented into individual words and translated" (Wirtz 110). At the same time, many laypeople in Cuba recognize words and phrases from the sacred environment and are familiar with the context in which they should be employed, but are at a loss to explain either the grammar or the lexical content of individual phrases, even though some elements may have drifted into the secular context. The presence of linguistic remnants from African languages in the mindset of Afro- and European-descendant Cubans has complexities that are peculiar to that society's interracial relationships. Both Guillén and Carpentier avail themselves of this heritage in their art.

As a native poet familiar with the diverse ramifications of his country's folkways and ethnology, Guillén's artistic force, at least in constructions where it concerns his Afro Cuban imagery, seems to rely on a combination of word, sound, and historical consciousness as the exegesis of his poetic effort. As he says in the opening stanza of "La vida tiene sus secretos":

> *La vida tiene sus secretos,*
> *pero tu puedes saberlos.*
> *Busca entre todos tus abuelos,*
> *a los más negros;*
> *ellos te dirán lo que aprendieron*
> *llorando*
> *lo que en sus largas noches*

les dijo el látigo.
(Augier 382)

(Life has its secrets
But you can unravel them
Look amongst all your grandparents
The blackest of them
They'll tell you what they learned
Crying
That which in the long nights
The whip told them.)

Here, an appeal to totemic spirits (*iba ibá*) seems to have become more generalized within the population than is usually considered. In essence, the poet's drive appears to be in the direction of the "where-is-your-grandma" syndrome with which the Puerto Rican poet Vizcarrondo also confronts his compatriots. In this sense, as Wirtz further explains, "What makes a particular interpretation good, in santeros' eyes, is not necessarily its etymological soundness...but its ability to reveal previously hidden knowledge, and make it relevant to the situation..." (119).

Other terms that Guillén employs are more commonly used in the secular sphere, although they may have started as part of the vocabulary of religious concepts. In particular, one can refer to *asere* and *chévere*, culled from the corpus of popular "Cuban speech." Both have evolved from the glossary of the Abakua secret society. *Asere*, originally a ritual greeting of salutation, is today generally accepted to mean "buddy," "friend," "dude," or "homeboy," depending on the context in which it is used. *Chévere*, based on the title of Ma'Kongo, a diviner and royal counselor of Old Calabar (Miller 168), is commonly used either as a substantive or a modifier, in the popular jargon of many Latin Americans, to indicate something or someone that is shrewd, clever, valiant, outstanding or remarkable, bold, audacious, intrepid, nervy, temerarious, or just plain "cool" in the urban sense of the word. Guillén's poem "El Chevere del navajazo/se vuelve el mismo navaja" ["That cool blade-swinging dude/ is himself the personification of a blade"] illustrates how Africanisms, in the Cuban literary space, can be constructed to convey imagery of life experiences. Seldom do these lexemes lend themselves to surface-level literal translations. As a native poet, Guillén nonetheless understood the social range of his lexicon and its perception in the native space:

> I don't doubt that many people will find these verses repugnant because they're thematically black and people oriented. I couldn't care less. Or better said: I am glad. Nevertheless they [meaning all Cubans] are participants in these very elements that make up the ethnic composition of Cuba [...]. The black man, in my opinion, has contributed essential ingredients for our mixture. (Prologue to *Songoro Cosongo*, qtd. in Zurbano 113 and 122fn6)

Additionally, it would not be uncommon to hear males, especially those from the popular segments of Cuba, and regardless of ethnicity, employ the phrase "*¡Asere qué volá!*" as a common greeting between social equals. However, Guillén used it in his verses of homage to the poet Angel Augier:

> *No señor, lo que él prefiere*
> *y a todos diciendo va*
> *si la ocasión lo requiere,*
> *es decir: Asere qué volá*
> (Augier 388)

> (No sir, what he prefers
> and as he'll tell everyone
> if the occasion requires him to,
> is to say: Hey dude, what's up!)

Guillén's approach is not exclusive to him. Novelists, poets, and lyricists in today's Cuba still find that African-based words, phrases, and portions of religious chants are important elements in their artistic output. The aim is to establish an image of Cuban authenticity. Thus, when one hears the rap group Orishas sing:

> *Viste asere/este no está en na'*
> [Hey homie did you see/this bro' ain't into nuttin']
> (From the "*Gladiadores*" ["The Gladiators"])

Aesthetics of Language as an Experience

Soy el tipo que camina/domina el territorio
con los ecobios, los propios
[I am the dude who strolls around/who controls the turf/
with the homeboys, yeh the homeboys] (From "Barrio")

mafereo ochún Elewa
[praises to the spirit of Eleggua]
. . . .
asoguere queremeye
(From "*Canto para Eleggua y Changó*" ["Chant to Elegua and Changó"])

from their albums *Emigrante* [The Emigrant], and *A lo Cubano* [The Cuban Way], there is no cultural confusion or conflict of comprehension for their audiences. Non-Spanish language items (*asere, ecobio*, and the chants) are readily accessible to the general public. The term *ecobio*, it should be mentioned, was originally used to indicate a ritual brother of the Abakua religion. In today's Cuba, it still connotes an amicable relationship between males. However, in keeping with the urban, secular atmosphere that now generates its use, for a popular English language equivalent the term "homeboy" seems to express more appropriately its secular use as opposed to a religious application. Recognition of the deep structure of the vocabulary and the spiritual basis of esoteric phrases is a national disposition. The observation has been made that "Cuban rappers are dynamically involved in redefining themselves both as peoples of African descent and as Cubans, more so than any other segment of today's Cuban society" (West-Duran, "Rap's Diasporic Dialogue" 31–33). Orishas, as a performing group, has declared that:

> [The] Afro-Cuban religion...has been with us since we were born....Whenever you find just one Cuban, in any part of the world, if he hears [the group] "Orishas," he will know that it's Cuban...[I]t has nothing to do with politics, just culture... (*Diario de Noticias*)

Consequently, the inclusion of the chant as a regular feature of their lyrics does not place the Orishas beyond the pale of cultural acceptance by the masses. However, the trend of including African-based vocabulary in musical compositions of a popular nature is not of recent vintage. Many ethnomusicologists and researchers of Cuba's musical scene have observed: "Afro musical traditions are deep-rooted, and hence Cuban rappers have drawn on Yoruba chants...to fashion a unique...Cuban style..." (West-Duran, "Rap's Diasporic Dialogues" 8). It appears that this reliance on chants is an element of deep-structured sensitivity that legitimizes the artistic ambience as being Cuban and soulfully black. It is with this understanding that one approaches the rap group Instinto and their rendition of Guillén's poem *"Quirino con su tres."* Here, *"tres"* refers to a musical instrument, native to Cuba, of six strings in three groups of two. In the poem, Guillén focuses on a black player of the *"tres"* instrument. Instinto, a female rap group, reworks the poet's material in order to highlight the art of Mercedes Valdez, a female singer of Yoruba chants. Valdez is not a contemporary of this group, and her performance style was different. Yet Instinto felt compelled to pay homage to her art form and at the same time recognize Mercedes the performer, consequently acknowledging their own African heritage. To include a phrase in the Afro Cuban style as part of their lyrics would spiritually connect them to Mercedes. Thus, they define themselves both culturally as well as spiritually.

> *...aprovecho y pido ya*
> *Unos aplausos que sean verdá*
> *Por Mercedes, efún beyá*
> *Que si no es por ella, no*
> *Canto ná.* (West-Duran, "Rap's Diasporic Dialogues" 29)
>
> (I take advantage of this moment and request
> A hearty and sincere applause
> For Mercedes, "efún beyá" [praises to her spirit]
> Since, if it weren't for her
> I wouldn't be singing at all.)

As indicated, the Yoruba expression *"efún beyá,"* with its religious overtones in a secular song, becomes a self-defining characteristic for

Aesthetics of Language as an Experience 131

Instinto. With the integration of religion, music, and culture, they not only pay homage to their African heritage but also stamp themselves as authentically Cuban.

As previously noted, there is some difficulty in producing a word-for-word translation of many of the religious-based phrases used in the secular arena due to the esoteric, nonproselytizing nature of the Abakua and Santería traditions from which they spring. The profound spiritual essence of some concepts is prudently hidden from the general public, by design. Nonetheless, various musicians who have belonged to these religious practices at one time or another have used sacred texts or liturgical forms in their performances, conscious that only a select few will have access to their depth, literally. Cuban rappers are only continuing a practice that began in the nineteenth century (Miller 177). In spite of this, not everyone agrees that these phrases are authentic. Some observers contend that their expressions are either novel or mere imitations of Yoruba and Carabali languages (Moore 199). Whether this is true or not, one has to admit that a certain reliance on a particular language form to establish perimeters of nationality and ethnicity might be seen as a subconscious reaction to a historical consciousness—that is, a direct relationship to Africa and blackness. In most cases, however, the sayings, legends, and chants that are presented to the Cuban public are the Spanish phonological version of actual Lukumi or Ki-Kongo phrases. They have been taken from the liturgy and prayers to African gods and spirits that traveled from the Continent to the Americas (in this case Cuba) with their worshipers and believers. For quite some time now, the philosophies of Afro Cuban religions and thought have been an integral part of Cuban life, and in the most favorable or optimistic interpretation, are at the foundation of Cuban culture.

In another illustration, if we were to focus on a single concept such as *rebambaramba* and look at its use by different strata of society, it would become clear that an understanding of certain Africanisms is not limited to certain social groups. Reportedly taken from the Abakua tradition as well (Miller 169), *rebambaramba* has served as the title of a classical poem by Nancy Morejón, the title of a ballet libretto by Alejo

Carpentier, and as a unifying element in the rap lyrics of the young Cuban duo Obsesión. Connotatively, *rebambaramba* refers to things in a state of confusion, an inordinate heap, and chaos. For Morejón, it becomes the frenzy of the black masses at carnival:

> *donde canta la conga*
> *su tonada mejor*
> *tango, tango real*
> *Todos somos hermanos*
> (Morejón, *Elogio y paisaje* 24)
>
> (where the conga sings
> its best tune
> tango, royal tango
> We are all brothers)

The metonymy inherent in *conga* and *tango* as national dances that also refer to groups of transplanted African peoples on Cuban soil reinforce the blackness of the ambience. Carpentier's libretto, with musical interpretation by Amadeo Roldan, similarly finds in the spirited dances and music of black Cubans the symbolism associated with African spirituality, such as the dance of the serpent. Additionally, there is a love triangle wherein the chaotic gradations of skin color become a thematic direction. It is culturally understood that without the African input, there would be no concept of miscegenation and culture of pigmentation in Cuba. For the rap duo Obsesión, *rebambaramba* is only a line in their rap song "Mambi": "*Esténse quietos que insurrecto y prieto es un lío. Rebambaramba*" ["Quiet down because to be both a rebel and a black man is no laughing matter. It's total confusion"] (Obsesión 210). Nonetheless, the word or thought coalesces disparate elements of the national consciousness that signify a black heritage: In the rap song, there is reference to Quintin Banderas as the representative "*mambi*," or black freedom fighter in Cuba's struggle for independence from Spain. Then there is the African-oriented lexicon used by some people as pejoratives to denigrate Cuban blacks (*niche, ñata, bemba*), which the rappers employ in an inverse role as a Gestalt patterning of racial pride:

> *Yo soy niche*
> ....
> *¡Escucha esto, Nicolás!*
> *Estoy rapeando al compás de*
> *mis pasas*
> *mi ñata, mi bemba, mi árbol*
> *genealógico*
> *mi historia, mis costumbres, mi*
> *religión y*
> *mi forma de pensar.* (Excerpted from "*Mambí*" by Obsesión)

> (I am Black
> ....
> Listen to this Nicolas!
> I'm rapping to the beat of
> my kinky hair
> my flat nose, my big lips,
> my family tree
> my history, my customs, my
> religion and
> my way of thinking.)

Morejón, without abandoning her aesthethics as a Cuban poet, considers the description of images by means of an African vocabulary to be a legitimate entity of the national literary paradigm. She would agree that to include words of an African origin in the lexicon and national literatures of Cuba in no way destroys the purity of a national language. "They are incorporated into the collective linguistic history" of the nation (Morejón, "La Poética de Nancy Morejón").

Generation after generation, this collective linguistic history has been accepted openly by some, and begrudgingly by others, as a component of the national social context. Isolated words and phrases that have found their way into the corpus of standard speech, song lyrics, and creative literature of the nation are not the same as a conglomeration of Yoruba or Kikongo patterns that become transformed into a Creole language. From her vantage point as an artist with words, Morejón also sees the phenomenon as follows:

> We have incorporated...an entire vocabulary of terms derived from Africa...analyzed by ethnic origin (Congo, Yoruba, Arará)... filtered into the body of the great Hispanic lexical tree. Popular Cuban speech registers an endless number of terms, idioms... [and] phonetic tones that hark back to the antecedents of our Cubanía. Even so, it would be both delusional and false to assert that a Creole exists in Cuba, or that these vestiges of African languages...lead a double life as a system of communication. They have no life...outside the rituals in which they are employed. (Morejón, "Cuba and Its Deep Africanity" 943)

This statement confirms that many Africanisms have now become integrated into the day-to-day system of standard communication in an isolated fashion. Their use adds to a Cuban essence—"cubanía," as Morejón declares. Cubanía for most non-natives can be quite an elusive term if they attempt to view it simply as "Cubanness." In Cuba, there is *cubanía, cubanidad,* and *cubaneo,* all referring to something that is generically Cuban. But cubanía, in addition to being something that is both abstract and ineffable (Caulfield 241–243), becomes for a writer such as Nancy Morejón:

> ...a state of mind that goes beyond skin color, beyond class or origins, beyond place of birth [i.e., locale within the geographical frontiers of Cuba as a nation], or ideological affiliation. It identifies us...in our shared expressions and cadences...in our facility for multidimensional oral expression... (Morejón, "Cuba and Its Deep Africanity" 938)

For example, in 1880, six years before the final abolition of slavery in Cuba, R. P. Zoell published a short story with the title "Manga-Mocha." By that date, facets of the African's life in Cuba, including his language and customs, had become fully integrated in the national psyche. In literature, this image was expressed with recognized Afro-lexical items to denote a mark of Cubanness. In spite of the fact that Africa was the foundation for his extra-Spanish lexicon, Zoell appeared quite secure and comfortable with his use of lexemes such as "*ñáñigo*," "*cheche*," and "*ñato*" to support his construct of Cuban blacks as part of the national scene. Rarely does he give an explication or clarification of the relationship of these words to the context. For Zoell, they are not included to lend an air of the exotic, but to provide the literary atmosphere with a feeling of the expected, that is, the culturally anticipated.

The reader intuitively perceives the semiology of this vocabulary (*ñáñigo*, etc.) and its relevance to a suggested phenotype. A pertinent example would be Zoell's use of "*cheche*," a Yoruba/Lukumi term that appears to have been in a state of linguistic flux at that moment in its Cuban usage. Initially employed to describe someone of low social life or with gangsterlike characteristics, it was evolving to also refer to the well-dressed paragon of sartorial elegance (Alvarez Nazario 266). Zoell, nonetheless, qualified his use of the word with an extension in standard Spanish, *baratero*:

> *No pudo menos de reconocer al cheche o baratero del Manglar.* (Sosa Rodriguez 418)
>
> (He couldn't help but recognize that tough dude or hustling gambler from the Manglar district.)

To provide a realistic environment for the context of the story line, there was an unavoidable reliance on lexical items that hark back to Africa. The social space for this short story's context revolved around the author's conception of "*un cuento ñáñigo*," or an Afro Cuban short story. Manga-Mocha was undoubtedly the projected *ñáñigo* and the character for whom the story was entitled. The author's aim was to denigrate the image of all members of this religious faction, that is, *el ñañiguismo* or the secret society of the *abakuá*. Zoell's negative drive was in keeping with the unflattering sentiment toward the sect that was in vogue at the time (Sosa Rodriguez 435). Stigmatized as a group, *ñáñigo* practices were outlawed in 1876. Nonetheless, the black, urban proletariat kept this ideology alive to the extent that even today in Cuba, it would be almost impossible to extricate philosophical elements of the Afro Cuban presence from the national fibers of Cuban identity, especially where language and certain attitudes of self-worth are concerned:

> *De él provienen fonemas, inflexiones de lenguaje y formas sintácticas de uso habitual, así como rasgos psico-sociales que sirvieron en el pasado para calificar a los ñáñigos de jaques petulantes, camorristas naturales proclives a la delincuencia...* (Sosa Rodriguez 124)
>
> (From this group [the *ñáñigos*] we have inherited the pronunciation of certain sounds, a particular tonality in the voice, verbal expressions that are in constant use, as well as socio-psychological tendencies that have led to the classification of *ñáñigos* as arrogant bullies [and] natural-born troublemakers prone to delinquent behavior...)

While the delinquent behavior mentioned in this reference is a subjective opinion that targets only one division (adherents of *ñáñiguismo*) of a larger whole (the Afro Cuban population), in a more objective analysis, inbred negative deportment has not been found to be part and parcel of all Cuban selfhood, as was demonstrated by the occupants of the flotilla of "*Marielitos*" that made their way to the shores of Florida in the 1980s. Some were professed criminals; others were law abiding, academically progressive individuals. Many were practitioners of Afro Cuban religions. Nevertheless, even with the exclusionary variable of negative social conduct, there is no doubt that to be Cuban and culturally integral, that is, to be totally Cuban in terms of culture, philosophy, and so forth, no omission can be made of Africa's imprint on the society as a whole—sociologically, linguistically, or psychologically. In this sense, most Cubans both on the island and in exile are familiar with the popular legend that has placed Fidel Castro under the protection of the Orichas, the African gods that are so popular and well known in Cuban culture. While giving his victory speech in Havana in 1959, a white dove descended and perched itself on Fidel's shoulder. This was a clear and irrefutable sign to many who were present that the power of *Olodumare*, the creator of the universe, had placed the Cuban leader in the protective care of the Orichas. Was this mass superstition or mass acceptance of a philosophical concept previously inculcated into the general culture? In essence, what the earlier quote and the legend of the dove imply is that to be Cuban is to admit to a multicultural heritage with African traits as one of its fundamental variables:

> El afrocubano—y ya aquí incluimos a negros, mulatos, blancos y amarillos—es decir, el "cubano de pura cepa," es culturalmente un mestizo. (Pomar 67)
>
> (The Afro Cuban—and here we include in this identity the black race, the mixed-race individual, the white race, and the yellow race—in other words " the real Cuban," is a multi-cultural being.)

The extent to which a culture of Afro Cuban fundamentals has imparted its elements to the mindset of the average Cuban can also be seen in the thematics of some of that country's films. One can refer, in particular, to the film *Patakin* (1983), made in Cuba and directed by Manuel Octavio Gómez. Neither the title, the names of the principal characters, the colors they wore (red for Changó, yellow for Ochún, or Caridad, her Christian name in the film), or the ethical theme of good over evil would have been beyond the scope of cultural comprehension for the average viewer, from the youngest to the oldest. The African-based vocabulary items in the dialogue appeared with normal frequency alongside the basic Spanish-language lexicon as a matter of common usage and with an aura of popular ambiance: "*Soy su ambia de infancia...*" ["I'm your childhood friend"]; "*Yo soy mamey, asere...*" ["I'm a cool guy, homie"]. Both *ambia* and *asere* entered the island by way of the enslaved African. Cuba, from its origins as a colony of Spain, soon found that both the recently arrived African captive and his native-born descendant would make their transported belief system into a bastion of that race's marginalized identity. As a result, Africans—after having supplanted the decimated indigenous Indian on the island and exceeding the Iberian European numerically—managed to transform their philosophical cosmovision into the metaphysical vision of all Cubans in general (Pomar 56). The stimuli that support the vibrancy of Africanisms in the Cuban linguistic system come from various sources of the African religious world. One such avenue has been the preservation of oral narratives from the corpus of Yoruba myths and fables called *patakin*, seen in the film by the same name. The notebooks that contain these legends, list of proverbs, and Yoruba/Spanish glossaries are reportedly well guarded and passed down from generation to generation to designated carekeepers (Duany 249). They offer a definitive example of how the linguistic patterns of Cuba's African communities spread from the specific to the general (see DeCosta-Willis 109). This is Excilia Saldaña's aim in *Kele Kele*, a collection of mythological Yoruba stories replete with the language of Lukumi storytellers. She initiates her revelation of these *patakin* with the following:

> I have come with the language of our ancestors, African and Spaniards…Cuba is a new and authentic product born of Spain and Africa…this fact is clearly visible in her dances, her music and her literature.
>
> *Kele Kele* speaks about a moment in the life of Ochún, the oricha. This is one of the most recognizable stories in our country…[and] forms a part of the popular psyche…
>
> Soon the old believers will fade away. Don't let these tales die along with them. Let us seek them out so that those that come after us will know them also. An African proverb of yesteryear says: "As each old person dies, a library goes up in flames." Let's make this library a part of the language of today. (Saldaña 7–13)

Saldaña's efforts to revive these stories serve the same subtextual purpose as the recourse to Africanisms that is used by other poets, lyricists, and novelists in Cuba. They maintain and support an affirmation of cubanía wherein Africa is an indelible unit.

Of course, Cuba, Mexico, Peru, Uruguay, and Puerto Rico, all mentioned in this essay, are not the only Latin American countries where remnants of African languages can be found integrated into the day-to-day national lexicon as the heritage of an African presence. Regardless of contemporary vacillations and/or denials of this reality, the entire Latin/Hispanic sphere inherited aspects of the cultures of Africa in varying degrees. Nonetheless, Cuba supersedes numerically all other polities in the area with whom it shares a Spanish linguistic heritage and where an African presence is a reality.

One must recall, in this respect, that Latin America as a sociogeographical concept is comprised of two major language areas: the Spanish-speaking countries of the Caribbean and Central and South America, and Brazil, the massive Portuguese-speaking country in South America. However, it must be clearly understood that the difference between Spanish as the native language in Cuba versus the Portuguese language in Brazil does not preclude the two countries from sharing equal access to African cultures as part of their native essence. Wherein for Cuba, one refers to its cubanía, for Brazil, it is the concept of *brasilianidade* that explicates its use and reliance on an inescapable cultural and historical link to Africa. Whereas Cuba's authenticity stems from its integration of Spain and Africa, Brazil is likewise an authentic product born of Portugal and Africa. One only has to consult her dances, her music, her religious practices, her foods, and her literature to confirm this fact, in addition to a broad range of phenotypes.

Gregorio de Matos (1636–1696), often considered to be the country's first Brazilian poet, referred to by some as the founder of Brazilian literature (Bates 83), and recognized as a major baroque poet of the seventeenth century, was not reluctant to include African and Amerindian words in his texts, despite his known ethnic prejudices and racial preferences. Fernando Da Rocha Peres, in a 1967 article entitled "Negros E Mulatos Em Gregório De Matos" ["Blacks and Mulattos in Gregorio de Matos"], refers to a word-list study in which some fourteen lexical items from African languages were used in de Matos' poetry: *banza, calundu, camba, corcunda, cochilar, jimbo, macuta, maribondo, mataco, mocambo, muxinga, quindim, senzala,* and *xingar* (67). This leads one to suspect that de Matos' public was familiar with and perhaps used, in popular speech, many of the same terms. For example, the word *jimbo* (alternative spelling "*gimbo*") appears on occasion in Matos' verses and leaves no doubt as to its popular usage:

> *Ambiciozo* [sic] *avarento*
> *Das próprias negras amigo*
> *Só por levar a gaudere*
> *O que aos outros custa* gimbo (Matos, as cited in Peres 61)

> (You're aggressive and greedy
> When it comes to Black women
> And try to get for nothing
> That for which others put out *cash*)

While the focus of the poet's verses here is on those who try to force their sexual attention on hapless slave women either through chicanery or prostitution, in another instance the popular expression for money (*gimbo/jimbo*) is presented in a more satirical light:

> *Pois no que toca a guardar*
> *Dias santos e domingos*
> *Ninguém vejo em mim que os guarde*
> *Si* [sic] *tem em que ganhar* gimbo.
>
> *Nem aos mizeros escravos*
> *Dão tais dias de vazio*
> *Porque nas leis do interesse*
> *É preceito proibido.*
> (Matos, as cited in Peres 72)

> (When it comes to observing
> Holy days and Sundays
> I don't see anyone keeping them
> If making money is involved.
>
> Not even the miserable slaves
> Are allowed to have these days off
> Because when it comes to self-interest
> It's a forbidden commandment.)

This sarcastic statement is intentionally directed at mocking the pious slaveholder who places making money above observing the precepts of the church. If the reader of that period were not acquainted with the vocabulary that Matos presented, why use it so freely? "*Gimbo*," presumably an expression of Congolese and Angolan origins (Peres 61fn11), is offered by Matos as if it were a standard Brazilian Portuguese lexeme.

African terms continue to be used in Brazil in both art and daily conversation, and after three hundred plus years, the vocabulary list has grown. Both Brazilian writers and the populace at large entertain the use of African terms as an inference of being authentically Brazilian.[6] Another relevant example of the acceptance of African loan words in the creative arts can be seen in the writings of Machado de Assis (1839–1908), long considered one of Brazil's greatest writers, if not the greatest. He carefully placed African terms in his texts, with an ulterior motive that was usually misunderstood. A biracial Brazilian, the son of a mixed-race father and a presumably white Portuguese mother, his peers often accused him of ignoring the plight and presence of his country's African descendants. Yet Machado created his novels with constructs that overtly presented the historical presence and social condition of blacks in the country, but at the same time covertly indicated society's condescension and neglect of the Brazilian African and the African descendant, not to mention the abuse they suffered. A careful reading of his art and an understanding of his literary aesthetics reveal that topics of race are couched in intricate and complex layers of social criticism. In spite of this, Machado has been strongly censured for what seems to be an almost intentional omission of blacks in major roles and characterizations in his works. Only black slaves, servants, or street urchins fill the vignettes of his works with manifest regularity, despite the fact that some descendants of Africans could be found at all levels in his contemporary society. Did he have a prejudiced aversion toward black people?

Given that Machado de Assis was known as an astute and clever practitioner of Brazilian Portuguese, questions arise as to whether he used Africanisms, in his mastery of the language, with a specific purpose in mind—perhaps as an aesthetically motivated artistic device. There is also the possibility that they were the only terms available to express a thematic concept. The emotive expressions such as *calundus* [negative attitude, irritability] or *muxoxo* [noise made with the tongue to indicate displeasure] were crafted into his texts to suggest either an awareness of Africans as part of the Brazilian community or as an indication of how ingrained the culture of those whom society disdained had become as part of the Brazilian whole. In context, one can look at his novel *Quincas Borba*, written within a time frame that is current with the period in which Machado lived. It appeared first in 1886 in serial form, and was published in its entirety in 1891. The dates are important for the novel's historical time frame. They represent the period when abolition was being heatedly discussed (1888) and when the aftereffects were being felt. The literary environment of the novel does not seem to be constructed around a theme of explicit blackness despite the historical moment. Yet the reader suspects that embedded within layers of interpersonal relationships there might be a motif of racial concerns. The language used in this novel appears to be standard and free of exoticisms, although the reader does encounter the occasional non-Portuguese word with its origin in an African language. For example, the term *moleque* is used throughout to refer to a young black person, either slave or free. Machado does not specifically say that the characterization is that of a black person, nor does he specify that a particular word is or is not from an African source. In the main, it was a Brazilian audience that read his works and with whom he shared linguistic traits culturally. *Moleque* had by then become socially ingrained as a national concept to refer to race (black or mixed) and status (lower class). The term is still in use in today's Brazil, even though it is no longer associated (at the surface level) only with Black youth. In its contemporary connotation, the meaning is less narrow. It is accepted as denoting all young males, but with a reference to blackness as a secondary inference—that is, certain urban behaviors and images elicit a labeling of *moleque*. In essence, when there is an implication of social negativism, the word still tends to be associated with a person who has an aura of inner-city, anti-social behavior and carries racial undertones. Irresponsible social behavior is now felt to be the core reference of today's *moleque*. Consequently, social status coupled with race has been relegated to historical memory.

If explicit blackness was not the literary backdrop that Machado used, neither did he write with the mindset of a "black author" on a mission of remonstrance. Africanisms, for him, were principally a constructive device that indicated an understanding and acknowledgment of Africa in the Brazilian environment. In other words, he saw them as fibers in the total fabric of Brazilian culture. His technique also called for him to show Africans from a humane perspective. In this light, their depiction is not limited solely to a reference of generic blackness—at least, that is the way they are portrayed in *Quincas Borba*. In this novel, for example, he affirms the African image to be a diverse race of people without resorting to rhetorically descriptive prose. To achieve the end result of ethnic diversification, he appeals to the ethnonomy of African groups that connotes individual characteristics. When a character in *Quincas Borba* indicates that for her daughter to either learn how "to speak French...or to speak Cabinda" would have been all the same to her, the question arises as to why Cabinda, and not Congo or Yoruba, the ethnic groups most commonly associated with Brazil? Was Cabinda a language, just a port of embarkation, or the name of an ethnic group? Machado understood that Africans had different ethnic origins with cultural characteristics that distinguished one group from the other. A European could be French, Italian, or Portuguese, yet belong to the same race. This fact was not lost on most Brazilians. The naming of specific ethnic origins—such as *Cabinda* and *Fula*—within the range of normal conversation had specific purposes. These two references, in particular, were his way of focusing on Africans as individual groups with different ethnic characteristics and qualities. Machado did not think that Africans should be grouped into one amorphous mass without precise human characteristics. For him, each ethnicity had a distinguishing feature. It should come as no surprise, then, that the author himself, a product of a society that emphasized and recognized gradations in skin color, saw the use of the term *fula* as a way to suggest distinctiveness in skin tone among Africans: "One of them, medium in stature, thin, with his hands tied, eyes lowered, Fula in color..." (Assis 61). The character that made this observation was not African, but a native Brazilian who spoke standard Brazilian Portuguese. The fact that one African was lighter in complexion than the other was of course the subtext of this character's observation. In juxtaposition, the darker-skinned African who appeared in the same vignette with the *Fula* was constructed by the author to be proud and self-assured even though he was being led to the gallows. Machado refuses to give this black man the image of the prototypically submissive and cowered slave of the nineteenth century:

> *Este outro olhava para a frente e tinha a cor fixa e retinta. Sustentava com galhardia a curiosidade pública.* (Assis 61)

> (The other one, uniformly jet-black in color, looked straight ahead. He haughtily stared down the public's curiosity.)

The observation that Africans were of different colors was not limited to Brazilians. Esteban Montejo, in the *Biografía de un cimarrón* [Biography of a Runaway Slave], who was Cuban and African, also mentioned this fact:

> *Cada negro tenía un físico distinto, los labios o las narices. Unos eran más prietos que otros; más coloraúzcos, como los mandingas, o más anaranjados, como los musongo. De lejos uno sabía a qué nación pertenecían.* (Barnet 150)

> (Each black person had his own distinct features, i.e., the lips or the nose. Some were blacker than others; more reddish like the Mandingos, or a deep tannish color like the Musongo. From a distance, one could tell the group they belonged to.)

Today, in Brazil, there are many who still refer to themselves as *Fula* for a classification by skin color. In the pigmentocracy of contemporary Brazil it is used to denote a subtle indication of some degree of discernible miscegenation, although in essence it could have been an inheritance from an African genetic mixture. Comprehension of the codes of color assigned to certain "in-house" classifications is often lost on those persons unfamiliar with Brazil's hierarchical scaling by color.

It is interesting to observe the aesthetic direction of Machado's writings of the mid-nineteenth and early twentieth centuries. Strategically placed and commonly used Africanisms are offered in many instances as telltale aspects of history, sociology, and even national psychology. Brazilian writers continue to employ these terms as part of the Brazilian base of their brand of the Portuguese language. One such word in daily use, "samba," is unquestionably seen as an icon of Brazilian culture. It arrived in Brazil with slaves from the Kimbundu region of Angola as a concept with layered meanings. One suspects that differentiations in significance were accomplished via morphological tone patterns. Today, "samba" is widely recognized worldwide as a lively Brazilian dance. It can also mean (according to context) a prayer to invoke the spirits of the ancestors, a plaintive cry, or a navel-bumping dance. This particular aspect of a word having multiple meanings is shared with other African descendants in the Americas. It is an acceptable word in Brazilian Portuguese and conforms comfortably to the morphological shapes of Portuguese grammar. The different contours that this African word assumes are found in the song "*Canta, canta minha gente*" ["Sing, sing my people"], as sung by Martinho da Vila. In the lyrics of this one song alone, da Vila lists for his audience the various styles of samba that are available: *o samba de roda, samba-canção, samba rasgado, samba de breque, o samba moderno, o samba quadrado, samba-enredo, samba sincopado.* Here the African substantive is modified and expanded in imagery when coupled with a Portuguese-language adjective. In addition, it becomes more fully integrated into the Portuguese lexico-grammatical system with an adjustment to morphemes similar to the Latinized base of most Portuguese words, as da Vila sings: "*sambando no asfalto*" ["dancing the samba on asphalt"] or "*um sambinho lento*" ["a slow little samba"]. Here, a purely African term in its Brazilian adaptation has become a normal item in the national linguistic paradigm. Da Vila assumes a fundamentally native stance with his lyrics to "*Canta, canta minha gente*" without focusing on one particular racial or ethnic entity.

The entire population of Brazil accepts and understands the concept of the samba as a representative part of the country's Gestalt patterning of nationhood.

At another social level, Brazilian rappers, much like their Cuban counterparts, find that Africanisms in their lyrics tend to raise the consciousness level of their listeners regarding black accomplishments and history. It is not that the black figures they sing about and the historical data to which they refer are unknown or lack prominence in the country. Their complaint is that blacks as a group, and in general, are not given credit for anything. To be belittled and ignored are acts that create angry, revolutionary lyrics. The group Rappin Hood with the song "Sou Negrão" ["I'm a Big Black Dude"] illustrates this attitude:

> We made history; we are lost in its memory...The verses of our samba-rap are intended to make the black man smile one day... therefore honor your race, honor your color. Don't be afraid to speak out, [but] speak with a lot of love. (Excerpted and translated from "Sou Negrão")

The fundamental concept of the song is presented in standard Portuguese, yet the group appears to intentionally support and culturally modify their lyrics with expressions from Brazil's available corpus of African-based entries: *bambas, samba, Zulu, Kizomba, capoeira, afoxé,* and *axé*. The tendency, not limited to this group alone, is seen as a form of protest—an active protest among many urban artists. For example, the group Z'Africa found that to resurrect the image of the black freedom fighter Zumbi, in their performance of *"O Rei Zumbi"* ["King Zumbi"], would not only be a reminder of black history but a call for hope:

> Quilombola *brasilificado nos* mocambos, *filho dos* quilombos *na* senzala *escura,*
> *E fria, vive uma esperança, em meio aos* banzos *ainda persiste um sonho.*
> Zumbi-zumbi oia zumbi, *salve o deus negro para uma sua ressurreição, pra*
> Outros um pesadelo.

(A hideout for runaway slaves within the Brazilian space, a child destined for the hideout [lives] in the cold, dark slave quarters [and] lives with hope; in the midst of the slave's nostalgic yearning there still remains a dream: Zumbi-zumbi, O' Zumbi, hail to the black god, for some [he is] the Resurrected One, for others [he is] a nightmare.)

Here, a cultural memory formed in Africa with terms such as *quilombola, quilombo(s), mocambo, senzala, banzo(s)*, and *Zumbi* is retrieved in a new space of oppression to conjure up hope for a better future.

In the contemporary arena of protests for rights, respect, and social and economic progress, Afro Brazilians have been wrongly accused of being complacent. This image, however, has been countered by research that places hip-hop artists emerging from the *"favelas,"* or shantytowns, as being at the forefront of a movement of race-consciousness (Gordon 1). It is a recognized fact that the vast majority of poor blacks and non-whites, along with a few who are accepted as white but exist at the lower socioeconomic strata, overwhelmingly people most *favelas* in Brazil. Confronted with this reality, there is an effort by the socially and economically privileged classes to continue to control both the economy and political policies of the country. They, on the whole, are white or appearing to be white and, to consolidate their position of favor, have adopted a strategy that declares any overt discussion of race to be deemed un-Brazilian. In such an environment, it is not surprising that the masses—predominantly black, politically ignored, and economically deprived—would consequently search for a vehicle to make their plight known. Based on custom and culture, the creative approach used by rappers from the *favelas* is underpinned with lexical symbols from an ingrained African heritage that is part of their country's national image. Their artistic direction has found currency as a nonviolent call for the country and for young, black Brazilians to consider their historical and psychological place in the racial makeup of the nation:

> Set within a Brazilian context of "racial democracy" where any discussion of race has historically been considered "un-Brazilian,"

rappers disrupt the desired silence around issues of race. Brazilian rap groups often write lyrics which overtly address race consciousness, racial identity, and racism...(Gordon 3)

Other creative media have also heeded the clarion call. As noted, standard Brazilian Portuguese, at least at the popular level, accepts Africanisms without fear of jeopardizing general intelligibility. Consequently, Brazilian readers of the popular novel *Cidade de Deus* [City of God] (1997) by Paulo Lins are certain to comprehend the following with all its deep-structure inferences:

> ...the hands of *Iemanja* [African goddess] over his head (11)
>
> ...and on the floor...where he had dragged his *bunda* [butt] during the first and second stages of his infancy (12)
>
> ...and, in order to do that, she had to smoke some *maconha* [pot, weed]... (248)
>
> After freeing herself from the *molecada* [mob of thugs]... (250)

For the average speaker of Brazilian Portuguese, the items that have been highlighted—*Iemanja, bunda, maconha,* and *molecada*—are not perceived as vocabulary that is alien to the native standard. Furthermore, when integrated into the general corpus of everyday vocabulary, none of the cited lexemes is viewed as a specific determinant for the race of the speaker or the listener. In other words, their use is not ethnically controlled or racially delimited. It should be pointed out, however, that these particular entries are all conventional indicators of a sociolect. Although now accepted as native Brazilian Portuguese, they each carry an inescapable historical and sociological link to African slavery. Thus, it has become unavoidable to acknowledge that a recognizable corpus of words with an African background, in active use throughout the country, has become another obvious element of black reality in Brazilian nationalism.

As seen with the previous examples and explanation, in addition to being an element of national imagery, the manner in which vestigial African vocabularies are used can also reveal the artist's personal relationship with both his or her ethnic environment and the aesthetic construction of the context. One can see this in the following quote from an online essay by Vargas Llosa: "Nothing teaches us better than literature to see in ethnic and cultural differences the richness of the human patrimony" ("The Premature Obituary of the Book"). This is also understood to mean that literature shows us language in context; language in context reveals the author's reaction to his environment, and likewise, the reactions of his ethnic characterizations in the literary environment to him.

In the final analysis, it should also be understood that the existence of an African lexicon in the creative arts of both Spanish and Portuguese speakers in Latin America may not be a linguistic inheritance imposed only by the factor of numbers, as inferred by G. R. Andrews in his review essay "Afro-Latin America: The Late 1900s" (363), but it may also be seen as the fundamental result of an active experience of black involvement in the national spaces of diverse Latin communities.[7] That is to say, the vocabulary found in the artistic output of the Hispanic/Latin sphere presents for the reader another vivid cultural expression of the Afro Latin/Afro Hispanic reality that has permeated the Latin American environment.

Works Cited

Aguirre Beltran, Gonzalo. *La Población Negra de México*. México, D. F.: Fondo de Cultura Económico, 1984. Print.

Alvarez Nazario, Manuel. *El Elemento Afronegroide en el Español de Puerto Rico: Contribución al estudio del negro en América*. San Juan, P.R.: Instituto de Cultura Puertorriqueña, 1974. Print.

Andrews, George Reid. *Afro-Latin America, 1800–2000*. New York: Oxford University Press, 2004. Print.

———. "Afro-Latin America: The Late 1900s." Review Essay. *Journal of Social History* 28.2 (Winter 1994): 363–379. Print.

Assis, Joaquim Maria Machado de. *Quincas Borba*. Ed. Massaud Moises. 4th ed. São Paulo: Editora Cultrix, 1957. Print.

Augier, Angel. ed. *Nicolás Guillén. Obra Poética Tomo II 1958–1985*. 3ra ed. Habana: Letras Cubanas, 2002. Print.

Barnet, Miguel. *Biografía de un cimarrón*. 2nda ed. México, D. F.: Siglo Veintiuno Editores, S.A., 1971. Print.

Basso Ortiz, Alessandra. "Los gangá longobá: El nacimiento de los dioses." *Boletín Antropológico* 2.52 (Mayo–Agosto 2001): 195–208. Print.

Bates, Margaret J. "A Poet of Seventeenth Century Brazil: Gregorio de Matos." *The Americas* 4.1 (Jul. 1947): 83–99. Print.

Bowser, Frederick P. *The African Slave in Colonial Peru: 1524–1650*. Stanford, CA: Stanford University Press, 1974. Print.

Boyd, Antonio Olliz. "The Concept of Black Esthetics as Seen in Selected Works of Three Latin American Writers: Machado de Assis, Nicolás Guillén and Adalberto Ortiz." PhD diss., Stanford University, 1975. Print.

Busdiecker, Sara. "Where Blackness Resides: Afro-Bolivians and the Spatializing and Racializing of the African Diaspora." *Radical History Review* 103 (Winter 2009): 105–116. Print.

Carroll, Patrick J. "Mandinga: The Evolution of a Mexican Runaway Slave Community, 1735–1827." *Comparative Studies in Society and History* 19.4 (Oct. 1977): 488–505. Print.

Caulfield, Carlota. Review: "Cuban Literature and Culture: Critical Junctures." *Latin American Research Review* 37.3 (2002): 231–246. Print.

Cruz, Celia. "Burundanga" lyrics. Web. 5 May 2010.

Cuba Literaria. "Nicolás Guillén Poeta Nacional de Cuba" Obras "El Apellido" Web. 6 May 2010.

da Luz, Eduardo. "Milongón de Reyes" lyrics. Web. 5 May 2010.

da Vila, Martinho. "Canta, canta minha gente." *Canta Canta Minha Gente*. RCA Victor, 1974.

DeCosta-Willis, Miriam, ed. *Daughters of the Diaspora: Afra-Hispanic Writers*. Kingston, Jamaica: Ian Randle Publishers, 2003. Print.

Diario de Noticias. "Entrevista a Orisha tras la grabación de 'A lo cubano.'" Web. 5 Jan 2009.

Duany, Jorge. Review: "After the Revolution: The Search for Roots in Afro-Cuban Culture." *Latin American Research Review* 23.1 (1988): 244–255. Print.

Garza, Cynthia. "Contemporary Cimarronaje: Teatro del Milenio's Kimbafá." *EMISFÉRICA* 5.2 (Dec. 2008): 1–3.

Gomez, Michael A. "African Identity and Slavery in the Americas." *Radical History Review* 75.111 (1999): 111–120. Print.

Gordon, Jennifer Roth. "Hip-Hop Brasileiro: Brazilian Youth and Alternative Black Consciousness Movements." Presented at the AAA Meetings. 18 Nov. 1999.

Guillén, Nicolás. *Obra Poética*. La Habana: Editorial Letras Cubanas, 2002. Tomo II 1958–1985. Tercera edición (ampliada). Print.

Hughes, Langston. *The Big Sea: An Autobiography*. New York: Thunder's Mouth Press, 1986. Print.

Ibáñez, Alberto. "Black in Mexico." *Inside Mexico* (Apr. 2007): 14–21. Web. 15 Apr. 2007.

Kennedy, James H. "Luiz Gama: Pioneer of Abolition in Brazil." *The Journal of Negro History* 59.3 (Jul. 1974): 255–267. Print.

La Onda Digital de Uruguay. No. 203, 14 al 20 de Setiembre de 2004. "Diálogo con la sicóloga Susana Rudolf y la estudiante Noelia Maciel." Web. 25 May 2007.

Lins, Paulo. *Cidade de Deus*. São Paulo: Companhia das Letras, 1997. Print.

Martinez Casanova, Manuel. "Religiosidad afrocubana y cultura terapéutica." *ISLAS* 44.133 (julio–septiembre 2002): 140–149. Print.

Megenney, William W. "Common Words of African Origin Used in Latin America." *Hispania* 66.1 (Mar. 1983): 1–10. Print.

———. "Some Lexical Linkages Between Africa and Venezuela." *Neophilologus* 76 (1992): 383–391. Print.

Miller, Ivor. "A Secret Society Goes Public: The Relationship between Abakuá and Cuban Popular Culture." *African Studies Review* 43.1 Special Issue on the Diaspora (Apr. 2000): 161–188. Print.

Miranda, Franklin. *Hacia una narrativa afroecuatoriana: cimarronaje cultural en Améria Latina*. Quito, Ecuador: Ediciones ABYA-YALA, 2005. Print.

Moore, Robin. *Nationalizing Blackness: Afrocubanismo and Artistic Revolution in Havana, 1920–1940*. Pittsburgh: University of Pittsburgh Press, 1997. Print.

Morejón, Nancy. "Cuba and Its Deep Africanity." *Callaloo* 28.4 (Fall 2005): 933–950. Print.

———. *Elogio y paisaje*. Habana, Cuba: Ediciones Unión, 1996. Print.

———. "Las poéticas de Nancy Morejón." Web. 24 Apr. 2007.

Murray, D. R. "Statistics of the Slave Trade to Cuba, 1790–1867." *Journal of Latin American Studies* 3.2 (Nov. 1971): 131–149. Print.

Obsesión. "Mambi (Rap)" *boundary 2* 29.3 (2002): 205–210. Print.

Orishas. "Canto para elewa y changó." *A lo cubano*. Universal Latino, 2000.

Ortiz, Adalberto. *Juyungo: Historia de un negro, una isla y otros negros*. Barcelona: Editorial Seix Barral, S.A., 1976. Print.

Palés Matos, Luis. *Selected Poems/Poemas Selectos*. Houston: Arte Público Press, 2000. Print.

Panford, Jr., Moses. "Hacia una revalorización de *Ecue-Yamba-O* de Alejo Carpentier: una perspectiva fanti." *Anales del Caribe* 21–22 (2003): 66–77. Print.

Peres, Fernando Da Rocha. "Negros e Mulatos em Gregório de Matos." *AfroAsia* 4–5 (1967): 59–75. Print.

Pérez-Sarduy, Pedro. *Las Criadas de la Habana*. La Habana: Editorial Letras Cubanas, 2003. Print.

Pomar, Jorge A. "El renacimiento religioso en Cuba." *Revista Encuentro de la Cultura Cubana* 12/13 (primavera/verano 1999): 56–67. Print.

Rappin Hood. "Sou Negrão." *Sujeito Homem*. Trama, 2003.

Rodríguez, Enrique. *Los Ñáñigos*. La Habana: Ediciones Casa de las Américas, 1982. Print.

Rodriguez, Romero Jorge. "The Afro Populations of America's Southern Cone: Organization, Development, and Culture in Argentina, Bolivia, Paraguay, and Uruguay." *African Roots/American Cultures: Africa in the Creation of the Americas*. Ed. Sheila S. Walker. Lanham, MD: Rowman and Littlefield Publishers, Inc., 2001. Print.

Romero, Fernando. "The Slave Trade and the Negro in South America." *The Hispanic American Historical Review* 24.3 (Aug. 1944): 368–386. Print.

Saldaña, Excilia. *Kele Kele*. La Habana: Editorial Letras Cubanas, 1987. Print.

Santos-Febres, Mayra. *Cualquier miércoles soy tuya*. Barcelona: Mondadori, 2002. Print.

Sones de Mexico. "Fandango" lyrics. Web. 5 May 2010.

Toña la Negra. "Yo soy mulata" lyrics. Web. 6 May 2010

Turner, Lorenzo D. *Africanisms in the Gullah Dialect*. Columbia: University of South Carolina Press, 2002. Print.

Valdés-Cruz, Rosa. *La poesía negroide en América*. New York: Las Américas Publishing Company, 1970. Print.

Vargas Llosa, Mario. "The Premature Obituary of the Book: Why Literature?" *The New Republic*. 5 May 2001. Web. 17 Sept. 2009.

Vass, Winifred K. *The Bantu Speaking Heritage of the United States*. Los Angeles: University of California Press, 1979. Print.

Vincent, Theodore G. "The Contributions of Mexico's First Black Indian President, Vicente Guerrero." *The Journal of Negro History* 86.2 (Spring 2001): 148–159. Print.

Vizcarrondo, Fortunato. *Dinga y Mandinga*. San Juan, P.R.: Instituto de Cultura Puertorriqueña, 1983. Print.

West-Durán, Alan. "Puerto Rico: The Pleasures and Traumas of Race." *Centro Journal* 17.1 (Spring 2005): 47–69. Print.

———. "Rap's Diasporic Dialogues: Cuba's Redefinition of Blackness." *Popular Music Studies* 16.1 (Apr. 2004): 4–39. Print.

Wirtz, Kristina. "How diasporic religious communities remember: Learning to speak the 'tongue of the oricha' in Cuban Santería." *American Ethnologist* 34.1 (2007): 108–126. Print.

Zurbano, Roberto. "El triángulo invisible del siglo xx cubano: raza, literatura y nación." *Temas* 46 (abril–junio 2006): 111–123. Print.

Essay III

An Aesthetic Experience

The Reality of Phenotypes and Racial Awareness in Dominican Literature

Julia Alvarez and Loida Maritza Pérez

¿Por qué quieres ser negro?
Eres indio
Indio claro
Dominicano
Indio claro
("Indio Claro" by Blas Jiménez)

(Why do you want to be Black?
You are Indian
A light-skinned Indian

Dominican
A light-skinned Indian)

National origin and race seem to function as inseparable conjuncts for many societies. Along with this idea, certain phenotypic images tend to surface as a subset of national race—with the result that prescribed racial characteristics become unqualified markers for inclusion within the parameters of that nation. Often, this prescription gives rise to "desired" or "imagined" phenotypes. Such seems to be the case for the Dominican Republic, where the corpus of sociological literature that studies the phenomenon of a prototypical national race grows continuously. However, the idea of race and national origin is not new nor is it limited to only one country in the Latin American sphere.

Juan Comas, in *Las razas humanas*, published in Mexico in 1946, questions whether the use of *"razas e idioma"* ["race and language"] such as in the term *"raza latina"*—Latin race—are coextensive. In a rhetorical sense, this leads him to likewise consider the exclusory concept embedded in the section *"Raza y Nación"* ["Race and Nation"] (7). In defining both elements, he finds that race, using the strictest criteria, is a conjunct of beings that possess the same genetic makeup (9). Nation, conversely, is fundamentally a historical and political notion that has absolutely nothing to do with the somatic types of the individuals that inhabit the spatial concept of a country (8).

While Comas' methods for arriving at his final determinations seem to be more empirical than scientific or theoretical, he emphatically agrees with the French anthropologist of his generation, H. Vallois, that no race is to be considered inferior to another (88). Furthermore, in biological terms, there is no such thing as pure races—*"razas puras"*—given that race mixing, *"mestizaje,"* has existed since the very beginning of humanity. While there may be groups of people who exhibit similar somatic differentiations, these characteristics are to be viewed as quantitative gradations rather than qualitative fact. Comas concludes that, *"El mestizaje, biológicamente hablando, no es bueno, ni malo; depende en todo caso de las características individuales de quienes sean sujetos...*" ["Miscegenation is neither good nor bad; one should take into account the individual characteristics of those who are affected by this human tendency."] (89). While it is not a matter of emphasis for Comas, there appears to be in his thesis evidence that along with miscegenation, there are gradations of mixture that represent a close proximity to the "norm" and also a deviancy from what the national psychology requires for its prototypical soma. The range of closeness to the national norm usually becomes codified in the national language. A specialized lexicon arises that describes and situates an individual along a prescribed locus for easy identification of phenotype. Such is the standard in most countries in the Americas where miscegenation is a historical fact. In the Spanish-speaking Caribbean, for example, terms such as *moreno, negro, mulato, trigueño, jabao, grifo,* and *pardo* are only a minute sampling of the myriad of standard lexical items that fall within the linguistic competence of most speakers when referring to a particular phenotype. In other words, this lexicon is recognized as describing a range of skin tones. Some of the terms used are flattering; others can be painfully pejorative.

The codification of skin tone as a morphological component of national awareness in the Dominican psyche has been internalized to function as an acceptable cultural sign. According to Daniel Chandler in his online essay "Semiotics for Beginners: Encoding/Decoding," there is recognition of the sign + comprehension of the intended meaning of the sign + interpretation of the sign in terms of relevance. Mayda Grano de Oro, in her article on the Dominican Republic, points out that the relationship between race and Dominican national identity has been a very important factor in the formation of the country. And although the Dominican Republic claims three different racial roots when defining its ethnic and racial composition—Taino (or Amerindian native), Spanish, and African—racism urges Dominicans to see themselves mainly as Hispanic and obliterate the concept of an African heritage while melding together the idea of Spanish and Taino roots. As a matter of fact, the tendency has become somewhat institutionalized wherein many light-skinned to dark brown Dominicans prefer to call themselves *"indio"* or Indian (i.e., a Taino descendant) as an official racial designation in order to avoid an association with blackness (Grano de Oro 8).

In order to support this national consciousness, the Dominican government institutionalized many of the racialized elements of that country's culture. For example, the word *"indio"* is commonly used to describe the great majority of Dominican mulattos or mixed-race individuals. In this sense, the Dominican government uses *"indio"* as a skin color descriptor on the national identity card that every adult Dominican must carry. Consequently, *"indio"* is no longer a slang term, but an official racial category, accepted and used officially for identification and classification by race. Most Dominicans are classified as *"indio."* Those with a much darker skin tone are labeled *"moreno."* Actually, very few Dominicans are labeled black, due to the term's pejorative connotation. This, in essence, sums up the "interpretation and evaluation" process of Chandler's observation of a sign, because for him, "what is 'meant' is invariably more than what is 'said'." The Dominican Republic is not the only Latin American country where attempts to subterfuge the native black image have become codified as national policy. Most countries throughout the region do not see the feasibility of including their black citizens in the national paradigm. For example, in a communiqué published online by the Venezuela Information Office, it is clearly stated that national blackness alone is not a preferred national identity:

> Abolition occurred in 1854, but freedom did not bring equality. Racism continued to flourish in Venezuela throughout most of the 20th century, and African heritage was denied through an emphasis on racial mixing. The *mestizo*, born of European, Indigenous, and African blood became a cornerstone of national identity…Since 2003, millions of Afro-Venezuelans have been issued national ID Cards guaranteeing them the citizenship rights they previously lacked. Article 56 of the 1999 Constitution guaranteed all persons the right to free registration with the Civil Registry Office, a measure that has allowed electoral participation among Afro-Venezuelans to grow tremendously. ("Afro-Venezuelans and the Struggle Against Racism")

How does creative literature approach the reality of the Dominican concern with phenotypes? If gradations in skin tones are a normal factor as to how an individual is nationally coded, what position will this coding take as an artistic construct? In order to arrive at a determination for these questions, it is important to look at recognized authors who write for both an internal and external market, but possess an internal vision. It is also of special interest to consider the author across cultures: race and identity as seen by the author in the Dominican Republic, as well as Dominican ethnicity and race as seen by the same author in situ by North Americans. For example, Julia Alvarez's *In the Name of Salomé* falls within this construct because of the ethnicity of the protagonist(s), the location(s) of the action, and the author's experience as a bilingual, bicultural writer. In an interview that focused on her artistic motives, Alvarez explained that she writes to find out what she is thinking and to find out who she is, in addition to trying to understand things (Requa, "The Politics of Fiction"). Apropos of the direction that will be taken in this study is the fact that the experience of women—especially women of color—has always interested Alvarez. Her statement, in the same interview, "But I don't want to deny my roots," is a very revealing thought.

Both Salomé and Camila, the protagonists of *In the Name of Salomé*, are Dominican women of color. This can be inferred because the author, Alvarez, does not identify them as white. The novel opens with a phenotypic description of Camila, without saying that it is she: "She stands by the door, a tall elegant woman with a soft brown color to her skin (southern Italian? A Mediterranean Jew? A light-skinned Negro woman who has been allowed to pass by virtue of her advanced degrees?") (*In the Name of Salomé* 1). It is interesting from a semiotic perspective to note that it is only the "light-skinned Negro woman" who must qualify with advanced degrees in order to be able to join the cadre of elegant, nonpale women. One later learns that these descriptions are a veiled reference to Camila, the Dominican co-protagonist. Of course, North American readers familiar with the unspoken code of phenotype and class in the racial ideology of the United States will tacitly understand these coded descriptions. Alvarez, as a bicultural author, comprehends this. She has learned that every culture has embedded its own set of signs that become part of a national ideology. These national signs or symbols generate both a meaning and an interpretation of the cultural vision, and likewise serve to identify the values of the culture (Bezuidenhout 1–3). It is determined that at this juncture in the novel, it is the author's inner voice that is describing Camila the Dominican, using a North American system of identification values that includes the mythology of the one-drop rule.[8]

In the Name of Salomé is considered by most reviewers to be a historical novel in which reality has been fictionalized. There are historical names, important dates in Dominican history, and factual occurrences that are easy to trace. The novel's plan of development addresses the life of Salomé Ureña, who remains an important figure in Dominican literature, even though she passed away more than a century ago in 1897. One sees later in the novel that the poet's daughter, Camila Henríquez Ureña, shares the role of protagonist with her mother. When Dominicans recall Salomé Ureña today, they see her as one of the greatest poets of the Dominican Republic, and even of the Americas. Certainly, as Franklin Gutiérrez points out, she is "*Figura central de la literatura dominicana del siglo XIX...*" ["The pivotal force of nineteenth century Dominican literature"] (175). Nonetheless, for political reasons, her daughter Camila, also a poet, did not see her work so widely disseminated in the Dominican Republic until after her death (88).

What is learned of the historical Salomé in this novel comes first by way of Alvarez's inner voice and later through reflections that she ascribes to the poet's daughter. The process of characterization weaves back and forth between (a) the author's creative projection of historical events and occurrences before and after the birth of Camila, and (b) an emotional attachment to space and race (Dominican ethnicity is seen as race) in the literary actuation of Camila who, as noted, is developed into a primary figure.

In both approaches, Alvarez offers the reader engrained, psychological, and cultural reactions to race and phenotypes in the Dominican

Republic. For example: "Gregoria was pale enough...but look at her grandmother" (*In the Name of Salomé* 19). The author's observation is based on a popular expression known in most of Latin America: "*¿Y tu abuela dónde está? Está en la cocina y se llama doña Tatá*" ["And where is *your* grandma? She's back there in the kitchen, and they call her Ole Mammy"]. This saying alludes to the fact that the lightest "latino" might have a black ancestor, who is usually hidden away. Alvarez also attempts to avoid the confusion of ethnicity and race in the United States where Dominicans are concerned: "You mean your mother was...a Negro? We call it mulatto. She was a mixture" (44). Even her outspoken friend Marion (from the United States) has always avoided the subject of Camila's race, as if to mention it were to bring up the unmentionable (160). And finally, Alvarez factors in, for comparison, the Dominican concept versus the universally accepted recognition of the term "*indio*" when applied to race, ethnicity, and identity. Pedro, Camila's brother, speaks:

> "Does he know about mama," Pedro asks, casting a knowing glance in Isabel's [his wife] direction. "Back home [in the Dominican Republic, the family is now in Cuba] everyone expects these mixtures." Isabel, herself, obviously has a little Indian in her golden skin, and a lot in her black hair, and dark almond-shaped eyes. (201)

However, Isabel is not Dominican. She is from Mexico, where there is a large indigenous and indigenous-based miscegenated population. Pedro seems to suggest that his mother's color—Salomé's phenotype—rightfully bestowed on her the Dominican classification of "*india*" as a deep structure module of racial classification. He obviously wanted to see some of his wife's Mexican Indian characteristics in his mother, a Dominican. This, undoubtedly, is ethnic symbolism used with the intention of demonstrating the subterfuge in racial identity in the Dominican Republic (African + European) versus the ethnic legitimacy that discloses racial identity in Mexico (Indigenous + European). That is to say, *Indio/India* in the Dominican Republic is a metonym for a presumed ethnicity based on the assignation of color. Alvarez is well aware of this cultural practice. She makes this exceptionally clear to the reader in her subtle comparison of Isabel, Pedro's wife, with Pedro and his mother Salomé: "Pedro and Max [his brother] have turned out to be the sons who look most like Salomé's side of the family, darker-skinned, a kink in their hair, all the telling features" (201).

Although the novel organizes its focus around the life of the Dominican poet Salomé Ureña and the relationship that she has with her offspring, especially her daughter Camila, there is no escaping the fact that Alvarez has intended for the question of race to help generate the theme. For example, the novel begins with Alvarez's inner voice offering the reader a description of Camila as someone of indeterminate race when she is seen in North American terms. In anticipation of how the novel will unfold, the author approaches the question of race and phenotypes on three distinct levels: in the United States, in the Dominican Republic, and in Cuba (another Hispanic country that shares similar patterns of miscegenation with the Dominican Republic, but not the national terms for identification).

In the United States, Hispanics and race are seen as enigmas. Where Camila sees white people as having "pale skin," "red hair," "blond hair," "fair skin," and some black Americans as being "light-skinned," North Americans seem to be confused by her ethnicity. She tries to explain to a white American student that her father (a white Dominican) had her mother's portrait touched up: "He wanted her to be prettier, Whiter..." (44). The puzzled white student looks at Camila and says: "You mean, your mother was a...Negro?" (44). Camila unhesitatingly replies: "We call it mulatto. She was a mixture..." (44). At least Camila understands that she is not white: "Of course the only apparently colored people in the room are up on the stage, and no one would guess that Camila, pale-skinned, with her wavy, marcelled hair, is one of them" (198). After all, she had an unforgettable welcome on her first visit to the United States as a young university student: "She remembers the first summer when some locals [from La Moure, North Dakota] left a burning cross on the

An Aesthetic Experience 165

lawn" (84). Previously undeterred by the warning signs with which Americans had confronted her regarding her race, Camila's inner voice now rationalizes her Dominican mindset that categorizes her as not black but "whitish." She is beginning to internalize the hypodescent rationalization of Americans. Finally, Americans seem reluctant to overtly bring up the subject of race: "Even her outspoken friend Marion has always avoided the subject of Camila's race, as if to mention it were to bring up the unmentionable. 'I don't care what you are,' Marion has often said to her" (160). Alvarez has built into the structuring of Marion's unbigoted thoughts and actions the fact that her family has a long history as New Hampshire abolitionists (201). This background of being active in a liberal sense where matters of race are concerned is undoubtedly the author's way of accounting for Marion's unbiased views when Camila's race is the focus. Camila's brother, Pedro, who is much darker than she, becomes disillusioned with the United States and wants to leave. He tells his colleagues that "[h]e cannot bear another winter [in Minnesota]." But privately, he has admitted to Camila that the difficulties he has encountered because of his color and accent have soured him toward the place (234). As a matter of fact, Pedro's negative experiences have made him painfully aware of the difference in attitudes between the Dominican Republic and the United States, especially the atmosphere where phenotype and racial awareness are concerned: "When he [Camila's white American boyfriend] meets me, he will know right away. [Pedro is alluding to the fact that he is not white]…Pedro's voice is edged with bitterness." And, "Camila remembers hard moments in Minneapolis for her brother, rentals suddenly unavailable, entry refused into certain clubs" (201).

If this can take place in a northern U.S. city like Minneapolis, what would the south be like for Pedro and Camila? There is a culminating scene that Alvarez creates to show specifically how white North Americans react toward the Hispanic image. It is seen when Scott Andrews, Camila's male, white American friend, extends her an invitation to visit a nearby café. Included, along with light-skinned Camila, are her darker-complexioned brother, Pedro, and his miscegenated Mexican wife, Isabel:

> Then, S. A. invited us all for refreshments at an elegant café nearby. Ay, Marion, what a painful moment. The establishment would not serve us. They said they did not have enough room for such a large party, but there were many empty tables, and we all guessed the reason. Pedro immediately turned on his heels and took Isabel home. (204)

Alvarez is careful, however, to let the reader know that she does not incriminate all Americans. After all, Camila's friend, Marion (with the abolitionist lineage), does not hesitate to take Camila home and introduce her to her family. Likewise, Scott Andrews shows a sincere, sentimental interest when he brings his sister Fanny to meet Camila. She, at first, wanted to accuse him of playing with her affections because she is not white:

> Suddenly, there he was ahead of us, S. A. in uniform, walking with an attractive young lady, as fair as he, her arm slipped in his...S. A. turns and takes in the whole family, at a glance. [He can see that they are not white.] I thought he would tighten his hold on his young White goddess, and walk off, but no. He hurried over. "So it *is* you, Camila! What a surprise!" My suspicions were all wrong. The fair companion was his sister Fanny, visiting from Concord. (203–204)

The author seems to indicate that there are individuals whose mindset, in matters of race, can run counter to that of American society in general. She has constructed Camila with the mental attitude of believing that with the exception of a few, it is the policy of society as a whole to reserve for both nonwhite North Americans and nonwhite Hispanics negative treatment:

> Camila thinks of the musicians on stage at the jazz club; how they came in a separate door; how she saw them on crates and eating outdoors when she and Scott left during a break in the music.

They could have been her brothers, especially the one that was light-skinned. (201)

Camila admits to herself that racially she shares much in common with the musicians, even though they are American: "Jazz! She thought jazz was the sassy music of White flappers with boyfriends in fur coats and Model T's. But jazz belongs to us, she thinks, the colored people, as they are called here" (198).

Was it the Dominican Republic that had prepared her to accept the identity of nonwhite, or was it the result of her treatment in the United States? Race in "*la patria*," as Camila calls her homeland, a place where social position or financial strength tend to mitigate the negative effects of an indeterminate racial phenotype, is compared to the racial/ethnic generalizations of the United States:

> "You are not nobody Camila" [Marion scolds]…"Camila's mother was a famous poet. Her father was president. Her brother was the Norton Lecturer at Harvard." Perhaps Marion thinks that…importance will stem the tide of prejudice that often falls on the foreign and colored in this country…How can Marion forget the cross burning on her front lawn that long ago summer when Camila visited the Reed family in North Dakota? (3–4)

Camila accepts the fact that her mother was not white and she makes it obvious that she empathizes with her mother's racial description. She did not like to be told that she looked like Pancho, her father. "She wanted to look like Salomé, the beautiful fantasy mother made up by a London painter" (149). Salomé's race is not open to conjecture. In a scene where Camila's maternal grandmother learns that her daughter, Salomé, has a relationship with Pancho, a suitor, and that it could lead to a more serious liaison, she counsels her:

> "I think you should accept his proposal…there is nothing, nothing that compares with the love of a man…I'll stand by you when the storm starts to blow, for there will be criticism…" [Salomé interjects a thought.] "Because he's so much younger?" [Her mother

replies:] "That, and he is White and we are mixed. His family has money and we have none." (236–237)

Pancho is white, young, and has money. Salomé is of mixed racial heritage, has no money, and is older than he. This combination could materialize into a true dilemma. However, the reader has already been led to understand that Pancho's interest in Salomé is based not on love, but on the fact that she has become nationally recognized as a gifted poet. The merits from her talent and acclaim would compensate for the racial and social imbalance. But then Alvarez carefully plants another symbol for the reader, another item to be considered in the interplay of ethnicity, race, and national awareness. She introduces the question of genotype versus phenotype. Salomé's mother continues advising her daughter:

"Then, of course, there is his Jewish religion…" "But the family has converted," I protested [Salomé interrupts]. Pancho had told me how his Sephardic grandfather had married a Dominican woman, and agreed to raise the children as Catholics. (137)

Central to the coded text/context that the author presents for consideration are the terms Sephardic and Dominican. Both imply an idea of miscegenation that is phenotypically visible. The Sephardim (Sephardic Jew) of Spanish or Portuguese origin is more Mediterranean in appearance and runs the gamut in skin tone from white to a deep, swarthy color. In contrast, the Ashkenazim or German, Polish and Eastern European Jew looks more European. To say that someone married a Dominican woman suggests an ethnic categorization that implies a racial description. Alvarez has carefully integrated the context with textual symbols for race. This becomes evident later in her thematic development when Pancho marries a supposedly white Dominican (after Salomé's demise) and he and his new wife have a son who is not white. At the core of the text is the hypothesis that race mixture in the Dominican individual has a history, is traceable, and operates on a continuum. To clarify and confirm her line of reasoning, the author allows Salomé to demonstrate her awareness of the imbalance between herself and Francisco (Pancho)

Henríquez, on both the social and racial levels, through a conversation that she has with her mother:

> "But mama...what if he finds out that he doesn't love me...?" "[S]hould you fall, you have a great net to catch you." "What net is that?"..."The poems you have written and the ones you will write." (137)

Pancho anticipates that Salomé will add prestige and status to his image because of her poetry. Salomé, reading between the lines of a letter he writes her and concluding that it is not a love letter, understands this:

> On the first day of the New Year, I received a letter from Pancho...Reading it through a first, and then a second time, I admit that I felt disappointed. The letter was three pages long, and not once was love or anything approximating love mentioned...he had come to realize...[that] I was the one poet of our nation who stood a chance of becoming a great poet for all times. (135–136)

Nevertheless, Salomé realizes that Pancho feels that she needs him to provide her with "the light of scientific truth," and [as she admits to herself] "to transfer all the scientific knowledge in his mind to mine" (136). Is this considered to be a gender or a racial slight? Salomé does become "*la musa de la patria*," the muse of the land of her birth (175). Pancho, subsequently, is allowed to become personal secretary to the president of "la patria." As a result, he is seen as an important political figure. Is one surprised to learn that after he has found the key to his success he moves on to other love conquests and marries the phenotype and social figure that he finds equal to his image? Salomé was not blind to Pancho's roving eye, nor was she oblivious to the type of women he preferred. As she says:

> On one occasion, however, he did not see me arrive, and I spotted him talking to Trini Villeta. Have I described Trinidad Villeta? She might have been Pancho's sister with the same rosy skin and dark eyes and black hair, which she wore in silky ringlets at her ears. (131)

Due to his new status, or perhaps because of his status and his political agitation, Pancho is offered a scholarship by the president to study in Paris. He extends his trip beyond the anticipated length of time—his studies are not the reason. Salomé accidentally discovers a letter Pancho writes to his brother wherein he admits to a long love affair in Paris with a French woman, with whom he has a child (231). When he finally returns to the Dominican Republic and to his wife and children, it is the next door neighbor, Tivisita, with whom he begins an affair: "Tivisita with a mass of auburn curls, and the dainty face of a porcelain doll" (265), "and hazel eyes" (279). Alvarez purposely uses these symbols of a genotypic legacy with their resultant phenotypic characteristics to disclose the mindset of Pancho. The construction is intended to dispel all doubt that race (with its subterfuge of color and phenotypic descriptions) is not important in this novel. Thus, it is significant to note that Pancho's paramour in France, Mlle. Chrittia is described as having "curly reddish hair, and grayish eyes" (272). To add more strength to her intention, the author structures her characterization so that Pancho and Tivisita marry within a year after Salomé's death (293) and start a family. The inner voice of the author advises the reader: "The oldest of Papancho's new family has a striking, indigenous look no one can trace to a known ancestor" (290). Pancho's youngest son with Salomé is quick to propose a Taíno connection for his half-brother. It is a suggestion that is coherently weak. However, the reader who has followed the author's logic and symbolism will recall that although Tivisita seems to be genetically monoracial and is phenotypically whiter than Salomé, she is still Dominican. As for Pancho, he too has Dominican ancestry (his grandmother). Nonetheless, he is phenotypically white. Which of the two, Tivisita or Pancho, is responsible for the non-Caucasoid traits of their child?

Did race matter in the Dominican Republic of the late nineteenth century, the era in which Alvarez's novel is set? If not race, were there particular phenotypes that were more preferable? To find the answers to these questions, one should note how Alvarez carefully leads the reader through a maze of encoded symbols that propose a discourse on racial theory in Dominican society. In this novel, there is a fusion of language and words as symbols. There is also the nonlinguistic system of attitudes and images associated with the meanings determined by the society in which they are used. This conforms to the common concept of reception theory, in which a meaning is not seen as a nondynamic property of a text, but is instead understood to be the result of the relationship between the creative project and its aesthetic realization by the reader. That is to say, the reader accepts no creative work passively. He or she interprets a text's meaning based on his or her individual cultural background. In essence, the author's intent is not obviously inherent within the text, but is created in the relationship between the text and the reader. For this reason, descriptions are fundamental for a complete comprehension of the author's aesthetics. Physical indications that imply race or phenotype are necessary for arriving at the realization of Salomé as symbolic of the author's literary "persona" and the reality of similar "personae" within the perimeters of Dominicanness or the aesthetics associated with a Dominican identity.

There are two protagonists in the novel: Salomé and her daughter, Camila. Camila accepts herself as someone who is not white, but she is introduced to the reader as a woman of indeterminate race. Alvarez covertly constructs a bloodline for the two protagonists, Camila and Salomé, that strongly suggests the relationship between genetics and phenotype:

The Great-Grandmother (Salomé's great-grandmother; Camila's great-great-grandmother):

> Gregoria herself, [Salomé's mother] was pale enough, and though she spoke of her grand-papa from the Canary Islands, all you had to do was look over her shoulder at her [Gregoria's] grandmother and draw your own conclusions. (19)

Grandmother (Gregoria's mother, Salomé's grandmother, Camila's great-grandmother): "Salomé and her sister Ramona were told by their White paternal grandmother that they looked like their maternal grandmother" (23).

Mother (Gregoria [Manina], Salomé's mother, and Camila's grandmother): "The marriage between Salomé's mother and father had been acceptable enough to his family...Gregoria herself was pale enough... but her grandmother?" (19).

Salomé (obviously not white): "The two of us [Salomé and her sister Ramona] with some color to our skin must have looked like somebody's chaperones" (129). After Salomé dies, Camila questions what she looked like. Ramona tells her: "Your mother was much darker, for one thing...." "As dark as me?" Camila wants to know. "Darker, Pedro's color with the same features." Camila, although light-skinned, is still not as white as her father's new wife and her half-brothers (281).

Camila: She is supposed to be more attractive than her mother...though she has never known if this is a euphemism for "Whiter, paler, more Caucasian in her looks" (204). Camila falls in love with an artist in Cuba: "I had fallen in love with the artist, his intensity, Africa in his skin—the things that connected me to my mother, not to him" (349).

Salomé's status as a miscegenated individual had been confirmed for her in no uncertain terms. It was her mother who advised her to accept Pancho's proposal and ignore the criticism that would surely come, because "he is White, and we are mixed" (137). On other occasions, Alvarez points out for the reader the physical traits in Salomé that highlight what her mother had confirmed: "Africa in her skin and hair" (94), "a broad nose" (87), and that "her hair still has an unruly kink" (105). Unlike the characterization of the women, the men (in the schematic outline that one finds when culling through Alvarez's symbols) are not identified overtly either as black or miscegenated. There is a strong suggestion, however, of the possibility that they may be white, if not genetically, at least phenotypically.

After Salomé's death and Pancho's entry into politics, he, his second wife, and all of his children go into exile in Cuba. The question of race becomes somewhat attenuated. Class and social position are given more importance. Nonetheless, Camila seems conditioned to see the world in binary terms of individuals who are white and those who are not, as if she had been psychologically conditioned in the Dominican Republic to make these observations. In Cuba, she meets Domingo, an artist who was asked to make a sculpture of her father after his death. She describes the artist as "a large mulatto with a handsome, big-featured face," who has "a voice that could sing a beautiful *Othello*, rich and full" (148). The juxtaposition of "handsome mulatto" and "Othello" are further additions to the author's system of codes to summon the reader's attention to the artistic creation of racial concepts. Alvarez seems to be following the plan that in order for a code or codes to be understood in literature (or a text), there must be factors of common access between the writer and the reader—for example, social context + denotation > connotation + social comprehension—versus an intellectual understanding void of its cultural meaning(s). Not all readers, it would seem, are able to decode a text to arrive at an interpretation and evaluation of its meaning. One might understand what is said (denoted), but to determine what is meant (connoted) requires peeling away layers of social context for a cognitive understanding.

In this light, it should be indicated that Domingo is part of the continuum of the racial environment that had been so pervasive in Camila's life in the Dominican Republic. Although Domingo is Cuban and they are in Cuba, race and phenotype establish a bond between the two that she could not form with Scott Andrew, the white North American. Camila feels a sense of trust that allows her to confide in Domingo that her mother, "the national poet…at thirty married a young White man from a prominent family" (160). She does not vacillate in telling him about Salomé, with "the full-lipped mouth, and the broad nose that the London based artist restructured to become aquiline, [and about] the discernible kink at the hairline in her tightly gathered hair. She derives satisfaction in talking about these things with Domingo" (160). Yet it would have been out of character for her to demonstrate this same kind of ethnic bond with Scott Andrews. As a matter of fact, the relationship between Camila and the Cuban sculptor rises to a level of confidence and trust that allows her to submit to him sexually, despite her ambivalent feelings about intimacy with men. Submission to Domingo becomes an act of feeling sheltered. He is a haven from the outside whirlwind of incomprehension (166). Their ethnic connection creates a comfort zone that acts to intertwine both their racial and political elements. The reader has already learned how an awareness of shared miscegenation has brought them together. Subsequently it is shown that the sculptor likewise empathizes with Camila's political causes: "Let me know how I [can] help you...I [would] like to join you...There is more to [my] life [than] art, Camila" (159).

Race is not the only context in the novel *In the Name of Salomé*, nor is it the only code available to the reader for a complete understanding of the novel. It is, however, part of a whole that provides the reader with a better understanding of the novel's integrity; better said, it enables the reader to decode the author's artistic honesty with greater accuracy. Undoubtedly, a concept of racial identity with a focus on national awareness addresses artistic concerns for Alvarez, much the same as encoding the Dominican Republic's political direction. She embeds historical data, imagery, and social occurrences with a focused accuracy that includes political facts about the time period of the novel. Her perspective includes not only Cuba, but also the Dominican Republic's relationship with the United States. This last aspect suggests a researched awareness of concepts of race in the United States as they relate to the Dominican Republic. With a stream of consciousness approach, she advises the reader that:

> President Grant to our north was sending a commission of American senators to study the idea of buying off part of the island and shipping some of their own Negro people to live here. A group calling itself the Ku Klux Klan was burning crosses in front of those Negro people's houses, so maybe they wouldn't mind coming. (61)

There is the inference that Salomé felt comfortable being nonwhite in the Dominican Republic of that era, and that perhaps others who were not white would enjoy the same security of person as she. As a matter of fact, U.S. history does show that one of President Ulysses S. Grant's most cherished projects was the annexation of Santo Domingo (former legal name of the Dominican Republic). He submitted his idea to the U.S. Senate by means of a treaty on January 10, 1870. This treaty was contingent on legislation to be passed by Congress to intervene in the persecution of U.S. black people by the Ku Klux Klan. The result was the Enforcement Act that strengthened the 14th and 15th Amendments. The central theme of Grant's proposal was designed to attract American investment to Santo Domingo, and to consider it as a place to send some U.S. blacks. In 1871 he appointed a commission (the Santo Domingo Commission) to study the feasibility of this action. It is interesting to note that the assistant secretary of this commission was the famous black civil rights activist and abolitionist, Frederick Douglass. Furthermore, when one studies the historical facts relevant to the author's spatial concerns and the time frame of her novel, one learns that she has made subliminal references to race and national awareness that are not overtly expressed but seem to be covertly understood. Research is undoubtedly an integral part of Alvarez's creative force. Take, for example, the black leader Frederick Douglass. According to history, by 1875 his son Charles Redmond Douglass had been appointed American consul in Puerto Plata, Santo Domingo. It was to Puerto Plata that Salomé retired to recuperate from an illness. A group of prominent nonwhite North Americans were living in the area during the time period of the novel. In addition to the Douglasses, a pioneering black American medical doctor by the name of Sarah Loguen Fraser was also a part of Puerto Plata's social scene. From her biography, one learns that in the spring of 1883 she was certified to practice medicine in Santo Domingo, but by law her patients were limited to women and children. Surprisingly, an African American woman was that country's first female physician. Her family prospered and enjoyed the company of political friends in high places, such as President Ulises Heureaux and General Gregorio Luperón (Luft, "Sarah Loguen Fraser, M.D., Class of 1876"). Perhaps it was because of their relationship with the latter that Loguen Fraser and her husband named their Dominican-born daughter Gregoria. Both Heureaux and Luperón are prominent black statesmen in Dominican history and are mentioned in Alvarez's novel. The literary vignettes of Alvarez seem to suggest that an anti–nonwhite climate against Dominican blacks, as such, was nonexistent. Evidently, American blacks with skills, education, and money shared this same atmosphere of racial neutrality. Dr. Loguen Fraser and her husband, a prosperous pharmacist in Puerto Plata, were accepted into the best social circles. Although Sarah Loguen Fraser died in the United States in 1933 and was buried in Washington, D.C.,

> ...in Puerto Plata, Dominican Republic, the Catholic Church held a high Mass [in her honor] and flags were hung at half-mast for nine days to mourn her death. Wreaths and flowers were placed on her husband's grave in remembrance of Dr. Loguen Fraser, the country's first woman doctor. (LeClair 123)

Yet, contrary to the acceptance of Dr. Loguen Fraser and her wealthy husband, there likely were anti-Haitian feelings during this period. This sentiment is subtly expressed by Torres-Saillant in his *Introduction to Dominican Blackness*:

> Dominicans commemorate the War of Restoration, fought against white Spaniards, with as much fervor as they do the War of Independence, fought against black Haitians. And the black General Luperón, who helped to restore the nation's sovereignty, inspires as much respect and admiration as the white creole Juan Pablo Duarte, the ideological founder of the Republic. Another salient figure of the Restoration War, [is] the black Ulises Heureaux, whose heroic exploits against the imperial Spanish army gained him national prestige [...]. (16)

This comment by Torres-Saillant corroborates Alvarez' thesis. In one section of the novel, she intimates this benign attitude toward some blacks with references to President Grant's realization of "Negro" persecution and the fact that some "Negro" people might like being sent to Santo Domingo to live. After all, the country did have a black person in the presidency. With this thought, she makes it appear that race relations in the United States were known to the Dominicans of that era and that associations between the races were not a problem unless it referred to the despised Haitians. Nonetheless, there was certainly a pigmentocracy in place that the author carefully encodes by means of relationships: that is, through Camila's maternal lineage and their spouses. Likewise, there are examples of native Dominican characters who, if one relies on the description of their phenotype, might be considered miscegenated. In this sense, the author employs the use of code words such as mixture, mulatto, a dusting of cinnamon, light-skinned, darker-skinned than, Africa in her skin (a hint of), indeterminate race, and so forth. These codes are offered by means of a nonintrusive comparison with white individuals, both native and nonnative. Her descriptive technique leaves no doubt as to her artistic intent: pale, color of fresh milk, rosy skin, and so on. North American individuals who are nonwhite, however, are referred to as "Negro" or "colored," and, rather infrequently, as "light-skinned." The one instance where there is an overlap of a Dominican and North American ethnic/phenotypic description is when a black American person reminds Camila of her brothers:

> Pedro and Max have turned out to be the sons who look most like Salomé's side of the family, darker-skinned, a kink in their hair, all the telling features....Camila thinks of the musicians on stage at the jazz club....They could have been her brothers, especially the light-skinned saxophone player. (201)

Here, there are explicit references to skin tone. In other instances, the jazz musicians are referred to as "colored people" (198) or with other ethnic/racial terminology: "the large Negro is playing the piano" (198). Certainly, bicultural Alvarez is conscious of the fact that in the United States the term "Negro" refers to an ethnic/racial classification, and was synonymous with "colored" during the time period of her story. Neither refers to a specific phenotype. American blacks were and still are seen as an ethnic/racial group regardless of their genotype (racially mixed) or phenotype (brown, light brown, reddish, etc.). The illusive one-drop rule is still standard fare in the warped racial psychology of most North Americans. The question posed is: Where are the black Dominicans, or those who are only slightly miscegenated, within the racial perspective of Alvarez's novel or in the author's reasoning? They are there, but the author's approach requires the reader to be familiar with Dominican history in order to decode their presence.

In the novel, one finds that the following are some of the symbols that tend to fill in the gaps on phenotype and national awareness:

> In May 1881 [President] Meriño abolished all civil rights...anyone caught bearing arms would be shot on the spot. [He] and his general Lilís [Ulises Heureaux] were deadly serious...Lilís had made Pancho the godfather to his firstborn. (181–185)

It is known that at one point in Dominican history, Ulises Heureaux had been Meriño's Minister of the Interior, and then succeeded him in 1882 as the elected president. He remained in office for seventeen years, holding the post on two separate occasions. Hubert Herring, in *A History of Latin America*, describes him as "the Negro Ulises Heureaux...tall, erect, and handsome...well educated, fearless, and versatile" (446). This North American historian is culturally programmed to make mention of Heureaux's race as an unavoidable necessity. Conversely, Alvarez, in her novel, makes no allusion to the race of this character. Nor does she supply him with a color description or specific phenotype as she does with other characters. The history surrounding this black president of Santo Domingo is well known. Sources advise that he was the "illegitimate son of a Haitian merchant" (Rogers 280). It is a fact that he knew the historical Salomé Ureña in real life and was familiar with her poetry. It is likewise traceable that he traveled in the circle of prominent black North Americans who lived in his country at the time, such as Sarah Loguen Fraser (Luft, "Sarah Loguen Fraser, MD (1850 to 1933)" 152). Are readers who are not familiar with Dominican history supposed to pass over the Ulises Heureaux symbolism even though it is one of racial contrast? In the accumulative sense, omission of his phenotype tends to clarify the author's position on race—that is, the Dominican Republic seems to be ignorant of its historical past where the race of important statesmen is a feature of their image.

Another coded figure who does not possess the characteristics of whiteness and who is based on a real person in Dominican letters is Gaston Deligne. Alvarez, in her construction, arranges for him to meet Salomé's boat when it stops in San Pedro de Macoris while she is on her way to Puerto Plata to recuperate: "He was dark-skinned, with...dark liquid eyes...Salomé felt that he was a gifted poet" (305). His biographers confirm that he was born in Santo Domingo and spent his later years in San Pedro de Macoris, where he is still celebrated as an outstanding poet. Alvarez only hints at his race—"dark-skinned"—without an overt ethnic classification. Was it his class that caused her to vacillate? Or is she being both specific and sensitive to the Dominican approach to phenotype and national awareness? Or is "dark" in this case equivalent to "*moreno*," in the Dominican cultural sense, and the connotation of this skin tone description is lost in the English translation? The novel was originally written in English. An interpretation into Spanish can confuse the cultural vagary of a symbol, especially when its use is literary. For example, Salomé says that she and her sister Ramona used to sing the following ditty, which evidently is part of Dominican folklore (Stinchcomb 7):

> I was born Spanish
> by the afternoon I was French
> at night I was African
> What will become of me!

Since Alvarez does not supply the reader with the Spanish counterpart for these lines (to accompany the original English), one questions how the following symbols are to be interpreted. Does Spanish only refer to "*española*" or is it a synonym for white? Does French mean "*francesa*" from Europe, or "*haitiana*" from black Haiti? Finally, by African, is this to be an interpretation of "*africana*" or "*negra*"? In the novel, there is a temporal context that may clarify the perception within its cultural parameter. The background offered is explained as: "We had fought off an invasion from Haiti, and soon we would fight a war with Spain" (*In the Name of Salomé* 13). The relationship of Africa to night is beyond a doubt symbolic as well as metaphoric. However, the Spanish-Haitian-African image does appear in the real, historical world of Dominicans as viable. Many Dominicans overtly and unabashedly retain a Spanish heritage as their racial basis, while they curse the Haitian invasion of 1821 that changed their political identity and for some their complexion. They are not wont to admit having an African admixture, and where not too visible it is denied outright.

In the racial climate of the Dominican Republic of today, it is both pejorative and offensive to openly classify someone as *"negro"* ["black"]. As a matter of fact, Wiarda, in *The Soul of Latin America: The Cultural and Political Tradition*, points out that

> for the Dominicans, it is no longer fashionable or acceptable to define their nationhood in racial terms. So the Dominicans as a nation are currently facing an identity crisis and casting about for a new, nonracial way of identifying their nationhood. (209)

With this in mind, it is interesting to focus on the one person who carries the burden of a definite black identity in the character construction of *In the Name of Salomé*. She is the family's nanny, Regina. The reader is not even sure if she is Dominican, given that she is the least developed of all the characters. What little is learned from her character design results in a figure of folklore: "Regina's skin is so black that whatever she says has to be believed" (320). When Regina speaks, Alvarez appears unsure of her development. Not only is the created "persona" of Regina confusing, it also lacks depth. After affirming that the spoken word of the family's nanny carries strong elements of truth, a few pages later Alvarez confronts the reader with: "'And I remember the day the world was made,' Regina says. Camila cannot tell if her nanny is teasing, because it is dark and she cannot see Regina's face" (322). Blackness, both definitive and concrete, appears to be the sole contributing element that Regina offers the novel's construction. Is she obscure and undeveloped on purpose, much like the black segment in the Dominican cultural and physical realities? It is understood that in Dominican society, racial blackness is not fully explored as a national paradigm, and if considered at all it is void of acceptance. For most Dominicans, Haitians are black and Dominicans are not. This psychological conditioning has developed into a national consensus.

In part, such reactions to race assigned to color must explain the linguistic observance in Dominican speech patterns of "light-skinned" as "*blanco*," or white, and why a dark-skinned Dominican takes strong offense at being called "*haitiano*," or Haitian. As one very dark-skinned informant replied to my question of why the term "*haitiano*" was so insulting: "*En mi caso y debido a mi color, lo percibo como 'prieto sucio'...y yo de prieto no tengo nada. Me pueden decir 'moreno' pero como buen dominicano que soy jamás acepto que me digan 'haitiano'.*" ["In my case, and because of my color, it's the same as being called 'a dirty black nigger'...and I am in no way a black nigger. You can call me 'brown,' but like the proud Dominican that I am, I'll never accept being called 'haitiano'"] (Oral Informant, Dec. 2006. Boca Chica, Dominican Republic).

Does Regina's lack of development transfer her into the proverbial "*doña Tatá*," hidden away in the kitchen? With other characters, Alvarez is sensitive toward miscegenation in the Gestalt patterning of their Dominican ethnicity. They represent a definite confirmation of racial intermixture in the development of the national prototype. Is Regina, who shows no signs of a mixed-race background, just as much a part of the "*patria*" as Heureaux (the son of a Haitian father), Deligne, and Salomé? Given that Dominicans are somewhat superstitious but deny a heritage of blackness, is the audience to question Regina's relationship to the national whole even though she is very black and superstitious? As Torres-Saillant suggests in *Introduction to Dominican Blackness*: "[There are some who] seek to dissociate themselves conceptually from the realm of Blackness [in order] to secure their Dominicanness" (46). Unfortunately, the reader, exposed to the miniscule image of Regina, may come away with the impression that absolute blackness is inconsistent with the concept of being Dominican. In spite of this, there is a covert symbol that appears to link the two female protagonists, either by design or circumstance, to an overlooked, shared relationship with Regina:

> So it is better if Regina stays below deck and...smell[s]...the smelly bottle she brought with her. When Camila puts her nose right against the opening [of the bottle], she smells her mother's room, an odd smell... (320)

The reader is thus faced with the three Dominican daughters of Eve, on a continuum: Regina as the purveyor of culture and ethnicity, Salomé as the transmitter of culture and ethnicity, and Camila as the recipient of culture and ethnicity, received in the name of her mother, Salomé. It has also been pointed out in *Introduction to Dominican Blackness* that for most Dominicans "the legacy of Black Eve remains submerged" (46), and

> While one can say that Dominicans of African descent have for the most part managed to evade the spiritual disfigurement that would come from accepting the tenets of a negrophobic discourse, their deracialized social consciousness and the lack of an education based on the liberatory self-assertion of our Black Eve, has caused them to settle for indifference as a way to deal with race-related questions. (39)

IMMIGRATION, PHENOTYPOCRACY AND NATIONAL IDENTITY IN THE LITERARY CONTEXT

> Dominicans do seem to have developed a mindset toward their African heritage and race that might appear at the surface level to connote an attitude of indifference or ignorance. The reality of being Dominican and not White in the United States, however, makes their reliance on phenotypic gradations somewhat nebulous. Not too surprising, the Dominican society is the pivotal starting point to consider Blackness in the Americas. The first African slaves who were sent to Spain's newly conquered lands entered through a port of the island that is known as Hispaniola, i.e., today's Dominican Republic/Haiti. July 1502 marked the start of the Black experience in this corner of the western hemisphere. The indigenous population, known as Taínos, that met both the Europeans and the Africans, began to die out almost immediately. In turn, Africans soon outnumbered the White colonists. (Torres-Saillant "The Dominican Republic" 110–111)

Today, although bipolar racial categories are predominant in the Dominican Republic, the myth of the Indian as a racial category is presumed in order to assuage an attachment to an African biological heritage:

> Your passport…
> Aquí está [Here it is]
> What is this business of "india clara"? ["light-skinned Indian"]
> ¿Dígame? [What?]
> No but's…
> That is my color. In Santo Domingo we were classified by skin color. I am "india clara," that means, "light Indian"…
> Indian is not a color …
> Pero, [But]
> No but's…Look, I don't have time for this kind of business… (Vicioso 27)

As mentioned in the previous section, to facilitate a self-perception of a prescribed ethnic acceptance, the Dominican government has institutionalized, for its nationals, a mindset with dubious elements of race. Nationally, the word "*indio*" is commonly used to describe the great majority of Dominicans who are slightly or to a greater degree miscegenated. "*Indio*," in this sense, became a skin color descriptor on the national identity card that every adult Dominican was supposed to carry. What was once a slang term became an official category. Also, most Dominicans, it appears, fall within the "*indio*" category. Those with a darker skin tone are labeled "*moreno*." Very few Dominicans are categorically classified "*negro*" or "black" given the negative connotation that this term carries (Sagas 7). As one observer has noted:

> [T]he varieties of skin color and phenotype do not fall into neat groups…Racial terms are by and large highly flexible, and Dominicans describe race with a plethora of color coded terms, ranging from coffee [*color café*], chocolate [*achocolatado*], cinnamon [*color canela*], and wheat [*trigueño*], to indio. (Howard 16)

Haitians are the demographic segment in the Dominican space that carry the burden of "black" as an ethnic indicator. Even Dominican citizenship, when not in jeopardy of summary rescission, might not be issued when solicited by the Haitian-descendant Dominican born within the political entity of the Dominican Republic. This is an action sanctioned by authorized approval, at least at the time of this publication.

Given the broad range of skin-tone classifications, with concomitant hierarchies—for example, white as superior and black as absolutely inferior—there is no doubt that the concept of an approved phenotype has become firmly fixed in the national consciousness (Sagas 7). Does this psychological attachment to skin tone always unfold in the same manner in the literature of Dominicans who immigrate to the United States? Does this national psychology continue in force when their art is created in this country, with a Dominican-oriented context and mindset? Is the style of ethnic/racial conceptualism that one finds in Alvarez considered the norm? Her ideology seems to accept blackness as a description of race, but only as a submerged part of an ethnic Dominican whole, a whole that has been somewhat mitigated.

Loida Maritza Pérez, the author of *Geographies of Home*, was born in the Dominican Republic in 1963 and came to the United States with her family at a very young age. Alvarez was born in New York City in 1950, but was raised almost from birth in the Dominican Republic. She returned to the States in 1960 at the age of ten. Both received their university education in this country, Alvarez at Middlebury and Pérez at Cornell. Both are bilingual and bicultural. This fact is quite evident in the manner in which both writers mold the context in which their theme and language unfold as concrete elements to develop their motif.

Geographies of Home is Pérez's first novel, and based on the many positive reviews by scholars and critics, it has been well received. However, while Alvarez has been tacitly associated with the group of writers classified as "of color" by some reviewers, in her essay "A White Woman of Color," she feels no remorse in declaring: "I am choosing to hold on to my ethnicity and native language even if I can 'pass.' I am choosing to color my Americanness with my Dominicanness even if it came in a light shade of skin color" (148). Pérez, however, seems to have been placed squarely in the camp of writers that identify with the African Diaspora. Her comments indicate that she accepts the placement:

> Our island was the first place on the continent to which African slaves were shipped...We share the blood of common ancestors. Language separates us, but our silence regarding our shared history also divides....We should refuse to be so easily fragmented—even by the unfortunate judgments some of us make of each other. (Esdaille "Same Trip, Different Ships")

What is readily noticeable in *Geographies of Home* is the Dominican *sabor* ["flavor"] that permeates each page. Unlike Alvarez, who stylistically layers *In the Name of Salomé* with different environments that are racially tangent to her story line but geopolitically diverse— the Dominican Republic, the United States, and Cuba—Pérez structures *Geographies of Home* within the closed environ of Brooklyn, New York. She then concentrates the bulk of her action inside the delimitations of a Dominican family unit, as these consanguine members interact with each other. The reader comes away with the feeling of having read a complex, multilayered saga of a poor, immigrant Dominican family transplanted to a poor, immigrant section of a borough of New York. Pérez has admitted that her inspiration to write this novel came from walking through the streets of Brooklyn, Queens, the Bronx, and Manhattan. The familiar smells and sounds of her homeland that she noted (such as the crowing of fighting cocks, etc.) moved her ("Pérez, An Interview"). Yet *Geographies of Home* is not a definitive text. Her intention was, as she says, "to write a narrative wherein I explore the lives of a particular family of specific means, living under specific circumstances. Any attempt to do otherwise would have resulted in stereotypes" ("Pérez, An Interview").

Consequently, one should assume that the manner in which she assigns phenotypic descriptions to each member of the family unit has its basis in the normal development of interaction in an average Dominican setting, and should not be interpreted as contrived or vacuous stereotypes. The candor of this author in assigning ethnic and skin-tone values so overtly contrasts with the subtle approach employed by Alvarez and suggests how ingrained the combination of phenotypology and national identity are in the Dominican psyche. Then again, Pérez's novel is different than Alvarez's in the use of social boundaries. The latter author focuses on a middle-class, highly miscegenated family to express her awareness of phenotypes and their effect on different societies. The artistically designed encounters of Alvarez are guided toward inter- or intra-action among groups more so than between family members. Pérez's characterizations, in contrast, are confined to one particular family, within the limited space that contains the family unit of mother/father/siblings. This arrangement enables her to provide the reader with observations on the family's range of phenotypes and the accompanying motives that assign them hierarchical values within this primary space. While an organization of this type shows cause and effect of action, at times it has the appearance of being psychologically rhetorical. In other words, Pérez, the author, responds to the question of how Dominicans think even before the question is posed. In this way, she uncovers each individual's relationship with others in the family group and makes it possible for the reader to understand what effect phenotype and national identity have on the Dominican society at large. She creates the impression of purposefully dispelling, with her constructs, the myth of a white, Hispanic, Catholic prototype: "The Dominican Republic has always defined itself as a nation in Hispanic terms: White, Catholic, European, Hispanic, Western" (Wiarda 209). For example, when queried on her choice of the Seventh-Day Adventist religion for a significant role in the lives of the family portrayed in *Geographies of Home*, Pérez replies:

> Because Latinos are usually portrayed as Catholic, I wanted to delve into one of the Protestant and increasingly proselytized religions such as that of Jehovah's Witnesses, Seventh-Day Adventist, Mormonism, Pentecostalism, or whatever. Choosing the most restrictive of these religions enabled me to provide more of a contrast with alternate forms of spirituality and folk religions. ("Perez, An Interview")

Protestant religions are certainly atypical as an image marker in Latino/Hispanic characterizations. Folk religions, conversely, are the prototypical examples usually anticipated in this context. Religious practices of this nature are often made to appear fundamental when class and ethnicity are beyond the social pale of the white middle- to upper-class individual with European genotypic ties or aspirations. In the environment that Pérez offers the reader, it is only Aurelia, the mother of the family in *Geographies of Home*, who on various occasions displays spiritual tendencies and practices of a folk nature. Although Aurelia's description infers an indeterminate racial classification, it excludes her from being considered white and middle class. Based on the folk imagery that Pérez has structured in the context, it is certain that a few readers, familiar with the belief system of some Dominicans, will accept it to be normal for Aurelia to keep her newborn daughter's name a secret. In this way, she protects little Marina from a premature death: "So until you turned three and strong, I called you ugly names to ward him [death] off..." (142). This is but one example of a Dominican cultural tendency that is still in use in West Africa today. In a certain sense, it recalls the "naming ceremony" of infants that the Akan of Ghana employ. Although modified, the relationship between the practice of Aurelia and that of the Akan is patent. Researchers have found that there are some tribes in Nigeria that also share Aurelia's habits:

> Almost universally in Africa a child has at least two given names... The Yoruba frequently give an appellation at birth...The first name given is often considered secret lest some supernatural power knowing it could harm the child. Among the Hausa this name is whispered into the ear of the newborn; only a second name is in daily use. (Pollitzer 111–112)

African-Christian syncretic religions in the Dominican Republic may appear to be hidden from general view (Howard 55). It was not a contradiction for Aurelia to attend a Seventh-Day Adventist church with her husband and still adhere to her ethnically oriented traditions. Torres-Saillant affirms that the persistence of a folk religion and other

African-descended practices may indeed be the syncretism inherent in Dominican culture that allows for the coexistence of these forms with other religious expressions of European origin (*Introduction to Dominican Blackness* 22).

Pérez is unequivocal in her assertion that the Dominican Republic does display viable and current proclivities of the black Diaspora. She confirms this in her novel with an approach toward Dominican blackness that is unswerving. It is as if to say that the African Diaspora in the Americas has resulted in many forms of expression, and the Dominican expression is but one of these forms. It is she who reminds us that the bonds of the Diaspora transcend literary icons. Pérez strongly declares that it is through the Diaspora that the blood of many ancestors is shared. "Language separates us, but our silence regarding our shared history also divides" (Esdaille 3), is her strong conviction. Notwithstanding the fact that both Alvarez and Pérez use aspects of phenotypic awareness to strengthen their Dominican theme, when one looks at the racialized overtures of each, there is a difference. Alvarez, on the first page of her novel, begins to integrate her development of phenotypes as a segment of a particular national identity. She does this with some vacillation. The racial identity of her novel's co-protagonist is conjoined with an ethnic image that makes her ethnic sketch imprecise: Southern Italian? A Mediterranean Jew? A light-skinned Negro woman? By contrast, the question of identity makes a determined entry on the first page of the Pérez novel. It is more direct, as she highlights the issue of race more than phenotype. Ethnicity is never a question: "The ghostly trace of 'NIGGER' on a message board hanging from Iliana's door failed to assault her as it had the first time she returned to her dorm room to find it" (*Geographies of Home* 1).

It is not until much later in *In the Name of Salomé* that Alvarez develops Camila's characterization to the point where racial slurs and slights are expected. From then on, the reader is led with full force into a world where race is bifurcated into a cosmos of phenotypic dichotomies: ethnically Dominican, Mexican, Cuban—that is, miscegenated—with Spanish as a native language, or ethnically Afro American, Afro Caribbean, Indigenous Mexican, and so forth. Miscegenation for this group is not discussed and is only briefly illustrated. Pérez's protagonist, Iliana, however, explains the author's position on race and ethnicity in more detail:

> She used to hate the question "Where are you from?"...Few of her classmates knew of the Dominican Republic and several of her Black friends assumed that she claimed to be Hispanic in order to put on airs..."We don't care where you come from! You be Black just like us [claimed the Afro American girls]!" "Nah, you speak Spanish. You one of us," her Puerto Rican friends would say. (190)

As Iliana further comments, her black friends frequently harassed her for hanging out with greasy "spics," and they (the "spics") in turn questioned why she wanted to be in the company of loud-mouthed "spooks" (190–191). Her phenotype placed her undeniably in the group of Afro Americans. Nonetheless, linguistically and culturally, she was classified as another member of the immigrant Hispanic community. But Iliana had not been able to fit comfortably in either group (191). Since Pérez confines her characters to one family unit, how did her protagonist's brothers and sisters react to the dilemma of phenotype and national ethnicity? For purposes of contrast, Pérez uses the image of Laurie, the wife of her brother Gabriel. He preferred white women, and accused black women of being the "ugliest, loudest and most demanding [sexually]" (107). No one in the family, however, seemed to like Laurie—neither Iliana's siblings nor her parents who defended family over everyone else:

> Laurie's green eyes widened. Her face turned a quick red. [S]he glanced at Gabriel, then at his parents, as if expecting them to come to her defense. When no one did, she jerked her head and, whipped her husband with her hair, [as she] stormed out of the room. "Then you wonder why she wants nothing to do with this family," Gabriel exclaimed. "What do you expect if whenever she comes down here someone in this house insults her?" (15)

Zoraida, Iliana's sister, generalizes when it comes to white people:

> Aurelia substituted the reprimand that had been on the verge of leaping off her tongue. Now let's be nice, she said. At least Laurie

> offered to make something. That's more than she's done any other time...Zoraida's mouth remained pursed in obvious distaste. That's White people for you. They offer you something nasty and expect you to be grateful. (268)

This is not to say that this family of different skin tones does not have idealized phenotypic standards:

> [Iliana] noticed that her sisters used language like a weapon to alienate and assault...Marina...was made fun of for her long, wide lips and kinky hair. Beatriz, who was beautiful, was ridiculed for her flat nose. (190)

As is normal for many families from different Hispanic countries and a common occurrence in the Dominican Republic as well, gradations in skin color and shading can run the gamut from deep chestnut brown to light olive. Torres-Saillant claims that because of a history of pervasive racial mixture one can chance upon two Dominican children who legitimately have strikingly different phenotypic characteristics, and yet they will belong to the same nuclear family unit and unhesitatingly identify themselves as biological siblings (*Introduction to Dominican Blackness* 51–52). This is the direction that Pérez follows as if it were indeed a normal manifestation. She artistically introduces the non-Dominican reader to a world where identifying skin tones and other racial characteristics are standard fare in everyday Dominican social interplay. One by one, a description of most of Iliana's siblings and of herself is provided. Although genotypically homogenous as a family, they are disparate in phenotypification.

Iliana:

> Her hair parted at the side and hanging limp, concealed the nut-brown forehead. Her lips, wide as Marina's but the length of Beatriz's, pouted so sullenly that despite chiseled cheeks and a nose her sisters envied as "White" she appeared the ugliest of the three. (41)

Marina:

> Before, she had been able to manipulate her reflection so as to see only her pale skin, shades lighter than any of her sisters and only slightly darker than Gabriel's wife [who is white]. That skin had blinded her to her kinky, dirt-red hair, her sprawling nose, her wide, long lips. (18)

Beatriz:

> Long, black hair curled loosely around her face. Its features, angular and severe enough to lend her a calculated look, appeared carved into the ebony darkness of her skin. (40) [Iliana] had heard even more about the beautiful child Beatriz had been with her dark, dark skin and head full of soft and blue-black curls. (185) Beatriz, who was beautiful, was ridiculed for her flat nose. (190)

Tico:

> Like Marina, he too possessed yellowish skin, a wide nose and long, full lips. (41)

Rebecca:

> [H]er skin yellowish, making her appear anemic…she raised her hand to her head and tucked strands of knotted hair under her hat. (60–61) …the hair she had once habitually straightened with a hot comb so that prospective husbands would believe it was naturally that way. (214)

Nereida:

> She was as light-skinned as Tico, Marina and Rebecca but with the chiseled features and high cheekbones of her darker siblings. (122)

Aurelia (Mother):

> …strands of hair plastered to her forehead…narrow purple lips… her olive skin…gave the impression of being sun kissed even in the midst of winter. (92)

Papito (Father):

> Papito had begun to oil his ashy skin and to slick his hair back with pomade. (153)

Although she has embedded her precise symbols of race identifiers, the author still finds the need to diffuse other characteristics of race so that they appear not as national markers but as spatial incidentals:

> Last of all, Iliana raised her eyes to the enlarged copy of the photo her mother had long ago preserved in one of the family's many albums. The blacks, whites and greys of the copy were so blurred that Aurelia and Papito each appeared to be of *indeterminate race*..." (44; emphasis added)

As shown, the description for Iliana's parents was not as complete as the physical outline offered for their children. The rhetorical question is how two people of "indeterminate race" could have such a wide range of phenotypically different children? With Alvarez, however, one sees that "indeterminate race" in her novel was a requisite marker to mask what might have been an accusatory factor of racial identification: "And these young Yanks (believe me, I have seen them over here) feel much more license with a foreign woman of *indeterminate race*" (*In the Name of Salomé* 244; emphasis added).

Nonetheless, neither author uses phenotype markers, racial consciousness, and ethnic affiliations as a negation of national awareness. On the contrary, they structure these symbols to confirm that ethnicity and race have the tendency to meld into a single unit. A particular phenotype, for these two authors, does not preclude membership in the national unit. A recent study explains that black Dominicans do not see blackness as the central component of their identity. For most, their nationality is valued instead, since this affirms their participation in a culture, a language community, and the sharing of a lived experience (*Introduction to Dominican Blackness* 26–27). A Dominican is Dominican first and then becomes tagged with skin tone and racial characteristics. In the United States, people are, of course, accustomed to the paradigm

An Aesthetic Experience 193

of race/ethnicity, and subsequently to a national affiliation (e.g., Black American, Afro American, White American, Asian American, etc.). To disqualify acceptance into the national unit in the Dominican Republic other factors would also have to be present, such as a deficiency in linguistic dexterity, a tactic once used by Trujillo during his administration, to separate darker-skinned Dominicans from Haitians (Howard 24). Notwithstanding this, and in spite of the absence of a binary approach to racial determination as in the United States (e.g., if not white then black; if not black then white), there is still a subtle bias in the Dominican Republic that favors the person with a fair complexion (Howard 17). The Dominican immigrant to the United States, however, learns that "black" is not an exact skin tone but operates as a racial/ethnic identifier. Pérez clearly shows her comprehension of this awareness with a dialogue that she designs between the protagonist Iliana and her sister Marina. As a defining context, the previous racial and phenotype descriptions for each family member culled from the novel should be referred to. Iliana has a discussion with her sister Marina:

> "Talking about men, have you hooked yourself a gorgeous blue-eyed hunk yet?"..."Blue-eyed wouldn't be my first choice," she [Iliana] muttered.
> "Why? What do you have against White people?"
> "I didn't say I had anything against them. And all Whites aren't blue-eyed." Marina snickered. "A big, Black stud. That's what you want "
> "Yeah." Iliana retorted. "A big-Black-man-with-a-great-big-[****]. What would be wrong with that if I did?"
> "Only that you could do better."
> "Better? What the hell is that supposed to mean?...Look at all your brothers."
> "Look at yourself" [Iliana says to Marina].
> "You're suffering from the same thing they are, thinking anything lighter must be better."
> "Give me a break, Iliana. How many Black people are at your school?"
> Iliana whirled around to face her sister. "What are you saying? That Blacks are inferior? Is that what you think about yourself?"

> "I'm Hispanic, not Black."
> "What color is your skin?"
> "I'm Hispanic!" (38)

The fact had been inculcated in Iliana that one could not assume that being Hispanic precluded the label of being black in the United States. Hadn't her counselors at school advised her while "smiling kindly" not to apply to university? "Besides people outside the city are not like us. Even just upstate they're—well—you know—racist. They won't want you there" (66). If the irony of this advice did not sink in at that moment, it certainly became clearer later on. For more than a year after entering the upstate university, Iliana had lived in such pristine conditions that she was deceived into believing, or wanted so desperately to believe that the abuses of life were a thing of the past, until she heard the word "'NIGGER' erupt from the lips of strangers..." (71).

It is important to stress that neither of the two novels, *In the Name of Salomé* nor *Geographies of Home*, used the concept of phenotype and national awareness as a primary motive. Yet the combination functions as one of the salient thematic concepts of the literary context. Camila, the offspring of Salomé, would have been devoid of depth and dimension without the personal adjuncts of race that identify her Dominican ethnicity. And Pérez, in the construction of her schema, shows that the psychological reaction of one family member toward another must include a consciousness of phenotypes. This phenomenon of color distinctions had been persistently taught from birth and, thus, is displayed in Pérez's characterizations as a normal reaction, sui generis. One could say, therefore, that color consciousness in the author's construction was either the confirmation of an ingrained Dominican awareness or an acknowledgment that the reaction to phenotypic differences is an integral part of being Dominican. Yet, for most students of the Caribbean sociocultural environment, these descriptions of differing pigmentations are not only Dominican but Caribbean cultural reactions to miscegenation, where skin tones are stratified into a hierarchy of acceptance or societal predilection.

The fact remains, nonetheless, that Alvarez and Pérez are Dominican writers. Phenotypic descriptions and designations are important elements in their literary planning. Both forge their individual styles within this perspective to assert that a concept of race and an idealized phenotype are important components in the cultural morphology of the Dominican whole. Their assertion makes use of symbols for genetically, phenotypically, psychologically, and spiritually oriented imagery. This approach should not be misinterpreted as either incrimination or rejection of the "Dominican way" of looking at the abstraction of race. One finds that both authors strive for the same goal. Each, with her own particular style, seeks to explain aspects of "Dominicanness"—that is, Dominican behavior, or perhaps that Dominican cosmovision that remains at the deep structure level of cultural utterances, like the linguistic terminology implies: an underlying marker with an implied meaning. What must be brought to the fore for those that do not share in this cosmovision is a surface structure analysis, or an interpretation of the meaning (i.e., of the assigned marker). In other words, reality (the deep structure) combined with society's interpretation of that reality (surface structure) should be the end result. Empirical observation, in this sense, leads us to conclude that most societies outside the Dominican cultural radius see the "*moreno* to *indio*" Dominican as racially black or black-related, and assign their own cultural meaning to a visual assumption. What the non-Dominican society must understand, according to the literary constructs of Alvarez and Pérez, is that for both authors considerations of phenotypes diffuse the semantic prime of the cultural concept of being black; that is, the context they provide affects the sense of what is said so as to communicate an intended meaning, as opposed to a literal meaning: the nuances of color in a national context. As an involved Dominican observer of race relations, Torres-Saillant has found that

> For Dominicans...to internalize extraneous paradigms of identity would be to disregard the complexity of their own national experience as regards interracial relations....Like...all other peoples dominated by the West, we come from a background that "taught us to experience Blackness as misfortune."...And to pass the test

of our moral strength it behooves us individually and collectively to stand up for what is Black in us as proudly as we do for our Dominicanness. (*Introduction to Dominican Blackness* 61)

Conclusion

"Your passport…"
"…What is this business of 'india clara'?"
"That is my color. In Santo Domingo…I am 'india clara,' that means 'indian'…"
"Indian is not a color…"
"…Look, I don't have time for this kind of business…

Y de hecho, nadie parecía tener tiempo para explicarme este "kind of business," que con tanto trabajo había tenido que internalizar a fuerza de desrizados y de crema Perlita para "aclarar" la piel; a fuerza de escuchar que tenía que casarme con un hombre blanco para "mejorar la raza"…por una terrible equivocación genética, o alguna venganza oculta, mi hermana y yo habíamos salido "indias claras" como mi padre, que realmente no era indio sino jabao, es decir, blanco,[9] *más bien rojizo, pero con el pelo "malo" y algunas pecas.*

Pero, es que en Santo Domingo no quedan indios! Me decían azorados mis amigos "indios" de Centro y Sur América…

Sí, pero es que allá estamos clasificados así. Yo soy india clara, si fuera más oscura fuera india-india y "si no tuviera remedio" fuera india-canela…

¿Y los negros?

Bueno, normalmente le pagan unos pesos al tipo de la cédula de identidad para que ponga "indio-canela" donde dice color…

¡Ah! (Vicioso 27)

(And as a matter of fact, no one seemed to have the time to explain "this kind of business" to me which I had taken so much effort to internalize through the force of hair straighteners and Perlita cream "to lighten" my skin, after constantly hearing that I had to marry a white man in order "to push the race ahead, lighten it up"… due to some terrible genetic mistake, or some occult revenge, my sister and I had come out "a light Indian color" like my father, who actually was not Indian but *jabao*-colored,[10] that is, white, or rather reddish, but with "bad" hair and some freckles.

"But, in Santo Domingo there are no longer any Indians!" My Indian friends from Central and South America would tell me, somewhat flustered.

Yes, but that's the way we are classified there. I am light Indian color, if I were darker, I might be Indian-Indian and "if there were no other way out" I would perhaps be a cinnamon-colored Indian...

And the Blacks?

Well, normally they give a few pesos to the guy in charge of the I.D. cards so that he'll write in "cinnamon-colored Indian" where it says color...

Oh!)

As the quote from Sherezada Vicioso shows, non-Dominicans become somewhat confused with the Dominican in-group approach to phenotypic descriptions. Consequently, through examples from the creative literature of Alvarez and Pérez, what this study has attempted to show is how race, phenotype, and national origin have become an integrated unit in the Dominican psyche. With both artists, these concepts give rise in their works to a prescription for racial characteristics that follow the national standards for those who look or do not look like a "native." In the Dominican Republic, it is commonplace to hope that the precepts of miscegenation will tilt more toward the diminution of a visible African admixture. The examination of two major examples of literature by Julia Alvarez and Loida Maritza Pérez shows, perforce, that race mixtures are foregone conclusions in character patterning. In Alvarez, the process was used to provide dimension in characterization and suggest a particular phenotype as a subset of the principal leitmotif. For Pérez, race mixture not only confirmed (in her terms) the gamut of phenotypes that Dominicans expect and accept in a close-knit family grouping, but the manner in which she considers this idea also affirms the Dominican relationship with its national culture of phenotypes. It is noticed that both authors employ a cultural mindset that presents them as writing within a true Dominican context. As Alvarez has said in an interview: "I write to find out what I'm thinking. I write to find out who I am. I write to understand things" (Requa). While each writer presents degrees of comprehension of the national behavior where a nonwhite phenotype is concerned, neither claims outright the notion that to be Dominican precludes an African genotypic heritage. They understand that it is this background that controls variations in skin color and facial characteristics in the national prototype. While the final quote from the creative work of Vicioso was not the major emphasis of this examination, it is concluded that she, as a Dominican writer, also confirms the conclusion that can be deduced from focusing on the works of Alvarez and Pérez: that it is deeply embedded in the Dominican psyche not to appear to be too African in phenotype. As indicated at the beginning of this study, such prescribed notions often result in desired or imagined standardized characteristics for a nation.

Works Cited

Alvarez, Julia. *In the Name of Salomé*. New York: Penguin Putnam, Inc., 2001. Print.

———. "A White Woman of Color." *Half and Half: Writers on Growing Up Biracial and Bicultural*. Ed. Claudine Chiawei O'Hearn. New York: Pantheon Books, 1998. Print.

Balaguer, Joaquin. *Historia de la literatura dominicana*. Buenos Aires: Guacalupe, 1972. Print.

Bezuidenhout, Ilze. "A Discursive-Semiotic Approach to Translating Cultural Aspects in Persuasive Advertisements." Web. 16 Apr. 2002.

Chandler, Daniel. "Semiotics for Beginners: Encoding/Decoding." Web. 11 Mar. 2008.

Comas, Juan. *Las razas humanas*. México, D. F.: Secretaría de Educación Pública, 1946. Print.

Esdaille, Milca. "Same Trip, Different Ships. Dominican Authors and African Americans." *Black Issues Book Review*, March 2001. Interview online. Web. 7 May 2002.

Grano de Oro, Mayda. "Dominican Republic." *Black World: News and Views of the Black World*. Web. 13 Nov. 2001.

Gutiérrez, Franklin. *Evas Terrenales: Biobibliografías de 150 autoras dominicanas*. Santo Domingo: Comisión Permanente de la Feria del Libro, 2000. Print.

Herring, Hubert. *A History of Latin America: From the Beginning to the Present*. New York: Alfred A. Knopf, 1972. Print.

Howard, David. *Dominican Republic: A Guide to the People, Politics and Culture*. New York: Interlink Publishing Group, 1999. Print.

Jiménez, R. Blas. *Exigencias de un cimmarón (en sueños)*. Santo Domingo: Editora Taller, 1987. Print.

LeClair, M. K., J. D. White, and S. Keeter. *Three 19th-Century Women Doctors: Elizabeth Blackwell, Mary Walker and Sarah Loguen Fraser.* Syracuse, NY: Hofmann Press, 2007. Print.

Luft, Eric v. d. "Sarah Loguen Fraser, M.D., Class of 1876: The College of Medicine's First African-American Woman Physician." *Alumni Journal Syracuse Medical Alumni Association* (Summer 1998): 14–17. Print.

———. "Sarah Loguen Fraser, MD (1850 to 1933): The Fourth African-American Woman Physician." *Journal of the National Medical Association.* 92.3 (Mar 2000): 149–153. Print.

Pérez, Loida Maritza. *Geographies of Home.* New York: Penguin Putnam, Inc. 1999. Print.

———. Geographies of Home. "An Interview with Loida Maritza Pérez." Reading Guides. Web. 10 May 2007.

Pollitzer, William S. *The Gullah People and Their African Heritage.* Athens: The University of Georgia Press, 1999. Print.

Requa, Marny. *The Politics of Fiction.* Web. 26 Apr. 2002.

Rogers, Joel A. *World's Great Men of Color.* Volume 2. New York: Simon and Schuster. Touchstone Edition, 1996. Print.

Sagas, Ernesto. "A Case of Mistaken Identity: Antihaitianismo in Dominican Culture." Web. 10 May 2007.

———. *Race and Politics in the Dominican Republic.* Gainesville: University Press of Florida, 2000. Print.

Stinchcomb, Dawn F. *The Development of Literary Blackness in the Dominican Republic.* Gainesville: University Press of Florida, 2004. Print.

Torres-Saillant, Silvio. "The Dominican Republic." *No Longer Invisible: Afro-Latin Americans Today.* Ed. Minority Rights Group. London: Minority Rights Publications, 1995. 109–138. Print.

———. *Introduction to Dominican Blackness*. New York: Dominican Studies Working Papers Series 1 (1999): 1–72. Print.

Venezuela Information Office. "Afro-Venezuelans and the Struggle Against Racism." Web. 20 Sept. 2007.

Vicioso, (Chiqui) Sherezada. "Dominicanyorkness: A Metropolitan Discovery of the Triangle." *La literatura dominicana al final del siglo: Diálogo entre la tierra natal y la diáspora*. Ed. Daisy Cocco Filippis. New York: Dominican Studies Working Papers Series 2 (1999): 1–94. Print.

Wiarda, Howard J. *The Soul of Latin America: The Cultural and Political Tradition*. New Haven, CT: Yale University Press, 2001. Print.

Introduction to Essay IV

Whether it is the prescient spiritual image of the "*fuku*" presence that Junot Diaz weaves into the construction of *The Brief Wondrous Life of Oscar Wao*, or the phenotypic changes that undergird the literary format of *In the Name of Salomé* by Julia Alvarez, there is an undeniable constancy that coalesces these works with others in the ever-growing canon of literature that articulates the Afro Latin image in the Spanish- and Portuguese-speaking Americas. The reader senses an unbreakable ligature that bonds them to identification with Africa, be it implicit or explicit, psychological or physical. Africa, perforce, becomes a comprehensive locus to which the Latin author can return (or begin) for an aesthetic impulse, an aesthetic direction, or an aesthetic truth. It appears, nonetheless, that this "going home" to a symbolic motherland remains physically unreachable; yet, for some authors it is ever present mentally. Both Diaz and Alvarez, as shown in the preceding essays, used the technique of an atmospheric Africa to give depth to their characterization in context. Perhaps the question of an Africa that remains perceptual but does not appear physically stems from an understanding that neither fictive characters nor the authors that design them are decidedly all "black" or all "white" in the ethnoracial evolution of their literary ambience or in the national environment that provides the self-identification of the author.

There is, in this sense, no denying that the Latin world functions within the concept of *"mestizaje"*—"mixed-race"—which has become intrinsic to its philosophies and is carried over to the aesthetics of its art forms, especially the literary arts. While an awareness of Africa's presence in the Latin environment is not new knowledge, the fact is still approached with skepticism, doubt, and with some reluctance to accept by many Latinos/Hispanics and most North Americans in particular. In a published debate in July 2009, it was contended that scholarly studies on Afro Latin America overpowered an equal amount of study on *mestizo* America. Following this statement, it was noted: "[t]his emphasis has resulted in a lopsided picture of how race functions in the region. This is especially noteworthy as the majority of countries in Latin America are *not* part of Afro Latin America" (Sue 1063). In spite of that researcher's conclusion, as early as 1915 the African American scholar/activist W. E. B. Du Bois had published a learned and practical view of the African contribution to Latin American life. Du Bois was even aware of some Africans being sent back to the Continent as penalty for mutinous acts against slavery. While not exactly hidden, the contemporary public at large is slowly being reapprised of the irrefutable verity of an African presence all across the Americas. In addition, Du Bois quotes from an even earlier study (H. H. Johnston, *The Negro in the New World* [1910]) that

> at the present moment there is scarcely a lowly or highly placed federal or provincial official at the head of or within any of the great departments of state [in Latin America] that has not more or less Negro or AmerIndian blood in his veins. (Du Bois 98–99)

Although some (both Latin natives and non-natives) are wont to ignore this genetic fact, others find reason to weave the perspective into the creative literature of their area:

El blanco que tuvo abuela
tan prieta como el carbón
Nunca de ella hace mención
Aunque le peguen candela
Y a la tía Doña Habichuela
Como que era blanca vieja
de mentarla nunca deja
Para dar a comprender
Que nunca puede tener
"El negro tras de la oreja."
(Juan Antonio Alix "*El negro tras de la oreja*")

(The white person with the grandmother
As black as a piece of coal
Would never make mention of her
Even if at the stake he would burn
Yet Doña So-and-So, his aunt
From a supposedly long line of whites
Is always and constantly mentioned
So as to confirm to all
That he could never be one of those
"With traces of blackness behind the ears.")

One cannot conclude that Juan Antonio Alix, a Dominican poet, necessarily limits his observations to his particular portion of the Latin sphere. At both the surface structure as well as the deep structure levels, the concept would be understood by a majority of native Spanish speakers. Most countries, however, have their own creative version of the same perspective. Andrés Eloy Blanco (discussed in Essay I) saw national considerations of race through his imagery of a native artist's deliberate "nonfocus" on the black people in the country they shared:

Si sabes pintar tu tierra/Así has de pintar tu cielo [If you know how to paint your homeland/That's how you should paint your heaven] ...*acuérdate de tu pueblo/Y al lado del angel rubio/Y junto al angel trigueño/Aunque la Virgen sea blanca/Píntame angelitos negros* [...remember your people/And alongside the blond angel/And together with the tan-colored angel/Even though the Virgin may be white/Paint, for me, some little black angels].

It is interesting to note that during the structuring of these verses, the poet opted for a dichotomy of white and black. However, at the end, the poet offers the listener/reader a truer image of the inherent ethnicity of "the people" [*tu pueblo*]: a blond angel, a tan-colored angel, and a black angel. Suffice it to say that in most Latin American countries, the "*trigueño*" or tan phenotype is accepted as a nonblack/or nonwhite entity. Given the social context, it may also be a euphemistically veiled insinuation of blackness, blackness with the possibility of some *mestizaje*, or mixture. For the poet Blanco, however, "*trigueño*" is not an amorphous ethnoracial concept, but a deliberate implication of race mixing.

Mestizaje in Latin America is not a new concept, nor is it uniform in its presentation in literature—or even in real life. One is reminded, in this respect, that literature takes a cue from real life. The concept of biracialism and/or multiracialism can be aesthetically presented either positively or negatively depending on the author's point of view. One can be mestizo with African roots or mestizo with Amerindian roots, although some would like to reserve the term to refer exclusively to the Amerindian/European mixture. Would this be a subtle rejection of the African and European or African and Amerindian genetic assimilation? The Dominican American novelist Julia Alvarez insightfully addresses this Latin problematic by openly declaring to her interviewer a lack of remorse in holding on to her ethnicity and native language even if she could "pass" (see Essay III). For her, there was no vacillation in admitting that her Americanness was colored with Dominicanness—the possibility of having nonwhite genes—albeit in a skin color of a lighter shade. This last consideration is the decisive component. In a January 2, 2009, interview on National Public Radio, in the segment entitled "Morning Edition," Laura Restrepo, a Colombian novelist, journalist, and political activist, responds to a question regarding her and the Colombian people's solidarity with President Obama in terms of race and ethnicity:

> We're sort of white; sort of black...a mixture of bloods. If you would see my skin, it's *whitish*, but not so much....We have Indian blood; we have Black blood. And then there's...plenty

of people...that are Black and that are Indian down here and... would belong to this mestizo race...And of course we see each other very close to a Black man like President Obama. We do feel that this is our victory. (Print copy of interview furnished by NPR; emphasis added)

It is in Restrepo's novel, *La novia oscura* [The Dark Bride], that the reader finds the dynamics of *mestizaje* from the author's personal reality factored into the construct of her artistic reality. The protagonists—Todos los Santos, of black and European heritage with white skin coloring, and Sayonara, the exotic, brown-complexioned beauty, offspring of a Guahibo Indian woman and a European descendant—are clearly designed to be representative of Restrepo's ethnoracial point of view with regard to the mixing of races. The competition between the two principal characters is based more on age and experience—both are prostitutes—than on the concept of "colorism" and racial superiority. Todos los Santos, the elder of the two women, befriends Sayonara with a maternal affection.

At the other extreme are the effects of the Spanish and African mixtures that are found in the Cuban space of Pedro Pérez-Sarduy's *Las Criadas de la Habana* [The Maids of Havana] in Essay II. References to miscegenation in Cuba abound in this novel, with repeated mention of diverse phenotypes that are the result of interracial relationships. Recall, in particular, Pérez-Sarduy's allusion to the character Basilia with built-in ethnic descriptors: "*Me preguntó Basilia, una sirvienta mulata jabá de pelo malo-malo...*" [Basilia, a light-skinned mulatta servant girl with exceptionally kinky hair, asked me...] (116). Such a reference is considered normal fare for the ethnic context in which the image is constructed (i.e., the national context for this description is Cuba and the depiction conforms to the psycholinguistic norm of the space). In contrast to the language used for Basilia, Restrepo in *La novia oscura* has another miscegenated Colombian character who is presented with a slightly opaque image when it comes to her ethnicity: "*...la señora Albita Lucía...pelo rojo crespo...una pecosa abundante y vivaracha de piel blanca...*" [Mrs. Albita Lucia...red, kinky hair, white skin with freckles, full-figured and lively...] (220). This is the same contextual image as Basilia from Cuba, where the African traits are more pronounced in the "hair quality." The effect of the imagery depends in large measure on how in tune the reader is with ingroup standards for race and ethnicity in a given Latin community. For example, the Dominican Republic does not transcribe "whiteness" with the same characteristics as Colombia. In this study, one ethnic description responds to the aesthetics of an African-descendant Cuban writer and the other conforms to the aesthetic requisites of a "whitish" Colombian author. Notice the latter's academic approach to her focus on the character's "whiteness" in the construction of the fictive persona's name: "Albita," etymologically rooted in the Latin lexicon "alba" (white, a white precious stone), and "Lucía," evolved from the Latin root "lux," as in light, sunlight. The imagery of neither the Cuban nor the Colombian author is aesthetically misconceived when considering both characters' ethnic morphology of skin color and hair quality. It is a given that *"crespo"* is the most common term to indicate hair that shows genetic African characteristics. As Blas Jiménez affirms in his poem "Pelo-Pelo-Pelo" ["Hair-Hair-Hair"]:

> *Mi pelo*
> *crece en mi piel*
> *piel negra*
> *mi pelo*
> *pelo que llevo en el cráneo*
> *pelo negro*
> ....
> *pelo que no se lo lleva el viento*
> ....
> *pelo bueno del negro*
> ....
> *filamento crespo*
> *filamento+filamento+filamento*
> *crea mi buen pelo*
> *un pelo crespo*
> *un pelo en afro*
> *un pelo de negro*
> *mi pelo.* (excerpted from *Exigencias de un cimarrón*)

(My hair
grows from within my skin
black skin
my hair
hair that's from my skull
black folks' hair
. . . .
hair that doesn't flow with the wind
. . . .
black folks' good hair
a kinky strand
strand+strand+strand
creates my good hair
hair that's kinky
an Afro type of hair
a black folks' hair
my hair.)

As shown, Africa's role in the overall ethnoracial composition of the Latin American scene can be overt or underplayed and psychological or physical for the creative artist. It depends on the artistic emphasis whether the relevant depiction of phenotypes may elude some observers, especially the non-native not accustomed to the culturally oriented morphological traits. More accessible to the majority listener/reader would be the aggressive stance also taken by Blas Jiménez in the verses:

> *Préstame tu fusil*
> *Préstame tu orgullo*
> *Préstame tus cojones de hombre*
> *Madre África.*
>
> (Lend me your weapon
> Lend me your pride
> Lend me your man-size balls
> Mother Africa.)

used to support the concept of *"liberación psíquica"* (Lewis, "Tipos/clasificación" 38) (e.g., mental liberation, mental independence, etc.).

This is likewise an instance of what was referred to in Essay I as the "decolonization of the mind" in the analysis of the poem "Hermano Negro." Undoubtedly, the writer's approach to Africa, although inspirational and mental, is nonetheless real for his aesthetic purpose. While Latin American poets and novelists of the twentieth and twenty-first centuries grapple with the poetic and real function of a personal Africa, nineteenth-century artists with an Afro Latin sensitivity also made attempts to reconcile an artistic relationship with the Continent. One such writer was Antonio de Castro Alves (1847–1871), a light-skinned, mixed-race Brazilian poet who became an ardent abolitionist and supporter of the rights of Africans in Brazil. His advocacy for a return to an idyllic Africa was more in support of his drive to free Brazil's slaves than an impulse to visit the "homeland." In his conception, it was a bucolic land, idealistically exempt of bondage, to which the freed slave could return. In his "Song of the African," he writes:

> My homeland has terrains as vast
> And boundless as the sea.
> With balmy palm trees in the sun;
> To there my thoughts do flee...("Canção do africano")

In contrast, Luis Gama (1830–1882), also a biracial Brazilian poet and abolitionist, lived with the social demon of "being too dark to pass." Unlike Castro Alves, whose connection to Africa was acquired through the time he spent with his father's slaves, Gama's relationship with his African ethnicity was direct and resolute. He knew that his mother had come directly from Africa and that he was the product of her relationship with a "white" Portuguese man who later sold him, his own son, into slavery. Gama's mother was a free woman, and under these conditions he had the status of being a free-born person. Nonetheless, in "Là vai verso," the poet unhesitatingly acknowledges the African source and social context of his inspiration:

Oh! Musa de Guinea, cor de azeviche
Estátua de granito denegrido. (Martins 93)

(Oh! Muse from Guinea, jet black in color
Statue hewn from denigrated granite.)

Here, slavery is recognized not as a perpetual bond, but as an experience from which the poet drew strength:

Escravo—não, não morri
Nos ferros da escravidão
Lá nos palmares vivi.

(Slave—no, I didn't die
Bound up in the chains of slavery
I lived there amongst the palm trees.)

For both Castro Alves and Gama, Africa offered an element of verisimilitude that would develop into an undeniable part of their aesthetic drive. But does one perceive in any of these creative artists a need to make the Continent a destination in real life?

Up to this point, it has been seen by means of references from the creative literature that Africa is indeed a viable entity to be considered in the national environment of the Latin American sphere. This is especially true for those who claim an Afro selfhood identity within the Latino demography. I have already expressed the view that not everyone shares in this acceptance, regardless of a visible and traceable affinity with the Continent.[11] Consequently, while the imagery of most writers can be perceived as symbols of their particular aesthetic view of people and nation, there may be a reluctance on the part of others to accept a full-fledged personal relationship with African blackness, the "*granito denegrido*" ("denigrated granite," that is, despised as a person, but valued as the entity that gave all countries in the Americas a competitive economic footing) that Gama mentions. Some literary critics[12] see it as the mestizo reality that leads to an *insoluble identity question* for some authors (Lewis, *Afro-Hispanic Poetry* 176–177; emphasis added). I refer to it as the "Hispanismo/Latinismo" ethnic syndrome—the ethnic imbalance of "neither-nor," that is, the genetic juxtaposition of unequal parts—in that blackness and black alliances are at psychological odds with the social perception of self where European traits are desired as a strong genetic contender or component. Still, there are some artists, along with laypersons in their national stratum, for whom the retention of African-related cultural traits serves, on a personal basis, as their irrefutable and accepted link to the Continent. For example, a cultural anthropologist from Kenya, while on a fieldwork project in the Andean region of Colombia, reported that she found people (Afrodescendants) where she lived who were insistent about their last names being from Africa:

> Carabali was only one of a number…[t]he same is with Lucumi… Angola, Congo, Viafara,…Mina,…Mosorongo, Quecu [Kweku is a Gold Coast/Ghana Ashanti name for a male child born on Wednesday] and a few others I don't recall…anymore. (Ng'weno, personal e-mail correspondence with the author)

Then, there are also others like President Hugo Chávez of Venezuela who, on more than one occasion, has recognized the genetic nexus that exists between the Americas and "Mother Africa," as he calls the Continent.[13] But, as previously indicated, not everyone is willing to embrace a connection with "Mother Africa," either for themselves or their country. In a paper prepared for members and committees of the United States Congress (November 2008),[14] it was acknowledged that some countries with large Afro Latino populations such as Brazil and Colombia usually do not provide good quantitative data by race. This, of course, makes it difficult to properly assess the socioeconomic position and health standards of the area's Afrodescendants. The negative approach that Brazil assumes regarding racial classifications and Afro Brazilianism has been studied extensively in the historical and sociological literature. Conversely, Colombia's racial patterns, not as well publicized as Brazil's, clearly reveal the problematic of ascertaining statistically "who is or who is not" in a more recent atmosphere. Colombia has the second-largest Afrodescendant population in the region after Brazil, and most analysts assert that Afro Colombians constitute between 19 percent and 26 percent of the Colombian population. Yet only 11 percent of this group self-identified as having an ethnic relationship with Africa.[14] It stands to reason that if conflicts of phenotypes and poverty, racism, and sociopolitical disenfranchisement comprise the inheritance that most Afro Latinos feel they have been bequeathed precisely because of their ethnicity, what incentive is there for Africa to serve as a palliative for their social ills? What is there to inspire the creative artist to explore the possibility of a more positive, more socially progressive African image in situ?

In Essay IV that follows, the Latin identity becomes an African experience back on the Continent, in real time and not as fiction, where the conflicts of phenotypes, poverty, racism, and sociopolitical disenfranchisement are not the currency of daily living. Groups of returnees did arrive at ports of the former Slave Coast (i.e., Bight of Benin on maps printed after 1820) and were subsequently referred to as "Afro Brazilians" even though not everyone was from Brazil; some actually were "Afro Latins" from Cuba and elsewhere. Collectively, they included former slaves, free mulattoe, and some enterprising whites (Strickrodt 215). This "going home," so to speak, of the Latin African, has relevant interest for both the creative artist and the layperson. For example, if Gama's mother were captured and deported, as rumored, would she have been returned to the Bight of Benin with one of the deported groups, or as a self-exiled individual? The surname she used, Mahim, indicates that she was a member of the Mahi whose ancestral home is in the region of the former Slave Coast. The exact positioning of tribal boundaries is a little uncertain since indigenous political boundaries were not the same during the slave era as they became after European colonialist powers decided to carve up the Continent (at the Berlin West Africa Conference, 1884–1885) for their own interests. What is clear is the presence, today, of descendants of Portuguese- and Spanish-speaking Africans all along the coast of West Africa, from Lagos in Nigeria to Accra in Ghana (Guran 2). It is to Ghana that our attention has been drawn precisely because of the scant attention it has received from historical sources as a locus of return from Latin America.

Works Cited

Castro Alves, Antonio de. "Canção do africano." Poem. Web. 9 May 2010.

Contreras, Joe. "Rise of the Latin Africans: A New Black-Power Movement in Central and South America." *Newsweek*. Web. 9 Jun. 2009.

CRS Report for Congress. "Afro-Latinos in Latin America and Considerations for U.S. Policy." Updated 21 November 2008. Print.

Guran, Milton. *Agudas: os "brasileiros" do Benim*. Rio de Janeiro: Editora Nova Fronteira, S.A., 1999. Print.

Jackson, Richard L. *Black Writers and Latin America: Cross-Cultural Affinities*. Washington, DC: Howard University Press, 1998. Print.

Jiménez, Blas R. *Exigencias de un cimarrón (en sueños)*. Santo Domingo, Republica Dominicana: Editora Taller, 1987. Print.

Lewis, Marvin A. *Afro-Hispanic Poetry, 1940–1980: From Slavery to "Negritud" in South American Verse*. Columbia: University of Missouri Press, 1983. Print.

―――. "Tipos/clasificación y géneros de la literatura afro-hispánica." *AMÉRICA NEGRA* 9 (1995): 33–47. Print.

Martins, Heitor. "Luís Gama e a Consciência negra na literatura brasileira." *AfroAsia* 17 (1996): 87–97. Print

Ng'weno, Bettina. Personal e-mail correspondence to the author. 28 Jul 2009.

Pérez-Sarduy, Pedro. *Las Criadas de la Habana*. Habana, Cuba: Editorial Letras Cubanas, 2003. Print.

Restrepo, Laura. "Colombian Journalist Gives Thoughts On War On Drugs and Future With Obama." Interview by Steve Inskeep. *Morning Edition*. National Public Radio. 2 Jan. 2009. Print copy of interview.

———. *La novia oscura*. Primera Edición Rayo. New York: Harper-Collins, 2002. Print.

Strickrodt, Silke. "Afro-Brazilians of the Western Slave Coast in the Nineteenth Century." Web. 15 Aug. 2009. <www.yorku.ca/nhp/jccurto/enslaving_connections/ch10.pdf>

Sue, Christina. "Debate: An Assessment of the Latin Americanization Thesis." *Ethnic and Racial Studies* 32.6 (Jul. 2009): 1058–1070. Print.

Essay IV

A Latin Identity, An African Experience

The Tabom Brazilians of Ghana

ABLEKUMA ABAKUMA WO

(A saying of welcome of the Gã Nation of Ghana, West Africa)

[Let all good people (even strangers) join us with their services]

The arrival of native peoples from various regions of the African continent to Latin America has left an indelible impact on life in all of the Spanish- and Portuguese-speaking spaces of the Americas. As examples in the previous sections of the creative literature of Latin America have shown, this presence has affected, in measures both large and small, the cultural fibers of most Latin American countries. Some, such as Puerto Rico, Cuba, the Dominican Republic, Colombia, Venezuela, and Brazil, would not have the definitive phenotype of their prototypical national image without the input of the African connection.

As seen in Essay III, the Americo-Dominican author Julia Alvarez capably shows this effect on the Latin image and the problem of colorism in *In the Name of Salomé*. The protagonists of her novel, Salomé and her daughter Camila, could not have been structured as paragons of the Dominican phenotype without a "touch of Africa" in their skin, as the author has said. From her perspective, it is the one thing that connects all miscegenated people:

> I had fallen in love with the artist, his intensity, Africa in his skin—the things that connected me to my mother, not to him. (*In the Name of Salomé* 349)

Even a country such as Argentina, which claims to be the sole predominantly Europeanized space in the Latin American geographical context in terms of culture and phenotype, cannot deny that its cardinal cultural icon, the tango, has African roots. This musical form was transplanted to the country during the epoch of slavery, an industry in which the Argentines also participated. Considering Argentina's allegation that it is a country with unmiscegenated, European roots, is it not incongruous, then, that the renowned Argentine musician, Luis Enrique Bacalov, would compose music for a classic liturgical Catholic mass ("*Misa Tango*") using the syncopated drumbeat of the tango as its underlying, driving force? Undoubtedly, the format that he chose for this composition must have reminded him of his native Argentina.

The fact that aspects of Africa are fully integrated into life in the Americas, in general, has not been lost from the cosmovision of artists who depict their environs honestly. According to the Dominican novelist Loida Maritza Pérez: "We [the people of color in the Americas] share the blood of common ancestors. Language separates us, but our silence regarding our shared history also divides [us]" (Esdaille, "Same Trip, Different Ships"). One has to question, nonetheless, the vacillation on the part of most Latin Americans to accept a deeply embedded African reality in their physical and cultural fibers, given that this presence cannot be so easily deracinated from the total spectrum of the Latin

American image. In the theoretical sense, it can even be said that Africa is a component that has become essential to the total Latin American presence, if not in terms of culture, then undeniably in the diversified physiognomy that spans the spectrum of skin tones from the deepest black to the palest white. As Luis Gama (1830–1882), the Brazilian poet and political activist, wrote:

> *Se negro sou, ou sou bode*
> *Pouco importa. O que isto pode?*
> *Bodes há de toda casta*
> *Pois que a espécie é muito vasta...*
> *Há cinzentos, há rajados*
> *Baios, pampas e malhados*
> *Bodes negros, bodes brancos,*
> *E, sejamos todos francos*
> *Uns plebeus e outros nobres*
> . . . .
> *Aqui, nesta boa terra,*
> *Marram todos, tudo berra*
> *Nobres, Condes e Duquesas,*
> *Ricas Damas e Marquesas*
> *Deputados, Senadores*
> *Gentis-homens, Vereadores,*
> *Belas damas emproadas*
> *De nobreza empantufadas*
> . . . .
> *Frades, Bispos, Cardeais,*
> *Fanfarrões imperais,*
> *Gentes pobres, nobres gentes*
> *Em todos há meus parentes.*
> . . . .
> *Pois se todos têm rabicho*
> *Para que tanto capricho?*
> *Haja paz, haja alegria*
> *Folgue e brinque a bodaria;*
> *Cesse pois a matinada,*
> *Porque tudo é bodarrada!*
> (Excerpted from "Quem sou eu?")

(If I'm Black, or a mixed-race animal
It matters little. What can it do?
There are all kinds of mixed-race animals
As the species is quite vast.
Some are dusky, some are streaked,
Reddish-brown, white-faced, or freckled,
Blacks that are mixed, Whites that are mixed
And, let's all be truthful about it
Some are just plain common people, and others nobility
. . . .
In this good country
Everyone butts, everything bleats
Noblemen, Counts and Duchesses
Wealthy ladies and Marchionesses
Congressmen, Senators,
The Gentleman, the Councilman
Beautiful, haughty ladies
From the conceited noble class
. . . .
Friars, Bishops, Cardinals
Imperial braggarts
Poor people, gentle people
My relatives are found amongst them all
. . . .
So if everyone has a tail that wags
What's all the fuss about?
Let's have peace; let's be happy,
Enjoy and celebrate our mixed-race heritage
And cut out all the gossip
We are all a bunch of mixed-race critters.)

In this poem, Luis Gama has used his art to parody a pejorative term ("*bode*" translates into English as "billy goat") used for mixed-race individuals in Brazil, while at the same time he approaches with sarcasm the question of miscegenation that is such a pervasive and established fact in Brazil and elsewhere in the Americas. Lost in the translation into English are the built-in nuances—the deep structure signification concerning race mixture that the poet crafts into his verses. In addition, there is a sense of implied mockery with his expansion of morphological constructions (e.g., *"bodarrada"* for the pivotal image of *"bode"*). The form is stretched and distorted with a hint of acrimony. This type of lexical construction—to modify the base form and give it additional meaning consonant with the sentiments of the speaker—is both possible and normal in Portuguese. In this case, the insinuated feelings are negative. Furthermore, the original lexical item in Portuguese assumes that the reader is familiar with terms such as *"bode"* [billy goat] and *"cabra,"* which carries a parallel reference to "goat." Both terms for "goat" are used in vernacular Portuguese to denigrate the obviously biracial person. Undoubtedly, it has not been lost on Gama that an African-based genetic manifestation is at the core of Brazil's national image. The same concept applies to Spanish-speaking countries as well. As a representative from Bacalov's presumably Caucasoid Argentina has said: "The culture of Africa has been inserted into our collective memory with deeply embedded roots, but we don't want to recognize it" (Magoo). As previous sections of this study have shown, most of Latin America would find itself devoid of its culturally identifying "Latin aura" without its African base and the indigenous Indian element. In retrospect, however, Spanish- and Portuguese-speaking Latin America are not the only areas where Europeans subjected Africans to their slavocracy, and where the ultimate aftereffect is the diversified skin tones of the descendant population. The Dominican author Loida Maritza Pérez, with her statement attesting to the "same trip different ships" reference, would be in total agreement with this observation.

The lyrics of Peter Tosh (1944–1987), the Jamaican reggae artist, also note:

> Don't care where you come from
> as long as you're a Black man, you're an African
> ....
> 'Cause if you come from Trinidad
> and if you come from Nassau
> and if you come from Cuba, you're an African.
> ....

> Not mind your complexion
> there is no rejection, you're an African
> 'Cause if you're plexion [sic] high, high, high
> if you're plexion [sic] low, low
> and if you're plexion [sic] in between
> you're an African. (Tosh, "African" lyrics)

While the repeated mantra of Tosh's verses is unquestionably the term "African" as a visible entity, the underlying philosophy, likewise unquestionable, is the close relationship that exists between color perceptions in the Americas and the image of Africa to express race. Tosh, who penned these lyrics in the mid-twentieth century, hailed from a geographical area in the Americas that is peopled predominantly by descendants of English and Gold Coast Akan forebears. Today, many of them display in their phenotype the results of various generations of interracial and intraracial mixtures.

In sum, what has been gleaned from the creative literature of Latin America is an Africa projected as a space that is not an abstruse, mythological entity created merely to satisfy the need for an imagined literary nirvana. It is a venue that is real, and from which people came with cultural attachments of languages, religions, and philosophies. Furthermore, the nineteenth-century Brazilian poet Luis Gama and the twentieth-century Jamaican lyricist Peter Tosh concur through their art that Africa supplied the physical representations in the Americas to produce the phenotypic paradigm that is so readily accepted as the Latin type. As demonstrated in Essay III on "Phenotypes and Dominicanness," what has been determined to be the Latin/Hispanic prototype, in the Dominican Republic, relies essentially on the more recent African input than on the alleged genetic remnants of a Taino Indian ancestral foundation. With the African continent playing such a vital role in the Latino physical and cultural composition, is there an interest on the part of Latinos in returning to the geographical source of these physical and cultural building blocks? Will the Continent itself ever have a psychological appeal for the miscegenated Latino artist, or even the unmiscegenated Latino artist, as an environment that is real and vibrant?

A Latin Identity, An African Experience 223

While it might appear to be rhetorically phrased, the question is nonetheless raised: Could Africa have been considered a viable venue to which (African) natives and their descendants might have wanted to return after being in the Americas? Why would they want to return? Africa, for many in the slave populations of the New World, must have resurrected memories of being sold as prisoners of war, wars that were the result of inter-ethnic conflicts, or of being handed over as pawns in exchange for a debt or some other obligation not of their making, but that of a militarily powerful chieftaincy. Still others must have recalled being captured and sold as the unwilling victims of ignorance, or as an expendable object that served to appease the human greed of both African chiefs and African merchants. Perhaps some had found themselves to be an item of profit in the scheme of European capitalism and an African chief's craving for a collection of cowries or some other valued commodity. Oral histories and traditional songs passed from generation to generation in Africa still relate the tragedy of Africans selling other Africans into slavery. As the Akan would say in "Life in a Foreign Land" ["Abrohkyir Abraboh"]:

> Life in a foreign land is difficult
> So let us love one another…oh, oh, oh
> A royal of this land
> Has become a slave
> In a foreign land.[15]

In the absence of written documentation for the period, from an indigenous point of view, the spoken word, in continuity, becomes an important source of historical reference, even when the possibility of edited details and the omission of motives are taken into consideration. In Ghana, for example, around the Volta region, there is the "Dzoglo Narration" attributed to the Lolobi/Akpafu, a division of the Ewe ethnic group. The Lolobi regularly narrate certain aspects of the slave-raiding period. In a certain sense, these tales serve as reference to their use of contemporary phrases such as "Dzoglo is alive." The narration, in essence, refers to the clever tactics used by one group to avoid subjugation and enslavement by another.

The story of Dzoglo recalls a historical event and confirms that in the past, slave trafficking by powerful Ghanaian kings in consort with their European allies did indeed occur. It accounts how Agor Koli tried to sell his hapless victims to Portuguese slave traders. Conversely, it also relates how brave King Ayi decided to resist the enslaving wiles of Togbe Agor Koli and move his supporters beyond the Togbe's grasp. King Ayi eventually settled his people in the Hohoe area of Ghana's Volta region. Despite the move, King Ayi's group again came face to face with the possibility of enslavement by the powerful Ashanti, a force that had recently arrived in the area. The Ashanti, it seems, intended to make Hohoe a slave-trading center. Wittingly, King Ayi's people managed to deflect attention away from themselves onto their neighbors, the Otuka, now known as the Lolobi and the Akpafu. Evidently, the Ashanti had not counted on the cunning stratagems of Dzoglo, the Lolobi's war leader. Forewarned by King Ayi's people, Dzoglo managed to thwart the efforts of the Ashanti. Nowadays, it is alleged that the popular phrase of the Lolobi/Akpafu that "Dzoglo is alive" is viewed as a protective password for anyone from the Lolobi/Akpafu faced with a situation of entrapment or capture (Simpson 29–30).

Did Africans of the Diaspora always consider the Continent to be a place of constant jeopardy? The evidence that slavery remained quite active in the region now known as Ghana is inescapable. Relative to other West African coastal areas, the physical structures that are still standing along Ghana's coastline serve as historical evidence of the active and nefarious transatlantic slave trade. The area's various forts, castles, and even residential houses containing preserved and tangible relics of the commerce in human captives are forceful reminders of these activities (Simpson 27). A tour through Elmina Castle, for example, led by a well-prepared Ghanaian docent with an overview that is based in part on factual documentation and in part on local oral history, can be a convincing and emotional experience. Likewise, a visit to the Franklin House at Jamestown, in the Osu area of Accra, Ghana's present-day capital, with its visible remains of shackles, chains, and holes through which slaves were fed, offers a view of human abuse and misery that is no less horrific.

A Latin Identity, An African Experience 225

Wars and enslavement were a realistic dimension of life on the continent of Africa. Such acts, nonetheless, did not completely efface memories of family and home or of life in a less volatile atmosphere for many who were held captive in the Americas. Antonio de Castro Alves (1847–1871), a mixed-race Brazilian poet of the nineteenth century, paints an ancestral motherland that is more idyllic than the environment that the African encountered in captivity:

> The slave sat in his narrow shack
> By embers in the sand;
> Within the dank room he intoned
> A song of his homeland;
> And as he sang nostalgic pangs
> Sent tears to moisten the sand.
> My native land is far away,
> Beyond the ocean blue
> More than this fairer land I love
> The home that I once knew!
>
> The sun beams down upon our beaches,
> Makes the sand there fiery hot.
> The beauty of our evening star,
> Once seen at dusk is ne'er forgot!
>
> My homeland has terrains as vast
> And boundless as the sea,
> With balmy palm trees in the sun;
> To there my thoughts do flee . . .
>
> And there we dance at eventide;
> The joys of life are manifold,
> For unlike here all men have pride;
> No human life for gold is sold.
> ("Song of the African," trans. from Portuguese by James H. Kennedy, "Núcleo de Pesquisas")

This interpretive imagery of a slave's nostalgic memories of Africa is presented as if it were a personal point of view. What references did the poet, who was never a slave, use as the basis for his construction? Castro

Alves was only seventeen years old when he penned these verses, and had never been to Africa. There is, nonetheless, confirmation of the fact that he came in contact with either transplanted Africans or their descendants in the Bahia of his day. The area where he lived was a noted center of strong African presence and of multiple and violent slave rebellions. Given the poet's dedication, from an early age, to abolition for the African slave, there is a strong possibility that he restructured some of the oral histories he may have heard firsthand in order to make these narratives conform to the idealism of his social policies. As the son of a medical doctor, he grew up surrounded by the attentions of his father's slaves, such as the elderly Leopoldinha who also functioned as his nursemaid. According to the poet's sister Adelaide, Leopoldinha and other Africans on their father's property regaled them with many stories of the slaves' life (Costa e Silva 13–14). This is consonant with the fact that throughout the Diaspora one discovers countless tales and personal histories that refer to the magnetic pull that the Continent exerted on Africans held in bondage far from her shores. As related by a captive who lived through a period of slavery in nineteenth-century Cuba, there was a belief that to escape the harshness of slavery, one could acquire wings through magical means and with self-imposed freedom fly back to a receptive Africa:

> Before, when the Indians were in Cuba, suicide did happen. They did not want to become Christians, and hanged themselves from trees. But the Negroes did not do that; they escaped by flying. They flew through the sky and returned to their own lands. The Musundi Congolese were the ones that flew the most; they disappeared by means of witchcraft...I know all this intimately, and it is true beyond a doubt. (Barnet, *The Autobiography of a Runaway Slave* 43–44)

The belief in such a force appears to have been common, as the concept was also portrayed in the Cuban film *La última cena* [The Last Supper] (1976). The moviegoer follows this aspect of the captive African's psychology in a vividly enacted scene of slaves fleeing dogs and overseers in order to avoid recapture. Entrapped captives commit themselves to a spiritual force, close their eyes, spread their arms to simulate wings in flight, and jump off a cliff in an act of liberation back to the Continent. This is but another instance where creative art bases its foundation and construction on the experiences of real histories. Consequently, it is observed in these examples from the arts how legends and narratives that have become a part of the slave's existence are often presented with an appeal to pragmatic results or circumstances. In a certain sense, they appear to have been a forerunner of Latin America's *realismo mágico*, that magical force that realistically resolves the irresolvable.

There was always a continuous flow of histories and tales about Africa that seemed to form the basis of the Africans' realistic concept of self in captivity. In the case of Brazil, cultural reinforcement for the African psyche would arrive from sources that are not often considered. For example, seagoing traffic between the Americas and the African continent was continuous during the long period of slavery. There are reports by historians detailing transatlantic slave-trade voyages that take into consideration accounts of African merchants and seamen who actually traveled beyond the coastline of their continent to reach the Americas. These crossway contacts seemed to endure in spite of the slave trade. However, connections with Bahia, Brazil, were closest and had the greatest social and cultural significance (Law and Mann 313–314). Through these channels of Africans meeting Africans, both social and mercantile networks were formed that facilitated the exchange of culture or the reinforcement of cultural traits, the transfer of new ideas, an awareness of news and social or religious currents, and trade in ethnic items that brought back memories of Africa as home:

> In the nineteenth century, if not earlier, the trade from West Africa to Brazil also included palm oil, kola nuts, black soap, calabashes, and various spices. The growth of Yoruba cults among slaves and ex-slaves in Brazil further created a demand for religious and ritual objects made in West Africa. (314)

This leads one to consider the fact that the institution of slavery, where Africans were concerned, was much more complex than has been reported in most accounts. In spite of the abject personal and familial misery that enslavement produced, losing one's own freedom did not seem to prevent some former captives to consider depriving others of the same right. It might come as a surprise to learn that:

> Many Afro-Latin returnees continued to travel back and forth trading in slaves and merchandise between the Guinea Coast and Bahia, Brazil. They tended to maintain ties among relatives, former owners, slaves and friends on multiple continents. (Matory, "Afro-Atlantic Culture" 36)

Commerce and material gain were not the only motivating reasons for intercontinental travel by Africans from the Americas, although, without a doubt, the need for African products in Brazil was a stimulus. Motives were varied and at times too entangled to unravel and explain logically. Some participants in this trade did become rich; others remained psychologically detached; and still others used their relationships as a means to help other Africans secure their release from bondage and go back to the Continent. Out of the many histories that unfolded during this era, a name often mentioned with regard to travel between the Americas and Africa is that of Martiniano Eloise do Bonfim (1859–1943). He was born in Bahia, Brazil, the son of a freed Egba import-export trader who himself had made the transatlantic roundtrip several times. In 1874 or 1875 (different sources give different dates), Martiniano traveled to Lagos with his father, and remained there for eleven years to acquire an education in secular subjects as well as in the Yoruba religious tradition. It was in Lagos that he underwent initiation as an *Ifá* diviner. *Ifá* is a system of divination wherein its practices become an avenue of communication between the spirit world and that of the living. The diviner, as someone well-versed in the literature (oral) and practices of this philosophy, is seen as a facilitator between the wisdom of the spirits or deity and the imparted prophecy to the living. Upon his return to Brazil, Martiniano became a major *babalawo* [priest, teacher] in the Candomblé religion. (Cohen 29; Matory, "The English Professors of Brazil" 79). There is also the example of Remigio "Adechina" Herrera (1811–1905), who arrived in Cuba, circa 1830, as a slave. Upon acquiring his freedom, he too is reported to have gone back to Africa for religious instructions that enabled him to return to Cuba and become a pillar of Santería, one of that country's still-active Afro Cuban religions (Cohen 29).

It is extremely important to understand that travel by Africans was crucial for an exchange of ideas regarding personal security and social conditions in Africa, especially when it concerned areas remembered as pivotal in the capturing and trading of slaves. It was this interchange between the African of the Continent and the African in the Americas that also served to maintain or reinforce ethnic concepts such as the strengthening of the principles of African religious traditions, as seen in the examples of Bonfim and Herrera mentioned earlier. Some of these philosophies (e.g., Candomblé and Santería) still remain vibrant throughout the Americas. Many of the freedmen who took part in the massive uprising in Bahia in 1835 were merchants as well as Islamic religious leaders. The latter individuals were known as *Malês* in Bahia. Through contact with seamen and fellow merchants who plied the Atlantic between the Continent and Bahia in particular, the leaders of the revolt (the *Malês*) appear to have been well apprised of the latest religious and political situations back on the Continent that would certainly affect their repatriation to the homeland (Farid 45). Therefore, when the Africans who had taken part in the 1835 insurrection received orders of deportation, the decision of where to settle on the Continent rested in large measure on what they had been told by other Africans who had recently traveled to Bahia. The corpus of news brought to Brazil by different, knowledgeable individuals was indeed valuable. Some of these sources, it is reported, were recent captives still being sent to replenish Brazil's labor resources (Diouf 172). Considering the various informants, it must certainly have been a compilation of different accounts that encouraged some prospective returnees to make their decisions of settlement in Africa based on carefully weighed odds. Therefore, it is determined that undoubtedly a good number of the former slaves who had intentions of returning to a home location farther inland ended up settling on the coast, where the threat of recapture was known to have decreased. The lingering fear of being re-enslaved remained a constant threat as the ex-captives learned of ongoing wars in the inland territories where they used to live (Codo 57). Nonetheless, Africans did return to the Continent, either in forced exile or of their own volition. Some of the coastal regions now viewed as safe havens in which to settle had not been the original ethnic enclaves for many of the returnees.

This brings to mind histories of returnees to Liberia from the United States and of those assisted to Sierra Leone by the British to areas that were not the birthsite of either group. The repatriation of these former captives has been widely publicized as the largest resettlements in Africa by ex-slaves. The common thought is that the returnees to Liberia and Sierra Leone were either the only groups to be repatriated or the only countries to which Africans were returned, or that groups sent to these countries were unique because of their numbers, as noted in the following statement:

> The largest groups of diaspora Africans who returned to the Continent were the settlers of Sierra Leone and Liberia in the eighteenth and nineteenth centuries, respectively. In 1816…European Americans established the American Colonization Society, and with the backing of the United States government shipped more than 15,000 people of African descent to the west coast of Africa between 1820 and 1890….Although some of the African Caribbeans came to Africa on their own, a group of 500 Jamaican Maroons were shipped to Nova Scotia in 1800 and then to Sierra Leone…A group of Barbadians who failed in a slave revolt in 1816 were also shipped to Sierra Leone… (Lake 24)

It is known, but does not often appear as a thematic drive in the creative literature of Latin America, that aside from those sent to Sierra Leone and Liberia by the British and European Americans, there were also ex-slaves who left Cuba in the nineteenth century to settle in Nigeria. Cuban sociologist Rodolfo Sarracino describes in his study *Los que volvieron a África* [The Returnees to Africa] how, during a trip to Lagos in 1980–1982, it was possible for him to make contact with some of the descendants of these returnees. It appears that when the possibility presented itself, black Cubans went back to Africa at various periods and for diverse reasons that in general were based on experiences of oppression and a feeling of personal insecurity. Of particular note to those interested in Cuban literature is Sarracino's comment on a declaration by the Cuban historian Juan Pérez de la Riva to the effect:

> ...la voluntad de regresar a la tierra nigeriana prendió en un número creciente de libertos, principalmente yorubá, después de la Conspiración de la Escalera en 1844, y continuó incluso después de la abolición de la esclavitud en 1886. (Sarracino 47)
>
> (...the desire to return to Nigerian soil overtook an ever-increasing number of freedmen, especially those of Yoruba descent, after the "Conspiracy of the Ladder" in 1844, and continued up to and even after the abolition of slavery in 1886.)

Africans and mixed-race Cubans, both slave and free, carried on a constant struggle against persecution and racism, and rebelled for the dignity of black people. Insurrections were many, and in this sense, the "Conspiracy of the Ladder" [*La Conspiración de la Escalera*] has been commented on repeatedly in Cuban history. The incident also figures prominently in connection with the unjust execution of a popular man of letters of that period. Accused of being actively involved in the alleged conspiracy that was purportedly aimed at fomenting an uprising of Cuba's black and mulatto slaves, the poet, Gabriel de la Concepción Valdés (1809–1844), lost his life at the hands of his Spanish accusers. Known in literary circles as Plácido, he was considered by many to be one of the greatest poets of romanticism in Cuba. Plácido, at the time of his death, was not a slave but a free man, a very light-skinned "person of color"; the illegitimate son of a biracial father and a white mother from Burgos, Spain. No proof was ever produced that conclusively linked Plácido to the "Conspiracy of the Ladder" he was accused of instigating. Evidently, his greatest crime was his "mark of color" together with his popularity as a poet, as a thinker, and as an advocate for those who were stigmatized by society because of their color. To the authorities, this combination of color, popularity, and control of word and thought posed a threat to social stability. In Plácido's mind, society had marked him with the stain that it had conjured up for people of his class and ethnicity.

Africanness meant blackness, and blackness was tantamount to slavery. Slavery was a mark of opprobrium. In keeping with this concept, on the way to his death Plácido is reported to have recited his poem *"Plegaria a Dios"* [A Prayer to the Almighty], where the idea of "stain and incrimination" poignantly surfaces from a locus within his being that begged to be exposed in his final hour:

> *Ser de inmensa bondad, Dios poderoso*
> *A vos acudo en mi dolor vehemente;*
> *Extended vuestro brazo omnipotente,*
> *Rasgad de la calumnia el velo odioso,*
> *Y arrancad este sello ignominioso*
> *Con que el mundo manchar quiere mi frente.* (Cited under
>   "Valdés, Gabriel de la Concepción)

> (Almighty God of abundant kindness
> In my impassioned pain, I cry out to you;
> Gather me up in your omnipotent embrace,
> Shred this hateful veil of slander
> And rip off this mark of ignominy
> That the world sees fit to stamp on my brow.)

Blackness in tandem with slavery is the badge of Africanness in all of the Americas, especially when it is phenotypically present. Its visibility—*"una mancha en la frente"* ["a stamp on my brow"]—an ignominious marking of shame, it renders the bearer inherently complicit in negative acts of sociopolitical behavior by means of calumny or alleged association. Plácido, however, questions whether his fate, because of his blackness, is the curse of "Destiny" (i.e., the divine will of the Almighty). If so, he accepts the decreed consequences to be meted out by man:

> *Mas si cuadra a tu suma omnipotencia*
> *Que yo perezca cual malvado impío,*
> *Y que los hombres mi cadáver frío*
> *Ultrajen con maligna complacencia,*
> *Suene tu voz, y acabe mi existencia...*
> *¡Cúmplase en mí tu voluntad, Dios mío!* (Valdés)

> (But if it should favor your most divine
> Omnipotence
> That I die as someone wicked [and] godless,
> And that men my cold corpse
> [Should] abuse with malevolent pleasure
> [Then] let your voice be heard and end my
> earthly being.
> With me, carry out your will, O God
> Almighty!)

Incidentally, the threat of rebellion that motivated Plácido's early death was named Conspiracy of the Ladder because "the ladder" (*escalera* in Spanish) was used as an anchor to which the slave was bound or restrained as he or she was subjected to torture for an alleged infraction. Symbolically, "the ladder" became an icon for the trappings of a system of oppression that had to be overthrown. Sarracino suggests that incidents of this nature induced a current of emigration to West Africa by those who were free and had the means to do so. By this date, conditions to travel by sea had improved and security on the coast of West Africa was more favorable (Sarracino 48).

Detailed accounts of Africans returning to the Continent from Cuba who had become acclimatized to a degree of Latin culture are not as aggressively exploited as literary themes as are narratives of their life as Cuban slaves. While reports of returnees from various Latin countries have remained scarce, perhaps the most underrecognized group of Africans to travel back across the Atlantic may be the Afro Brazilians of the 1835 uprising in Bahia. As in Cuba, novels, short stories, poems, and essays in Brazil abound that also focus on the African as a slave. Still, the imagery of Brazilian returnees to Africa remains almost a blank page where creative artists are concerned. One wonders, in this respect, if the motifs in the creative literature of Brazil find it important to recall that while the Africans that rebelled had sailed westward to Brazil as slaves, their eastward return to Africa saw them free of bondage. Indeed, there were some slaves and some free Africans who did not take part in the uprising. Still, many from this particular group also decided to return to the Continent in self-exile. Likewise, others were expelled whom the authorities in Brazil considered a threat to the country's stability. In general, there appears to have come into play a fear and repression of "Africanness," or specifically, blackness. Barickman in his assessment of the period alleges that:

> No sooner was the Malês revolt crushed than authorities in Bahia unleashed a wave of repression against African slaves and especially against freed Africans...Thus on 13 May 1835, the Bahian legislature approved provincial law number 9, allowing authorities to bring charges of insurrection against any and all freed Africans arriving in Bahia from elsewhere in Brazil. (301)

Punishment was dispensed in forms that were either corporal or psychological or both. Hundreds of free Africans, mostly Muslims, apart from the harsh public lashings they received were either shipped by force from Bahia or aggressively encouraged to abandon the area and leave behind whatever possessions they might have accrued. In November 1835, two hundred men and women were shipped off to Whydah in today's Republic of Benin, even though that was not necessarily their point of embarkation into Brazilian slavery. What laid ahead for them was unknown. The uprising had occurred on January 24–25, 1835. Even after this date, the public continued to clamor for Bahia to actively rid itself of all rebellious individuals and their cohorts, specifically African Muslims. As the Minister of Justice in Rio declared, "[it is necessary] to expel from Brazilian territory all those freed Africans who represent a danger to our tranquility" (302).

Rebellions by captive Africans in Brazil were by no means a new phenomenon. As early as 1807, some of the Hausa populations, the majority of whom were Muslims, had begun to agitate for their freedom and create massive problems between masters and slaves. The decades between the early part of the nineteenth century and the fulminating outburst of the Malês in 1835 were never moments of total quiescence among the slave populations. João José Reis, who has published extensively on this subject, cites that: "Slave revolts and conspiracies occurred in Bahia in

1807, 1809, 1814, 1816, 1822, 1824, 1826, 1827, 1828, 1830, 1831 and culminated with the great urban uprising of 1835" (119). Perhaps the explosive image created by the insurrection of the Malês has loomed so impressively in Brazilian history because of the sheer size of the masses. The intent was for a vast throng of combatants to take to the streets of Bahia at one time in an attempt to gain control of the capital (Viana Filho 217–218). The numbers given for the Africans who took part are never exact, and vary from 300, per bin Farid in his study, to the 1500 mentioned by Viana Filho in the cited reference.

Regardlesss of the actual number of participants, the well-planned struggle by Afro Brazilians in 1835 is recorded in history as "The Revolt of the Malês." The term "Malê," accepted by many to designate the Muslim leaders in Bahia, appears to have evolved from the classical Arabic "*mu'allim*" (Kent 356). Basically, betrayal by other Africans has been determined to be the cause of the insurrection's defeat. Kent lists the informers as Duarte Mendes and his wife Sabina da Cruz, "free Africans [who] informed on and…prevented the success of [the] planned insurrection of 1835." In 1848, some thirteen years after their services to the authorities in Bahia, the couple was officially recognized for their efforts by having their taxes cancelled by a "grateful Legislature" (349).

By 1836, Africans, subdued and oppressed, had begun to seek refuge en masse in Nigeria, as well as in areas that are currently called Benin, Togo, and Ghana. Nonetheless, in each of these regions of resettlement there had previously been some groups more closely associated with the raiding and selling of slaves than others. Ghana (i.e., the Gold Coast), Togo, Benin, and Nigeria all form part of the Bight of Benin. According to some reports, six of every ten slaves that landed in the New World from the Bight of Benin between 1662 and 1863 were sent to Bahia (Law and Mann 312). While enslavement of Africans by other Africans was a fact of life, not all ethnic groups participated. Without a doubt, the odds against recapture or the assurance of freedom from enslavement must have been the stimuli that tacitly induced some and strongly encouraged others to rejoin a once lost environment or reclaim a longed-for cultural space. In most circumstances, repatriation to Africa, whether by forced or voluntary initiative, now created a new atmosphere of self-expression ad libitum for the returnees from Brazil. While conditions on the Continent may have changed somewhat, it should not be overlooked that in the main, most returnees had acquired cultural traits different than those with which they had been transported to Brazil. Additionally, their descendants who accompanied them back to Africa were more psychologically Brazilian than they were native African. Furthermore, the fact should not be overlooked that some of these Brazilian Africans had acquired skills unknown in Africa; others had become financially independent through thrift and ingenuity.

As previously noted, the 1835 rebellion in Bahia of both slave and free Africans under the leadership of the Malês unleashed a volatile wave of oppression and retaliation. As previously stated, apart from the harsh public lashings, hundreds of free Africans, mostly Muslims, were either expelled by force from Bahia or aggressively encouraged to abandon the area by laws or threats that targeted their freedom and tranquility. Measures such as obligatory deportations by the Bahian authorities, together with self-imposed deportations by those who could afford to do so, became the order of the day. To compound the issue and further threaten the atmosphere of tranquil living, it was proposed that all free Africans be repatriated. This action led to a decree issued in March 1836 to the effect that all persons suspected of having taken part in the rebellion should be exiled from Brazil, even those who had not been sentenced. The proposal became law in May 1836 (Diouf 174).

The first contingent of Africans to arrive in Whydah, Dahomey, around this time was well received by local authorities. Because of the various aptitudes that the returning Africans demonstrated, a high value was placed on their expertise, which understandably became a sought-after commodity. Village chiefs allotted them land on which to start their own settlements, and on which they could cultivate foodstuffs for their people. Not surprisingly, when word of this favorable reception traveled back to Bahia, hundreds more opted to sail "home." Unlike the projects of Sierra Leone and Liberia, which received financial assistance from Europeans and European Americans, the movement from Brazil back to the Continent was somewhat different. Because of acquired skills and talents, a few of the liberated Africans had managed to accumulate varying degrees of economic stability after their release from bondage. This group proved to be quite instrumental in both providing for itself and in assisting kinsmen and others in resettlement on the Continent. There is, for example, the report of Antonio da Costa and João Monteiro, both reportedly rich. Together they chartered a British boat to take them, their families, and 150 other free Africans back to their native soil. Safe arrival at the coast of Africa enabled some members from this group to disembark in the ports of Elmina, Winneba, and Agoue in April 1836 (Diouf 175). These particular locations should be kept in mind, since African Brazilians had previously landed on the coast between 1831 (some say 1829) and 1835 (others cite 1836), due to prior deportations (Akurang-Parry, "A Smattering of Education" 50fn58). Although the Gold Coast's Accra is usually considered to be the focal point of Brazilian return, Elmina, Winneba, and Agoue likewise serve as areas to be studied as ports of disembarkation.

As indicated, after the 1835 revolt the authorities in Bahia considered the return to Africa to be a palliative for civil unrest. Some of the same ports in the Gold Coast (Ghana), Benin, Togo, and Nigeria that now received the returnees had previously witnessed the active exportation of slaves to Bahia and other areas in the Americas (Dickson 99). The political climate had now changed and the coastal areas had come under the protection of the British, who had a policy of controlling or abolishing slavery. A less volatile environment created the atmosphere that facilitated the return to some of West Africa's coastal areas, even though trafficking in slaves was still a source of income for some African kingdoms. While the policy of extradition covered many Brazilian Africans, not all returnees left Brazil under orders of deportation by the authorities. There are examples like the ex-captive who, in order to escape the backlash aimed against the majority of Africans, decided to sell his property and abandon the country. The return on his investment allowed him to bankroll a voyage back to the Continent on a chartered British boat and also assist in leading some two to three hundred individuals out of Bahia back to Lagos. This port was the site from which many of the now returning bondsmen had been sold and transported. Even before the uprising, freedom from enslavement in Brazil had long been a goal for the ex-captives. But in the aftermath of the rebellion, manumission had now become a relative term. Freedom from slavery now included physical and mental oppression as major factors. It is interesting to note that this same African referred to previously as a leader for repatriation had made the transatlantic trip westward to Brazil as a captive some fifteen years earlier. Sixty of the individuals who now accompanied him back to Africa had formerly sailed with this benefactor on the same slave ship westward as fellow captive cargo. Reportedly, they were coreligionists. This bond might perhaps attest to the solidarity of Muslims in Bahia as a unified community. However, their close relationship might also have been a continuation of ethnic bonds that had started back on African soil and continued in America (Diouf 175).

* * * * * *

When Africans arrived in the Americas, they brought with them a legacy that today has become inextricably intertwined in the cultural and physiognomic characteristics of all regions in the area. Will returnees to Africa make a similar impact on the cultural and artistic spaces to which they were repatriated? For example, in the area of Bahia, the revolt of the Malês is still recorded as a singular event in the oral and artistic histories of Bahians, in particular those who are African-related. As the musicians/composers Luis Carvalho de Jesus (Luis Bacalhau) and Juraci Tavares would pen:

> *Estampidas ecoam, Liberdade, Liberdade.*
> *1835, Salvador, Levante Malê na cidade.*
> *À frente Calafate e Licutan*
> *No 25 de janeiro, o Ramada*
> *Dia da glória, grande Glória*
> *A Revolta dos Malês*
> *Página viva mudando a História* (Excerpted from *"Buscando Outra Sociedade"* by Luis Bacalhau and Juraci Tavares)

A Latin Identity, An African Experience 239

(The alarm cries out: Freedom, Freedom,
1835, Salvador, the Malê rebellion in the city
Under the leadership of Calafate and Licutan
On January 25th, a banner day
Day of glory, great glory
The Rebellion of the Malês
A page out of life changing history)

Other Brazilian artists, such as the composer Tom Zê and the singer Virgínia Rodrigues, have also paid homage in their creations to the rebellious Malês, but are not as specific as the lyricists of *"Buscando Outra Sociedade."* In the folk history of Brazil, the insurrectionary Malês have acquired an iconic image of being nonsubmissive, Afro Brazilian rebels. Yet, their return to African soil as the sequel to the group's uprising has not enjoyed the same interest or artistic expression. Notwithstanding the omission, many of the rebellious Africans were forced to return to their roots, and a new life of social and political expansion became their goal. A return to the Continent was not just a mere retracing of the steps that were taken prior to being sent to the Americas in captivity. Acceptance and accommodation in a new sociopolitical environment would now become integral factors in the Africans' need to replant their disrupted roots.

> ...Kwaku Ankra...[was] Accra's leading slave trader until his death in 1840. Ankra founded an *oblempon*, or "rich man's" stool, which remained a source of alternative authority within Otublohum...His clout was demonstrated in 1836 when a party of ex-slaves deported from Bahia in Brazil landed in Accra. The returnees, most of whom were Muslims originally from the Sudanic savanna, were incorporated into Otublohum under the personal patronage of...Ankra....Within a few years of their arrival a number of Tabons had emerged as wealthy entrepreneurs, having forged commercial links with fellow returnees in the ports of the Slave Coast. (Parker 14–16)

Some of the skills and commercial traits that the returnees acquired during their sojourn in Brazil were a testament to the extent of their acculturation, and helped to set them apart from the native population on the Continent. In Ghana, for instance, returnees from Brazil differed from the native population due to their advanced ideas and agricultural know-how. They introduced methods of crop irrigation and new crops of vegetables and plants such as mango, cassava, and beans. Not only did they make advancements in architecture, but they are still recalled for having started, in 1854, the first tailoring shop in the country, appropriately called Scissors House (Schaumloeffel). Dan Morton, a descendant of the Brazilian returnees and an active member in the community, continues the tradition established by his ancestors and is recognized today as the eminent dean of "haute" tailoring in Accra.

The expressions of assimilation that the returnees had acquired in the New World were varied, prominently noticeable, and served to highlight their Brazilianness or their Latin culture. Pierre Verger, commenting on the contact that travelers made with Afro Brazilian families in Whydah (Dahomey) during the years 1843–1850, found that the area was a transplanted corner of Bahia, Brazil. This image was displayed not only by the ostentatious lifestyle of the middle-class Brazilian household, but also in the many examples of Brazilian cuisine and Brazilian entertainment accompanied by songs in Brazilian Portuguese (Verger 371–375). Nowadays, however, some 170-plus years after resettlement, there is scant evidence of a firmly planted, vibrant Brazilian culture in most of the locations of the African repatriation. Nonetheless, a strong psychological affiliation with Brazil persists. Examples of Brazilian architecture, in some areas, are perhaps the most vivid examples of the returnees' cultural contribution. In Accra, one speaks of the iconic "Brazil House" in the Jamestown area. In Lagos, Nigeria, Afro Brazilian ex-slaves with Portuguese-sounding surnames like da Silva, da Costa, da Rocha, and Soares, although a small minority, likewise made an important contribution to the city's architecture. It is said that the contemporary Yoruba bungalow and its various subtypes have their origins in Brazil. Afro Brazilian carpenters not only built houses for themselves and their fellow countrymen in Lagos, but also erected several major public structures including Shitta Bey Mosque, the Central Mosque, and

Holy Cross Cathedral. These buildings demonstrate strongly the fact that many of the returnees had worked in the building trades in Brazil (Vlach 4–8). But the Portuguese language, a feature that once had set the Brazilian Africans apart from the various national groups on the African coast, has ceased to be the principal mode of communication for most of the returnees' descendants. M. E. Dakubu, in her sociolinguistic history of Accra, claims that the Latin African returnees from Brazil in the Accra area found no need to continue using Portuguese by the second generation. They had become fully integrated into the Gã-speaking society through the Otublohum quarter (149). Consequently, for the Brazilian African community—as for most other residents in the areas where they settled—Gã and English became the requisite languages of social, political, and economic acclimation and progress.

A conversation with the Brazilian segment in Ghana today reveals that there is still a permanent attachment to their Latin American roots. The community in Accra uses as its clan identity a name that is constructed from a combination of two words in Portuguese: *está*>[ta] and *bom*>[bõ], orthographically represented as "bon" or "bom." Together, the two morphemes have evolved into the ethnonym "Tabõ," with the graphic representation of "Tabon" or "Tabom." The Gã language has totally supplanted whatever oral facility in Brazilian Portuguese the returnees and their descendants might have had. When questioned on this subject, a young graduate student of linguistics at the University of Ghana, Legon, who is attached to the Tabom, produced a brief list of some twenty entries that showed a column of standard Portuguese words translated into English and Gã. They were, he said, a representative sampling of the Portuguese lexicon that is found in the Gã spoken in Accra. This is the version that became the principle language, the mother tongue, or the hereditary language for the Brazilian Africans. For speakers of standard Portuguese, the majority of the words on the list would be recognizable even in isolation—that is, separated from the linguistic environment of Gã. For example, "*o bolo*" in Portuguese becomes "*abolo*" in Gã, a type of corn cake. In Portuguese, the word refers to cake made of any type of flour. There were other identifiable words that appeared to have undergone phonemic shifts due to the influence of area languages such as Twi, or perhaps had become phonemically overwhelmed by the dominant Gã with which spoken Brazilian Portuguese, at one time, competed. There is a comparable set of Portuguese lexical items found in Nii Josiah-Aryeh's *Inside Ghana's Democracy* (21). Yet, in a conversation with a Fante-speaker also from Accra, there were words on these lists that he also recognized as part of his corpus of words in Fante, an Akan dialect. This leads the outside observer to consider that perhaps the Portuguese vocabulary used by the Gã might not be the residue of what was introduced by the "Tabom," but are words inherited from the earlier Portuguese presence on the Gold Coast.

Portugal had a long history of activities in the coastal area of the Gold Coast, known today as Ghana. The Portuguese founded the famous Elmina Castle in 1482. They interacted with the locals and introduced Christianity into the region. As is often intimated by native historians: "The Portuguese...brought the Bible and Christian ideas," on the one hand, and "took away gold and slaves with the other" (Josiah-Aryeh, 20). Many of their mulatto children were taught "presumably" (as Dakubu indicates) in Portuguese and Latin. Alongside formal Portuguese, conditions also existed for the development of a Portuguese-based lingua franca with local characteristics. At the end of the seventeenth century, representatives of European trading nations employed Portuguese as a normal medium for trade. Then, by 1700, Portuguese seems to have become a true lingua franca on the Gold Coast. Its use in Accra, in particular, was motivated by commercial reasons. The Danes, the Dutch, sailors, and traders all spoke it after being introduced to the Portuguese colonies in the Far East and in other parts of Africa, for example, Cape Verde and São Tomé. In short, up to the nineteenth century, Portuguese was not an alien mode of communication on the Gold Coast. However, there apparently was not enough spoken Portuguese reinforcement by the time the Tabom arrived to prolong its use by the descendants of the new returnees. Thereafter, English as the language of trade and colonization replaced Portuguese on the Coast (Dakubu 142–150). But, as some residents of Accra claim, there are remnants of Portuguese in the Gã that everyone speaks natively, even though many do not recognize its integration into the mother tongue. In an article entitled "A Traditional Poetry of the Gã of Ghana," Abarry, the author, transcribes the following verses:

> The Gas were still in celebrations when their
> elders went into *Konfrensi* [council]
> Indeed, Gas were still in celebrations when their
> elders went into *Konfrensi*. (Abarry 498)

The Gã to English translation gives "council" as the meaning of "*Konfrensi*." Nonetheless, in the citation, speakers of Portuguese will unfailingly recognize "*Konfrensi*" as having evolved from the standard Portuguese word "*conferência*." Both "conference" in English and "*conferência*" in Portuguese have their etymological root in the Latin term *conferentia* (sng.), *conferentiae* (pl.). However, I am more inclined toward a consideration of Portuguese as the source for this word's entry into the lexicon of the Gã to convey the significance of "conference," as noted, as well as "confab," "palaver," or "council." As indicated, "[t]he Portuguese trade left a considerable legacy of Portuguese words which now form an integral part of the Gã language..." (Josiah-Areyeh 21).

* * * * * *

The earlier references to African returnees to the Continent, including both Brazilian and Cuban Africans, do not appear to have captured the interest of Latin American artists. The image of the African as a "Latino" returnee to the Continent is a somewhat opaque figure in the contemporary creative literature of Latin America (emphasizing the imagery of being a returnee or descendant now established on African soil). When treated, if treated at all, the probability of such an experience usually takes the aesthetic form of myth or legend (Barnet, *Biografía de un cimarrón* 40). The same cannot be said of historians who have studied the black Latin presence in Africa. There are several contemporary studies that have focused on the Afro Brazilian communities that were established in nineteenth-century West Africa. Nonetheless, references seem to concentrate on areas that today fall principally along the perimeters of Benin and Nigeria. By contrast, there has been a diminution of investigation into the image and heritage of the African Brazilian communities of Togo and Ghana (Amos 293). In Togo, there is the legacy of the Olympios, whose progenitor, Francisco Olympio Silva, was reportedly born in Salvador, Bahia, on July 24, 1833, some two years before the Malê uprising. He is said to have arrived in Africa in 1850 and subsequently founded a dynasty that is acknowledged even today. At the time of Togo's independence from France in 1960, Francisco's grandson, Sylvanus Epiphanio Kwami Olympio, was that country's prime minister. When Togo later adopted a presidential form of government in 1961, Sylvanus Olympio became its first president. The new leader's genealogy could not have been more Latin American, while at the same time containing strong African roots. Francisco Olympio Silva, the famed ancestor of Sylvanus' patrilineal lineage, was born in Brazil, the son of a Portuguese father and a mother of African and Amerindian origin (295). Sylvanus' mother, Constancia Talabi Pereira dos Santos, was the daughter of Antonio Pereira dos Santos. Antonio, the matrilineal grandfather, had arrived in Agoué (Dahomey) around 1836, the period of the great African exodus from Bahia after the Malê uprising. The arrival dates of 1836 and 1850 for the president's respective grandfathers illustrate quite clearly the ongoing attraction that Africa had as an environment for positive resettlement.

While the success of the Olympio family stands out in the contemporary history of Togo, other Brazilian African families also made a strong impact on the tribeless but clan-strong society into which the descendants became integrated. Politics was not the only arena where their presence was felt. It is a well-known fact, for example, that religion is paramount in Brazilian culture. During the period of return in question, most Africans in culturally Brazilian households in Togo acknowledged an allegiance to either Catholicism or Islam, the same as their counterparts in Brazil. However, notwithstanding the fact that most Brazilian Togolese were Catholic, one of the first prominent leaders of the Protestant church in Togo was Robert Domingos Baeta, whose father,

João Gonçalves Baeta, had come to Africa from Brazil in 1850 along with the dynastic linchpin Francisco Olympio (299). Islam, as noted, was likewise strong among the Africans of nineteenth-century Brazil. Consequently, when one refers to the Latin-surnamed Geraldo, Santana, Pereira, Aguiar, and Reis families of Lomé, the capital of Togo, as belonging to the Nago (Yoruba) group of returnees, the assumption is that these Africans with a Brazilian heritage undoubtedly were Yoruba Muslims who arrived in Togo by way of Nigeria and Dahomey, today's Benin (300).

Sylvanus Olympio's presidency was not long-lived—he was assassinated in 1963. Nonetheless, with his rise to power as leader of the country that had received his ancestor as a returnee from bondage in Brazil a little over 100 years earlier, the social strides of the Brazilian Africans can be viewed as epical in nature. Togo was not, however, the only locale that gave witness to the phoenix-like rise of returnees from enslavement to the upper echelon of acknowledged patricians. There is the case of the exceptional Tabom clan of Ghana.

The area now known as The Republic of Ghana, formerly the Gold Coast, likewise accepted onto its shores both deported and self-exiled ex-slaves from Brazil. They became known as the "Tabom," with a variant spelling of "Tabon".[16] There are only a few detailed studies devoted exclusively to the presence of Brazilian returnees in Ghana. The most accessible—Schaumloeffel and Amos-Ayesu—corroborate what the chief of the group, "Tabom Mantse Nii Azumah V," told this author in several meetings held in August 2007 at that leader's Dansoman, Accra, premises. Prior knowledge of the hierarchical position of the clan's leader, Nii Azumah V, led to the viewing of certain aspects of the protocol that resulted in these sessions being as informative as the results of the interviews. Access to Nii Azumah V was not direct, initially. Befitting his image as the recognized chief of a clan, with a status that presumably has royal authority, the introduction was suitably dignified and above all, respectful. It was obvious that the group had now coalesced from several nonrelated groups of Brazilian returnees into an ethnic whole with an established social and political ranking.

Today's Tabom headman is a direct descendant of one of the first leaders to reach the Gold Coast in the nineteenth century. According to Amos and Ayesu (40), Kangidi Asuman reportedly arrived in the area around 1829. However, the oral history related to me by the chief's brother, Alexander Arunah Nelson, gives the year of his ancestor's arrival as 1836. Mahdi Adamu, in *The Hausa Factor in West African History*, cites A. Addo-Aryee Brown as confirming the arrival of Usuman Kangidi [*sic*] to Accra circa 1836 (135). It would not be unreasonable to speculate that there is perhaps the possibility that Kangidi Asuman (later known as Azumah Nelson) did arrive at the earlier date, but the community itself perhaps did not become recognized as fully integrated with the Otublohum faction of the Gã until the later year mentioned. There is also the likelihood that another core group arrived in 1836, after the Malê uprising in Bahia, to join the Brazilians who were already in place. Two of the persons who supposedly returned around this date were Malê (i.e., Mallam or Malam, a Muslim teacher, scholar, or leader), as per the Mahdi Adamu reference. He names them as Malam Aruna and Malam Mama Sokoto (135). The fact remains that by 1836, Brazilian Africans had made a name for themselves as a group that was socially aggressive and that as an entity, was apart from other ethnic factions in the Gã territory. As a matter of fact, the Dutch commander of the region where Nii Ankrah, the leader of the Otublohum, received the Brazilians complained in a letter dated 16 August 1836 that he did not feel as kindly toward "those people" (i.e., the Tabom) as did Chief Ankrah. The commander objected to the welcome mat being extended to this new aggregation of people without his permission (Amos and Ayesu 40). It seems that he was not totally satisfied with their behavior. Whatever the date, without documented proof, either in the form of a ship's manifest or a log, some details of the Tabom's arrival are sure to be chronologically revised, exchanged with other facts, or blurred with time.

The core of the Tabom as a group is said to have traveled from Brazil to Lagos in Nigeria, then to Ghana on a ship by the name of H. M. S. or S. S. *Salisbury*.[17] Online information lists this vessel as being in service from 1814 to 1837, at which point it was sold to the Spanish fleet.

In 1835 it was in dry dock. If in 1836 the *Salisbury* was put back into use for the British fleet, it would have seen only one year of service before being sold. Costs certainly would have controlled the option of traveling on a steamship (S. S.) with a commercial function, or on a vessel of the British crown (H. M. S.) that was perhaps fully or partially subsidized. João José Reis advises that another ship, the *Nimrod*, was put into use to transport Africans from Bahia to the Continent after the 1835 revolt. This vessel left Bahia, according to the Reis account, a year after the uprising, on 25 January 1836 (481–482). He sheds further light on this movement with the indication that most of the returnees who were free defrayed their own passage, but it is not known whether this was full passage or partial passage. Conversely, the Bahian government is said to have paid for those who rebelled and were now considered personae non gratae. Circumstances notwithstanding, because of public flagellations and aggressive harassment, there is the sense that an atmosphere of rapacious oppression evolved in Brazil that caused some Africans to abandon the country at all costs. Reis further reports that a good many of the returnees had been in Brazil for a long time and that some had even purchased their freedom. In addition, others had begun to establish economic interests that they were now forced to leave behind. Not everyone that left had taken part in the rebellion. Nonetheless, due to the ruling class' perceived need to maintain control over matters of race, and since this control was seen as a coefficient of economic stability, a good many of the Africans who returned had become victims of both ethnic and racial persecutions. The authorities and other interests wanted to rid the country of real or imagined troublemakers. In addition to physical oppression, given that most of the rebellious Africans were Muslims, an aggressive campaign of Christianization began to take root (485–499).

In retrospect, if the head of the Brazilian immigrants, Azumah Nelson (posthumously honored as Nii Azumah I), was recognized for his leadership that covered the period from approximately 1836–1865 (Schaumloeffel 41–42), then an arrival date earlier than 1836 seems plausible. One must keep in mind that a span of time would have been necessary for the various families—Azumah Nelson, Mahama Nassau, Vialla, Manuel,

Zuzer, Gomez, Peregrino—who were recognized as being the pioneers, each with its own particular leader, to come together and organize as a cohesive group. Furthermore, there was the need to adjust to the linguistic requirements and sociocultural imperatives of the Gã-speaking community they shared. The Tabom had arrived together in Ghana from Brazil speaking Portuguese, in addition to Hausa, Yoruba, and a few other languages that were alien to the Gã quarter. But as previously noted, "An event that might have prolonged the use of Portuguese in Accra...was the arrival...in 1836 and after of the Portuguese-speaking Brazilians... known as the 'Tabon' people" (Dakubu 149). The Tabom's command of the Portuguese language fell into disuse. Evidently, there were other, more pressing exigencies that would have enabled them to be accepted as functional residents within the prescribed tribal and utilitarian parameters of their hosts. Much to their advantage, the Tabom had acquired two superior benefactors who had immediate control over the protocol of accessibility and acceptance: Nii Tackie Kome I, the supreme chief of the Gã kingdom, and Nii Ankrah (Schaumloeffel 42). Still, it could only have been after an assessment of their proven worth to the Gã polity that the Tabom would have become attached to the sector controlled by Gã Mantse Ankrah and consequently have been integrated into the Otublohum district (per Nii Armah Josiah-Aryah).

Another factor that probably contributed to their acceptance was the fact that Azumah Nelson's son, Alasha, had developed a strong friendship with Tackie Tawiah, the grandson of the supreme chief Tackie Kome I. According to Azumah Nelson V, the Tabom Mantse, his ancestor Alasha Nelson and Tackie Tawiah (subsequently Tackie Tawiah I) had become friends before the group's arrival on the Gold Coast. It was not clear from the Chief's account whether this meeting took place during the group's brief stay in Nigeria, Benin, or elsewhere. Given that Tackie Tawiah I was known to be a merchant who traveled extensively, and given that transatlantic travel by some Africans was not unknown, the question was raised concerning Bahia as a possible meeting place. This query also remained without a certain reply. The Chief was positive, nonetheless, that Tackie Tawiah I was the one who extended the invitation to the Brazilians to settle in the area controlled by the Gã. The Tabom leadership accepted the offer, arrived in the new African space, proved themselves with abilities learned in Brazil, and merited becoming endowed—"enstooled"—according to custom and culture with the inception of an inheritable lineage under the direction of the Nelson bloodline. Today, the Tabom chief and his community march equally with all the peoples of the Gã nation, fully entitled under the Gã adage "Ablekuma abakuma wo" that accepts all people, even strangers, as long as they contribute to the good of the whole.

The dichotomy of being descendants of Brazilians ethnically, while advocating a new dimension of authentic Africanity, might suggest either a conflicting image or a difficult explanation. Yet, when talking with today's members of the Tabom community, there is always a feeling that after several generations they have become confident in their self-identity as full-fledged natives of the African environment they now inhabit. Leading Tabom members willingly provided information on the group's origin and offered anecdotes from their oral history. One might be tempted to say that this was a collective "griot" endeavor. However, one cannot overlook the fact that the Tabom, as a clan, did not begin its group history until after they had arrived on the Gold Coast in the nineteenth century. Before then, their beginnings were disparate and related only by the institution of slavery in Brazil. Their histories give the Tabom a clear link to a mutual identity. In this way, the descendant of the African Brazilian who established the first tailor shop in the country and the representative from whose family the chieftaincy is inherited both take pride in their legacy as progeny of Brazilians. In addition to this heritage, the tailor and the Chief felt equally secure of being firmly established entities of the Gã nation, as did others in their society. Notwithstanding the perceived image of being native Africans with a political allegiance to Ghana and a social connection to the Gã society, everyone who called himself or herself a Tabom demonstrated fierce pride in their clanship based on a Brazilian ancestry. Still, no one that this writer spoke with had ever visited Brazil or speaks Portuguese. The customs and celebrations their ancestors acquired in Brazil and brought with them to the Gold Coast have receded to become a blurred memory. It was possible to discern (in 2007) that among the various members of the community there was an avid curiosity in all things Brazilian. Brazil's first black ambassador to Ghana had also discovered the group's unswerving allegiance to a Brazilian image when he took up his post in Accra in 1961. At an audience held with a delegation from the Tabom community, J. Fortunato Antonio Nelson, the group's Prince Regent at the time, read a statement from his father, Nii Azumah III, who was in office from approximately 1936 to 1961. Among other declarations of sentimental attachment to Brazil, the Prince Regent stated:

> It's true that none of us here has ever visited Brazil, but that's not important. We still consider Brazil to be our motherland, and we have anxiously looked forward, Mr. Ambassador, to this moment of reconciliation, here in Ghana. And may I further add that we accept it to be our obligation to offer you this reception in view of the fact that you, Mr. Ambassador, are the legitimate representative from the country that, as I have already said, we look up to as our mother-country. (Dantas 48)

This acknowledgement of Brazilian identity and allegiance, delivered in Africa, was made in the Gã language by the Prince Regent as the appointed spokesperson for the Tabom community. There was simultaneous interpretation into English by an English-speaking member of that community. A staffperson of the Brazilian Embassy then rendered the English translation into Portuguese, the native language of the Brazilian ambassador, an African descendant. Brazilian Portuguese for Ghana's African Brazilian community had become relegated, at this juncture, to a few surviving family names. Some of these were now orthographically misspelled and phonemically mispronounced due to a decline in the control of spoken and written Portuguese (e.g., Vialla = Vieira, Zuzer = Souza, Maslieno = Marcelino, etc.). As the ambassador was likewise told in that meeting in 1961: "These Brazilians used to speak Portuguese [upon their arrival here], but they also understood and spoke Yorubá and Hausa, languages of Nigeria" (46). The Yoruba and Hausa components

A Latin Identity, An African Experience 251

mentioned in this observation would confirm the fact that most of the rebellious Africans of the 1836 uprising were Muslims, as many of the Yoruba- and Hausa-speaking groups of Nigeria were adherents of Islam. Adamu in his study also notes that "significant in attracting other Muslims from the interior...in the second half of the nineteenth century was the settlement in Accra of a sizeable number of liberated African slaves from Brazil." He continues on to list the names of the pioneering Brazilians, and reminds his readers that it was not possible to ascertain how many were Hausa, "though at least the Imam was" (135).

The historical symbolism of the meeting of the Tabom delegation must not have passed unnoticed by Ambassador Dantas. This commission of Ghanaians was the beneficiary of the historical uprising in Bahia that has been referred to as "The Revolt of the Malês." The Malês, as noted, were enslaved and ex-slave Muslim leaders in Bahia who had made a valiant attempt to overthrow their oppressors. Even those who had previously acquired their civil freedom before the rebellion demanded an inalienable right to religious expression, (i.e., the Islam that had traveled with them from Africa versus the Christianity that was imposed in the West) under slavery. Ambassador Dantas' position in Brazil, as a descendant of Africans, was linked to the struggle for civil and religious freedoms in which the ancestors of the Tabom community had engaged. At the moment of the ambassador's meeting with the contingent from the Tabom community, approximately 125 years had passed since the forebears of this group had left Brazilian shores as former slaves. They had now risen, socially, to the pinnacle of one of the traditional nations of their new homeland. Furthermore, those Tabom descendants who had subsequently received the benefits of a university education and advanced degrees had been appointed to or had risen to posts of ultimate responsibility in Ghana. By the same token, Ambassador Dantas, as both an African descendant and a Brazilian diplomat, was a rarity in his country. He was witness to the limited possibilities for further advancement by members of his race that existed at that moment in Brazil's history. When questioned by students at the University of Ghana about Brazil's alleged policies of racial discrimination, —"*Não há discriminação no*

Brasil?" [Doesn't Brazil support discrimination?], the politically careful ambassador refrained from giving a direct answer in his official capacity as an appointed spokesperson of his country's government. All in all, the students understood the body language of his silence, coupled with a frown and a raised eyebrow. "An answer is not necessary," replied the student who had raised the question (39).

In his memoir, Dantas recalls how his nomination to the ambassadorship in Ghana by President Jânio Quadros had caused him to be the object of much criticism. The basis for these remarks, as Ambassador Dantas explains, was none other than the same racial prejudice that had thwarted the upward mobility of other black Brazilians (51). The opposition's principal argument was that he was not a career diplomat, but a journalist. They tended to overlook the fact that the country had never allowed any person of African descent to enter the school of diplomacy up to that moment in the 1960s. As a matter of fact, it was not until much later, in 1978, that a young woman designated as black was accepted to pursue studies at the Rio Branco Institute, the school that trained Brazilian diplomats. Much to her surprise, Monica Menezes Campos, the student in question, was transformed into a cause célébre by the national press. The media made a concerted effort to show that racism had at last been eliminated from the institution that prepared candidates for the diplomatic corps. Be that as it may, the duplicity of Brazil's racial policies became patently clear when Menezes Campos herself commented that for all intents and purposes she had changed overnight from being commonly accepted in Brazil as a "mulata," or person of mixed racial heritage, to being listed as black with her new appointment (Nascimento 278). This ethnic modification, in a few words, speaks to the false perception supported by Brazilian rhetoric that mixed-race individuals of African and European heritage and Afrodescendants with little or no European admixture are to be considered racially different.

For President Quadros, Dantas' appointment had been a brave political move, given the long history of social and political antipathy toward the descendants of Africans on the part of the white and almost-white establishment in Brazil. President Quadros seemingly had wanted to promote a more liberal agenda concerning race when he made the following statement:

> As to Africa, we may say that today it represents a new dimension in Brazilian policy. We are linked to that continent by our ethnic and cultural roots and share in its desire to forge for itself an independent position in the world of today...I believe that it is precisely in Africa that Brazil can render the best service to the concepts of Western life and political methods. Our country should become the link, the bridge, between Africa and the West, since we are so intimately bound to both peoples. In so far [sic] as we can give the nations of the Black continent an example of complete absence of racial prejudice... (Quadros 24)

This statement was a typical example of the Brazilian saying, "*só para inglês ver*," which means, in other words, that it was only for "show and tell" and had no underpinning of truth. This was clearly substantiated by Ambassador Dantas' silence when queried by the Ghanaian student regarding race relations in Brazil. In the absence of instances of racist antagonism and negative racialist rhetoric in his country, the ambassador should have enthusiastically denied the African student's claim or at least replied emphatically in the negative. Race relations have often remained in the foreground of Brazil's foreign policy, especially where Africa or African descendants are concerned. President Quadros intended to have his nation play a special role in what was considered the nonwhite world with the establishment of embassies in Nigeria, Senegal, and Ghana. In addition, his administration provided *Bolsas de Estudos*, that is, scholarships for African students to pursue academic courses in Brazil in critical fields of study and research. Because of or in spite of these efforts, his presidency was cut short. Under pressure from the military junta and those with opposing policies they wished to see in place, President Quadros was forced to turn in his resignation after being in office for only seven months (February to August 1961). His successor, João Goulart, did not fair much better, given that the military junta did not support his liberal African initiatives (similar to those of Quadros) either. On April 1, 1964, also under

President John F. Kennedy receives the credentials of Ghana's Ambassador Miguel A. Ribeiro at the White House in Washington, D.C., April 25, 1963. Ambassador Ribeiro is a direct descendant of the Tabom returnees from Bahia, Brazil to the Gold Coast (Ghana). (Photo courtesy of the John F. Kennedy Presidential Library, Boston Massachusetts. Photographer: Abbie Rowe.)

pressure from the military, Goulart left for Uruguay in self-imposed exile. By 1965, successive regimes had drawn closer to Europe and Portugal and to the latter's efforts to thwart the movement for independence in its African colonies of Angola, Mozambique, Cape Verde, and Guinea-Bissau (Moore 395). Dantas, perhaps disillusioned by the turn of events, or in all likelihood encouraged to do so because of the turn of events, drafted his resignation to hand in to Quadros' successor, Goulart, before this latter president also left office:

A Latin Identity, An African Experience 255

> [Undated]—I am finally planning to return to Brazil, within a month or so. As a matter of fact, I have outlined my position for President Goulart, requesting my release from this honorable post. I would like to stress that not much has been done with regards to improving our commercial initiatives... (Dantas 95)

In contrast to the lack of opportunities that Afro Brazilians experienced in Brazil during this period because of their race, the president of Ghana would appoint a leading member of the Tabom African Brazilian community to be his country's ambassador to the United States. This appointment happened within the same period that Dantas was planning to resign from his diplomatic post in Ghana, given that his fellow Brazilians found his blackness to be an impediment for a position of that caliber. In the final analysis, one African-descendant Brazilian feels stymied because of his race, while his counterpart in Africa is elevated in rank despite being a descendant of Africans from Brazil. According to an official communiqué of the U.S. Department of State, dated in Washington on 26 April 1963, the U.S. Embassy in Ghana was notified that:

> Ghanaian Ambassador Ribeiro [Miguel Augustus Ribeiro] presented his credentials to the President [John F. Kennedy] April 25 after which a frank and pleasant conversation took place in a cordial atmosphere. The Amb [sic] conveyed the greetings of President Nkrumah and expressed appreciation for [the] assistance that US is providing to Ghana. (Department of State, Central Files, POL 17–1 Ghana)

Considering the years that had passed since the abolition of slavery and the purported policy of racial democracy in Brazil, it seems somewhat incongruous that Ambassador Dantas, unquestionably considered to be a native Brazilian of African descent, would have to contend with a non-supportive constituency in his homeland solely because he was black. In contrast, Ambassador Ribeiro, the descendant of Africans who had left Brazil due to intimidations and expulsions over matters of race, forced labor, and religious concerns, received full support from the government of his ancestors' adopted polity. The Tabom had received full integration and rights within the social and political communities of the Gã nation, one of the endemic tribal groupings of Ghana.

When one considers the returnees from Brazil as a whole, the Ribeiro family exemplifies the many Tabom family groups that have made noteworthy contributions to Ghana's positive image. Among the Ribeiros are several well-known barristers, a filmmaker, and a nationally and internationally recognized surgeon, Bernard Ribeiro, CBE, who at the time of this publication holds the presidency of the Royal College of Surgeons in the United Kingdom. Not long after Brazil's ex-captives had settled in the Gold Coast, a Ribeiro made his presence known in the area of education with lasting effects. Aware that good schooling would be the key to more solid advancements for his descendants, Francisco Ribeiro agitated the European authorities for schools of better quality, more rigorous studies, and a higher level than what was then being offered:

> [T]hroughout the period of Dutch rule [mid-seventeenth to mid-nineteenth centuries] Kinka [the Dutch section of Accra] remained without a school. This became a major issue in Accra in the years following the departure of the Dutch [1868], when notables of all three towns, led by the Wesleyan-educated Brazilian returnee, Francisco Ribeiro, repeatedly demanded improved access to English-language education for their children. (Parker 82)

Kinka was the Gã name for the section of Accra now known as Ussher Town. Boahen, a native Ghanaian historian, informs his readers in *Mfantsipim and the Making of Ghana: A Centenary History, 1876–1976* that the need for advanced education had become dire, especially in the Gold Coast of the British. Colonialism had created a need for the assistance of "native agents" in the administration of its day-to-day affairs: "However, while appreciable strides had been made in the field of elementary education by the early 1860s, there [still were] no provisions whatsoever for secondary or grammar school education in the country" (8–9). Francisco Ribeiro's efforts, starting around 1865, and those of his like-minded associates finally led to the Cape Coast establishment in 1876 of the Wesleyan High School. Recognized as the first secondary school to be established in the Gold Coast, its British name with Methodist roots was ultimately changed to a name in the language of the Fanti: *Mfantsipim*. While a Tabom descendant—along with other visionaries of his time—was instrumental in seeing that the academic requisites of that period would be put in place for the advantage of their children, it would not be remiss to say that an important educational legacy was also started. Some of Ghana's most learned leaders have gotten their academic start at Mfantsipim, most notably the internationally recognized Secretary General of the United Nations (1997–2007) and Nobel Prize awardee (2001) Kofi Annan. Mr. Annan's name appears on Mfantsipim's rosters for the years 1954–1957.

The social advancements of the Brazilian Africans who returned to settle in the counry known today as Ghana are a testament to the keen intellect, the progressive vision, and the upwardly mobile possibilities of a people not fettered with the barrier of rejection because of phenotype, or denigrated by a history that tied them to African slavery. As a matter of fact, for the Tabom, while blackness still equates with Africanness, the image of Africanness does not automatically correspond to slavery as it does for their ethnic brothers and sisters still in the Americas, notably Brazil. Nonetheless, the question does arise: When the descendants of former slaves meet the descendants of former slave owners on an equal footing socially, economically, and academically, will there be a psychological shift in how each views the other? Quite recently, the great-granddaughter of one of the pioneer returnees was vetted by Ghana's parliament and subsequently appointed by President Kufuor (2001–2009) to become Ghana's first female Chief Justice of the Republic. Georgina Wood (née Lutterodt) (formally addressed as "Her Ladyship") assumed office on June 15, 2007, as Ghana's twelfth Chief Justice since that country's independence in 1957. With a traceable biological link to the returnees to Ghana from Brazil, Madame Wood's apical rise in political, judicial, and social status stands as an iconic exemplification of the Tabom's desire for the better life that Brazil's volatile ambience of racial and religious strife could not afford their families at the time of their exodus. Tabom oral history informs us that Chief Justice Wood's great-grandfather, Mahama Nassau, a Brazilian ex-slave and a principal figure among the seven named pioneering family groups that reached the Gã territory of the Gold Coast in 1836, acquired the land and erected the first structure where today's symbolic "Brazil House" now stands.

This building is indeed a tangible monument to the philosophical dreams and ambitions of those men and women who returned to Africa from captivity. Their willpower and determination enabled them to surmount the injurious effects and history of their enslavement. Consequently, with education, intellect, and the will to succeed, the foundation was prepared for various generations of descendants to become involved in the affairs of the State that had received them. Of paramount interest, in this sense, is the aforementioned appointment of Georgina Wood as Ghana's Chief Justice. According to Ghana's constitution, the Chief Justice is fourth in line for the presidency. Of special note, also, is the fact that Justice Wood, subsequent to her appointment as Chief Justice, was likewise the recipient of the Order of the Star of Ghana (7 July 2007), the country's highest honor for distinguished services to the nation. The history of the returnees to the Gold Coast also includes the fact that they were not blocked into strict religious channels, even though most returnees were alleged to be Muslim. For example, Chief Justice Wood's great-grandfather, Mahama Nassau, arrived in the Gold Coast as the spiritual leader of the Muslims in his group. He was literate in Arabic and after getting settled, opened a Koranic school in his house (Amos and Ayesu 18, 21). Unlike her ancestor, the Chief Justice is Christian and an active member in a church that is affiliated with a Protestant denomination: The Assemblies of God.

In addition, other Tabom descendants have become practicing members in a variety of denominations and religious faiths that have proselytized in Africa. Nonetheless, it should be noted that for many in the Tabom group an ongoing interest in European-based religions has not precluded a still-active participation in the worship of "Shango." This is one of the Yoruba deities that was taken to the Americas in the dungeon-holds of slave ships or acquired in the Americas from fellow enslaved Africans. In this sense, the African Brazilians of Ghana share traits with others in the African Diaspora, where firm roots of African religious philosophies still remain

A Latin Identity, An African Experience 259

Chief Justice Georgina Theodora Wood, the twelfth Chief Justice of the Supreme Court of Ghana and the first woman to occupy that position. She is a direct descendant of the Tabom returnees from Brazil to the Gold Coast (Ghana) in the early nineteenth century. (Photo courtesy of Emmanuel Quaye, photographer. Accra, Ghana)

implanted in American spaces that include Cuba, Brazil, Venezuela, Trinidad, Haiti, Colombia, and the United States.

As if by a decree of fate, the Chief Justice's ancestral relationship with Brazil has been scheduled to transcend the negative image of her Brazilian ancestor's exile back to the Continent. Ironically, where circumstances forced Mahama Nassau to leave Brazil because of his race and religion, his great-granddaughter was invited to the country as a person of superior social and juridical ranking, race notwithstanding. As Ghana's President of the Supreme Court, Judge Wood accepted an invitation to be the guest of Justice Ellen Gracie, who likewise is Brazil's first female President of the Federal Supreme Court. On May 12, 2008, Chief Justice Wood read a paper before Brazil's federal organization entitled "The Praxis of Present Day Constitutional Control." In her discourse she alluded to the similarities that could be observed in the Constitutions of both countries (i e., Brazil and Ghana), and placed special emphasis on the prioritization of issues of human rights. While the assembly did not fail to acknowledge Ghana's Chief Justice as the descendant of Afro Brazilians who had returned to Africa, it did not elaborate on the conditions that had required the return. The fact that she stressed the need to reduce the distance that existed between the legal text and its practical application must have been of special interest to the Brazilian jurists who were present (*Notícias STF*).

The examples of Ambassador Ribeiro and Chief Justice Wood are concrete references that illustrate the Tabom's full integration into the body politic of Ghana. Had the Gã nation, a native group that was well entrenched in its culture and politics, rejected the Tabom on the basis of being ex-slaves, these returnees to Africa would not have been able to produce the results seen in Ribeiro, Wood, and in others. Their advancements clearly illustrate what can be accomplished when people are willingly received and respected by an agency with which they are unrelated in culture and language. As a proverb of the Akan people of Ghana succinctly says: "*Akoa mpow a nna ofir ne wura*" [If a slave looks nice, then it is because of the master].

Even in the face of social challenges, some Tabom descendants have had the wherewithal to surmount barriers of ethnicity and be accepted as positive representatives of the Ghana of their immigrant ancestors. In this light, the most impressive image is of the Peregrino family. Among them, Francis Zaccheus Santiago Peregrino requires special consideration for the role he played on the international scene. As a backdrop, we again refer to the fact that the majority of the returning families were alleged to have been strict practicing Muslims. The leaders of the insurrection in Brazil that instigated the return to the Continent, in the main, were adherents to Islam. A few families converted to Christianity upon arriving in the Gold Coast, or prior to their arrival had been summarily invested with a sufficient amount of religious trappings to nominally consider themselves Christian. Conversion was an act that may have been carried out with or without their volition. Technically, all Africans were supposed to be Christianized upon arrival in Brazil. But for many, Islam and Islamic practices remained a pragmatic approach to self-identity, respect, and brotherhood. Notwithstanding needs, actions, and designs, and in spite of the ulterior motives of the slave owner and the inwardly guarded conviction of the enslaved, surnames for some Africans were made to conform to recently adopted or imposed European religious affiliations, while other retained surnames showed cultural ties transferred from Africa to Brazil. In addition, there were names that identified ownership attachments, acquired in Brazil under the system of slavery. The fact that some families returned to the Gold Coast with the names Abu, Adama, Azumah, Aruna or Haruna, and Yusif does suggest a retained association with the Islamic religion. These surnames could possibly have been a preslavery African transport. Other names (Nelson, Morton, etc.) appear to be Anglo and Christian and demonstrate an acknowledgment of the British that were politically and militarily in place when the Tabom ancestors settled in the Gold Coast. For example, the complete nomenclature of today's chief, Nii Azumah Nelson V, includes not only Azumah, but also Abdulai (James Abdulai Nelson). Yet, per his admission to this author, the chief is not a Muslim but a practicing Presbyterian, although his ancestors were followers of Islam. Still, other surnames of Tabom families (e.g., Manuel, Gomez, Costa, Ribeiro, and Peregrino) are deceptively Latino and presumably Christian as opposed to Muslim. In spite of this perception, to many researchers of Iberian cultural traditions, Manuel, Gomez, Peregrino, and Costa often appear as the family names of Iberian Sephardim (i.e., Spanish and Portuguese Jews). However, Jonathan Schorsch, in *Jews and Blacks in the Early Modern World*, declares:

> A 1773 "vocabulary" of Hebrew, English, and Spanish, produced by a Sephardic Jew in England, embedded Kushites [i.e., Blacks] within the orderly conceptual framework of the new era. In the sixteenth chapter…appeared words connected…with family, the cycle of life, the family of nations. [There are three columns of words listed, with (a) with Hebrew script, (b) the English

transliteration, and (c) the Spanish language equivalent as follows, excluding the Hebrew script]:

The Cradle	La Cuna
Native	Nativo
Inhabitant, inhabitants	Morador, moradizos
A Foreigner, Foreigners	Peregrino, peregrinos
A stranger, strangers	Estrangero, estrangeros
A strange language	Barbaro
The people	Pueblo, pueblos
A nation, nations	Pueblo, pueblos
A nation, nations	Gente, Gentes
An Ethiopian, Ethiopians	Ethiopeo, Ethiopeos (277)

Of interest to this study is the observation by Schorsch that these concepts somehow referred to the Sephardim concept of blacks (Kushites), as well as the appearance of the term *"Peregrino"* translated in the work that Schorsch alludes to as "Foreigner." Would these connections in some way lead the observer to consider that the Peregrinos who returned to the Gold Coast as a family of liberated black slaves had had an association with Brazilian Sephardim during their stay as captives in Brazil? At one period in Brazil's history, there was a sizeable presence of Spanish- and Portuguese-speaking Jewish residents, especially during the period when the more tolerant Dutch protected the area. The Dutch as a military force invaded the Brazilian territory and remained there from 1630–1654. When the Portuguese again took control, their religious intolerance affected most of the Sephardim. Because of the negative bias toward their group, the Iberian Jews either abandoned the territory or were expelled by the Inquisition. From the late seventeenth century throughout the eighteenth century, Brazil was not an optimum place for Judaism to be openly practiced. Nonetheless, some Jews, under the guise of being *"conversos,"* or New Christians, remained in Brazil while subscribing to the Jewish faith of their forefathers behind closed doors. When Brazil achieved independence from Portugal around

1822 and found itself in need of lighter-skinned immigrants to offset the overwhelming imbalance of African phenotypes found in its slave and ex-slave population, the country readjusted its mindset to receive some openly declared adherents to Judaism. A few that arrived at the beginning of this era came mainly from North Africa. Others who were already in the country now had the option of either making an open profession of their Jewish faith or remaining silent because of the uncertainty of their reception in a predominantly Christian environment. Regardless of the personal position, the Sephardim presence was again in evidence in Brazil.

This observation is merely an introduction to the reality of a Sephardic group in Brazil that might possibly account for the Tabom surnames that are associated with the Sephardim; it may even be a hint at the reason for some of the phenotypes that belied miscegenation among the Tabom. The main thrust of this study is not aimed at a focus on the Jewish relationship to Africa, or an investigation of a Jewish correlation to African slavery in Brazil or the rest of the Americas, although Jews in the New World were also involved in the industry of transporting, selling, and buying Africans and procreating miscegenated offspring. Nonetheless, one is forced to notice the Sephardic names among some of the Tabom returnees to Africa that stand out in the midst of the names of alleged Muslims who were deported or who exiled themselves back to the Continent. In this respect, of all the names listed, Mammon Peregrino seemed to have the most unlikely given name and surname to be associated with a person who claimed to be a follower of Islam. The combination of Mammon and Peregrino is not generally associated with Islam or found exclusively among Christians. Both Mammon and Peregrino do come into play, however, as appellations associated with families of Sephardic origin, and have been found on lists (as per the example shown) that are specific to the Safarad lineage. Schorsch's mention of the term "Kushites," the biblical Black nation, attracted our attention. While this list offers "foreigner" as an English equivalent for the Spanish term "*peregrino*," it is just as valid to translate it as "wanderer" with reference to the image usually associated with a characterization of the

Jewish person. Although some Spanish and Portuguese Jews adopted surnames that they felt described them or the places from which they had come, others had names assigned to them by religious authorities (e.g., The Holy Office) according to perceived characteristics. If the Mammon Peregrino of this study returned to Ghana from Brazil as an unmiscegenated black or biracial ex-captive, what would have been his relationship to Brazil's Sephardim community? Under what conditions had he been integrated with that society or with the Muslim society with which he is listed? Mahdi Adamu says that Peregrino, along with Usuman Kangidi and others, were "either Muslims before [they arrived in Brazil] or became converts during slavery" (135). Was Peregrino's affinity with Iberian Jews consanguineous if he was biracial, or did he bear this surname as a mark of having been someone's property? The thought that there might have been close alliances between Sephardim and Africans, in a sociohistorical sense, is not capricious folly or mere speculation. As Jonathan Schorsch also says in his study:

> Early Modern Catholic Iberian discourse generally scorned Jews and linked them, implicitly and sometimes explicitly, with denigrated Africans…marginalized and often persecuted, *conversos* and Sephardim of the sixteenth through the eighteenth century [and] resorted to hegemonic discourse about Blacks to construct their own identity. (Schorsch, "Blacks, Jews and the racial imagination" 109)

An example of this line of reasoning can be seen in a historically recorded account of a Sephardic man, coincidentally named Peregrino, who confirms the notion that Africans and Iberian (Sephardim) Jews were not unknown to each other, and did maintain intimate relationships. Jacob Peregrino, born Jerônimo Rodrigues Freire in Tancos, Portugal, fled Portugal in the early seventeenth century to settle in Amsterdam, away from the grasp of Portuguese Inquisitors. Later, he was registered as a merchant on the coast of Senegal in a region of the Senegambia known as the Petite Côte. His son, Manuel, appears to have committed a grave offense against African protocol by having a serious, illicit, and quite intimate relationship with the daughter of a Wolof king in the region. Perhaps this particular affair was viewed as a sensitive breach of royal etiquette because the young girl was of aristocratic heritage and Manuel was not, for as one researcher has found, there were other liaisons that did not merit the same recrimination:

> ...they [the Sephardim] clearly developed significant interpersonal bonds with the peoples of the coast [Petite Côte of Senegal] as evidenced through the sexual relationships that developed. Moreover, their stimulating exposition of the possible Jewish origins of some of the mulatto presence on the coast is placed in an interesting light by the evidence of the numerous African and mulatto members of the Sephardi [sic] community of Amsterdam in its formative years. (Green 178–179)

While some Western groups feign an air of incredulity when confronted with the reality of interethnic/interracial sexual encounters, the biracial results of human sexual attractions and/or human sexual victimizations belie the denials. Can it be confirmed, then, that the Sephardim took their biracial offspring and other Africans to Amsterdam as family members, servants, slaves, or lovers? What extant records have brought to light is the fact that African Jews were physically present in seventeenth-century Holland. For example, it was ruled in 1647 that a separate space had to be found in the cemetery of Beth Haim in which to bury blacks and mulattos (Green 179). This request highlights the reality that it had been only thirty years prior (in 1614) that the first segment of Beth Haim (in the environs of Amsterdam) was purchased at Ouderkerk aan de Amstel as an exclusive burial site for the "white" Sephardim. In the meantime, Jacob Peregrino's life "ended...on the coast of Africa, in isolation from the 'pure blood' of his fellow Sephardim of Amsterdam," the result of debts that precluded his return to Europe (Green 182). It is almost certain that he was not the sole example of the Judeo ethnoreligious community that was found in Africa. There is evidence that Portuguese Jews did convert Africans to Judaism in Holland. One nonetheless questions whether the Sephardim subscribed to the practice of converting their African slaves to Judaism during their stay with the Dutch in

Brazil. It is difficult to find absolute proof that Africans were categorically encouraged to adopt the religion of their Portuguese or Brazilian Jewish masters. Schorsch concluded that:

> In those parts of Brazil conquered by the Dutch, Jews were pretty much free to treat their slaves according to their religious dictates…[T]he dearth of available documentation allows us to reconstruct the religious life of Jews and their slaves only inferentially. [However]…one scholar stated that "a few of the Jews were mulatto half-caste" [and in this light] a closer look is warranted. (Schorsch, "Blacks, Jews and the Racial Imagination" 219)

"A closer look" will reveal more than just a few individuals who carry the phenotypical stamp of interracial parentage based on a Jewish heritage. There can be no denying the fact that what went on behind the closed doors of Brazil's secret Jews in terms of ritual, beliefs, and social practices was not always documented. It is also common knowledge that miscegenation was not the exclusive domain of one religious sect only. Historian Josiah-Aryeh's recent declaration that his "father was partly descended from Brazilian immigrant settlers in Accra and had smooth wavy hair" (*Ghanaweb*, "Nostalgia from Nii Armah Josiah-Aryah") is a strong inference that some of the returnees arrived from Brazil with the prototypical traits of a mixed racial heritage. The ethnic basis of such miscegenation is not always revealed, that is, whether the non-African source is Jewish, Christian, or of no religious affiliation. If there were biracial offspring in Amsterdam who could claim Jewish parentage, there were no legal restraints in Brazil to preclude the same from taking place.

The actuality of so many New Christians in Bahia, the area from which Mammon Peregrino left to go into exile in the Gold Coast, might have justified in some way Bahia's nickname as the Capital of the Crypto-Jews[18] (Simms 428). There were those who felt, nonetheless, that "[b]y the early nineteenth century, most New Christians in Brazil had lost their Jewish identities…" (and perhaps had become mainstream Christians or freethinkers) (Levine 46). If this were so, why would Mammon Peregrino, a black man, leave Bahia in the early nineteenth century as a

Muslim with a common Sephardic name? If it actually were common practice, as Farid has declared, for slaves to be baptized upon arrival in Bahia and given a Christian name (24), why would Mammon retain this connection to a Sephardic identity, unless the family that gave him this surname overtly posed as New Christians, and Mammon in some way shared a relationship with them? The religion that Mammon practiced in Ghana has not been brought to light with official documentation, although from the oral histories that were offered to us it is presumed that he was Muslim, like the majority of the group that returned to Africa with him.

In this respect, one takes into consideration the pressure that might have been placed on Mammon Peregrino to become Muslim around the period of the uprising in Brazil, were he not a practicing Islamist already. At one point, prior to the 1835 uprising, a call had gone out for the unity of all Muslims in the area, with a declaration of jihad against whites and Creoles (i.e., blacks born in Brazil who were either Christian or practitioners of traditional African religions). At the same time, there were incidents of African intolerance toward other Africans who did not accept Islam. Africans who embraced the Catholic faith were singled out as polytheists and pagans. They were labeled *kafirs*, and looked down on with much disdain (Farid 42–43). Peregrino's case might have been exceptionally sensitive since he was undoubtedly either a freed person or a slave allowed to work independently (a so-called "*escravo de ganho*") whose obligation required that he report to his owner with a certain amount of his earnings. A "*de ganho*" slave was usually semiskilled or even fully skilled in the craft of a tailor, blacksmith, stoneworker, carpenter, mason, barber, musician, painter, and so forth (Farid 22). As a tailor, other Africans in his community must have been acquainted with him and his religious practices. Peregrino is still remembered in the oral history of today's Tabom descendants as having been a tailor of merit (Amos and Ayesu 44). His exodus from Bahia, at that unsettling moment in its history, could have been propelled by any number of relevant factors, including his nonwhite color or his civic status of being either a slave for hire or a freed person of some economic means. Then, it also could have been his professed or presumed religious affiliation (i.e., a perception of Peregrino as Muslim, or even as Jewish) which would have still been problematic for him. All Africans, especially Muslims, had become an anathema in Bahia. Even if for some reason, there might have been a suspicion of a connection with New Christians, Peregrino's persona in Bahia would have been subject to harassment. After the Malê revolt of 1835, there prevailed an atmosphere of hysteria. It was an environment of vehement white racism, racial persecution, and government-sanctioned violence against the African community in general (56).

To have Peregrino as a family name, in the nineteenth-century Brazil from which Mammon Peregrino left, was no guarantee that it still belonged to practitioners of the Jewish faith, but the image is intriguing and calls into question the free-will changing of a name when one's social environment accepts such an act. If nothing else, Peregrino was African or an African descendant, and the social atmosphere in Bahia had become challenging for him. The bias of white Christians during this period in Brazil's history strongly manifested itself against African culture, particularly the African Islamist. A decree was put into effect that levied a fine of 50,000 reis upon masters who neglected to instruct their slaves in matters of the Christian religion, and most of all, baptize them. Passed during the years 1835–1840, these laws were aimed at regulating the organization of Africans on every level and even went so far as to prohibit freed Africans from trading or reselling basic necessities (Farid 57). Under all measures, the laws and attitudes would have affected a person like Mammon Peregrino, whether he was a Muslim, suspected Jew, New Christian under suspicion of practicing Judaism, or a freed person with some economic stability that needed to be stifled. As of 2010, Peregrino as a surname is still quite present in contemporary Ghanaian society. It has given rise to a dynasty associated with Islamic Ghanaians/Nigerians of some social ranking (the Peregrino-Brimah clan).

In "Sou Brasileiro: História Dos Tabom, Afro-Brasileiros Em Acra, Ghana," Amos and Ayesu make reference to returnees of the Peregrino family without mentioning Mammon:

> ...some of the Muslim immigrants, from the Hausa ethnic group, could not have spent much time in Brazil. Such was the case of Adsuma Maryamu Matta, one of the first immigrants, and a good representative of this scenario. Adsuma was a Nigerian-born Hausa. When she left Brazil, she brought along two children (Claude or Cláudio and Zaqueu Francisco Santiago Peregrino), and gave birth to a third (J. P. Mattier) on board the ship headed to Africa. Later she had three more children in Accra (Adelaide Maria, and twins Ahotei and Ahotey). (53, original parentheses)

At this juncture, it can be assumed that of Adsuma's offspring, perhaps Zaqueu Francisco Santiago might be able to claim descent from Mammon Peregrino. This has not been confirmed. While Amos and Ayesu do not specifically link Mammon Peregrino to Adsuma Maryamu Matta (Zaqueu's mother) in their listings of spousal and parental connections, it has been determined that Adsuma's six children had different fathers (Amos and Ayesu 62). Zaqueu is identified with the Peregrino surname, and it is with him that subsequent Peregrinos with a Tabom heritage are associated.

While the name Mammon Peregrino is unusual for a practicing Muslim and more in keeping with that of a New Christian or a Sephardic Jew, Zaqueu's name, Zaqueu Francisco Santiago, is just as interesting, given that he had Muslim parents, or at least that his mother, Adsuma Maryamu Matta, a Nigerian Hausa, was Muslim. Francisco and Santiago are the names of Christian saints, and are commonly used as given or baptismal names by Christians in Portuguese- and Spanish-speaking countries. Zaqueu (Zacchaeus), while not as common as the names of the two saints, is likewise the name of a Biblical figure who decided to follow Christ:

> (1) Jesus entered Jericho and made his way through the town.
>
> (2) There was a man there named Zacchaeus. He was one of the most influential Jews in the Roman tax-collecting business, and he had become very rich...
>
> (5) When Jesus came by, he looked up at Zacchaeus and called him by name. "Zacchaeus!" he said. "Quick come down! For I must be a guest in your home today."

> (8) Meanwhile, Zacchaeus stood there and said to the Lord, "I will give half my wealth to the poor, Lord, and if I have overcharged people on their taxes, I will give them back four times as much!"
>
> (9) Jesus responded, "Salvation has come to this home today, for this man has shown himself to be a son of Abraham. (10) And I, the Son of Man, have come to seek and save those like him who are lost."
>
> [Holy Bible NLT Luke 19.1–10]

A Jew that followed Christ! Was Adsuma's choice of name for her son another indication of a New Christian contact in Brazil? Did Zaqueu's mother make such a contact or does this in some way refer to Mammon? Is this an indication of her familiarity with the Bible? It would not have been unusual for a Muslim to know characters and stories from the Old and New Testaments, as the Koran speaks often of these holy books. Bibles were even available in Arabic (Diouf 112). What relationship did she share with Mammon Peregrino or with a person with the Peregrino surname who linked this surname to one of her children? It is easy to see, from the questions raised, that the returning Brazilian Africans had a wide range of personal histories that were more complex than might appear at first glance. Just because one is captured into slavery does not mean that one is captured without a history, or cannot subsequently acquire one. Zaqueu Francisco Santiago Peregrino, born in Brazil and raised in the Gold Coast, had five children: one son, Francisco Zaccheus Santiago Peregrino, born in Accra around 1851, and four daughters (Brimah 30–31). Zaqueu Francisco, who reportedly became the owner of a tobacco plantation, must have acquired a solid financial footing in his community. His daughters all married into prominent Gold Coast families, while the son, Francisco Zaccheus, was sent off to England at an early age to pursue his studies.

It must be pointed out that while religious and racial persecution were two of the principal motives that encouraged the Tabom group to abandon Brazil, their religiosity did not appear to have been hemmed in by unbending orthodox boundaries, as some historians have suggested.

A Latin Identity, An African Experience 271

Perhaps a more realistic perspective can be gleaned from the inference by John Parker in *Making the Town: Gã State and Society in Early Colonial Accra*:

> The arrival of the Tabons [sic] from Brazil in 1836 represented the first influx of Muslims into Accra....these ex-slaves and their descendants, while retaining a distinct identity based largely on their continuing adherence to Islam, became recognized as very much a part of the Gã community. (164)

While Parker does not overtly indicate the status of non-African religions in the area, it is known that the Gã had already begun to feel a pull toward Christianity from the proselytizing of colonial missionaries. Parker's continuing observation reveals that, "In contrast with the Tabon [sic] returnees, these later Muslim settlers remained aloof from indigenous [Gã] affairs" (164). In other words, it does not seem likely that the Tabom could have become fully integrated with the Gã (as they so successfully did) and remain predominantly Muslim. Among today's Tabom descendants, Islam no longer figures as the religion of the majority, and most of the Tabom who still reside in Accra have assumed a Gã cultural image while viewing their Brazilian heritage as an important subunit of their total identity. Still, within the diverse religious circles of today's Tabom, there are some practicing Muslims in the Accra area who trace their ancestry to the pioneering Islamic returnees from Brazil. Fatima, one of the daughters of Zaqueu Francisco—"a local aristocrat with the aura of elder statesman, and a member of a class of earlier immigrants from Brazil"—married a wealthy Muslim, Chief Alhaji Brimah I. He was a migrant to Accra from Nigeria (Brimah 30). Today, members of the Peregrino-Brimah clan can be found not only in Ghana and Nigeria, but also throughout Europe and the United States. There are some who have made a strong impact on Accra's Islamic community. One of the sons of Alhaji Brimah I and Fatima, Chief Alhaji Amida Peregrino Brimah, became chairman of the Council of Muslim Chiefs of Ghana and head of its Muslim community in the 1970s (Brimah 71). In contrast, another one of the children of the Islamic Adsuma Maryamu Matta, identified as Adelaide Maria Peregrino (was there perhaps some relationship with Mammon Peregrino?), married John Plange, scion of a notable Gold Coast family with strong political ties. John Plange (1820–1899) was a member of the Teiko Tsuru We ruling house, Abola quarter, and eventually was recognized as an ordained Methodist minister. He was among the first generation of indigenous Methodist pastors in the Gold Coast (Parker 156). Yet, Adelaide Maria's niece, Fatima, who formed the alliance with the Muslim chief, as indicated, acquired the reputation of being a model orthodox Muslim wife. In contrast, Francisco Zaccheus Santiago Peregrino, Adelaide Maria's nephew and more than likely the grandson of Mammon Peregrino, is not recognized either for Christian principles, in particular, or for being a steadfast follower of Muslim orthodoxy above everything else. He was, however, internationally distinguished as a staunch proponent of human rights for all black men. Francisco Zaccheus Santiago Peregrino, born in Accra as a Tabom descendant, died in Cape Town, South Africa, of a heart attack at the New Somerset Hospital on November 19, 1919 (Saunders 88).

As previously indicated, at an extremely young age, Francisco Zaccheus Santiago Peregrino was sent to England (ca. 1860) to continue his education. He never returned to the Gold Coast. Nonetheless, wherever he went he would consistently refer to himself as a native of the Gold Coast, and that is how he has been remembered in various countries by diverse cultures. Late in the 1880s, he transferred to the United States and for a period resided in Buffalo, New York. There, he made his presence felt by launching a newspaper for black readers called *The Spectator*, and edited it from Albany, New York (Saunders 81). During his almost ten-year sojourn in the States, Peregrino traveled widely, familiarized himself with the pitfalls and advancements of American racial politics, and forged alliances with some of America's best-known black leaders of the day. It was undoubtedly his acquaintance with the efforts of the black American educator Booker T. Washington that led him to attempt an introduction of the Tuskegee educational system into South Africa and to send South African students to Tuskegee Institute. Peregrino and Washington maintained an active relationship, by correspondence, of intellectual cooperation and philosophical concern for the black man despite the fact that one was in South Africa and the other in the United States (Harlan 464).

In 1876 Francisco Zaccheus Santiago Peregrino married Ellen Sophia in Birmingham, England. An Englishwoman, she and two of their younger children later accompanied him on his trip to the United States. In July 1900, however, they sailed back to England to attend the first Pan African Conference in London, where Peregrino agreed to be the Cape Town, South Africa, agent for the Pan African Association (or Society, as it was sometimes called). Perhaps he was encouraged to accept this position because his eldest son, Francis Joseph Peregrino, had already settled there and had assumed the duties of principal for an educational and cultural organization called The Progressive Institute. This position required Francis Joseph to be directly involved with the African community. Francisco Zaccheus, the father, was highly in favor of activities of this nature. While still in his early twenties, the younger Francis became known for a series of lectures he published in London under the title "A Short History of the Native Tribes of South Africa and Their Manners and Customs" (Saunders 82). The elder Francis arrived in Cape Town, South Africa, in September or November of 1900. Within six weeks of his arrival, the first issue of his paper, *The South African Spectator*, was on sale. The paper's motto clearly explains Peregrino's vision as its editor, along with his civic stance in his newly adopted country: "Anti-racial, Cosmopolitan, Unprejudiced and Politically Independent" (African American Archives of the WRHS).

A statement found in "The Black Press in South Africa and Lesotho" might help to clarify why Peregrino's journal was such an important addition to the South African scene:

> The South African Press has been a sectional press throughout its history. *Race*—not language, religion or culture—has proved to be the dominant characteristic of this sectionalism, moreover, which has given the press in this country a unique status among the world's mass media of communication. (Switzer vii)

Peregrino, as a Pan Africanist, used his newspaper to promote the interests of both a "Coloured" and an African readership. It was obvious that for him, the concerns of race were paramount. During his first year in Cape Town (1901), he formed the Coloured Peoples' Vigilance Society, which aimed "to foster friendly relations between all people in South Africa who are not known as White" (Switzer vii). Furthermore, in the course of that first year, he was chosen to deliver an address before the visiting Duke of Cornwall on behalf of the Coloured people of South Africa (Saunders 84). Peregrino was also instrumental in establishing the Native Press Association (NPA) in 1904 with the aim of eliminating political party and ethnic 'tribal' differences between African newspapers in the early 1900s. The NPA most likely reinforced an informal news exchange service, already in existence, among various black publications of the day (Switzer 19). Clearly, Peregrino made a niche for himself in the area's society and in a very short time rose to become one of the two or three leading black residents of Cape Town (Saunders 84). Given the racial climate of the South Africa of that day, might he not have been considered simply "nonwhite"? Did the Peregrinos return to Africa from Brazil as miscegenated Africans?

It is important to remember the background that brought Peregrino to the station in life he attained in South Africa. He never denied that he was a Gold Coast national. It was something that he remembered and claimed with pride. But he was not an ethnic Ewe, Hausa, Fanti, Dagoma, Dagari, or Gã, among other myriad ethnic groups that are located within the geopolitical space of the Gold Coast. Nor was he in some way psychologically controlled by a heritage of ethnocultural norms. In essence, Peregrino was a black man with roots formed in Brazil and transplanted to a Gold Coast society that accepted his ancestors for their skills, stamina, resolve, and intellect. This is not to say that the area of settlement or even the Gã were ignorant of the fact that his ancestors had been held in captivity. It does, however, strengthen the position that when the African concept of being a captive who is sold is compared with the mindset that Westerners have toward an individual who is bought as forced unpaid labor, it carries entirely different connotations. As the Akan are wont to say: "*Owu nnyim akoa, nnyim ohdishi*" ["death treats the slave and the royal alike"]. In other words, death visits all humans on equal terms.

Most ethnic communities in Ghana still have in their collective memory a lexical entry that refers to the condition of being a slave:

Twi	Akoa
Fante (Akan)	Donkor
Ewe	Kluvi
Hausa	Bawa [m], Bawia [f]
Gã	Somolo
Dagbani	Dabri
Dagaare	Nora or Gbangba
Frafra	Dabri

Even so, it is not unusual in today's Ghana and in the lexicon of the Akan linguistic family, to encounter the surname "Donkor" (a derivative of "*odonkor*," i.e., slave or forced laborer) that originally referred to captive individuals. It no longer burdens the carrier of this name with the image of being a slave. Peregrino's Tabom roots, in this sense, seemingly never hobbled or entangled him with the inferiority complex of being the descendant of slaves. To the contrary, he considered himself to be a model African, a paragon of what the African person could attain and become. "He believed firmly that 'Coloured' and African in South Africa should recognize their common Blackness..." (Saunders 88). It was said that Peregrino preferred to use the "Coloured" category to include all people who were not European or white. At times, however, he proposed that the category exclude Bantu speakers (Besten 95fn13). Access to European culture, it would seem, was the principal factor that modified his concept of who was or was not "coloured." He, himself, was tribeless. Would this classify him ethnically as "nonblack" or coloured?

Yet his newspaper, *The South African Spectator*, had sections devoted to diverse ethnic interests such as those of the Indian population as well as speakers of Xhosa (Switzer 58). After reviewing the political life and journalistic goals of Peregrino, the author of "New Negro Modernity and New African Modernity," an unpublished paper read at a forum in Zurich in January 2003, concluded that:

> ...it was the Ghanaian F. Z. S. Peregrino, exemplifying the blending of New Negroism and New Africanism, who actually brought Pan-Africanism to South Africa and articulated its ideology in the pages of his *South African Spectator* newspaper in Cape Town. (Masilela 28–29)

Can it be said with any certainty that it was Peregrino's Tabom roots that encouraged him to consider in a positive light not only Africans and their mixed-race descendants in the Diaspora, but those same ethnicities on the Continent as well? Peregrino was still very young when he left the Gold Coast for his schooling under the British. Although he was able to maintain contact through correspondence with friends and relatives back in his home country, what would be the aftereffects of his social environment as a nonwhite youth in mid-nineteenth-century England? In the end, he did marry an English woman and had offspring who were biracial.

As previously mentioned, one of his sons commendably proved his resolve toward achieving progress and fair treatment at a very young age while working in South Africa. Apparently he was following his father's philosophy of equality for all persons of color. There is all the reason to believe that, based on his personal experiences, Peregrino's global vision (of "ethnic Blackness," as a continuum) appeared to be the force behind his drive "to foster friendly relations between all people in South Africa who are not known as White...to instill, if possible, a little race pride in the Colored or Black man" (Saunders 84–88). This personal viewpoint undoubtedly encouraged him to make references in his articles to Ethiopians in the Bible, to Hannibal—who for him was "one of the noblest men who ever lived"—to Alexandre Dumas, Senior and Junior; to the mulatto presidents of Latin America; and to

Toussaint L'Ouverture of French-speaking St. Domingo (Haiti) (Saunders 84–86). Indeed, one of the greatest legacies that Peregrino left to his memory was his image as a fighter for the rights of all people who were not white, be they native Africans or not. Among the first Afro-Caribbean immigrants to participate in South African politics was the Pan-Africanist Henry Sylvester Williams from Trinidad. Peregrino was among those who accepted Williams' ideals and made them known in *The South African Spectator*. For a time, Williams shared offices with Peregrino, and he, in support of Williams' Pan-Africanist goals, made it known in an editorial that: "[I am] proud to be one who aspires not to be White" (Cobley 361–363).

Recognition of the Peregrino heritage of black unification is not limited solely to South Africa. In a 2005 thesis from the National University of Rwanda, it was acknowledged that:

> In short, "The Gladiators" and *A Walk in the Night* both aim...at highlighting the importance of a collective action against white supremacy. Like *Peregrino*, who "placed strong emphasis on the need for Black unity, denouncing coloureds who felt superior to Africans"...La Guma, in the novella and short story in question, wanted coloureds to forget the small differences and put all their energy into the common struggle with all the oppressed. (Ntaganira 38; emphasis added)

There is no doubt that even as someone who was far from the direct inspiration of the Gold Coast and his Tabom roots, Peregrino managed to assume a leadership role with confidence and to become a strong advocate for a positive image of the black man.

To promote a model that speaks in a positive manner for people of African descent seems to be one of the hallmarks of the Tabom group. Their arrival and settlement in Ghana did not represent one tribal ethnicity in particular, but comprised a disparate collection of individuals from diverse tribal backgrounds with one overarching goal: social progress and respect for a person irrespective of religion or tribal affiliation. Instead of disbanding and going separate ways, they selected a leader to represent their group as a whole and rallied together under his direction. The position of leadership for the Tabom, as a united body of people, has never gone unfilled since their arrival on the Gold Coast. Although reportedly there was a period (i.e., 1981–1998) when the principal office of chieftaincy may have been lacking the confirmation of a head person, group cohesion and recognition of an interim figure of authority, invested in a person of confidence, served to preserve the community's solidarity. Today, the chieftaincy role continues under the aegis of the Nelson family. Their authority to direct the clan was bestowed by the Gã sovereignty on Azumah Nelson, the recognized headman of the returning Africans from Brazil. Posthumously, he was recognized with the title Nii (i.e., Chief or head person) Azumah I, initiating the respected chieftancy lineage of the Tabom clanship. In continuation, the second person to assume this pivotal role in the clan, João Antônio Nelson, adopted the title Nii Azumah II in honor of his father. The Nelsons, I was informed, have retained leadership responsibilities for the Tabom community since the authority of a Chief was instituted and recognized.

Conversely, while the question of hereditary or assigned chieftaincy is not within our purview to judge, it can nonetheless be ascertained that as an agent for the preservation of social cohesion, a clan leader seems to have a legitimate raison d'être, at least for the Tabom. It is not difficult to find in Ghana an overall dynamic of Ghanaian identity, the same as one would find in other political territories a Liberian, Nigerian, Ivorian, or Burkinabé national. Still, ethnosegmentations of Ewe, Hausa, Akan, and even Fanti as a unit of the Akan whole surface in conversations and social interactions as normal ethnic ideologies for the country's demographic landscape. Although a relatively small country in area, Ghana has an extremely diversified population with an estimated calculation of some 60 to 100 distinct tribal groupings and more than 52 major languages. The distinct tongues and offshoot dialects that have stemmed from these communities are a concept apart. In spite of this, Ghana's Vice President Alhaji Aliu Mahama was able to confirm at a meeting with the House of Chiefs of Ghana's northern region that:

> We are one people, irrespective of religion, tribe, political affiliation or social status. Whether one is Muslim, Christian or Traditionalist, Ghana is big enough to accommodate all of us. (*Daily Graphic*, "We are Ghanaians First" 23)

Each chief at that meeting represented a tribe or subtribe, with its correlative language and culture. Were the Tabom present in such a meeting, their unity as an identifiable community would be represented by their Chief.

Although the Tabom have become essentially a unit of the overall Gã Gestalt patterning of today, there is no denying the fact that they did not originate as an endogenous element of the Gã nation to which they now belong. Their oral histories and verbal memories, which express the foundational culture for most African societies, are different. Of primary note is the fact that the Gã, as a nation of people, have retained in the description of their beginning and identity a tradition of having migrated from Canaan, through Egypt. They claim a connection with the Hebrews and Hebrew customs, as well as a relationship with the Cushite kingdom that gave them one of their great rulers, "Ayi Kushie" (Ayi of Kush). It was he who led them from the east westward, through Nigeria to Togo. But Ayi of Kush died before reaching the settlement where the first Gã capital was established in the Gold Coast (*Ghanaweb*, "Nostalgia from Nii Armah Josiah-Aryeh"). The Gã still retain, in the recollection of their past, thousands of years of traditions, experiences, and migrations on the African continent. However, retrospection on their precaptivity period before arriving in Brazil does not seem to play a part in the day-to-day activities of the Tabom. Over the years, they have adjusted their cosmovision, as a clan, to the cultural uniqueness of the Gã and have joined in that group's ethnic-based observances and celebrations as willing and knowledgeable participants, in spite of their image as historical newcomers. This fact does not prevent the Tabom from celebrating an event such as "Homowo," for example, even though the occasion is not related to their origins. "Homowo" is a special occurrence that recalls the annual Gã festival commemorating the triumph of an abundance of crops over

Hereditary chief of the Tabom Nii Azumah V, a direct descendant of returnees from Brazil to the continent of Africa in the early decades of the nineteenth century. (photo from the author's personal collection)

famine during the Gã's long, millennial trek westward toward their final Gold Coast settlement. In the Tabom community, everyone participates in the occasion with verve, enthusiasm, and knowledge of the tradition, as if it were a part of the oral history they transferred from Brazil. Today, the Tabom are without a doubt an established entity of Ghanaian ethnography. But their collective history, prior to arrival in Ghana, does not correspond to the country's overall ethnopolitical structure. By this, it is meant that their memoirs may not compare chronologically to that of the Ashanti, the Ewe, or other groups found in the country. Nevertheless, they are indisputably bona fide Ghanaians. They see themselves as Ghanaians with an African Brazilian heritage. In this light, the internationally known boxer Azumah "The Professor" Nelson, recognized nationally to be of Tabom ancestry and a cousin of the Tabom Chief Nii Azumah V, is invariably referred to as "a native [son] of Ghana, and the first inductee from that country to enter the International Boxing Hall of Fame in the first year of eligibility" (*Ghanaweb*, "Boxing Hall Enshrines Azumah"). This recognition was bestowed on the boxer in 2004. Today, he is being hailed for his Azumah Nelson Foundation (AZNEF), which aims to provide social services to the poor and needy of his country through the mechanisms of sports and education. A proposed multisports complex will sit on a fifty-acre site purchased by this Tabom boxer and is to be equipped with modern sports and educational facilities.

At one time or another, all Africans have belonged to an identifiable ethnicity and in cases of intermarriage, identity has often been resolved by traditions of matrilineal or patrilineal exigencies. Today's Tabom are not exempt from this practice. Although many of the Tabom returnees had obvious identities—such as Yoruba or Hausa—when they left Brazil to return to Africa, few, if any, passed on to their descendants in Ghana notions of the exact location in the kingdoms of the Yoruba nation (or passed on histories of Hausa migrations on the Continent) to confirm the origins of their ancestors (Schaumloeffel 121). The authors of the UNESCO study on the oral tradition and the slave trade in Nigeria, Ghana, and Benin report that:

> One important observation from the culture of the Tabon [sic] is that during social gatherings organized by the group, songs are usually rendered in Yoruba, a language that is ironically not understood by the singers. Similarly, dances that accompany the

songs are the same as those found among the people of Lagos Island and Warri in the delta state of Nigeria. (Simpson 31)

Some of the returnees are said to have spent time in Nigeria after leaving Brazil, before finally settling in the Gold Coast. Kangidi Asuman, who later became Azumah (or Asumah) Nelson (Amos and Ayesu 40) and leader of the Tabom, serves as a relevant example that confirms a Nigerian connection for some of the members of the group. It is clear that Usuman/ Asuman/Asumah/Azumah appear to be phonemic transcriptions of a variant pronunciation of the Arabic/Muslim name "Uthman." Kangidi is a place name in Nigeria, also associated with the name of a person in the history of that country. Kangidi Asuman/Azumah Nelson is known to have arrived in the Gold Coast with a Nigerian wife. Before being captured and sent to Brazil, was he originally from Nigeria? If so, upon his return to the Continent, why did he leave Nigeria to subsequently settle in the Gold Coast? What aspects of Yoruba/Nigerian culture did he and his wife pass on to their children?

It was not unusual for descendants of the Yoruba in the New World to refer to themselves as Nagos in Brazil or Lukumí in Cuba. Today, adherence to the Candomblé religion in Brazil and Santería worship in Cuba is directly tied to the strong Yoruba (i.e., Nago and Lukumí) presence that arrived in the two areas. Perhaps it was because of their vast numbers in both countries that acknowledgement and acceptance of these religious forms are no longer confined just to the African descendants of the Nago/Lukumi groups. Today, adherents to African-based religions among the European-descendant population can also be found in both Brazil and Cuba. In addition, concepts of Yoruba heritage appear in songs, in popular speech forms, and in the creative literature as part of the national culture expressed in Spanish or Portuguese. Nothing comparable seems to have pervaded the overall cultural framework of the Tabom. Schaumloeffel found that only remnants of Yoruba culture surfaced in some songs and stories that were performed at social meetings of the Tabom. However, it was mainly a tradition perpetuated by the elder women of the group (124).

With consideration for the presumed Hausa name of pioneers such as Adsuma Maryamu Matta, inquiries to informants in Ghana's present-day Hausa community recognized the name as that of a female Hausa Muslim. Nevertheless, after allowing for phonemic shifts that occur with time and orthographical changes or uncertainties, the name remained swimming in the vast ocean of tribal migrations without the possibility of pinpointing, in the case of Tabom descendants, a specific locale of genesis. Given that the primary mode of communication for the Tabom individual in Accra is no longer Yoruba, Hausa, or even Brazilian Portuguese, could it be that aspects of their history faded along with the languages they had received from their ancestors? Most mental images and concepts of history and origin, brought with the ancestors from Brazil, are now challenged by time and superseded by their Gã acculturation. However, as Nii Azumah has said, he and the elders meet periodically to revive and keep alive clan secrets in order to make sure they remain ready for transferral to the next person that inherits the "stool" of authority.

Today, while a majority of the Tabom practice Christianity and some follow Islam, Nii Azumah did not deny that conscious notions of a spiritual relationship with "Shango," a Yoruba orisha or deity, still remain in their catalogued memory. As for this aspect of their identity, their relationship with "Shango" gives them much in common with the descendants of diasporic Africans found in Brazil, Cuba, Venezuela, Puerto Rico, Trinidad, and other countries of the Americas, regardless of the national language they now speak. This attachment to a Yoruba religious philosophy remains a constant in the Diaspora even though the predominant religion of a particular country might be Catholicism or Protestantism. There was some reluctance, nonetheless, on the part of the Tabom members present at our meeting to divulge why the emphasis was only on Shango when the collectivity of deities worshiped in Cuba and Brazil is so diverse. Shango (with an orthography of Changó in Cuba, Xangô in Brazil, and Shango in English-speaking Trinidad) is the spirit god of thunder from the vast pantheon of Yoruba deities brought from the Continent to the Americas. While Nii Azumah V did not mention other divinities from the same Yoruba source, from a contemporary point of view this raises the question of Islam, the religion with which the Tabom returned to the Continent. Was worship of the Yoruba diety also recognized and practiced by returning Muslims? Given the orthodox approach to which Muslims presumably are held, the combination of Islam and Shango might appear unlikely. Yet, the dichotomous concept in and of itself might be a clue toward joining broken threads of the group's oral history. Could the majority of the returnees have been of Yoruba origin or come under strong Yoruba influence, as opposed to a Hausa affiliation? Muslims in the Yoruba kingdoms were known to be more accommodating than Hausa Muslims, for example, and allowed the practice of traditionalist beliefs to continue alongside Islamic patterns of worship. Yoruba Islam, it is reported, is more complex than it appears at first. Studies point to the fact that the Yoruba who returned to the Continent after bondage in Brazil brought a rather progressive Islam with them that in some measure even affected those who had been left behind in Africa (Kenny n.p.). And when commenting on the slave uprising in Bahia that propelled the return of Yorubas, Hausas, Ewes, Minas, and so on back to the coast of Africa, Farid also found that Yoruba participation in leadership roles had a significant presence (Farid 55). This leads to the perception that the majority of the Afro Brazilian returnees, including the headman Azumah Nelson, might have been from the Yoruba-speaking regions or had at least been in close contact with Yoruba leaders.

Beyond the general classification of "retained Yoruba concepts," it was not evident in our conversations with the Chief whether these remnant cultural artifacts have served as definitive identification of a specific African locus of origin for the clan. They are viewed only as confirmation of the generalization: "coming from Nigeria." In this respect, the Tabom, although they have relocated to the mother continent, share much in common with other African descendants in the Diaspora of the Americas who now find themselves extricated from an ongoing oral history in the millennial griot tradition. They are all, nonetheless, still required to look upon themselves as an ethnic whole. It is in this sense that the Tabom are identified as "African Brazilians." Psychological adjustments for specific occurrences that had defined time and space in the life of the original returnees prior to their new beginnings on African soil undoubtedly molded the social structure and symbols of cultural heritage that were to be transferred.

Today's Tabom, as descendants with an immediate ancestral past that gave origin to their clan status, seem to have coalesced their transplanted ancestry into a consciousness of self and presence. This reality was subsequently translated and depicted as logo for their cultural flag. As a Tabom standard, it is displayed at gatherings and official functions, carried in ceremonious parades, or placed alongside the chief as another symbol of clan authority and unity. The flag with its logo summarizes in its design the group's history before arriving in the Gold Coast. Consequently, the official banner has abstract references to the clan detailed in green and yellow, the national colors of Brazil, together with the image of Islam's crescent moon and star, and a phrase in Yoruba whose exact meaning is no longer accessible to all individuals in the group. One perceives in this display a historical trajectory that has begun to fade with the generational divide.

Although Nii Azumah has a lucid and well-organized recollection of his group's history in Ghana, their reality prior to captivity in Brazil presented understandable lacunae, even for him, when recounting their ancestors prearrival in the Gold Coast. There were important elements available in the chief's narration, such as his ancestors' brief stay in Nigeria, confirmation of Tackie Kome's friendship, and Gã encounters with the Tabom prior to their settlement in the coastal area. There was even a recollection of the place of departure from Bahia for the seven groups, with a probable name of "Antonio." Few details were conclusively or definitively expanded. There remains to be determined who among the ancestors had still been in captivity or was free prior to the 1835 uprising in Bahia. Is one to expect that such information would have been freely given to an outsider? For clarification of the transfer of African culture prior to captivity in Africa, it would help to know who had been a recent arrival to Brazil before the uprising, and precisely from where in Africa the majority of the ancestors had come. How many of the ancestors had been a *"Crioulo"* [African-descendant born in Brazil]? It is important to recall, however, that the Tabom as a Brazilian Portuguese-speaking ethnic entity had originally formed their diasporic image in Brazil only to solidify its significance in the Gold Coast. In this light, did all family histories run parallel prior to their return to Africa?

As indicated, the clan was given its cohesion as such in the early decades of the nineteenth century (1836) with the arrival to the Gold Coast of Brazilian Africans in seven individual groups. Each party consisted of ten members. The recognized leader at the head of each section appeared to owe allegiance only to the members of his assemblage. Why were they organized into seven groups with a fixed number of people in each unit? Was this a prior arrangement with the Gã leadership? Was this an organized grouping that put the Brazilians under the protection of the *"Sete Potências"* [Seven Powers] of the Yoruba belief system, i.e., the Seven African Powers? And why did each group have exactly ten members? Was this arrangement settled upon in Nigeria? Why? These are questions that remained unanswered in our conversations with clan members. However, Michael Tetteh, a Gã-speaking friend who is not a member of the Tabom community, discussed at length the history and culture of his group, the Adangbe (Gã-Adangbe). As they are closely associated with the Gã, he suggested that some answers might be found in the culture of this group, with which the Tabom became assimilated. Politically, the Gã, Ningo, Pampram, Ada, Krobo, and so on are similar in culture and have been classified into one big tribe that goes by the name Gã-Adangbe. Based on oral histories, the organization of certain facets of their infrastructure (he referred to this as "quarters," i.e., areas or districts) is based on the number seven. Seven represents the actual or surmised number of groups with which the Gã-Adangbe arrived along the coast. And, Tetteh relates, "This honorable tribe of people stretches right along the coast from Ada in the East to Accra proper in the West."[19] Would an organization into the prophetic number seven have made the Tabom newcomers more acceptable, if they were to pattern their arrival to conform to an established mythological image? The question still remains as to how they could have been introduced to the concept of "seven" as a special feature of the area's culture. Were the Tabom prepared for this while still in the American phase of their Diaspora? A history with various dimensions that have to be retrieved is one of the legacies of a diasporic existence. Even though as Brazilians, they may have been formed into a cohesive group of like-minded individual families, there apparently was no concept of being a Tabom or of belonging to one particular and distinctive ethnic clan until their return to Africa.

Nevertheless, as refugees in the Gold Coast who coalesced into one mega unit of kindred purpose and a similar language (all were reportedly conversant in Brazilian Portuguese), it appears that seven individual oral histories were supplanted by one overarching, collective biography with clear delineations of time and space. In accounts not written by the Tabom, the approach taken usually makes reference to a "Brazilian" heritage or lineage without the details of their Yoruba, Hausa, or other ethnic history and affiliation prior to their Gold Coast settlement. Thus, for associates from their group, such as the Peregrinos, who offered so much to the clan's image of self-pride and black progress, not much is known about the background that formulated this mindset. For many of the people that the Tabom encountered on their return to the continent of their ancestors who were already settled, there was an unbroken chain of continuous history. The author of *Inside Ghana's Democracy* offers us a relevant case in point. Before beginning his discussion of the political atmosphere of the country, he introduces himself to his readers as follows:

> The yard in which I grew up was surrounded by [the] ancient housing of my matrilineage. It was typical traditional housing named after the founder, a smith. It was called Ofori Solo We…As a smith, Ofori was reputed in household folklore to have been the first settler at Adadentam or Adentam…He was joined by a group of fishermen from Asere, the core Ga settlement in pre-colonial Accra. To date, the Adentams, with names like Ayi, Armah, Dedei, Korkoi, Adaku, bear the purest Ga names among the inhabitants of Jamestown.…For some strange reason the paternal section of my matrilineage claim allegiance to the Sempe quarter of Jamestown…Members of Ofori Solo We were also among the earliest settlers at Bortianor and Kokrobite where they constitute one of the main royal houses. (Josiah-Aryeh 2)

But then, equal importance is given to the fact that there are other ethnicities in his ancestral environment:

> The great featherweight Azuma Nelson shared many things in common with me. Our mothers were friends and *paternally*, we both have black Brazilian antecedents. His father, a cheerful tailor, lived at Mamprobi where Azuma learnt his trade and flourished. (4; emphasis added)

How expansive would the boxer Azumah Nelson be, in contrast, when recounting his ethnic lineage? Part of Tabom's collective memory in Ghana includes the fact that in 1854, they became the founders of the First Scissors House, which was the first tailoring shop in the country. Among the various responsibilities and activities of this new enterprise was the task of providing the Ghanaian army with uniforms. Even today, the most celebrated and accomplished tailor in Accra is Mr. Dan Morton, the official chairman of the Tabom community.

Much can be said about the success of the Tabom in Ghana and their integration into the Gã nation. The relationships they have acquired in that country, especially through marriage, seem to be complex and extended. However, when one attempts to compare their Ghanaian kinships with a Brazilian lineage, the latter appears truncated and less expansive. This lack of depth in family extensions is particularly noticeable where a protracted listing of genealogical references is anticipated, as in the customary African framework. Perhaps this is how the clan has designed the social model of their image for extragroup and national consumption. There is the possibility that their genealogical referencing prior to and during their stay in Brazil might detract from clan cohesiveness. This is not to say that lineage and heritage do not come into play in the Tabom cultural framework. After all, succession in the chieftaincy rank depends on an understanding of its seemingly dichotomous structure: while Nelson descendants reign supreme in its hierarchy, the group's "stool" or invested authority alternates between progeny from the house of the Alasha Nelson family and their counterparts from the Aruna Nelson branch. The previous chief, Nii Azumah IV, was officially recognized as a scion of the Alasha Nelsons. It stands to reason then that the ruler, Nii Azumah V, would have to be from the house of the Aruna Nelson family.

Careful observation leads one to intuit that there are aspects of the group's oral history that must remain reserved, and are to be shared only with the inner circle. Consequently, some of the questions raised may have in-house answers that might not be for outgroup consumption. Schaumloeffel reports that for the person who is to assume the highest rank of authority within the Tabom clanship,

> [there is] a period of learning, in which the future leader of the community is visited by elders, who tell him the "secrets" of the ancestors, the history of the clan and transmit their experiences accumulated orally from generation to generation...[with the aim] of always respecting their history, traditions and customs. (72)

This confirms the intuition that mere membership in the Tabom clan does not expose everyone to the maximum profundity of the group's ancestral well, and what it entails both philosophically as well as psychologically. It can only be surmised that embedded in the secretive nature of these "sessions of preparation" would be references to the pre-Brazilian African experiences and histories of the principal ancestors, if not to all the forefathers and foremothers of the group. With Tabom names such as Shalah, Aruna or Harun, Alii, and Musa, among others, it is certain that such orthodox Muslim designations must have had a pre-Brazilian connection. Matters of this nature are usually attached to an oral history. Today, however, most of the Tabom hold on tenaciously and quite overtly to the concept of a Brazilian-African Latino ethnic affiliation, and tend to avoid the impression of appearing psychologically deracinated from Brazil, in spite of that country's history of African enslavement.

Still, the Brazilian roots transplanted by returning Africans are firmly implanted in diverse facets of Ghanaian life. For example, one can trace in the name of Bishop Aruna Kojo Nelson, a Tabom ordained into the Anglican ministry in 1932 (Schaumloeffel 85), the historical trajectory of a clan that adopted not only Christianity in a new space, but adapted to the culture of the new land. The combination of "Aruna-Kojo-Nelson" hints at Muslim and Ghanaian characteristics, with elements of both. Aruna, an Islamic Yoruba designation for "Aaron," one of the prophets (Arun<Harun and Aruna<Haruna) teams up with the Ghanaian nomenclature "Kojo," given to a male child born on Monday. This allows for a comfortable integration of cultural adaptations. However, adaptations can assume an entirely different dimension. For example:

> ...the names of twelve Gã leaders liable to furnish carriers were added to the requisition forms provided by the government. These included three oblempon stool holders of the Otublohum quarter: Chiefs Antonio Ankra and John Vanderpuye of the Dadebanwe, and John A. Nelson, the leader of the Tabon community. (Parker 143)

Nelson, who as a stool holder assumed the title Nii Azumah II, was born in Brazil and arrived in the Gold Coast at an extremely young age. It is highly unlikely that his Brazilian name was anything other than João Antonio. Yet the English language sources that were consulted have adopted the Anglicized version of his name, John Anthony (John A.) (Schaumloeffel 42). The responsibilities that various Tabom members were allowed to assume in the society at large gives one the sense that slavery in Brazil was no longer viewed as an albatross or an impediment. To the contrary, postslavery in the Gold Coast, for the returnees and their descendants, had become a metaphor for progress or social mobility.

The Embassy of Brazil in Accra has officially recognized the Tabom as descendants of ex-captives who left their Latin American space in the nineteenth century. Acknowledgment of the group by the Brazilian government, along with aid from UNESCO and other organizations, have facilitated restoration of the iconic "Brazil House." Originally, finances to purchase the land on which "Brazil House" is located and construction of the building, with its colonial Brazilian architecture, were the personal challenges of a returning Tabom group leader, Maama Nassau.[20] The uniquely styled building, when it was first erected, was one of the first stone structures in the area. In this respect, the trailblazing achievements

A Latin Identity, An African Experience

Nii Azumah V, the hereditary chief of the Tabom, descendants of returnees to Africa from Brazil, greets President of Brazil Luiz Inácio Lula da Silva at the reconstructed nineteenth century "Brazil House" in Accra, Ghana. (photo courtesy of Emmanuel Quaye, photographer. Accra, Ghana)

of the Tabom did not stop with their arrival. Today, the community continues to make its presence known and felt through noteworthy accomplishments. In this context, one considers Ghana's first female Chief Justice, Georgina Wood, whose great-grandfather was the pioneering Nassau and who recalls having lived in Brazil House as a child. Today's restored edifice, modeled on a colonial-era mansion of Bahia, Brazil, will function as the reception center for the Tabom chief and serve as a museum and cultural site to promote the group's image, as well as a center for the Tabom community at large. Brazil's president, Luiz Inacio Lula da Silva, in a recent visit to Ghana and to the reconstructed building, paid homage to the Tabom with the declaration that: "The house honours the memory of...great people" (*Daily Graphic*, "Brazil President Visits Brazil House in Accra"). One wonders, nonetheless, what thoughts must have occurred to the Brazilian contingent that accompanied Pres. Lula da Silva upon seeing their head of state being formally received by the descendant of former slaves from their country. As the official representative of the Tabom, Nii Azumah V wore the august trappings of his high-status office: a crown, gold-decorated sandals, and a toga of expensively woven cloth. A formal entourage of Tabom elders accompanied him, giving official recognition and support to the protocol of the chief's station as they and he received the president from Brazil.

The Tabom community enjoys a distinguished image in Ghana with a brief but respected history. The paternal lineage of Chief Azumah V can be traced to one of the first Brazilian leaders that arrived in the Gold Coast approximamtely 180 years ago. This pioneering figure, Kangidi Asuman/Azumah Nelson, was subsequently endowed with the title "Nii" and became Nii Azumah I. It was through him that the group's chieftancy was initiated. From then to now, terminating with the present-day authority of Azumah V, they are:

a. Nii Azumah I — great-grandfather of Azumah V
b. Nii Azumah II — great-uncle of Azumah V
c. Nii Aruna I — grandfather of Azumah V
d. Nii Azumah III — uncle of Azumah V
e. Nii Azumah IV — cousin of Azumah V/eldest son of Azumah III
f. Nii Azumah V — present leader of the Tabom clan

To date, the historical and contemporary presence of the Tabom in Ghana appears to be a dimension of the aftermath of slavery that is rarely approached or even considered in the creative literature of Latin America. Isn't their existence just as viable for literary exploration as African slavery? The Tabom are only one such group in just one of several countries that received returnees. There are similar returnee groups in other African countries. What happens to the concept of Diaspora as institution when the despised and enslaved African returns to the Continent after the ravages of slavery have taken their toll psychologically? Not all Africans on the Continent, at least at the surface level, tend to view slavery as a permanent status. For some groups, it can be a misfortune of time and place:

> My children "ei"
> (Yes)
> What do you fear?
> (We fear the tiger)
> The tiger is not back from hunting
> So you can play
> (The children start playing in the open field)
> The TIGER is coming "o-o-o"
> All the children run to avoid capture.
> ("Me mba ei…Seboh no reba…", Akan children's game)[21]

In the Gold Coast, the Twi- and Fanti-speaking Akan, neighbors of the Gã who accepted the Tabom, saw their ranks depleted by the slave catcher, the human tiger. The same misfortune befell the Ewe, Hausa, and other African nations in the Gold Coast or in West Africa as a whole. All native groups recognize that a set of unexpected circumstances can translate freedom into captivity despite predetermined boundaries of ethnicity or rank. Again, to borrow from the wisdom of the Akan: "*Owu nnyim akoa, nnyim odeshe*" ["death treats the slave and the royal alike"]. In the final analysis, the lives of all men are intertwined: "*Odeshe annko a, akoa guan*" ["When the nobleman refuses to fight, it is the slave that will run away"].

For the Gã, it was consideration of the person, not previous enslavement, that enabled them to open up their lands to the acquired skills and aptitudes of the Brazilian Africans—united under the clan name "Tabom"—and to offer them a refuge from rejection and exploitation: "*Ablekuma Abakuma Wo.*"

Works Cited

Abarry, Abu. "A Traditional Poetry of the Ga of Ghana." *Journal of Black Studies* 14.4 (Jun. 1984): 493–506. Print.

Adamu, Mahdi. *The Hausa Factor in West African History.* Ibadan, Nigeria: Ahmadu Bello University Press, 1978. Print.

Aguirre Beltran, Gonzalo. *La población negra de México.* México, D. F.: Fondo de Cultura Económico, 1984. Print.

Akurang-Parry, Kwabena O. "Rethinking the 'Slaves of Salaga': Post-Proclamation Slavery in the Gold Coast (Colonial Southern Ghana), 1874–1899." *Left History* 8.1 (2002): 33–60. Print.

———. "A Smattering of Education and Petitions as Sources: A Study of African Slaveholders' Responses to Abolition in the Gold Coast Colony, 1874–1875." *History in Africa* 27 (2000): 39–60. Print.

Alvarez, Julia. *En el nombre de Salomé.* Trans. Dolores Prida. New York: Vintage Books, 2002. Print.

———. *In the Name of Salomé.* Chapel Hill, NC: Algonquin Books, 2000. Print.

Amos, Alcione M. "Afro-Brazilians in Togo: The Case of the Olympio Family, 1882–1945." *Cahiers d'Etudes africaines* 162. XLI (2001): 293–314. Print.

Amos, Alcione Meira, and Ebenezer Ayesu. "Sou Brasileiro: História dos TABOM, Afro-Brasileiros en Acra, Gana." *Afro-Asia* 33 (2005): 35–65. Print.

Bacalhau, Luis et al. "Buscando Outra Sociedade." Web. 17 Mar. 2010

Barickman, B. J. "Reading the 1835 Parish Censuses from Bahia: Citizenship, Kinship, Slavery, and Household in Early Nineteenth-Century Brazil." *The Americas* 59.3 (Jan. 2003): 287–323. Print.

Barnet, Miguel, ed. *The Autobiography of a Runaway Slave: Esteban Montejo*. Trans. Jocasta Innes. New York: Pantheon Books, 1968. Print.

———. *Biografía de un cimarrón*. México, D. F.: Siglo Veintiuno Editores, SA. 1968. Print.

Besten, Michael Paul. "Transformation and Reconstitution of Khoe-San Identities: Aas Le Fleur I. Griqua Identities and Post-Apartheid Khoe-San Revivalism (1894–2004)." Diss. Geboren te Roma, Lesotho, 1969. Print.

Boahen, A. Adu. *Mfantsipim and the Making of Ghana: A Centenary History, 1876–1976*. Accra, Ghana: Sankofa Educational Publishers, 1996. Print.

Boyd, Antonio Olliz. "The Concept of Black Esthetics as Seen in Selected Works of Three Latin American Writers: Machado de Assis, Nicolás Guillén and Adalberto Ortiz." PhD diss., Stanford University, 1975. Print.

Boyd and Abudu, Gabriel Asoanab. "Piedra Pulida: Nancy Morejon's Tribute to Nicolás Guillen." *Singular Like a Bird: The Art of Nancy Morejon*. Ed. Miriam DeCosta-Willis. Washington, DC: Howard University Press, 2001. 245–262. Print

Brimah, M. A. P. *A Migrant African Chief*. Baltimore: Noble House, 2001. Print.

Cobley, Alan Gregor. " 'Far from Home': The Origins and Significance of the Afro-Caribbean Community in South Africa to 1930." *Journal of Southern African Studies* 18.2 (Jun. 1992): 349–370. Print.

Codo, Bellarmin C. "Returning Afro-Brazilians." *From Chains to Bonds: The Slave Trade Revisited*. Ed. Doudou Diene. New York: Berghahn Books, 2001. 55–64. Print.

Cohen, Peter J. "Orisha Journeys: The Role of Travel in the Birth of Yoruba-Atlantic Religions." *Archives de Sciences Sociales Des Religions* 117 (janvier–mars 2002): 17–36. Print.

Costa e Silva, Alberto da. *Castro Alves*. São Paulo: Companhia das Letras, 2006. Print.

Daily Graphic. "Brazil President Visits Brazil House in Accra." Web. 21 Apr 2008.

———. "We are Ghanaians First." 23 Aug 2007. Print.

Dakubu, M. E. Kropp. *Korle Meets the Sea: A Sociolinguistic History of Accra*. New York: Oxford University Press, 1997. Print.

Dallek, Robert. *An Unfinished Life: John F. Kennedy, 1917–1963*. Boston: Little, Brown and Company, 2003. Print.

Dantas, Raymundo Souza. *África Difícil (Missão Condenada: Diário)*. Rio de Janeiro: Editora Leitura, S. A., 1965. Print.

Department of State, Central Files, POL 17 – 1 GHANA. 26 Apr 1963. "Telegram from the Department of State to the Embassy in Ghana." Web. 11 April 2007.

Dickson, K. B. "Evolution of Seaports in Ghana: 1800–1928." *Annals of the Association of American Geographers* 55.1 (Mar. 1965): 98–111. Print.

Diouf, Sylviane A. *Servants of Allah: African Muslims Enslaved in the Americas*. New York: New York University Press, 1998. Print.

Esdaille, Milca. "Same Trip Different Ships: Dominican Authors and African Americans (Interview)." *Black Issues Book Review* (Mar. 2001). Web. 7 May 2002.

Farid, A. A. Muhammad Shareef bin. *The Islamic Slave Revolts of Bahia, Brazil*. Pittsburgh, PA: Institute of Islamic-African Studies, 1998. Print.

Ghanaweb. "Boxing Hall Enshrines Azumah." Web. 15 Apr 2008.

———. "Nostalgia from Nii Armah Josiah-Aryeh" Web. 19 Jan 2007.

Green, Tobias. "Further Considerations on the Sephardim of the Petite Côte." *History in Africa* 32 (2005): 165–183. Print.

Harlan, Louis R. "Booker T. Washington and the White Man's Burden." *The American Historical Review* 71.2 (Jan. 1966): 441–467. Print.

Holy Bible, New Living Translation. Wheaton, IL: Tyndale House Publishers, Inc., 1996, 2004.

Josiah-Aryeh, Nii Armah. *Inside Ghana's Democracy.* Milton Keynes, U.K.: Author House U.K.: Ltd., 2008. Print.

Kennedy, James H. "Nucleos de pesquisas em tradução e estudos interculturais." *Translating Poetry* (Sept. 2006) Depto. De Línguas e Letras. Universidade Federal de Espíritu Santo. Web 16 Jun. 2007.

Kenny OP, Joseph. "The Spread of Islam in Nigeria: A Historical Survey." Reading. Conference on Shari'a in Nigeria Spiritan Institute of Theology, Enugu (22–24 Mar. 2001). Print.

Kent, R. K. "African Revolt in Bahia: 24–25 January 1835." *Journal of Social History* 3.4 (Summer 1970): 334–356. Print.

Lake, Obiagele. "Toward a Pan-African Identity: Diaspora African Repatriates in Ghana." *Anthropological Quarterly* 68.1 (Jan. 1995): 21–36. Print.

Law, Robin. "The Evolution of the Brazilian Community in Ouidah." *Slavery and Abolition* 22.1 (2001): 3–21. Print.

Law, Robin, and Kristin Mann. "West Africa in the Atlantic Community: The Case of the Slave Coast." *The William and Mary Quarterly* 56.2 (Apr. 1999): 307–341. Print.

Levine, Robert M. "Brazil's Jews during the Vargas Era and After." *Luso-Brazilian Review* 5.1 (Summer 1968): 45–58. Print.

Lucía, Daniel Omar De. "Sociedades de retorno en África Occidental: siglos XVIII–XX." *El Catoblepas* 14 (abril 2003): 1–27. Print.

Magoo, Eduardo. "La Buenos Aires negrera, tanguera y kilombera." Web. 23 Sept. 2008.

Masilela, Ntongela. "New Negro Modernity and New African Modernity." Reading. Black Atlantic: Literatures, Histories Cultures Forum. Zurich, Jan. 2003. Print.

Matory, J. L. "Afro Atlantic Culture: On the Live Dialogue Between Africa and the Americas." *Africana: The Encyclopedia of the African and African-American Experience*. New York: Basic Civitas, 1991. 36–44. Print.

———. "The English Professors of Brazil: On the Diasporic Roots of the Yoruba Nation." *Comparative Studies in Society and History* 41.1 (Jan. 1999): 72–103. Print.

Montgomery, Mary E. "The Eyes of the World Were Watching: Ghana, Great Britain, and the United States, 1957–1966." PhD diss., University of Maryland, 2004. Print.

Moore, Z. L. "Out of the Shadows: Black and Brown Struggles for Recognition and Dignity in Brazil, 1964–1985." *Journal of Black Studies* 19.4 (Jun. 1989): 394–410. Print.

Nascimento, Abdias do et al. "Reflections of an Afro-Braziliano." *The Journal of Negro History*. 64.3 (Summer 1979): 274–282. Print.

Naval Database. *Salisbury*, 1814. Web. 25 Jan. 2008.

Noticias STF. "Presidente da Suprema Corte de Gana destaca importância do intercâmbio entre judiciário." Web. 21 Aug 2009.

Ntaganira, Vincent. "Alex La Guma's Short Stories in Relation to 'A Walk in the Night': A Socio-Political and Literary Analysis." MA thesis. University of the Western Cape, South Africa, 2005. Print.

Parker, John. *Making the Town: State and Society in Early Colonial Accra*. Portsmouth, NH: Heinemann, 2000. Print.

Pérez-Sarduy, Pedro. *Las Criadas de la Habana*. La Habana, Cuba: Editorial Letras Cubanas, 2003. Print.

Pérez-Sarduy, Pedro, and Jean Stubbs, eds. *Afro Cuban Voices: On Race and Identity in Contemporary Cuba*. Gainesville: University Press of Florida, 2000. Print.

Quadros, Jânios. "Brazil's New Foreign Policy." *Foreign Affairs* 19.1 (1961–1962): 19–27. Print.

"Quem sou eu." Luis Gama. *Jornal de Poesia*. Web. 16 Jun. 2007.

Reis, João José. *Rebelião escrava no Brasil: A história do levante dos malês em 1835*. São Paulo: Companhia Das Letras, 2003. Print.

———. "Slave Resistance in Brazil: Bahia, 1807–1835." *Luso-Brazilian Review* 25. 1 (Summer 1988): 111–144. Print.

Reis, João José, and Eduardo e Silva. *Negociação e Conflito A Resistência Negra No Brasil Escravista*. São Paulo: Companhia Das Letras, 2005. Print.

Rodrigues, Jose Honório. "The Influence of Africa on Brazil and of Brazil on Africa." *The Journal of African History* 3.1 (1962): 49–67. Print.

Saunders, C. "F. Z. S. Peregrino and the South African Spectator." *Quarterly Bulletin of the South African Library* XXXII (1977–1978): 81–90. Print.

Sarracino Magriñat, Rodolfo. *Los que volvieron a África*. La Habana, Cuba: Editorial de Ciencias Sociales, 1988. Print.

Schaumloeffel, Marco Aurelio. *TABOM: The Afro-Brazilian Community in Ghana*. Bridgetown, Barbados: Schaumloeffel Editor/Custom Books, 2009. Print.

Schorsch, Jonathan. "Blacks, Jews and the Racial Imagination in the Writings of Sephardim in the Long Seventeenth Century." *Jewish History* 19 (2005): 109–135. Print.

———. *Jews and Blacks in the Early Modern World*. New York: Cambridge University Press, 2004. Print.

Simms, Norman. "Being Crypto-Jewish in Colonial Brazil (1500–1822): Brushing History against the Grain." *Journal of Religious History* 31.4 (Dec. 2007): 421–450. Print.

Simpson, Alaba. *Oral Tradition Relating to Slavery and Slave Trade in Nigeria, Ghana and Benin*. Paris: United Nations Educational, Scientific and Cultural Organization, 2004. Print.

Switzer, Les, and Donna Switzer. *The Black Press in South Africa and Lesotho: A descriptive bibliographic guide to African, Coloured and Indian newspapers, newsletters and magazines 1836–1976*. Boston: G. K. Hall & Co., 1979. Print.

Tosh, Peter. "African" lyrics. Web. Jun. 2007.

Valdés, Gabriel de la Concepción. "Plegaria a Dios." Poetas Cubanos. Web. 15 Dec. 2007.

Verger, Pierre. "América Latina in África." *África en América Latina*. Ed. Manuel Moreno Fraginals. México, D. F.: Siglo veintiuno editores, s. a., 1977. Print.

Viana Filho, Luis. *O Negro na Bahia: Um Ensaio Clássico Sobre A Escravidão*. Rio de Janeiro: Editora Nova Fronteira, S. A., 1988. Print.

Vlach, John Michael. "The Brazilian House in Nigeria: The Emergence of a 20th-Century Vernacular House Type." *The Journal of American Folklore* 97.383 (Jan.–Mar. 1984): 3–23. Print.

Epilogue

The Tabom unbdoubtedly see themselves today as a Latin community transplanted to Ghana. They function as a collective whole whose unifying ethnic bond or clanship stems from the group's common heritage as descendants of ex-enslaved Portuguese-speaking immigrants from Brazil. They are, without a doubt, an ethnoracial link to the African-descendant Brazilians one finds in that country today, and by extension, to all black people whose ancestors were dropped off at different ports in Latin America. While on the whole, many of the ancestors of the Tabom—during precaptivity—were originally from different areas in Africa and possessed diverse ethnonyms, after captivity and during their stay in Brazil, these affiliations, although still alive, apparently began to assume less importance. It became a given, therefore, that after returning to the Continent and settling in the Gold Coast, unity as a group with a common goal for survival and progress would become the main focus. This was precisely the observation made for another community of Brazilian Africans that returned to Africa and put down roots in Benin (formerly Dahomey), a region east of the Tabom's Gold Coast area:

> *Os antigos escravos que retornaram tinham diferentes origens étnias e só estavam unidos pelo passado comum vivido no Brasil.* (Guran 270)
>
> (The former slaves that returned were all from different ethnic origins, and were only united by the [slave] past they shared in common in Brazil.)

Regardless of the loss of a native identity, it should always be understood that there is no such thing as a generic African and that each African taken into slavery came originally from a definite region and had an identifiable kinship group with a corresponding culture of which they were aware. Assimilation, nonetheless, became a means of survival in a new environment. What was left for the newly arrived clan of settlers was a perceived unity, in an ideal sense. It stemmed principally from an ethnic relationship that became strengthened by a common mission. The result joined one African from Brazil to the other and then each individual to the continent of Africa by reason of ancestry or actual birth. Perhaps to their mutual benefit, while in Brazil their sense of group unity did not preclude Africans from acquiring aspects of Brazilian culture, which by its nature had become a hybrid of Portuguese and African components. Even the Portuguese language, their main mode of communication, became Africanized to a certain extent. As various sources report, Africans were literally converted into Brazilians by default:

> *Tendo vivido no Brasil...esses africanos retornaram à África não "africanos" como tinham chegado na Bahia, mas "brasileiros," ou seja africanos abrasileirados...Esses africanos e descendentes de africanos depois da sua estada no Brazil...retornaram à África "abrasileirados"...nos seus diversos hábitos, gostos, costumes e mesmo nos seus vícios.* (Guran 270)
>
> (After having lived in Brazil, these Africans returned to Africa not as the Africans they were when they arrived in Bahia, but as Brazilians, that is, Brazilianized Africans...These Africans and their

descendants after living in Brazil returned to Africa Brazilianized in their diverse habits, tastes, customs and even in their vices.)

Having established that the ancestors of the Tabom returned to Africa with a new and somewhat expanded awareness of themselves and the American world, what is the legal and cultural status of these Brazilian-related Africans today? While none of the informants who were consulted would say that dual citizenship had been discussed openly, the government of Brazil has publicly acknowledged the Tabom and has accepted their assertion of Brazil as their locus of origin. The authorities likewise recognize the community as part of Brazil's historical patrimony, and it is common practice for Brazil's head of state, President Lula da Silva, to visit the community whenever he is in Ghana. As an iconic symbol, these descendants of former slaves from a Latin American country are a reminder of the many links that comprise the long chain of the African Diaspora—a human cordon that stretches from the Continent to all of the Americas and back again. They are visible, tangible, and credible evidence of the role that African peoples played in the economic and social history of the Spanish- and Portuguese-speaking Americas. Moreover, they have fashioned a positive image for themselves in Ghana with proof of the intellectual, economic, and civic contributions that society gains when stultifying prejudices are not allowed to eclipse human qualities. An impression of this nature should provide an aesthetic inspiration for Afro Latin artists, especially those writers who still approach Africa in "the search for a positive ancestral model," as one literary critic has commented (Lewis 176). Unfettered opportunity supported by preparation, intelligence, and drive supplant the racism and phenotypic entitlements these Brazilian Africans would have had to confront in race-conscious Brazil. In this respect, one can compare the societal advances of the Tabom in Ghana with that of their African-descendant counterparts in Brazil. Mention was previously made in this study of the president of Ghana's Supreme Court, Georgina Wood, the great-granddaughter of a Tabom pioneer. In a country of approximately 22 million inhabitants and scores of ethnic divisions, her appointments (in 2002 as a Supreme Court judge and in 2007 as its chief judge) demonstrate the recognition given to intellect, talent, and solid academic preparation over ethnic preference (she and the president that appointed her do not belong to the same ethnic group), social bias, gender prejudice, or some other contrived, discriminatory practice. In contrast, it was not until 2003 that a black man (categorically identified as such) was appointed to the Brazilian Supreme Court, well over a century after the abolition of slavery in that country, a country with over four times more African descendants than Ghana's total population. The reported figures indicate that approximately 90 to 95 million Brazilians are identified as black in a total population of 190 million. When confronted with this fact, Brazilians who are hypersensitive to the fallacies of their policy of "racial democracy" counter that Joaquim Barbosa (the black man that Brazil's president Lula da Silva appointed to the Supreme Court) is not the first black supreme court judge, but the third. This might be true if Brazil's declared ethnic categories were not so movable ad libitum. Records show that Hermenegildo de Barros (1919–1937) and Pedro Lessa (1907–1921) indeed were nonwhite federal jurists. However, the two are usually referred to as "mulatto"—de Barros was considered "a dark mulatto," while Lessa was termed "a light mulatto." Likewise, depending on the social context, both might be claimed under the rubric of "*pardo*," another catchall heading for multiracial individuals. Yet when it is a matter of ethnoracial listings, Brazil claims that there is a definite distinction between mixed-race and nonmiscegenated peoples. If so, on what grounds are de Barros and Lessa now being claimed as the first two "black" Supreme Court judges? With allowances for the doubt of an identifying ethnic context, whether the image of just three black judges since abolition and the founding of the Republic of Brazil stands as a symbol of racial progress or not goes without comment. It appears that the reliance on phenotype makes "racial democracy" elusive and not applicable to everyone. Following the same line of reasoning, the reader should refer to Essay IV—which introduced the Tabom—where there was mention of a young Brazilian woman (Monica Menezes Campos) who, though classified "*mulata*," was selected to study at the Rio Branco

Institute for career diplomats because of the complaint that no blacks had ever been nominated to prepare for the diplomatic corps. With all seriousness, she remarked that overnight she had stopped being a mulatta to become "Black"! Then too, there is the case of the internationally famous writer, Machado de Assis, recognized in all circles as "mulatto" while he was alive, but listed as "white" on his death certificate. Thus, due to his indisputable fame he attained in death the social benefits that eluded him while alive. In all fairness when discussing Brazil's approach to questions of race and ethnicity, it should be noted that their seventh president, Nilo Peçanha (1909–1910) was always acknowledged as nonwhite, but was a light-skinned Brazilian.

The psychological rationale appears to be that the darker skin tones denote a closer relationship to African blackness in the Latin context, and this blackness, in turn, is a direct connection to slavery. This was precisely the inference found in the aesthetics of Alvarez and Perez in Essay III. Still, in spite of volumes of research (mainly accessible to academics) that postulate an ongoing blackness and a historical African existence in Latin America, with visible evidence that establishes the reality of their presence in the area, it was and is not difficult to find opponents to the idea of there being strains of Africa in the genetic pool of the Latino/Hispanic prototype. As the Venezuelan political activist Jesus "Chucho" Garcia has noted:

> ...the official versions of Venezuelan history, akin to the histories of the rest of so-called Latin America, reduce Africa's contributions mainly to drums and "witchcraft." (Garcia 284)

Under this guise, African contributions that relate to phenotypes and philosophies are glossed over or ignored in favor of the much-touted European and Amerindian components of the Latin American national image. In the analysis of Alvarez's novel *In the name of Salomé* in Essay III, the Ureña brother who married the Mexican woman with indigenous features wondered—it was more a silent wish—if the Dominican mulatto physiognomy could be confused with the Indian phenotype of his Mexican wife. The common assessment of this perspective is that bias against certain ethnoracial types is supported with the intent to "modify the ethnic composition of our people" (Garcia 284). Be that as it may, with the advent of media globalization and more access to educational opportunities (e.g., Brazil has just begun to grapple with issues of "affirmative action" for increased access by nonwhite students to state universities), African Latinos, Afro Hispanics, Black Latins, Black Hispanics (oxymorons or a question of ethnogenesis?) in ever-increasing numbers have begun to overtly challenge the official versions of their Eurocentric national histories and ethnic propaganda with investigative proof of their own, as the following statement affirms:

> In 1985, I made my first trip to the Republic of the Congo in search of information about Venezuela's historical relationship with Central Africa. My purpose was to demystify the African, particularly the dominant Central Bantu presence in Venezuela, in order to fill in the African absence in the construction of our national identity. (Garcia 284)

Not only in Venezuela but also in most Latin American countries in general, when the issue of national identity becomes a reason for embarrassment in the mind of the controlling sector, national histories can be adjusted in order to present the most favorable image. As a result, usually a racial component suffers:

> In Ecuador, as elsewhere in Latin America…the official imagination of national identity has been constructed since the colonial period by the white and white-mestizo elites around the notion of *mestizaje* (race mixing); it is "an ideology of *blanqueamiento* (whitening)…." Despite its obvious intention to render racial and ethnic diversity invisible, this Ecuadorian ideology of national identity imposes a racist reading on the map of national territory, which consists of conceiving rural areas as places of racial inferiority, indolence, backwardness (if not savagery)…areas, mostly populated by nonwhites…my intent is to locate blackness within the cultural topography of Ecuadorian society… (Rahier 421, original parentheses)

Nevertheless, in the final analysis, the prototypical Latin/Hispanic national image depends more on suppositions based on phenotypes than on traceable genotypes for the promoted national image. In his study of the racial scene in Ecuador, Rahier found that ethnic groups were identified as indigenous, blacks, mestizos, white-mestizos, and whites. The white-mestizo/white segment controlled social, political, and economic powers. As for black Ecuadorians, "they remain invisible. Afro Ecuadorians constitute the ultimate Other [sic], some sort of historical aberration, a noise in the ideological system of nationality..." (422). This observation, in a sense, confirms the aesthetic truth that the Ecuadorian novelist Adalberto Ortiz structures into his tale of *Juyungo*, a world of diverse ethnicities and legendary histories. As the novelist informs the reader, black history in Ecuador is a matter of versions—but whose version?

>...*Y ustedes han de saber que nuestra raza, es decir nuestros antepasados, no eran naturales de estas tierras.*
>—*¿Y de dónde eran, entonces?*
>—*De un lejano continente que se llama Africa.*
>............................
>—*Una cosa que siempre me ha llamao la atención es por qué habemos tanta gente morena por estos lados.*
>............................
>—*Porque, según cuenta...allá por el año 1553 frente a las costas de Esmeraldas, naufragó un barco negrero que llevaba veintitrés esclavos negros y negras, los cuales aprovecharon...para ganar tierra e internarse en estas montañas. Otros aseguran que los esclavos se sublevaron y, acabando con la tripulación, encallaron la nave y saltaron.*
>............................
>—*A esto se agrega que hay y ha habido siempre una afluencia de gente de color desde Colombia.*
>—*Así es...porque allá se dizque está el negro que tetea, al menos en el río Patía...* (Ortiz 185)

>(All of you must know that our race, that is our ancestors, are not from these parts.
>—So, where are they from?

—From a faraway continent called Africa.
....
Something that's always struck me is why there are so many Black people in this region.
....
Well, according to what they say…around 1553, a slave ship foundered off the coast of Esmeraldas with twenty-three black men and black women slaves who took advantage [of the situation] …to make it to land and flee into the mountains. Other [versions] assure us that the slaves mutinied, did away with the crew, ran the ship aground and jumped overboard.
....
Another version adds that there is and always have been an influx of people of color from Colombia.
—Well that must be it…since they say that over there Black people are limitless, at least along the River Patia…)

Whatever the version, it becomes apparent from Ortiz's interpretation that black Ecuadorians have never been apprised of the facts of their history. Later, it is learned from the novel's construction that to keep a person in ignorance was a form of subjugation. Ecuador, in this respect, is no different than other Latin countries with its hierarchies of phenotypes that function behind the manipulation of power, economic and social entitlements, and historical omissions. The history of the Barbosa appointment to Brazil's Supreme Court becomes all the more suspect in this light. Nonetheless, for the Latin American scene, it is almost a truism to declare that power controls experiences and creates complex convolutions where race and ethnicity are involved. Overt racial bigotry is often disguised by covert machinations or by allusions to the leveling effect of *mestizaje* or race mixing. To illustrate this point, one can refer to an online article with the intriguing title: "Colombia borró de la historia a su único presidente Negro" ["Colombia erased its only Black president from history"]. The author of the article claims that:

> Alvaro Uribe is not Colombia's 84th president, but its 85th due to an historical incident that historians attribute to racism: that

country had a black president in the mid nineteenth century that was literally washed out of all historical records: Juan José Nieto Gil. (Guillén n.p.)

Apparently, Nieto Gil's administration was short-lived, only lasting from 25 January 1861 to 18 July 1861. Be that as it may, the fact that he existed as one of Colombia's presidents is not conjecture, given that accounts of him and his administration were rediscovered during the course of fieldwork undertaken by a Colombian sociologist, Orlando Fals Borda. At the same time, an oil painting of Nieto Gil happened to be retrieved from its obscure location. An examination of the painting is said to have offered proof that the rediscovered portrait had been touched up to make the subject appear whiter than he was at the time of the original sitting. This practice has been known to exist not only in Colombia but in other areas of Latin America as well. For example, Machado de Assis, the Brazilian writer often referred to in these essays, has the visual identification of a dark mulatto in his early portraits, so unlike the white person that he represents in pictures during his later years of national fame. For Nieto Gil, it was concluded:

> *Sin embargo, con la restauración de 1974, reapareció el hombre negro original, que en realidad se cree fue más bien un mulato caribe de los que en todo caso, en Colombia son considerados negros.* (Guillén n.p.)
>
> (However, with the 1974 restoration, the original Black man reappeared; in all events he is believed to be a mulatto from the Caribbean area, the type who if anything at all is considered Black in Colombia.)

The reluctance to recognize or accept blackness in Latin America's positions of power is not relegated to the nineteenth century. As a matter of fact, it is not a secret that even today (2010) much of the vehement opposition toward President Hugo Chávez in Venezuela and elsewhere in the Americas stems from his open admission of a Black/African heritage. Then there is the physiognomical evidence that supports this assertion.

In an online paper entitled, "Multiculturalismo y racismo en la época de Chávez: Etnogénesis afrovenezolana en el proceso bolivariano" ["Multiculturalism and racism in the Chavez era: Afrovenezuelan ethnogenesis in the Bolivarian process"], the author quotes from a statement by William Lara, Venezuela's Minister of Communication and Information (2006–2008) that fundamentally was only for domestic consumption. The international community would never discuss these matters openly, and in the United States the catchphrase "of Hispanic origin" conveniently skirts around and disguises sensitive implications of racial ambiguity:

> ...*Desembozadamente los voceros de tales sectores destilan su veneno racista contra el líder barinés satirizando el color de su piel y su fisonomía. Empero, no es la herencia africana e indígena que corre por la sangre de Chávez la razón principal de los desbordamientos biliosos...si el presidente...se deja domesticar y se convierte en el instrumento de tales grupos para que recuperen el poder político perdido y aumenten su prevalencia económica ya no lo llamarán zambo y le prodigarán amores y con refinada hipocresía le aceptarán como uno de los suyos.* (Ishibshi n.p.)

> (Unabashedly, the spokespersons for these districts let their racist venom ooze out against our leader from Barinas, making fun of his color and features. However, the African and indigenous heritage that run through Chavez' veins are not the principal reason for these bilious excesses...if our president...were to allow himself to be manipulated and be converted into their puppet so that these groups could regain their lost political power and increase their economic might, they would no longer call him a "Black-Indian" but would shower him with love and refined hypocrisy, while accepting him as one of their own.)

The fact that President Chavez is obviously a miscegenated person, like the vast majority of the politically and socially impoverished in most Latin American countries, blatantly exposes the "hypocrisy" of the ruling class' willingness to accept "him as one of their own"—that is, allow him to be accepted as an honorary "whitish" member of their society, but only with conditions attached that are in their favor. Consequently, based on the foregone evidence, it appears indisputable to this author that all of the instances of denigrations, slights, omissions, and hegemonic phenotypes—discussed in this study—stem from the undeniable actuality of Africa's presence in Latin America and the attempt to conceal the reality of its identity.

In conclusion, while the Tabom view themselves as a link to that African presence still found in the Americas, each of these groups—the Tabom in Africa and the African-descendant groups in Latin America—has a societal image that is quite unlike that of the other. Yet they are still part of the same set of circumstances inherent in the maxims: "Same ship, different ports" or "Same trip, different ships," with the exception of an extension which the Tabom have appended to include the phrase: "…and back to home port." With their return to Africa, the Brazilian Africans in Ghana enhance the ethnogenesis of the African Latin image as an uprooted people conjoined by a common history that encompasses both Latin America and Africa.

Thus, it becomes only logical to question whether there is a correlation or thematic interconnection that in some way ties the four essays of this study together. While each was designed as a separate discourse, interconnectedly they lead the reader to consider, fundamentally, the presence of Africa in the Americas as reality converted into an aesthetic drive. In this sense, there appears to be an artistic aim by the writers and lyricists discussed in the first three essays of showing how the African manifestation is integrated into the various societies as more than a legacy of myths, drums, and so-called witchcraft (malefic spirituality). For example, the *"fukú"* imagery that Junot Diaz reveals in *The Brief Wondrous Life of Oscar Wao* is no longer seen as just a negative force, but also functions as a protective shield for the Continent's descendants transferred to a hostile environment in the Portuguese- and Spanish-speaking Americas. Whereas Africa's *"axé/aché"* (i.e., positive *"fukú"*) might not have been a dimension of life anticipated by Europeans—the controlling forces—in contrast, the color-changing genetic input willingly or unwillingly contributed by New World Africans and their progeny produced another dimension that the controlling society anticipated would eventually be subsumed and revert to the much desired "norm" of European whiteness as a predominant physiognomy. Given that phenotypic whiteness signaled power and control, as the human masses of the regions turned darker and darker, population-wise, the whitening process ("*branqueamento*" in the Portuguese of Brazil, or "*blanqueamiento*" in Spanish-speaking areas) became societies' teleological direction, as the white skin-tone aesthetics of Alvarez, Perez, and Restrepo so clearly illustrate in their novels. Latin America's African-descended peoples and those who listen to their voice clearly understand that abolition of slavery and the progression of time have done little to resolve the mindset that inferior/superior humans are decreed by color. Some contend that Latin America has had almost three centuries to ponder and rectify the controversy.

What have abolition and time achieved in race relations for the Afro Latin or Latin Africans? In today's ethnoracial environment, when the black Brazilian compares the truth of his or her spatial context with that of their North American counterparts—in terms of abolition and the progression of time for both communities—and discovers how infinitesimal their social progress and acceptance have been, the rallying cry of U.S. President Barack Obama ("Yes we can!") assumes a different perspective.

For African Brazilians, rather than reacting with positive responses, the maxim evokes a series of questions: "*Nós quem?*" ["We, who?"]..."*E também podemos o que?*" ["And also we can do what?"]:

> *Para nós negros(as), maioria da população brasileira segundo dados recentes da IBGE [Instituto Brasileira de Geografia e Estatística], seria bom elegermos um(a) presidente negro(a)? Ou no caso da Bahia, estado em que ¾ da população é negra, nós nos contentaríamos com a justa eleição de um(a) governador(a) negro(a), ou com um(a) prefeito(a) negro(a) em Salvador, maior cidade negra do mundo, fora da África? Seguramente a resposta é sim...É muito provável que a nossa auto-estima e a nossa autoconfiança, massacradas por séculos de opressão escravista e exclusão racista aumentariam significativamente...[P]or que em um país*

Epilogue 313

de maioria negra,...nunca tivemos sequer um(a) candidato(a) negro(a) à presidência da república e o número de governadores(as) e prefeitos(as) negros(as) que já existiram é tão insignificante, em termos estatísticas, que mal nos lembramos de seus nomes? ("A eleição de Barack Obama" [The election of Barack Obama])

(For us, as Black people, the majority of Brazil's population according to recent data of the IBGE [Brazilian Institute of Geography and Statistics] would the election of a Black president [male or female] be in our favor? Or in the case of Bahia, a state where ¾ of the population is Black, would we be happy with the fair election of a Black governor [male or female], or with a Black mayor [male or female] for Salvador, the largest Black city in the world outside of Africa? Naturally, the answer is yes. And undoubtedly this would significantly raise our self-esteem, and our self-confidence, massacred by centuries of oppression under slavery and racist exclusion...we have never even had a Black candidate to the presidency, and the number of Black governors and mayors that there have been have been so numerically insignificant until we hardly remember their names?)

This last statement, published on the Web page of the Brazilian Black Researchers Association, clearly highlights the dilemma that not only Brazil but most Latin American countries have with their black communities. Societies can assume a position of denial toward black people as an official segment of the demography; they can feign indifference; or they can assume a complex attitude of recognition, with the norm being more than likely a combination of all of these elements. Brazil, as indicated previously, has a policy of "racial democracy," which officially recognizes the black population, but infers that a lack of social and economic mobility is due principally to "class differences" and not to restrictions based on color. Consequently, when read in conjunction with the beginning essays, the Tabom surface as part of the historical ethnogenesis of black Latinism—a Latinism that shares more in its slave-oriented existence in Latin America than in an Africanized-European culture—and offer a demonstrated example of life after slavery without the lingering aftereffects of denigration and oppression targeted at individuals and groups because of color and a history of enslavement for the economic empowerment of the oppressor. Contrarily, the welcomers of the Tabom hailed the arrival of Africans from the New World back to the Continent precisely because their labor and skills would serve the best economic interest of the host society. As a paragon of blackness, void of the negative impact of slavery in all the dimensions found in Latin America, can the experiences of the Tabom, in their new cultural space, provide the aesthetic material that counters myth with reality? As the Gã said when welcoming the African Brazilians ashore on the Gold Coast in 1836: *"Ablekuma Abakuma Wo."*

Works Cited

"A eleição de Barack Obama e o dilemma racial brasileiro: ou porque o Brasil ainda está longe de ter um presidente negro." Associação brasileira dos pesquisadores(as) negros(as). 8 Sept. 2009. Web. 11 Oct. 2009.

Garcia, Jesus Chucho. "Demystifying Africa's Absence in Venezuelan History and Culture." *African Roots/American Cultures: Africa in the Creation of the Americas.* Ed. Sheila S. Walker. Lanham, MD: Rowman and Littlefield Publishers, Inc., 2001. 284–290. Print.

Guillén, Gonzalo. "Colombia borró de la historia a su único presidente negro." *El Nuevo Herald.* 12 Nov. 2008. Web. 2 Jul. 2009.

Guran, Milton. *Agudás: Os "brasileiros" do Benim.* Rio de Janeiro: Editora Nova Fronteira, S. A., 1999. Print.

Ishibshi, Jun. "Multiculturismo y racismo en la época de Chávez: Etnogénesis afrovenezolana en el proceso bolivariano." Web. 2 Oct. 2009.

Lewis, Marvin A. *Afro-Hispanic Poetry 1940–1980: From Slavery to "Negritud" in South American Verse.* Columbia: University of Missouri Press, 1983. Print.

Ortiz, Adalberto Juyungo. *Historia de un negro, una isla y otros negros.* Barcelona: Biblioteca Formentor Seix Barral, 1976. Print.

Rahier, Jean Muteba. "Blackness, the Racial/Spatial Order, Migrations, and Miss Ecuador 1995–96." *American Anthropologist* 100.2 (Jun. 1998): 421–430. Print.

NOTES

1. The bibliography of Africa's presence in Mexico has made giant strides within recent years (see Ben Vinson III. "Afro-Mexican History: Trends and Directions in Scholarship." History Compass 3. 1 [2005]: 1–14). The journal *Callaloo* likewise affords the interested reader or researcher lists of sources that substantiate the presence of African descendants in this area: Charles H. Rowell, "Africa in Mexico. A Reading List." *Callaloo* 27.1 (2004): 172–173 and Charles H. Rowell, "Africa in Mexico. The Editor's Notes." *Callaloo* 29.2 (Spring 2006): 397–400. We also recommend www.Afromexico.com, the Web site of Bobby Vaughn's "Black Mexico."
2. In Spanish "mulato" is the correct orthography. The dictionary is published in Spanish.
3. Bracketed gender references indicate that the corresponding word in the original quote in Spanish carry morphemic endings that innately infer gender. For example, "mestizo vs mestiza" both translate to "mestizo" in English, while "español vs española" translate to "Spanish."
4. The conclusions were the same, but Aguirre Beltran used a slightly different arrangement. Morner appears to have updated the list.
5. "Might" is used to suggest "probability." The area is heavily miscegenated with a genetic base of African and indigenous Indian elements.
6. The cultural magazine *Brazzil*, in its online publication of November 1999 focused on Brazil's most popular dictionary of the Brazilian Portuguese language, the Aurélio, in particular, the Novo Aurélio Século XXI [New Aurelio Century 21], which had just been published, to comment in depth on its popularity. It appears that the dictionary is used by academics, students, and the general public at large in Brazil, even though as the description claims: "The Aurélio is not the most complete dictionary in Brazil. The Michaelis Moderno Dicionário da Língua Portuguesa [The Modern Michaelis Dictionary of the Portuguese Language] has 201,174 terms, 30,000 more than the Aurélio…The new words introduced in the [Aurélio] dictionary are slang, as well as medical, scientific, and computer terms which have appeared in the last 13 years. Two thousand new words are Africanisms." Web. 30 January 2009. http://www.brazzil.com/pages/p08nov99.htm.

7. In a 2005 publication, a focused investigation of the African presence in Latin America and the stages (e.g., Bozal talk, Creole, etc.) that the transplanted African went through in the acquisition of communication in standard Spanish makes it quite clear that the process was not completely passive. On the contrary, it was interculturally dynamic: "The African contribution to the Hispanic American lexicon is undisputed...[there are] hundreds of Africanisms found in the local level in dialects of Spanish throughout the Caribbean and South America..." (Lipski, John M. *A History of Afro-Hispanic Language: Five Centuries, Five Continents*. Cambridge: Cambridge University Press, 2005).
8. In the United States, unlike most countries in Latin America, there is the practice of applying a rule of hypodescent, often called the one-drop rule, to determine a person's race. Accordingly, it defines black as a person with any known (or admitted) African ancestry, no matter how many generations in the past this mixture may have occurred in someone's lineage.
9. While the Spanish term "blanco" literally translates into English as "white," in the Dominican vernacular "blanco" is often a synonym for "tez clara," or "light" in complexion. This is confirmed by the use in this short transcription of the term "jabao" as an equivalent phenotype for "blanco." (Refer to "mi padre...jabao, es decir blanco.") A true Caucasian is never referred to as "jabao." This latter description is reserved for individuals whose facial characteristics and hair quality denote a definite African admixture in spite of their light skin color.
10. See note 9.
11. An interesting treatment of this concept can be found in Stanley Cyrus, "Ethnic Ambivalence and Afro-Hispanic Novelists," *Afro-Hispanic Review* 21.1–2 (Spring–Fall 2002): 185–189.
12. For a comprehensive list of critics of Afro-Hispanic literature, refer to: Antonio D. Tillis, "Afro-Hispanic Literature in the US: Remembering the Past, Celebrating the Present, and Forging the Future." *IPOTESI, Juiz de Fora* 12.1 (Jan/Jul 2008): 21–29.
13. Refer to Joe Contreras, "Rise of the Latin Africans: A new black-power movement in Central and South America" in the online version of *Newsweek*, 9 June 2009. http://www.newsweek.com/2008/05/31/rise-of-the-latin-africans.html.
14. See CRS Report for Congress, "Afro-Latinos in Latin America and Considerations for U.S. Policy." Updated 21 November 2008, especially page CRS-5.

15. Edmond Adoko, oral informant, personal communication with author, August–December 2007; January–March 2008. This is part of a collection of Akan sayings, tales, and poems given to me by informants in Ghana while doing research there on the Akan's oral history of slaves being sent to the Americas.
16. The difference between the [m]=[n] spelling is inconsequential since both nasalized consonants represent the approximate sound of a terminal position vowel that carries an inherent nasal quality. The [m] corresponds to the original Portuguese graphology, while [n] is the English counterpart. For this project, we shall adhere to the "Tabom" spelling as accepted in Brazil and Portugal unless a quote is taken from a source that uses the "Tabon" variant.
17. While no written or printed information has ever come to light, as of yet, regarding an S. S. *Salisbury*, there is information concerning an H. M. S. *Salisbury* that can be found online under the Naval Database heading http://www.pbenyon.plus.com/18-1900/S/04065.html.
18. Undercover practitioners of Judaism.
19. Michael Luther-Tetteh, oral informant, personal communication with author, August 2007–present.
20. This spelling alternates with Mahama in different documents.
21. Edmond Adoko, oral informant, personal communication with author, August–December 2007; January–March 2008.

INDEX

Abakua, 85, 91, 102–103, 123–124, 127, 129, 131, 135
Abarry, Abu S., 242
Accra, 213, 224, 237, 239–242, 245–246, 248, 250–251, 256–257, 266, 269, 270–272, 283, 286–288, 290–292
aché, 4, 311
adelantar la raza, 22
Adsuma, Maryamu Matta, 269, 271, 283
aesthetics, xvi, xxiv, xxv, 305, 312
　black, 6, 20, 23, 25, 28, 33, 38, 43–44, 57, 66
　racial, 14
Africa late en la mexicanidad, 2, 9
Africa (Mother), 209, 212
African American, xxi, xxiv, 175, 204, 273
　ancestor, 23, 114, 117
　Brazilian, xxvi, 233, 235, 239–240, 243, 255, 260, 284
　continent, xxv, 20, 52, 82, 100, 222, 227, 255, 279
　descendant(s), xvii, xx, xxiii–xxiv, 2, 6, 8, 28, 48, 59, 68–69, 87, 89, 96, 103–104, 108, 110, 112, 141, 145, 250–251, 255, 282, 285
　Diaspora, 20, 30, 33, 41, 89, 103, 185, 188, 258
　Jew(s), 265
　Latino(s), xxiii, xxvi
Africanness, 232, 234, 257

Afro Bolivian, 89–90
　Brazilian, xxvi, 147, 260
　Caribbean, 38, 111, 188, 277
　Colombian, 21, 28, 213
　Cuban, 47–48, 85, 100, 104, 122, 124–126, 129, 131, 135–137, 229
　descendant, xxiv, 21, 89, 126, 212, 252
　Dominican, 33, 35, 42
　Ecuadorian, 100, 307–308
　Hispanic, 13, 149
　Iberian, 13
　Latin, xxiv, 2–10, 13, 17–25, 29–33, 41, 43, 82, 149, 203, 210, 213, 228
　Latin America, 103, 149, 204
　Latinism, xvii, xxii, 42
　Latino, xvii, xix, xxi–xxiii, 5, 44, 52–53, 72–73, 95, 99, 212–213
　mestizo, 10–11, 107
　Mexican, 10, 66, 104, 107
　Peruvian, xx, 9, 86, 88
　Puerto Rican, 38, 41, 109, 112
　Uruguayan, 21, 108
　Venezuelan, 288
Agoue, 237, 244
Aguirre Beltran, Gonzalo, xviii, 9–10, 53–54, 59–61, 73, 317
Akan, 187, 222–223, 242, 260, 275, 278, 293, 319
Alasha Nelson, 288
Alix, Juan Antonio, 205
Almoravids, 14

Alvarez, Julia, 33–34, 161–181, 184–188, 192, 195–198, 203, 206, 218, 305, 312
Alvarez Nazario, Manuel, 5, 82, 119, 135
ambia, 137
Amerindian, 8–11, 55–57, 60–61, 64, 87–90, 114, 139, 159, 204, 206, 244, 305
Amos (and Ayesu), 244–246, 258, 267–269, 282
Andrews, George Reid, 103, 149
"Angelitos negros," 16–17, 106, 205
Angola, 145, 212, 254
Ankrah, Nii, 246, 248
Annan, Kofi, 257
aphorism, xv, 97
Arará, 91, 99, 134
Argentina, xix, 18–20, 218, 221
Aruna Nelson, 288–289
asere, 127–129, 137
Ashanti, 212, 224, 281
Assemblies of God, The, 258
Asuman, Kangidi, 246, 282, 292
Autobiography of a Runaway Slave.
See *Biografía de un cimarrón*
axé, 4, 146, 311
Ayi Kushie, 279
Ayllón, Eva, 88
Azumah Nelson, 246–247, 278, 282, 284, 292
Azumah Nelson V, Nii, 248, 261, 281, 292
Azumah "The Professor" Nelson, 281, 288
Azumah II, Nii, 278, 290, 292

Babalú, 102
Baca, Susana, xx, 9
Bacalov, Luis Enrique, 218
Baeta, João Gonçalves, 245
Baeta, Robert Domingos, 244
Bahia, 226–229, 233–240, 244–248, 251, 254, 266–268, 284–285, 291, 302, 313
Bakongo, 120–122
"Balada de los dos abuelos," 86
Bamba, La, 9–10, 20, 107
Bantu, 28–29, 82, 93, 100–101, 104, 109, 120, 122–125, 275, 306
Batista, Fulgencio, 17–18
bemba, 92–93, 106, 112, 133
Benin, xxv, 234–237, 244–245, 248, 281, 302
Berlin West Africa Conference, 213
Bight of Benin, 213, 235
bilongo, 91
Biografía de un cimarrón, 144, 243
biracial, 12–13, 15, 31, 34, 48, 64–67, 93, 141, 210, 221, 231, 264–266, 276
Black, xviii, xx–xxiii, 1–2, 5–9, 12–27, 30–39, 41–54, 57–63, 66–73
Black Cuban, 91
Black Enterprise, xxi
Black heritage, 19
Black Latin, xxi, xxiii, xxvi
Black music, xx, 9
Black people, xxi–xxii, 5, 10–12, 22–24, 35, 38–40, 45, 47, 53, 69, 87–88
Blanco Meaño, Andrés Eloy, 16–17, 205–206
blanqueamiento, 306, 312
Bolivar, Simón, 17
Bolivia, 19, 89
branqueamento, 312
brasilianidade, 139

Brazil House, 240, 258, 290–292
Brazilian African, 257, 270, 286, 289, 293
Brief Wondrous Life of Oscar Wao, 3, 5, 203, 311
British, xxiv–xxv, 49, 104, 110–111, 230, 237, 247, 256–257, 261, 276
Buganda, 111
"Buscando outra sociedade," 238–239

Cabinda, 109, 143
Calabar, 97, 102, 114, 123, 127
Campos, Monica Menezes, 252, 304
candomblé, 120, 228–229, 282
Cape Coast, 15, 256
Cape Verde, 242, 254
Caribbean, xviii, xxi, 5, 7, 20, 28–29, 33–35, 91–92, 103–104, 111, 114–115, 139, 159, 194, 309, 318
Carpentier, Alejo, 92, 123, 126, 132
Castro Alves, Antonio, 210–211, 225
Castro, Fidel, 17, 136
Caucasian, xx, 8, 71, 172, 318
Cavero, Arturo "El Zambo," 89
Central Africa, 120, 306
Central America, 7, 20, 103
Central Mosque, 240
Chalá, Ana, 18
Chambacú, corral de negros, 21–22
Chandler, Daniel, 159–160
Changó, 48, 101–102, 129, 137, 283
Chávez, Hugo, 18, 212, 309–310
chévere, 127
Chile, xix, 8, 19
Chinese, 18, 47–50
chino, 14, 60–61, 118–119
Christian, 137, 187, 242, 258, 261–263, 266–269, 272, 279
Christian (New), 268–270

Christianity, 8, 242, 251, 260, 271, 283, 289
Cidade de Deus, 148
cimarrón(es), 105, 144, 208, 243
cocolo, 34–35
Colombia, 5, 8, 26, 208, 212, 217, 259, 307–309
colorism, xxv, 65–66, 73, 207, 218
color indio, 57
Comas, Juan, 158–159
conga, 91, 132
Congo, 10, 93–94, 97, 99, 102, 108, 110–111, 114, 120–125, 134, 143, 212, 306
Conspiración de la escalera (Conspiracy of the Ladder), 231
Conversación en la catedral, 87
Cortés, Hernán, 54
corrido, 61–63
cosmovision, 4, 6, 33, 100–101, 138, 195, 218, 279
creole, 88, 104, 134, 176, 318
crioulo, 285
Cualquier miércoles soy tuya, 28, 32, 116
Cuba, xviii, 1, 7–8, 18, 29, 47–51, 55–56, 83–84, 91, 94, 96–103, 119–139, 163–164, 172–174, 185, 207–208, 213, 217, 221, 226–233, 259, 282–283
Cuban color, 51, 55–56
cubaneo, 134
cubanía, 134, 138–139
cubanidad, 124, 134
Cubanness, 124, 134–135
cueca negra, 90

da Luz, Eduardo, 108–109
da Vila, Martinho, 145

Dahomey, 236, 240, 244–245, 302
Dantas, Raimundo Souza, 250–255
Deligne, Gaston, 179, 181
Deusa Negra, A., xxii
Diaz, Junot, 3, 5, 33, 44, 52, 203, 311
Dominican Republic, xvii–xix, 1–2, 4, 7–8, 37, 41–44, 55–56, 91, 158–167, 170, 173–193, 197, 208, 217, 222
Douglass, Frederick, 175
Duany, Jorge, 35–38, 138
Du Bois, W. E. B., 204
Dutch, 34, 104, 242, 246, 256, 262, 265–266
Dzoglo, 223–224

East Africa, 111
ecobio, 129
Ecuador, xix, 306–308
Ecue-Yamba-O, 92
"El apellido," 121
Elemento afronegroide en el español de Puerto Rico, El, 82
Eleggua, 102, 129
Elmina, 15, 224, 239, 242
Embassy of Brazil, 290
England, xviii–xxiv, 261, 270, 272–273, 276
Equatorial Africa, 12
Esdaille, Milca, 33
ethnography, 11, 281
ethnonym, 109, 241, 301
ethnoracial, xx, 8, 12, 15, 21, 29, 40, 42–43, 48, 52–53, 62, 71, 86, 112, 117, 123, 206–209, 301, 304, 306, 312
eurocentric, 19, 53, 111, 306
Europe, xxv, 8, 13, 15, 19, 179, 265, 271
Ewe, 223, 274–275, 278, 281, 293

Fajardo-Acosta, Fidel, 72
Fals Borda, Orlando, 309
Ferré, Rosario, 38–39, 41
Franco, Jean, 43
Franklin House, 224
Fraser, Sarah Loguen, 175–178
fufu, 5
fuku, 4, 5, 203, 311
Fula, 15, 143–144

Gã (Ga), 17, 241–243, 246, 248–250, 256–260, 271, 274–275, 278–279, 283, 285–290, 293, 314
Gambia, The, xxiv
Gabon, 105
Gama, Luiz (Luis), xxiii, 210–211, 219–222
Gangá, 99–100
García, Alan, 89
García, Jesus "Chucho," 305–306
genomic, 8, 11, 27, 31, 66
genotype, 27, 107, 114, 168, 177
Geographies of Home, 36, 184–188, 194
Gold Coast, xxiv–xxv, 212, 222, 235, 237, 242, 245–262, 266, 270–282, 285–287, 290–293
Golden Law, 119
Gómez, Manuel Octavio, 137
Gorostiza, Celestino, 64–65, 72–73
Goulart, President João, 253–255
Grant, Ulysses S., 174
Guayama, 110, 112, 114
Guerrero, Pedro, 104
Guerrero, Vicente, 104–105
Guillén, Nicolás, 52–53, 85–86, 121–122, 125–130
Guinea Bissau, 254

Haiti, xviii, 47, 83–84, 104, 179, 182, 259, 273
Haley, Alex (*Roots*), xxiv
Hansen, Terrence L., 61
Haro, David, 10, 107
Hausa, 187, 234, 246–251, 269, 274–275, 278, 281–284, 287, 293
Henríquez Ureña, Camila, 162
"Hermano Negro," 45–49, 210
Hernández Cuevas, Marco Polo, 2, 9, 11, 57, 60–62
Herrera, Remigio "Adechina," 228–229
Herring, Hubert, 178
heterogeneous, 8
Heureaux, President Ulises, 175–178
Hispanic, xvii–xviii, xx, 1, 7, 13, 23, 28, 41, 44, 50–52, 59, 96–99, 134, 139, 149, 159, 164–166, 186–190, 194, 204, 222, 305–306
Hispanic American Historical Review, xviii
Hispaniola, 1, 3–4, 182
Holy Cross Cathedral, 241
homogenous, 190
Hughes, Langston, 85–86
hypodescent, 165, 318. *See also* one-drop rule

Ibáñez, Alberto, 11, 107
Iberian Peninsula, 2, 12–13, 90, 138, 261–264
Ibn Hamid, 14
indentured, 48–49
Indian color, 56, 197. *See also* color
indio
indigenous, xix, 7–8, 20, 30, 32, 53–59, 117, 137, 160–163, 170, 182, 188, 213, 221–223, 271–272, 305, 307, 310, 317

indio, 55, 57, 95, 157, 160, 163, 183, 195–196
Instinto, 130–131
interethnic, 8, 223, 265
interracial, 265
intraracial, 30–31, 222
In the Name of Salomé, 161–163, 174, 179–180, 185, 188, 192, 194, 203, 218, 305
Ireme, 102
Islam, 8, 244–245, 251, 260–263, 267, 271, 283–284

jabao, 23, 29, 94, 114, 196–197, 318
Jamestown (Accra), 224, 240, 287
Jaramillo, Juan, 54
Jew(ish), 161, 168, 188, 261–270
Jiménez, Blas, 157, 208–209
juju, 5
Juyungo, 100, 307

Kennedy, James H., 225
Kimbundu, 145
Kinka, 256

La casa de la laguna, 38, 42
La ciudad de los perros, 87
ladino, xviii
Lagos, 213, 228, 230, 237, 240, 246, 282
Language Duel/Duelo del lenguaje, 39
La Negra Hipólita, 17
La Negra Matea, 17
La novia oscura, 207
Lara, William, 310
Las criadas de la Habana, 81, 90–92, 102, 120, 207

Latin African, 213, 241
Lazarillo de Tormes, 11, 14–15
lengua, 91
Liberia, xxiv, 99, 230, 236
lingua franca, 242
Lins, Paulo, 148
Lisbon, 13
Los que volvieron a África, 230
Lukumí (Lucumí), 99, 123–124, 126, 131, 135, 138, 212, 282
"Luis Bacalhau," 238
Luperón, General Gregorio, 175–176

Machado de Assis, Joaquim Maria, 141, 305, 309
Magoo, Eduardo, 221
Mahama, Alhaji Aliu, 278
Mahama Nassau, 247, 257–259
Mahin, Luiza, xxiii–xxiv
"Majestad Negra," 109–114
Malê, 235, 238–239, 244, 246, 268
Malinche, 54
Mambí, 132
Mandinga, 105, 112
Marielitos, 136
Martínez, Casanova, 91–92
Matos (Mattos), Gregorio de, 139–140
mauchi, 90
"Mayombe-bombe-mayombe," 125
mestizaje, 51, 57, 59–60, 70–73, 158, 204, 206–207, 306, 308
mestizo, white, 306–307
Mexican Revolution, 69
Mexico, 7, 9–10, 19–20, 26, 53–68, 70–73, 104–107, 138, 158, 163, 317
Mfantspim, 257

Miranda, Franklin, 100
miscegenation, xxv, 8, 11, 15, 21–22, 26–30, 35, 54–60, 67, 73, 83, 94, 103, 114, 122, 132, 144, 159, 164, 168, 174, 181, 188, 194, 197, 207, 220, 263, 266
moleque, 142–143
Monteiro, João, 237
Montejo, Esteban, 144
Moore, Robin, 131
Moore, Zelbert, 254
Morales, Evo, 89–90
Morejón, Nancy, 51, 55–56, 131–134
Morner, Magnus, 58–59, 317
morphology, xxii, 23, 31, 42, 55, 62, 93–94, 117, 195, 208
Morton, Dan, 240, 288
Mozambique, 10, 107, 109, 254
mulato oscuro, 14, 31, 42, 117
mulatto, dark, 119, 304, 309
Muslim, 234–239, 245–247, 251, 258–265, 267–272, 279, 282–284, 289–290

Nago, 245, 282
negro retinto, 23, 118
Nelson Alasha, 248, 288
Nelson, Alexander Arunah, 246
Nelson, J. Fortunato Antonio, 250
Nelson, James Abdulai, 261
Nelson, João Antonio, 278
New Spain, 57, 105
Nigeria, 102, 123, 187, 213, 230, 235, 237, 240, 244–253, 271, 279, 281–286
Nimrod, 247
noesis, xvii
North Africa, 263

Oaxaca, 105, 107
Obama, President Barack, 34, 206–207, 312–313
Obatalá, 102
Obsesión, 132–133
Ochún, 102, 129, 137–138
Ogún, 3, 5
Olodumare, 137
Olympio, Sylvanus Epiphanio Kwami, 244
Olympio Silva, Francisco, 244–245
one-drop rule, 59, 96, 162, 177, 318. *See also* hypodescent
Oricha, 3–5, 126, 136–137
Orishas (vocal group), 128–129
Orixá, 3–4
Ortiz, Alberto, 100, 307–308
Osu, 224
Otublohum, 239, 241, 246, 248, 290
Ovando, Nicolás, 15

Palés Matos, Luis, 41, 83–84, 109–112, 114
Palo Monte, 91, 120, 123, 125
Panford Jr., Moses, 1–2, 123–124
Paraguay, 19
Patakin, xvii, 137–138
patronymic, 121–122
Pedroso, Regino, 45–53
Peña Gómez, José Francisco, 36
Peregrino, Francis Joseph, 273
Peregrino, Francis Zaccheus Santiago, 260
Peregrino, Francisco Zaccheus Santiago, 270, 272–273, 276
Peregrino, María Antonia, 105–107. *See also* Toña La Negra
Peregrino, Pablo "El Negro," 106

Peregrino, Zaqueu Francisco Santiago, 269
Peres, Fernando de la Rocha, 139–141
Pérez, Loida Maritza, 33, 36–37, 184–198, 218, 221, 305, 312
Pérez de la Riva, Juan, 231
Pérez-Sarduy, Pedro, 81, 90–98, 101, 120, 207
phenotype, xix, xxii–xxiii, 7–8, 18, 21–22, 30, 33, 37, 51–61, 106, 135, 159, 161, 163, 165, 167–173, 177–179, 183–186, 188–198, 206, 217–218, 222, 257, 304–305, 318
phenotypocracy, xxv, 182
physiognomy, 24–25, 29, 36, 93, 219, 305, 312
pickaninny, 61
pigmentocracy, 42, 102, 144, 177
Plácido. *See* Valdés, Gabriel de la Concepción
Plange, John, 272
"Plegaria a Dios" (A Prayer to the Almighty), 232
Portugal, xviii, 2, 12–13, 90, 139, 242, 254, 262, 264, 319
Protestant Church, 244
Puerto Rico, xvii, 5, 7–8, 28–29, 32, 38, 41, 82–84, 91, 109–119, 138, 217, 283

Quadros, President Jânio, 252–254
Quimba, 87–89
Quincas Borba, 142–143

racial democracy, xv, 147, 225, 304, 313
racial parameter(s), xxii

racism, xix, 6, 14, 36, 44, 49–50, 73, 148, 159–160, 213, 231, 252, 268, 303, 308, 310
racist attitude(s), 7, 49
Rappin Hood, 146
"Raven and the Lily, The," 13–14
razas humanas, Las, 158
realismo mágico (magical realism), 227
rebambaramba, 131–132
Regla Arará, 91
Regla Conga, 91
Regla de Ocha, 91
Regla de Palo, 91
Reis, João José, 234, 247
Restrepo, Laura, 206–207, 312
returnee(s), xxiii–xxv, 102, 213, 228–233, 236–247, 254–263, 266, 268, 271, 280–285, 290–293
Revolt of the Malês, 235, 238, 251
Ribeiro, Francisco, 256
Ribeiro, Miguel A., 254–255, 260
Rio Branco Institute, 252
Rodrigues, Virginia, 239
Rojas González, Francisco, 66–73
Roldán, Amadeo, 132
Romero, Fernando, xix–xxii, 87

Saldaña, Excilia, 138
Salisbury, HMS, 246–247, 319
samba, 90, 140, 145–146
Sanfancón, 48
San Lorenzo de los Negros, 105
Santa Bárbara, 48
santería, 48, 91, 120, 123, 126, 131, 229, 282
Santo Domingo, 4–5, 175–179, 183, 196–197
Santo Domingo Commission, 175

Santos, Antonio Pereira dos, 244
Santos, Constância Talabi Pereira dos, 244
Santos-Febres, Mayra, 28–32, 38, 115–119
Sarracino, Rodolfo, 230–233
saya, 89–90
Schaumloeffel, Marco Aurélio, 240, 245, 247–248, 281–282, 289–290
Schorsch, Jonathan, 261–266
Scissors House, First, 240
semiotic, xxii, 24, 28, 113, 122, 161
Senegal, 253, 264–265
"Sensemaya," 125
Sephardim, 168, 261–265, 269
Seven African Powers, 286
Shango, 258, 283–284
Shitta Bey Mosque, 240
Sierra Leone, xxiv, 99, 230, 236
Silva, President Luiz Inácio Lula da, 291–292, 303–304
skin color, xix, 22, 37, 42, 44, 51, 64, 132, 134, 143–144, 160, 183–184, 190, 198, 206, 208, 318
Slave Coast, 213, 239
slavery, xvii, xix, xxiii–xxiv, 3–4, 20, 47, 49–50, 73, 88–89, 93, 99, 102–103, 105, 117, 119, 124, 126, 134, 148, 204, 210–211, 218, 223–227, 231–238, 249, 251, 255, 257, 261–264, 270, 290, 292–293, 302–305, 312–314
social reality, xxvi, 2
Sociedad Secreta Abakuá, 91
Son Jarocho, 107
"Sou Negrão," 146
South Africa, 272–277
South African Spectator, 273, 276–277

Index

"Soy su ambia," 137
Spain, xviii, 2, 11–15, 56–57, 82, 90, 100, 119, 132, 137–139, 179, 231
Stinchcomb, Dawn F., 2, 179

Tabom, 101, 241–242, 245–261, 263, 267–272, 275–293, 301–304, 311–314, 319
Tabom chieftancy, 278, 292
Tabon, 239, 241, 245, 248, 271, 290
Tackie Kome I, 248, 285
Tackie Tawiah I, 248
Tavares, Juraci, 238
Tinhorão, José Ramos, 12–13
Togo, xxv, 235, 237, 244–245, 279
Tom Zé, 239
Toña La Negra. *See* Peregrino, María Antonio
Torres-Saillant, Silvio, 4, 55, 176, 181–182, 187, 190, 195
Treaty of Peking, 49
Trujillo, Rafael, 55, 193
Truque, Carlos Arturo, 23–25, 28
Twi, 104, 242, 275, 293

Uganda, 110–111
United States, xxi, xxiv–xxv, 34, 37, 52, 93, 96, 98–99, 103–104, 117, 119, 161–167, 174–177, 182–185, 192–194, 212, 230, 255, 259, 271–273, 310, 318
Ureña, Salomé, 162, 164, 178
Uruguay, xix, 21, 108–109, 138, 254
Ussher Town, 256

Valdés, Gabriel de la Concepción, 231–233. *See also* Plácido

Valdez, Mercedes, 130
Valens, Richie, 9, 107
Vargas Llosa, Mario, 86–87, 149
Vass, Winifred, 104
Vera Cruz, 10
Verger, Pierre, 240
Vicioso, Sherezada (Chiqui), 183, 196–198
Vizcarrondo, Fortunato, 112–115, 127

Washington, Booker T., 272
West Africa, 4, 108–111, 187, 213, 217, 227, 233, 293
whitish, 97, 102, 165, 206, 208, 310
Whydah, 234, 236, 240
Winneba, 237
Wolof, 122, 264
Wood, Chief Justice Georgina Theodora, 257–260, 291, 303

Yanga, Gaspar, 105, 107
Yemayá, 102
Yoruba, xxiv, 19, 99, 120, 122–123, 126, 130–135, 138, 143, 187, 227–228, 231, 240, 245, 248, 250–251, 258, 281–287, 290

Z'Africa, 146
Zaire (Democratic Republic of the Congo), 10
zamba malató, 9, 60, 89, 310
zambo, 60
Zapata Olivella, Manuel, 21–22, 25, 28
zemba, 90
Zoell, R. P., 134–135
Zumbi, 146–147

LaVergne, TN USA
10 July 2010
189005LV00003B/3/P